CII® Certificate in Financial Planning
CF2 INVESTMENT AND RISK

2010/11 tax year edition

Study Text

This **Study Text** provides full coverage for Paper CF2 *Investment and Risk* of the Chartered Insurance Institute's® Certificate in Financial Planning

Visit www.bpp.com/financialadvisers for more information

BPP LEARNING MEDIA

Fourth edition September 2010

ISBN 9780 7517 9259 1

(previous edition ISBN 9780 7517 6879 4)

British Library Cataloguing-in-Publication Data

A catalogue record for this book
is available from the British Library

Published by

BPP Learning Media
BPP House, Aldine Place
London W12 8AA

www.bpp.com/learningmedia

Printed in Great Britain

All our rights reserved. No part of this publication may be reproduced, stored in a retrieval system or transmitted, in any form or by any means, electronic, mechanical, photocopying, recording or otherwise, without the prior written permission of BPP Learning Media.

We are grateful to the CII® for permission to reproduce the syllabus.

Chartered Insurance Institute® and CII® are registered trademarks. The CII® does not endorse, promote, review or warrant the accuracy of the products or services offered by BPP Learning Media.

© BPP Learning Media 2010

A note about copyright

Dear Customer

What does the little © mean and why does it matter?

Your market-leading BPP books, course materials and e-learning materials do not write and update themselves. People write them: on their own behalf or as employees of an organisation that invests in this activity. Copyright law protects their livelihoods. It does so by creating rights over the use of the content.

Breach of copyright is a form of theft – as well being a criminal offence in some jurisdictions, it is potentially a serious beach of professional ethics.

With current technology, things might seem a bit hazy but, basically, without the express permission of BPP Learning Media:

- Photocopying our materials is a breach of copyright
- Scanning, ripcasting or conversion of our digital materials into different file formats, uploading them to facebook or emailing them to your friends is a breach of copyright

You can, of course, sell your books, in the form in which you have bought them – once you have finished with them. (Is this fair to your fellow students? We update for a reason.) But the e-products are sold on a single user license basis: we do not supply 'unlock' codes to people who have bought them secondhand.

And what about outside the UK? BPP Learning Media strives to make our materials available at prices students can afford by local printing arrangements, pricing policies and partnerships which are clearly listed on our website. A tiny minority ignore this and indulge in criminal activity by illegally photocopying our material or supporting organisations that do. If they act illegally and unethically in one area, can you really trust them?

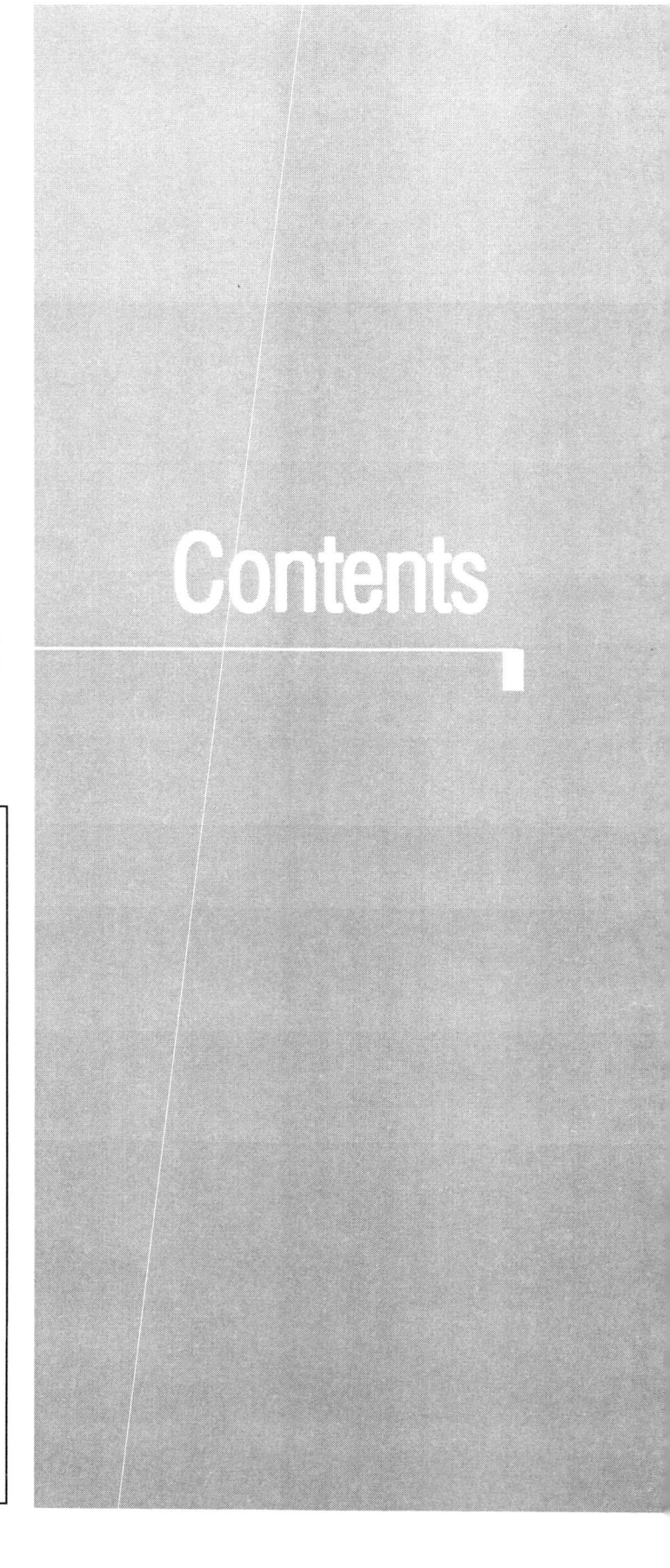

Contents

Introduction

	Page
Using this Study Text	iv
Syllabus summary	v
Syllabus details	vi
Website links	xii
Examination format	xiii
Tackling MCQs	xiv

Chapters

		Page
1	Socio-economic trends	1
2	The economic framework	17
3	Economic analysis	37
4	Taxation	63
5	Cash deposits	93
6	Government securities and corporate bonds	111
7	Equities and derivatives	137
8	Property	169
9	Commodities and alternative investments	187
10	OEICs and unit trusts	195
11	Investment trusts	227
12	Life assurance company products	249
13	Tax incentives, tax wrappers and tax planning	281
14	Socially responsible and ethical investment	307
15	Risks and return	319
16	Investment planning and management	341
17	Regulation	361

Tax Tables

409

Index

417

Using this Study Text

This Study Text provides comprehensive syllabus coverage for candidates sitting Paper CF2 *Investment and Risk* of the Chartered Insurance Institute's® **Certificate in Financial Planning**.

The Study Text contains:

- A list of topics covered in each chapter
- Clear, concise topic-by-topic coverage
- Examples and Exercises to reinforce learning, confirm understanding and stimulate thought
- A roundup of the key points in each chapter
- A quiz at the end of each chapter
- A bank of practice questions, with answers

We recognise that most students have only **limited time for study** and that some study material available on the market can be very time-consuming to use. **BPP Learning Media** has prepared study material which provides you with what you need to secure a good pass in your exam, while making effective use of your time.

Updates to this Study Text

There is a free Budget Updating Service for users of BPP's Study Text. For information on Updates to this Study Text, go to our website at **www.bpp.com/learningmedia**. If you do not have Internet access, please telephone our Customer Service Team on 0845 0751 100 for further information about available Updates.

Plan your exam practice and revision

How can you give yourself the best chance of success in your exam? As well as studying the material in this **Study Text** fully, plan your **exam practice** and **revision**.

Exam practice

BPP's long experience in preparing students for exams shows that **question practice** is a vital ingredient in exam success. Question practice will improve your exam technique and help to build confidence for tackling the exam itself. It can highlight problem areas and remind you of key points.

Revision

The syllabus for your examination is published by the Chartered Insurance Institute (CII) and is very wide-ranging. In your **revision** during the run-up to the exam, you will want to focus your revision on ensuring that you recall what you have studied. BPP's **Passcards** present key facts for your subject in a visually appealing style, to remind you of key points.

Call BPP Learning Media on 0845 0751 100 to order Study Texts, i-pass and Passcards for other CII® Certificate in Financial Planning examinations.

Syllabus summary: Investment and Risk

	Summary of learning outcomes	Number of questions in the examination *
1	Understand the macroeconomic factors that affect investment returns	6
2	Understand the basic principles of taxation applying to the investments of UK resident and domiciled individuals	8
3	Understand the following asset classes, their main features and suitability for different consumer circumstances: • Cash deposits • Government securities and corporate bonds • Equities • Property	25
4	Understand the following packaged products, their main features and suitability for different consumer circumstances: • OEICs and unit trusts • Investment trusts • Individual Savings Accounts (ISAs) • Onshore and offshore life assurance company products	20
5	Understand the role of ethical investment and socially responsible investment in financial advice	2
6	Understand how investment returns are related to investment risk and how that risk is measured	8
7	Understand the risks faced by investors and how an investor's risk profile is determined	7
8	Understand the importance of asset allocation in the investment process	5
9	Understand tax planning strategies	6
10	Understand how other issues affect investment planning	4
11	Understand the importance of keeping up to date with trends and changes in the legal framework for providing advice	2
12	Analyse consumers' circumstances and suitable investment products, taking account of any existing arrangements	4
13	Apply suitable investment product solutions to specific consumers' circumstances	3

* The test specification has an in-built element of flexibility. However, the number of questions testing each learning outcome will never change by more than plus or minus 2.

INVESTMENT AND RISK

Syllabus details

Syllabus Item			BPP Study Text Reference (Chapter – Section)
1		Understand the macroeconomic factors that affect investment returns	
1.1		The main long-term UK socio-economic trends	
	1.1.1	Ageing population	1-1
	1.1.2	Rising living standards	1-2
	1.1.3	Growth of the service sector and other changing patterns of the UK economy	1-4
	1.1.4	Productivity of capital and labour	1-3
	1.1.5	Wealth and income distribution	1-2
	1.1.6	Technological change	1-3
1.2		The global factors that affect investment returns	
	1.2.1	International markets	2-3
	1.2.2	Globalisation of trade and finance	2-5
	1.2.3	European economic and monetary union	2-6
	1.2.4	Political factors	2-4
1.3		The role of government and central banks	
	1.3.1	Fiscal and monetary policy	2-1
	1.3.2	Measuring money supply	3-5
	1.3.3	Inflation	3-3
	1.3.4	Deflation	3-3
	1.3.5	Disinflation	3-3
	1.3.6	Interest rates	3-4
1.4		Balance of payments	
	1.4.1	Capital and current account	3-6
	1.4.2	Exchange rates	3-6
	1.4.3	The importance of the balance of payments	3-6
1.5		The economic and financial cycles	
	1.5.1	Global influences	3-2
	1.5.2	National income	3-1
	1.5.3	The main stages of economic and stock market cycles	3-2
	1.5.4	Longer term growth trends	3-2
1.6		The role of financial investment in the economy	
	1.6.1	Primary markets – how investment markets introduce new funds to business and the government	2-3
	1.6.2	Secondary markets – how markets enable investors to adjust their investments to suit their needs	2-3

Syllabus Item		BPP Study Text Reference (Chapter – Section)
1.7	**The key economic indicators**	
1.7.1	Gross Domestic Product (GDP)	3-1
1.7.2	Retail Prices Index (RPI) and the Consumer Prices Index (CPI)	3-3
1.7.3	Public Sector Net Cash Requirement (PSNCR)	2-1
1.7.4	Volume of fixed investment	3-1
1.7.5	Volume of consumer spending	3-1
1.7.6	Money stock	3-5
1.7.7	Foreign exchange rates	3-6
1.7.8	Bank rates and London Interbank Offered Rate (LIBOR)	2-2
1.7.9	Gilt yields	2-3
1.7.10	Stock market indices and benchmarks	2-3
2	**Understand the basic principles of taxation applying to the investments of UK resident and domiciled individuals**	
2.1	**The key principles of Income Tax**	
2.1.1	Liability to Income Tax	4-1.1
2.1.2	Allowances	4-1.4
2.1.3	Reliefs	4-1.4
2.1.4	Rates	4-1.5
2.1.5	Grossing up interest and dividends	4-1.3
2.1.6	Employed and self-employed income	4-1.3
2.1.7	Priorities for taxing different classes of income	4-1.5
2.2	**The key principles of Capital Gains Tax**	
2.2.1	Liability to CGT	4-2.1
2.2.2	Disposals	4-2.1
2.2.3	Death	4-2.1
2.2.4	Deductions	4-2.3
2.2.5	Losses	4-2.3
2.2.6	Main exemptions	4-2.3
2.2.7	Basic calculation of chargeable gains	4-2.3
2.2.8	Entrepreneurs' relief	4-2.3
2.3	**The main features of Stamp Duty Reserve Tax on securities**	4-4

INVESTMENT AND RISK

Syllabus Item		BPP Study Text Reference (Chapter – Section)
3	**Understand the following asset classes, their main features and suitability for different consumer circumstances**	
3.1	**Cash deposits**	
3.1.1	Main types of deposit account – instant access, notice and fixed rate	5-3
3.1.2	Characteristics and past performance:	5-1
	• liquidity	5-1
	• rates of interest	5-1
	• real returns	5-1
	• institutions	5-2
	• statutory protection	5-1
	• risk factors	5-1
	• foreign currency deposits	5-1
3.1.3	Taxation of deposit interest – savings income, tax deducted at source, offshore accounts	5-4
3.1.4	ISAs	5-5, 13-2
3.1.5	National Savings and Investments – deposit products including Guaranteed Equity Bonds	5-6
3.1.6	Stakeholder Saving products, including Child Trust Fund	13-2, 13-3
3.2	**Government securities and corporate bonds**	
3.2.1	Main characteristics of fixed-interest investments – nominal value and market price, coupon, redemption date	6-1
3.2.2	Gilts – government guarantee, short, medium and long-dated gilts, past performance, gilt strips, risk	6-2
3.2.3	Index-linked gilts – returns on income and capital, risk	6-2
3.2.4	Corporate bonds – borrowers' risk ratings and effects on yields, past performance	6-3
3.2.5	Other types of bonds – Permanent Interest Bearing Shares, zero coupon bonds, deep discounted bonds, convertible loan stock	6-3, 6-4, 6.5
3.2.6	Investment returns and risk – running yields, yields to redemption, capital returns, volatility, yield curves	6-7, 6-8
3.2.7	National Savings and Investments – fixed-interest investments	5-6
3.2.8	Mechanics of dealing, including costs of purchases and sales	6-6
3.2.9	Taxation of government securities and corporate bonds – interest and capital gains/losses	6-6
3.3	**Equities**	
3.3.1	Main types of share – ordinary and preference	7-1
3.3.2	Characteristics of equity-based investment:	7-4
	• individual company performance	7-4
	• main factors that affect company profits and share values	7-4
	• size of company and market liquidity	7-4
	• sectors and markets	7-4

INTRODUCTION

Syllabus Item		BPP Study Text Reference (Chapter – Section)
3.3.3	Investment ratios, measuring performance and their limitations – price earnings ratio (PE), earnings per share, dividend yield, dividend cover, borrowing, net assets	7-5
3.3.4	Market behaviour – what makes markets fluctuate, fundamental analysis and market psychology	7-4
3.3.5	Past performance and volatility – growth and dividends	7-4
3.3.6	Stock market indices – main UK and overseas indices	7-6
3.3.7	Mechanics of dealing, including costs of purchase and sales	7-2
3.3.8	Taxation of dividends	7-2
3.3.9	Derivatives – futures and options, main features and uses	7-7
3.3.10	Employee share schemes and incentives	7-3, 13-6, 13-7
3.3.11	Alternative Investment Market shares and unlisted securities – tax characteristics, past performance in terms of risk and returns	7-4
3.3.12	Mergers and acquisitions	7-4
3.3.13	Primary and secondary markets	7-1
3.3.14	Main components of company accounts that affect investment returns	7-5
3.4	**Property**	
3.4.1	Characteristics of commercial and residential property investment:	8-1, 8-2, 8-3
	• returns from rent and capital growth	8-5
	• supply and demand	8-1, 8-2, 8-3
	• risks	8-1, 8-2, 8-3
	• quality of tenants	8-1, 8-2, 8-3
	• occupancy levels	8-1, 8-2, 8-3
	• liquidity	8-1, 8-2, 8-3
	• depreciation	8-1, 8-2, 8-3
	• maintenance costs	8-1, 8-2, 8-3
3.4.2	Past performance – differences between commercial and residential property (buy-to-let), key determinants of past investment returns, volatility, income and capital returns	8-1
3.4.3	Borrowing – its effect on risk and returns	8-1
3.4.4	Transaction costs – commissions, fees and Stamp Duty Land Tax	8-1, 8-2, 8-3
3.4.5	Taxation issues – taxation of rental income, interest relief, Capital Gains Tax	8-2, 8-3
3.4.6	Indirect property investment vehicles – unit trusts/OEICs, property shares, life assurance property bonds, offshore funds, Real Estate Investment Trusts (REITs)	8-4
4	**Understand the following packaged products, their main features and suitability for different consumer circumstances**	
4.1	**OEICs and unit trusts**	
4.1.1	Structure of OEICs (investment companies with variable capital – ICVCs) and unit trusts – the common characteristics of funds and the main differences	10-2, 10-3
4.1.2	Range of funds – different UK fund classifications, hedge funds, limited issue funds, tracker funds	10-4
4.1.3	Charges and pricing – initial and annual charging structures, single and bid/offer pricing, dilution levies	10-2, 10-3

INVESTMENT AND RISK

Syllabus Item		BPP Study Text Reference (Chapter – Section)
4.1.4	Taxation onshore and offshore:	10-2, 10-3, 10-6
	• taxation within the funds	10-2, 10-3, 10-6
	• taxation of UK individuals and trustee investors	10-2, 10-3, 10-6
4.1.5	Recognition by the FSA of offshore funds	10-5, 10-6
4.1.6	Structured investment funds – equity index-based and equity-based growth and income funds	10-7
4.1.7	Relative merits of direct investment versus investment in funds	10-1
4.1.8	The process of buying and selling OEICs and unit trusts	10-2, 10-3
4.1.9	Fund supermarkets and wraps	10-4
4.2	**Investment trusts**	
4.2.1	Basic structure and characteristics:	11-1
	• closed ended structure	11-1
	• differences between closed and other funds	11-1
	• range of investment trusts	11-1
4.2.2	Main different classes of share:	11-4
	• ordinary	11-4
	• income	11-4
	• zero dividend	11-4
	• capital	11-4
4.2.3	Dealing	11-2
4.2.4	Pricing and net asset value (NAV)	11-3
4.2.5	Premiums and discounts	11-3
4.2.6	Gearing – advantages and drawbacks in terms of risk and flexibility	11-3, 11-4
4.2.7	Performance of investment trusts – risk and returns	11-3, 11-4
4.2.8	Taxation – dividends, capital gains of investment trusts and for the investors who own them	11-6
4.2.9	Warrants	11-5
4.3	**ISAs**	
4.3.1	Structure – components:	13-2
	• stocks and shares, cash	13-2
	• annual investment limits	13-2
4.3.2	Charging – initial and annual charges for direct investments and collectives, stakeholder standards	13-2
4.3.3	Tax treatment – interest dividends, mixed bond funds, capital gains;	13-2
4.3.4	Eligibility – age, residence	13-2
4.3.5	Transfers – restrictions, rules	13-2
4.3.6	Death of the investor	13-2

Syllabus Item		BPP Study Text Reference (Chapter – Section)
4.4	**Onshore and offshore life assurance company products**	
4.4.1	Structure and characteristics of life assurance funds and products	12-1, 12-2, 12-3, 12-4
4.4.2	Qualifying policies – maximum investment plans and other endowments	12-7
4.4.3	Traded endowments	12-5
4.4.4	Charges – initial and annual	12-3, 12-4
4.4.5	Taxation – onshore and offshore, within the fund and for the investor	12-7
4.4.6	Differences between life assurance bonds and OEICs/unit trusts	12-6
4.4.7	Structure and characteristics of purchased life annuities	12-8
4.5	Multi managers – manager of managers and fund of funds	10-4
4.6	Venture Capital Trusts (VCTs) and Enterprise Investment Schemes (EIS) – structure, tax characteristics, past performance in terms of risk and returns	13-4, 13-5
4.7	Exchange Traded Funds	10-4
4.8	Child Trust Funds	13-3
5	**Understand the role of ethical investment and socially responsible investment in financial advice**	
5.1	Socially responsible investment – definition of socially responsible investment	14-1
5.2	Ethical investment – definition of ethical investment and the criteria used for including or excluding companies in ethical funds	14-1, 14-2
5.3	Implications for investment performance	14-2, 14-3
6	**Understand how investment returns are related to investment risk and how that risk is measured**	
6.1	Principles of investment risk	15-1, 15-3
6.2	Inflation and investment returns – the difference between nominal and real returns	15-2
6.3	The effects of compound and simple interest	15-2
6.4	The time value of money	15-2
6.5	Varying investment returns from the main different asset classes – risk-free rates of return and the risk premium	15-6
6.6	Measuring risk – volatility, the significance of standard deviation as a measure of volatility, the importance and limitations of performance data	15-4
6.7	Sharpe Ratio	15-6
6.8	Measuring total return and the significance of beta and alpha	15-2
6.9	Investment portfolio planning and reducing risk through diversification – systematic and unsystematic risk, diversification across shares, sectors, markets and asset classes	15-5
7	**Understand the risks faced by investors and how an investor's risk profile is determined**	
7.1	The importance of affordability and suitability in making financial planning decisions	16-3, 16-4
7.2	Main types of risk for investors – equity capital risk, currency risk, interest rate risk, institutional risk, regulatory risk, income risk, inflation risk, shortfall risk, legislative risk, counterparty risk	15-3

INVESTMENT AND RISK

Syllabus Item			BPP Study Text Reference (Chapter – Section)
7.3	Objective factors to determine an investor's risk tolerance – timescale of investment, age, commitments, wealth, life cycle		16-3
7.4	Subjective factors to determine an investor's risk tolerance – attitudes and experiences		16-3
7.5	Methods of assessing an investor's risk tolerance		16-4
8	**Understand the importance of asset allocation in the investment process**		
8.1	The definition and importance of asset allocation – achieving objectives, reducing risk, need for review		16-2, 16-3, 16-4
8.2	The underlying composition of funds – managed funds, with-profits funds and other funds		16-2
8.3	Sample asset allocations for different types of investors		16-3
8.4	Different approaches to asset allocation		16-1, 16-5
8.5	Quantitative and qualitative statistical data		16-1
9	**Understand tax planning strategies**		
9.1	Basic Income Tax and Capital Gains Tax computations – personal allowances, non-savings income, savings income, dividends, life assurance bond profits, chargeable gains		4-1.5, 4-2.3
9.2	Basic investment tax planning – use of personal allowances, spouses' personal allowances, children's tax position, pension contributions, use of ISAs, use of Capital Gains Tax exemptions, tax deferral, use of life assurance bonds, entrepreneurs' relief		13-8
9.3	Criteria for selecting a tax planning strategy		13-8
9.4	Rules and procedures relating to personal tax calculations		4-1.2, 4-2.3
9.5	Tax calculations		4-1.5
9.6	Legal requirements applying to confidentiality and disclosure of personal tax information		13-8
10	**Understand how other issues affect investment planning**		
10.1	Charges, their impact on returns, reduction in yields		16-5
10.2	Active investment management		16-1
10.3	Passive investment management		16-1
10.4	The relationship between investing and borrowing		16-3
10.5	Alternative investments (gold, art, antiques), commodities and alternative energy		9-1, 9-2
10.6	Advantages and disadvantages of using past performance		17-6
10.7	Advantages and disadvantages of using aggregation and consolidation services		16-5
10.8	Implications for the consumer of closed and/or underperforming funds		12-2
11	**Understand the importance of keeping up to date with trends and changes in the legal framework for providing advice**		
11.1	Existing regulations and forthcoming changes in regulation and legislation affecting investment advice and the investment market		17
11.2	Trends in case law affecting investment advice		17

Syllabus Item		BPP Study Text Reference (Chapter – Section)
12	**Analyse consumers' circumstances and suitable investment products, taking account of any existing arrangements**	
12.1	Factors shaping consumers' circumstances	16-1, 16-3
12.2	Affordability and suitability	16-3, 16-5, 17-7
12.3	Methods of identifying and reviewing suitable product solutions	16-5
12.4	The impact of new solutions on existing arrangements	16-5
13	**Apply suitable investment product solutions to specific consumers' circumstances**	
13.1	The range of solutions available to suit different types of circumstance	16-5
13.2	The criteria for matching solutions to consumer needs and demands	16-5
13.3	Factors influencing the way in which recommendations are presented	16-6
13.4	Confirm consumers' understanding of recommendations	17-7
13.5	Consumer rights and the regulatory requirements that apply to the provision of investment advice	17

Website links

Organisation	Information included	Website address
Association of British Insurers	Insurance topics	www.abi.org.uk
Association of Investment Companies	Investment trust data	www.aitc.co.uk
BPP Professional Education	Study material and Updates	www.bpp.com/learningmedia
Chartered Insurance Institute®	Cert FP exam information	www.cii.co.uk
Debt Management Office	Details of gilts	www.dmo.gov.uk
Department for Work and Pensions	State benefits	www.dwp.gov.uk
Ethical Research Service	Research on ethical investments	www.eiris.org
Financial Services Authority (FSA)	Regulatory information	www.fsa.gov.uk
FTSE	FTSE indices	www.ftse.com
HM Revenue & Customs (HMRC) – practitioners' area	Technical tax information	www.hmrc.gov.uk/practitioners
HMRC	Child Trust Funds	www.childtrustfund.gov.uk
Investment Management Association	Unit trust and OEIC/ICVC data	www.investmentuk.org
National Savings and Investments	NS&I products	www.nsandi.com
Office for National Statistics	Demographic, economic and other statistical information	www.statistics.gov.uk
Pension Service (part of DWP)	Information on state pensions and other benefits	www.thepensionservice.gov.uk
Pensions Regulator	Regulator of work-based pensions	www.thepensionsregulator.gov.uk

Examination format

The examination consists of **100 Multiple Choice Questions**. Each **multiple choice question** will consist of a problem followed by four options, labelled A, B, C and D, from which you are asked to choose the one correct or best response. One mark is awarded for each correct response. No marks are deducted for incorrect responses.

The **duration** of the examination for CF2 is **two hours**.

The nominal **pass mark** for the exam is **70%**. There is no pre-defined quota of passes, but the actual pass mark may be varied depending on the difficulty of the question paper, to ensure a consistent standard.

In the examination, pay particular attention to words in the question that are emphasised in **bold** type, for example: **maximum**, **minimum**, **main**, **most**, **normally** and **usually**. Negative wording is emphasised by the use of capital letters, for example **NOT** and **CANNOT**.

When do changes become examinable?

The CF2 examination will be based on the legislative position in England **three months** before the date of the examination.

What skills are tested?

The CF2 syllabus requires the ability to **apply and analyse knowledge and understanding** of the subject matter.

Candidates may be tested at the following **cognitive skill levels**.

- **Knowledge.** Candidates are required to know and be able to recall factual information. Typically questions may ask 'What', 'When' or 'Who'.

- **Understanding.** Candidates must be able to link pieces of information together in cause and effect relationships. Typically questions may ask 'Why'.

  Questions set on an 'understand' learning outcome can test either knowledge or understanding or both.

- **Application.** To answer application questions, the candidate must be able to apply his/her knowledge and/or understanding to a given set of circumstances. Typically questions may require candidates to 'Calculate' – for example, 'Calculate liability to Income Tax'.

  Questions set on a 'be able to apply' learning objective can test knowledge and/or understanding as well as application.

- **Analysis.** Candidates must be able to analyse a set of circumstances and use that skill to be able to make calculations, differentiate between important aspects or identify courses of action. Typically questions may ask 'How' - for example, 'How would you classify?'

  Questions set on an 'analyse' learning outcome can test understanding, application or analysis.

Tackling MCQs

Multiple choice questions (MCQs) each contain a number of possible answers. You have to choose the **one** option(s) that **best** answers the question. The incorrect options are called distracters.

There is a skill in answering MCQs quickly and correctly. By practising MCQs you can develop this skill, giving you a better chance of passing the exam.

You may wish to follow the approach outlined below, or you may prefer to adapt it to suit your own learning style and needs.

Step 1. **Note down how long** you should allocate to each MCQ. For example, since you have 100 questions to answer in 120 minutes, you have 1.2 minutes on average to answer each question. For a group of 10 questions, you have 12 minutes. You will probably not spend an equal amount of time on each MCQ. You might be able to answer some questions instantly while others will take more time to work out.

Step 2. **Attempt each question**. Read the question thoroughly. A particular question might look familiar to you, but be aware that the detail and/or requirement may be different from any similar question you have come across. So, read the requirement and options carefully, even for questions that seem familiar.

Step 3. Read all the options and see if one matches your own answer. Be careful with numerical questions, as the distracters are designed to match answers that incorporate **common errors**. Check that your calculation is correct. Have you followed the requirement exactly? Have you included every stage of the calculation?

Step 4. You may find that none of the options matches your answer.

- **Re-read the question** to ensure that you understand it and are answering the requirement
- **Eliminate any obviously wrong answers**
- **Consider which of the remaining answers** is the **most likely** to be correct or best and select that option

Step 5. If you are still unsure, **continue to the next question**.

If you are nowhere near working out which option is correct after a couple of minutes, leave the question and come back to it later. Make a note of any questions for which you have submitted answers but you need to return to later.

Step 6. **Revisit questions** you are uncertain about. When you come back to a question after a break, you may find that you are able to answer it correctly straight away. If you are still unsure, have a guess. You are not penalised for incorrect answers, so **do not leave a question unanswered!**

Investment and Risk

chapter 1

Chapter topic list

1	Demographic profile of the UK	2
2	Household income, wealth and living standards	8
3	Productivity and technology	10
4	Sectors of the economy	11
	Key chapter points	13
	Chapter quiz	15

Socio-economic trends

INVESTMENT AND RISK

CHAPTER LEARNING OUTCOMES

1 **Understand** the macroeconomic factors that affect investment returns

   1.1   The main long-term UK socio-economic trends

        1.1.1 Ageing population.
        1.1.2 Rising living standards.
        1.1.3 Growth of the service sector and other changing patterns of the UK economy.
        1.1.4 Productivity of capital and labour.
        1.1.5 Wealth and income distribution.
        1.1.6 Technological change.

1 Demographic profile of the UK

Learning outcome

1.1.1 Ageing population

Introduction

We start our studies by looking at features of the population of the UK. Social factors and economic factors are, of course, interrelated in various ways. If we are to understand people's investment needs, we should gain an overall understanding of the socio-economic trends making the UK what it is today.

1.1 Collecting the figures

Demography is the study of **populations** using statistical methods through **census** returns and other surveys. In the United Kingdom, a full census of the population is carried out every ten years. The last census was in 2001 and the next will be in 2011, though estimates are made each year and the latest figures available at the time of writing were for 2008

Many important facts about a country's demographic profile are collected by government to aid planning. Originally, the UK government conducted its census as a population count alone, but more recently additional information about the population has been requested. Apart from the census, other official surveys and information sources provide demographic information.

The UK government publishes various statistics every year, as a result of its various data collection exercises. Two examples are the **Annual Abstract of Statistics** and **Social Trends**. Both contain population data, although **Social Trends** goes into more detail about people's habits. Summary Census information can also be viewed at **www.statistics.gov.uk**. Some data comparisons from the past and projections into the future are given below.

1.2 Population size

The population of the UK as a whole grew significantly during the 20th century, but this growth is **expected to level off** during the 21st century.

1: SOCIO-ECONOMIC TRENDS

In every year since 1901 (with one exception – 1976), there were more births than deaths in the UK. The population has grown due to natural change. Until the mid-1990s, this natural increase was the main driver of population growth. Since the late 1990s, there has been a continuing natural increase, but net international migration into the UK from other countries has been an increasingly important factor in population change.

Population of the United Kingdom

	2021 projected '000s	2008 '000s	2001 '000s	1991 '000s	1901 '000s	% change 1901–2001
England & Wales	59,620	54,450	52,042	51,100	32,528	60
Scotland	5,411	5,169	5,062	5,107	4,472	13
Northern Ireland	1,927	1,775	1,685	1,601	1,237	36
United Kingdom	66,958	61,394	58,789	57,808	38,237	54

You can see from the figures above how the last century saw a significant **increase in population**, particularly in England & Wales. The increase is projected to continue.

The current population of the UK is 61.4 million people.

1.3 Gender distribution

UK population by gender

	2016 projected Millions	%	2001 Millions	%	1991 Millions	%	1901 Millions	%
Males	32.0	49.4	28.6	48.6	28.3	49.0	18.5	48.4
Females	32.8	50.6	30.2	51.4	29.5	51.0	19.7	51.6
Total	64.8	100.0	58.8	100.0	57.8	100.0	38.2	100.0

There is a slightly greater number of women than men in the population, reflecting the fact that women generally have a longer **life expectancy** than men. However, there are more males below the age of 65 than females reflecting the fact that there are more male births than female births.

1.4 Age structure

The **age structure** of the population is of particular concern to planners and business organisations.

The population increases mentioned above have not occurred for all age groups. While the proportion of the population aged 65 and over has increased, the proportion of the population below the age of 16 is less now than it was thirty years ago. The percentage of people aged 65 and over increased from 13 per cent in mid-1971 to 16 per cent in mid-2007. Over the same period, the percentage of the population under 16 fell from 25 per cent to 19 per cent.

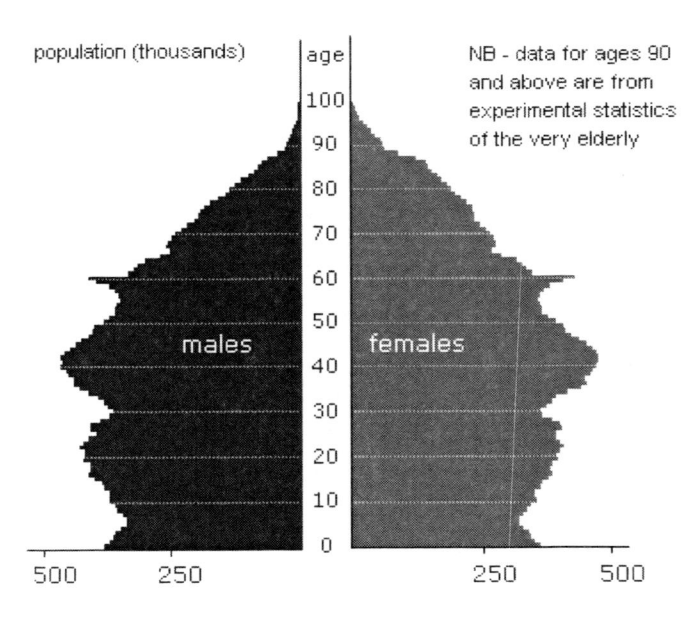

Age and gender structure of the UK population (2007)
Source: Office for National Statistics

The age structure, as with population size generally, depends significantly on birth rates and death rates. Importantly, of course, the age structure depends not only on the **current** birth rate, but also on that of previous years. For example, there was an increase in the numbers of births immediately following World War II and another, as these 'baby boomers' themselves had children, in the 1960s.

In 1961, 12% of the population were 65 or over. This is expected to rise to 24% by 2031. The table below illustrates trends for the age structure.

UK population age structure

	Under 16 %	16-24 %	25-34 %	35-44 %	45-54 %	55-64 %	65-74 %	75+ %	Total Millions
1961	25	12	13	14	14	12	8	4	52.8
1996	21	11	16	14	13	10	9	7	58.8
2007	19	12	13	15	13	12	8	8	61.0
2021 (proj)	18	11	13	12	13	14	11	9	62.2

In 2007, the average age of the UK population was 39.0 years, an increase on 1971 when it was 34.1 years. In 2007, around one in five people in the UK were aged under 16 and one in six people were aged 65 or over.

1: SOCIO-ECONOMIC TRENDS

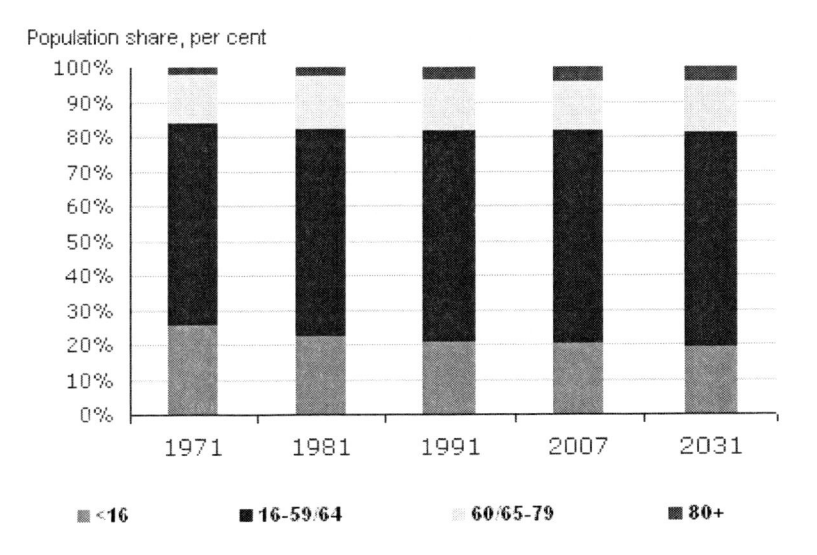

Ageing population
Source: Office for National Statistics

The effect of greater life expectancy is that a larger proportion of the population will be senior citizens (say, 65 years or over) and unlikely to be working.

(a) A country with an **expanding population** will have **larger proportions of children and old people**, and **lower proportions of people of working age**.

(b) A country with a **declining population** will eventually have a **large proportion of old people** and **reducing proportions of people of other ages**.

1.5 Implications of an ageing population

Generally, the **working population** must create a country's economic wealth. With more people at retirement age, and also more young children, the proportion of the population which is working will be lower, and the proportion that is non-working and dependent on the working population will be higher. This puts an extra burden on the working population, which must pay, through taxes, for expenditures on:

- State old age pensions
- State health care
- State education and training of the young

It can be seen that, while the **working** population is fairly constant as a percentage, there is a shift in the relative proportion of elderly and young dependants. This has been occurring since 1961 and continued in the 1990s. This long-term shift is important for the following reasons.

(a) Elderly dependants have **different needs** (for long-term health provision, for example) to younger people whose needs are for education and so on. Planners must take this into account when allocating resources for social provision.

(b) The elderly, as a **market segment**, will become increasingly important, while adequate **retirement planning**, as the **Financial Services Authority** has emphasised, needs to be encouraged.

(c) The decline in the number of young people will mean that organisations might have to change their **recruitment policies** or **production methods**. There will be fewer young people, and more competition for them.

INVESTMENT AND RISK

1.6 Ethnicity

Ethnic minorities form around 8% of the UK's population. About half the UK's ethnic minority population lives in London and the South-East, comprising 12% of the population there, as opposed to 4% in the North.

Social Trends has reported that ethnic minority populations are younger (around one in three under 16 as opposed to one in five otherwise) than the average population.

1.7 Regional distribution

As well as changes in aggregate population numbers, there are changes in where people choose to live and work. Different **regions** may have different birth and death rates. In aggregate, these differences can have a significant influence on social provision (eg schools, hospitals) and infrastructure (eg roads).

Over the last twenty years or so, there has been a shift of population from cities and built-up areas to non-metropolitan regions. This can be caused by differing birth and death rates in the various regions, or internal or external migration.

Some of these trends may reverse over the next few years. There is pressure from government on local authorities in South-East England to build more homes, and create new or greatly expanded towns. There is also pressure to build on 'brown field' sites (sites of previous development) in cities.

1.8 Family

Demographic information is also used to map the social units in which people live (eg family size). Some trends in the UK are as follows.

- More and more people **live alone**, with one-person households accounting for 30% (6.5 million) of all **households** in 2001 (compared to 12% in 1961). Three-quarters of these are occupied by a woman living on her own. This fact could be reflected in advertising for a bank's mortgage service, for example. Instead of featuring couples buying a house, it may feature an individual buying a flat.
- At 2001, **married couples** made up 50.7 per cent of the adult population and 45% of households. However, the percentage of married couples in the population is declining. In 1991 it was 55%, in 1981 it was 64% and in 1971 it was 68%. This contrasts with the increase in the percentages of single (never married) people and **divorced** people. Marketers and advertisers have been criticised for advertising which does not reflect the realities of family life in the UK, but an idealised version of it.
- Almost 30% of households in England and Wales contain **dependent children** and one in nine have children under five years old. Of all households with dependent children, 59% are married couple households, 11% are cohabiting couples and 22% are lone-parent families (26% in London).
- 9.6% of households in England and Wales are lone-parent and over 90% of these are headed by a woman. Two thirds of **lone-parent households** have **dependent children** and the remaining third contain only **grown up children**.

1.9 Family life cycle

An example of a use of demography in the marketing of financial and other products and services is **family life cycle** (FLC). This is a summary of demographic variables.

```
        Age
+       Marital status
+       Career status
+       Whether have children
        ─────────────────────
        Family life cycle
```

Family life cycle is able to identify the various stages through which households progress. Particular products and services can be target marketed at people who occupy specific stages in the life cycle of families.

(a) **Single adulthood**

Individuals may have high disposable income; although they are at a low point on the career ladder, they will have few financial commitments. They will be able to indulge in activities such as attending concerts or dining out. With no family responsibilities, there may be little planning for the future, and only limited funds available for saving and investment.

(b) **Young married couples with no children**

This can be a prosperous period with two incomes and no costs of children. Couples may have the income to afford luxury purchases such as overseas holidays or fashionable clothing. However, there may be more concern about the future, for example taking out mortgages or pensions.

(c) **Married couples with dependent children**

Disposal income may fall as children consume resources of money and also time, thus leaving less time for other lifestyle activities.

(d) **Empty nesters**

These middle-aged people whose children have grown up and left home were the marketer's holy grail. Having no responsibilities and with mortgages paid off, they were seen as a wealthy market. In practice, matters have not worked out like this.

1.10 Problems with family life cycle

(a) **Caring**

'Empty nesters' are increasingly responsible for caring for their elderly parents, a burden on time and expense. This is a direct consequence of the ageing population. So, one set of responsibilities is merely exchanged for a new one.

(b) **Paying for care**

Empty nesters might have expected to benefit financially from the inheritance of their parents' wealth. However, as people are expected to pay for long-term nursing care, the elderly are frequently using up their capital in this way.

(c) **Job market**

Problems with the job market for young people mean that, anecdotal evidence suggesting, they stay home for longer before moving out. The vagaries of the labour and property markets have much to answer for.

(d) **Redundancy**

People of late middle age might be more likely to be made redundant in firms which are removing middle management layers.

INVESTMENT AND RISK

2 Household income, wealth and living standards

> **Learning outcomes**
> 1.1.2 Rising living standards
> 1.1.5 Wealth and income distribution

2.1 Interpreting the data

Comparing people's living standards might seem to be a simple matter. Surely, all we need to do is compare income after direct tax and social security contributions to see how well off people are? In reality, it is not so simple.

Collecting and presenting data relating to **wealth** and **living standards** raises problems, and such data should be viewed with a critical eye. The State (the Government) levies taxes and pays out benefits. Wealthier households tend to be **taxed more than** they **benefit**, and poorer households **benefit more** than they are **taxed**.

2.2 UK wealth and income distribution

2.2.1 Income distribution

The following graph shows the changes in the distribution of UK income from 1977 to 2007. In 1977 the top fifth earned 36% of the total income but this has risen to 42% in 2007. In contrast, the bottom fifth of the population earned 10% of total income in 1997, this has now fallen to 8%. It is clear, therefore, that the income gap between the highest and lowest earners has widened markedly over this period, income inequality has increased.

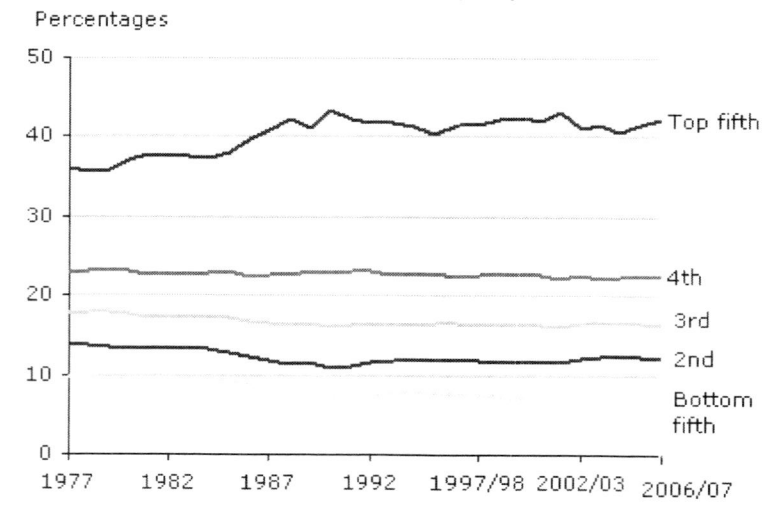

Household income by quintile group
Source: Office for National Statistics

2.2.2 Wealth distribution

The following table shows the distribution of UK wealth from 1976 to 2003 (the latest dates available).

1: SOCIO-ECONOMIC TRENDS

United Kingdom — Percentages

Marketable wealth

Percentage of wealth owned by:

	1976	1986	1996	1999	2000	2001	2002	2003
Most wealthy 1%	21	18	20	23	23	22	24	21
Most wealthy 5%	38	36	40	43	44	42	45	40
Most wealthy 10%	50	50	52	55	56	54	57	53
Most wealthy 25%	71	73	74	75	75	72	75	72
Most wealthy 50%	92	90	93	94	95	94	94	93
Total marketable wealth (£ billion)	280	955	2,092	2,861	3,131	3,477	3,588	3,783

Marketable wealth less value of dwellings

Percentage of wealth owned by:

	1976	1986	1996	1999	2000	2001	2002	2003
Most wealthy 1%	29	25	26	34	33	34	37	34
Most wealthy 5%	47	46	49	59	59	58	62	58
Most wealthy 10%	57	58	63	72	73	72	74	71
Most wealthy 25%	73	75	81	87	89	88	87	85
Most wealthy 50%	88	89	94	97	98	98	98	99

Share of wealth
Source: Office for National Statistics

In the UK, a large proportion of wealth is held as **property**, and so increases or falls in property prices can affect wealth significantly. In 1971, 26% of personal sector wealth was in dwellings. By 1991 this had risen to 36%, before falling to 26% in 1995 as a result of declining house prices. Since then, house prices have risen again significantly.

We can see from the data above that the wealthiest 1 per cent owned approximately a fifth of the UK's marketable wealth in 2003. In contrast, half the population shared only 7 per cent of total wealth. The results are even more skewed if housing is excluded from the estimates, suggesting this form of wealth is more evenly distributed.

Wealth is considerably less evenly distributed than income, and life cycle effects mean that this will almost always be so. People build up assets during the course of their working lives and then draw them down during the years of retirement, with the residue passing to others at their death.

2.2.3 Household expenditure

The patterns of household expenditure show the general increase in the standard of living over the period from 1971 to 2007. In 1971, food (the absolute essential) consumed 21% of average income, whereas this had declined to 9% by 2007.

INVESTMENT AND RISK

	1971	1981	1991	2001	2007
Food and non-alcoholic drinks	21	17	12	9	9
Alcoholic drinks and tobacco	7	6	5	4	4
Clothing and footwear	9	7	6	6	6
Housing, water and fuel	15	17	18	19	20
Household goods and services	7	7	6	6	6
Health	1	1	2	2	2
Transport	12	15	15	15	14
Communication	1	2	2	2	2
Recreation and culture	9	9	10	12	12
Education	1	1	1	2	2
Restaurants and hotels	10	11	12	12	12
Other	7	7	11	11	11

Household expenditure by purpose
Source: Office for National Statistics

When expenditure patterns are examined, we find that **wealthier professionals** spend less of a **proportion** of their total income on food and housing, and more on leisure, than do unskilled manuals. This does not imply they spend less in absolute terms: they have more available to spend on other things.

2.3 Earnings growth

In the early years of the 21st century, growth in earnings for the UK has been more subdued relative to the late 1990s. For example, the **Average Earnings Index** grew by 3.8 per cent in 2002 and 3.1 per cent during 2001, compared with 5.5 per cent for 1999 and 4.5 per cent for 2000.

Growth in earnings can vary widely between sectors. 2001/2002 was the first sustained period since 1993 in which **public sector** (government) employees' earnings growth was higher than for the **private sector**.

2.4 Earnings and living standards

In considering trends in households' income over time, we can adjust the money income received by inflation to establish the change in **real incomes.** If people's real incomes are increasing and the population is more or less stable, this increase in real incomes is reflected in growth in **national output.** As real incomes rise, as they do in periods of economic growth, people can buy more goods and services than before. Their '**living standards**' in an economic sense are increasing. During a recession, which is conventionally defined as a period of at least two quarters of falling output, overall living standards will fall. Of course, even in a recession, there will be some whose incomes increase, although the overall impact will be a loss in living standards.

3 Productivity and technology

Learning outcomes

1.1.4 Productivity of capital and labour.
1.1.6 Technological change.

3.1 What is productivity?

Economists identify four **factors of production** in the economy: **Land, Labour, Capital** (ie machinery and plant) and **Enterprise.** These factors are combined in various ways, in order to produce goods and services.

Productivity is a measure of the efficiency with which factors of production are used. It can be calculated as the total output divided by the number of units of a factor of production – for example, the number of persons employed (to measure the **productivity of labour**), or the number of machines used (to measure the **productivity of capital**).

Substitution between factors of production (for example, between labour and capital) may take place provided that substitution is practical or technologically feasible (for example, machines can be made to do the work previously carried out by labour, or that labour can physically do the work of machines). Substitution is likely when the price or productivity of one factor of production **rises relative to another**. If wages go up, the marginal cost of labour will rise, and firms will want less labour at this higher cost. Labour will also become more expensive in relation to capital, and there will be some **substitution of capital for labour**. The net result of an increase in wages will be a reduction in the quantity of labour employed – unless the productivity of labour can be increased at the same time, to strengthen the demand for labour.

Increases in productivity create greater economic wealth and boost real household incomes. By producing more with the country's factors of production, there are more goods and services available for people to use and consume.

3.2 Technological change

The development of new **technology** is behind much of the increases in productivity that create economic growth. New technologies can produce significant leaps forward in economic conditions. The mass production made possible by the Industrial Revolution of the late 18th century was fuelled by advances in the spinning of cotton and the development of steam power. Electrification and the development of motorised transport were further major technological changes.

We are now in an age when **computerisation** is making major changes to the economy and to how businesses organise their operations. The development of the **internet** is still in progress, and everyone has seen that the internet has wide-ranging implications for how businesses communicate with customers and how information is disseminated.

The availability of fast and efficient **telecommunications** enables a shift to new ways of employing staff resources and reaching customers. In the past, workers may have had to relocate to where employers delivered their services. Now, a bank, for example, may '**outsource**' many staff functions involving communication with customers to overseas call centres: extensive branch networks have become a thing of the past for many financial services companies, and many functions have been centralised.

4 Sectors of the economy

Learning outcome

1.1.3 Growth of the service sector and other changing patterns of the UK economy.

4.1 Primary, secondary and tertiary sectors

A distinction can be made between **primary**, **secondary** and **tertiary** sectors of the economy.

- The **primary sector** of the economy consists of industries which produce **raw materials** such as crops and minerals. These are sometimes called **extractive industries**. Over the long term, the trend for the UK is one of decline in this sector when measured in terms of its share of gross domestic product (GDP).

Viewed against the process of economic growth, this declining share reflects **the rising absolute level** of output of other industries.

- The **secondary sector** consists of industries which **process raw materials**, and is broadly referred to as **manufacturing industry**. This sector normally grows rapidly during the early stages of economic development. The UK has reached a later stage of decline, mainly due to the **decline** of **manufacturing**, which is the part of the sector most heavily involved in international trade, as opposed to construction and energy and water. The decline in the secondary sector has led to a **reduction in employment** in the sector bringing some problems of severe unemployment in regions which have been heavily dependent on particular industries.

- The **tertiary sector** is made up mainly of **goods distribution and service industries**. It is often referred to as the **service sector** of the economy. This sector has become the predominant provider of employment and output in the UK economy in recent decades. A major reason for the continuing growth in this sector has been the rapid expansion in the banking, finance and insurance sectors.

4.2 The tertiary service sector

Within the tertiary **service sector**, the rising share of **banking, finance and insurance** reflects a number of factors.

(a) London has built on its reputation as one of the leading financial centres of the world, and in many areas (for example, currency trading) it is pre-eminent. The strong position of 'the City' (the London financial community) makes it a large exporter of financial services.

(b) Increasing affluence and changing social factors (eg increasing levels of owner-occupation of housing) have increased domestic demand for financial products of various kinds (eg current accounts, mortgages and insurance products).

(c) Events such as the abolition of exchange controls in 1979 and the deregulation of financial markets during the 1980s (for example the Stock Exchange 'Big Bang' and the Building Societies Act of 1986) served to free up supply as well as intensify competition in this subsector.

There is much fiercer competition than there used to be between **financial institutions** for business. For example, building societies have emerged as competitors to the banks, and foreign banks have competed successfully in the UK with the big clearing banks. Insurance companies have diversified their range of products, including moves into banking by some. Banks themselves have changed too, with some shift towards more fee-based activities (such as selling advice and selling insurance products for commission) and away from the traditional transaction-based activities (holding deposits, making loans).

4.3 Profitability of sectors

Profitability can be measured as the net rate of return on capital employed, after allowing for depreciation of assets. In general, the **service sector** has higher profitability than the **manufacturing sector**: this reflects the fact that the manufacturing sector is more capital intensive, and so involves more capital expenditure on fixed assets.

Key chapter points

- The UK population is increasing slowly. In aggregate, the age structure is shifting towards a higher proportion of elderly people. There is a slow increase in single person households, but most people live as part of larger units. Around 8% of the UK population belong to ethnic minorities.

- With more older people, and also more young children, the proportion of the population that is working reduces, and the proportion that is non-working and dependent on the working population increases.

- Living standards rise when incomes increase by more than the rate of inflation.

- The value of property is a significant part of personal sector wealth in the UK.

- Productivity is a measure of how much output is produced by factors of production. Factors of production are land, labour, capital and enterprise. Increases in productivity, for example those produced by technological developments, create economic wealth and enhance household incomes and therefore living standards.

- A major factor behind the growth in the tertiary service sector of the economy has been the rapid expansion of the banking, finance and insurance sectors.

1: SOCIO-ECONOMIC TRENDS

Chapter Quiz

1. How often does the national Census take place? .... (see para 1.2)
2. Outline some of the implications of an ageing population. .... (1.6)
3. What is an 'empty nester'? .... (1.10)
4. Which better reflects changes in living standards: increases in money income or increases in real income? .. (2.4)
5. Define 'productivity of labour'. .... (3.1)
6. What is the meaning of 'outsourcing'? .... (3.2)
7. Explain what is meant by the primary, secondary and tertiary sectors of the economy. .... (4.1)

chapter 2

The economic framework

Chapter topic list

1	The role of government	17
2	The role of central banks	22
3	Capital markets and money markets	23
4	International trade	27
5	Globalisation	30
6	European Economic and Monetary Union	31
	Key chapter points	34
	Chapter quiz	35

INVESTMENT AND RISK

Chapter Learning Outcomes

1 **Understand** the macroeconomic factors that affect investment returns

    1.2   The global factors that affect investment returns:

           1.2.1   International markets.
           1.2.2   Globalisation of trade and finance.
           1.2.3   European economic and monetary union.
           1.2.4   Political factors.

    1.3   The role of government and central banks

           1.3.1   Fiscal and monetary policy.

    1.6   The role of financial investment in the economy

           1.6.1   Primary markets – how investment markets introduce new funds to business and the government.
           1.6.2   Secondary markets – how markets enable investors to adjust their investments to suit their needs.

    1.7   The key economic indicators

           1.7.3   Public Sector Net Cash Requirement (PSNCR).
           1.7.8   Bank rates and London Interbank Offered Rate (LIBOR).
           1.7.9   Gilt yields.
           1.7.10 Stock market indices and benchmarks.

1 The role of government

Learning outcomes

1.3.1   Fiscal and monetary policy.
1.7.3   Public Sector Net Cash Requirement (PSNCR).

1.1 Economic policy aims

As well as providing a legal and regulatory framework for economic activity, the government plays a role in managing the economy. Among the aims of a government's **economic policy** may be the following.

    (a)   To achieve **sustainable growth** in national income per head of the population. Growth implies an increase in national income in real terms. National income grows through expansion of economic activity: more goods and services become available for people to consume. The idea of sustainable growth implies that the fluctuations of the business cycle are avoided and that output grows on a steady upward trend. This is generally seen as the most important goal of a government's economic policy.

    (b)   To **control inflation** in prices. This has become a central objective of economic policy in many countries in recent years.

    (c)   To achieve **full employment.** Full employment does not mean that everyone who wants a job has one all the time, but it does mean that unemployment levels are low, and involuntary unemployment is short-term.

(d) To achieve a **trade balance** – that is, a balance between exports and imports. The wealth of a country relative to others, a country's creditworthiness as a borrower, and the goodwill between countries in international relations might all depend on the achievement of an external balance over time. Deficits in external trade, with imports exceeding exports, might also be damaging for the prospects of economic growth.

It should be noted that some of these are conflicting aims. Where aggregate demand in the economy exceeds the available resources we will experience inflation with full employment. Where aggregate demand is below the available resources we will experience unemployment and, consequently, little inflation. Under normal circumstances, inflation and unemployment are negatively correlated with one being high when the other is low.

1.2 The changing emphasis of economic policy

The **emphasis on different policy objectives** has changed over time in line with political, social and economic events. The objective of full employment was central to policy in developed countries following the Second World War. Later, other macro economic objectives came to the fore. Explicit policy commitments have been made by governments at different times in different countries to the objectives of low inflation, balance of payments equilibrium and sustainable development of the economy.

Sustainable development describes a pattern of economic growth at a local or a national level which is stable over the long term and is unlikely to be a victim of its own success. Sustainability implies that there will always be sufficient natural, financial and human resources available to meet future growth. Sustainable development has been particularly used to describe growth which does not destroy the natural resources which are vital to further production.

To try to achieve its intermediate and overall objectives, a government will use a number of different **policy tools** or **policy instruments.** These policy tools are not mutually exclusive and a government might adopt a **mix of policies** to achieve its economic objectives. Conflicts may arise between different objectives, meaning that choices have to be made. Two main areas of policy are **fiscal policy** and **monetary policy**.

1.3 Fiscal policy

Fiscal policy is government policy on taxation, public borrowing and public spending.

- **Direct taxation** is taxation of incomes.
- **Indirect taxation** is taxation of products and services, for example value added tax.

The amount that the government must borrow each year is now known as the **Public Sector Net Cash Requirement** (PSNCR) in the UK. Its former name was Public Sector Borrowing Requirement (PSBR). The public sector net cash requirement (PSNCR) is the annual excess of spending over income for the entire public sector – not just the central government.

A government might intervene in the economy by:

(a) **Spending more money** and financing this expenditure by borrowing

(b) **Collecting more in taxes** without increasing spending

(c) **Collecting more in taxes** in order to **increase spending**, thus diverting income from one part of the economy to another

In the UK in 1998, the newly elected Labour government introduced a Code for Fiscal Stability. This Code set out five principles used to guide fiscal policy: transparency, stability, responsibility, fairness and efficiency.

The government introduced two rules that would govern **UK fiscal policy**.

- The so-called **golden rule** states that, over the course of an economic cycle, the Government will borrow only for investment purposes. Current spending will not be funded by borrowing over the period as a whole. In other words, the Government will aim for the current budget to be in balance or in surplus over the economic cycle as a whole.

- The **sustainable investment rule** states that the ratio of public sector net debt to gross domestic product will be maintained at a stable and prudent level over the economic cycle. A prudent level, it is suggested, would be below 40%.

1.4 Fiscal policy consequences

A government's **'fiscal stance'** may be **neutral, expansionary** or **contractionary**, according to its overall effect on national income.

(a) **Spending more money** and financing this expenditure by borrowing would indicate an expansionary fiscal stance. Expenditure in the economy will increase and so national income will tend to rise, either in real terms, or partly in terms of price levels only: the increase in national income might be real, or simply inflationary. This may be referred to as **fiscal easing**.

(b) **Collecting more in taxes** without increasing spending would indicate a contractionary fiscal stance. A government might deliberately raise taxation to take inflationary pressures out of the economy

Collecting more in taxes in order to **increase spending**, thus diverting income from one part of the economy to another would indicate a broadly neutral fiscal stance.

If a government raises taxes and spending by the same amount so that the government's overall budget remains in balance, there will be an **increase in aggregate monetary demand**. This is because taxpayers would have saved some of the money they pay in increased tax and the government spends all of it within the economy. (This effect is called the **balanced budget multiplier**.)

Since government spending or tax reductions might be inflationary, and higher domestic prices make imports relatively cheaper and exports less competitive in foreign markets, fiscal policy has possible implications for the **balance of payments** (discussed later in this Study Text).

Fiscal policy could be used in an attempt to reduce unemployment and provide jobs. For example:

- More government spending on capital projects
- Government-funded training schemes
- Taxation of companies on the basis of the numbers and pay levels of employees

Government spending, however, might create inflationary pressures, and inflation tends to create more unemployment. Fiscal policy must therefore be used with care, even to create new jobs.

The impact of changes in fiscal policy is not always certain, and fiscal policy to pursue one aim (eg lower inflation) might for a while create barriers to the pursuit of other aims (eg employment).

Government planners need to consider how fiscal policy can affect **savers, investors** and **companies**.

(a) The tax regime as it affects different savings instruments or property ownership, for example, will affect **investors'** decisions.

(b) **Companies** will be affected by tax rules on dividends and profits, and they may take these rules into account when deciding on dividend policy or on whether to raise finance through **debt** (loans) or **equities** (by issuing shares).

1.5 Fiscal policy and the Budget

A feature of fiscal policy is that a government must **plan** what it wants to spend, and so how much it needs to raise in income or by borrowing. It needs to make a plan in order to establish how much taxation there should be, what form the taxes should take and so which sectors of the economy (firms or households, high income earners or low income earners) the money should come from.

This formal planning of fiscal policy usually follows an annual cycle. In the UK, the most important statement is **the Budget**, which takes place in the spring of each year. The Chancellor of the Exchequer also delivers a Pre-Budget Report each autumn. The Pre-Budget Report formally makes available for scrutiny the government's overall spending plans.

Because of the annual planning cycle of government finances, fiscal policy cannot be very responsive to shorter-term developments in the economy. For shorter-term fine-tuning of the economy, the government may need to use **monetary policy**.

1.6 Monetary policy

Monetary policy is the area of government economic policy making that is concerned with changes in the **amount of money** in circulation – the **money supply** – and with changes in the **price of money** – **interest rates**. These variables are linked with **inflation** in prices generally (hence indirectly to unemployment), and also with **exchange rates** – the price of the domestic currency in terms of other currencies. Tight control of the money supply should keep inflation low with the unfortunate trade-off of high unemployment.

In the next Chapter of this Study Text, we look at how the supply or stock of money in an economy affects inflation and other economic variables.

Although the control of inflation has remained the main objective for some time, the UK current monetary policy framework has evolved from changing circumstances in recent decades.

Up to the 1970s, monetary policy included direct **controls** on the amount of **lending** that banks were allowed to undertake. In the 1980s, the framework of monetary policy involved trying to control the overall supply of money in the economy. Targets were set for the growth of money (notes, coins, bank deposits) and interest rates were varied accordingly. However, measures of the amount of money in the economy did not always prove to be a reliable guide to demand and inflation. As a result, by the mid-1980s monetary policy came to be based on an assessment of a wider range of economic indicators rather than a single measure of money supply growth.

One aspect of this was that there were exchange rate targets, with the object of linking monetary policy and inflation in one country with that of another or others. For a period in the late 1980s, the target exchange rate was three Deutsche Marks to one pound (DM3 = £1). In 1990, the UK entered the **European Exchange Rate Mechanism (ERM)**. Monetary policy had to be set so that the pound would not strengthen or weaken by more than a certain amount against other ERM currencies.

In 1992, differing economic conditions across Europe created tensions between setting interest rates to maintain the exchange rate target and the exchange rate required for the domestic economy. There was strong growth and inflationary pressure in Germany, following its reunification. This made German interest rates high. On the other hand, the UK, was emerging from a recession, with slow growth and falling inflation. Maintaining sterling's position in the ERM limited the scope for reducing interest rates below the German levels to a rate that would have been better for the UK economy. Investors lost confidence in UK policy and did not want to hold sterling. Downward pressure on sterling led to a **suspension of ERM membership** on 16 September 1992 and a sharp depreciation of the sterling exchange rate.

After sterling's exit from the ERM, the UK Government adopted an **explicit target for inflation** for the first time. Instead of targeting the exchange rate or some other variable as a means of controlling inflation, a rate for inflation itself was targeted. Interest rates were to be set to ensure demand in the economy was kept at a level consistent with a certain level of inflation over time. If interest rates are increased consumers have less cash available to spend, weakening consumer demand and asset prices. If rates are decreased it will have the opposite effects.

INVESTMENT AND RISK

2 The role of central banks

> **Learning outcome**
> 1.7.8 Bank rates and London Interbank Offered Rate (LIBOR).

2.1 Central banks

A **central bank** is a bank which acts on behalf of government. You will probably also have heard, for example, of the **Federal Reserve Bank** – the central bank of the USA – and the **European Central Bank** – the central bank of the Euro currency zone. The central bank for the United Kingdom is the **Bank of England**.

2.2 The Bank of England

The Bank of England ('the Bank') is a nationalised corporation run by a Court of Directors, consisting of the Governor, Deputy Governor, and some Executive Directors and part-time Directors.

The following are functions of the Bank of England.

(a) It acts as **banker to the central government** and holds the 'public deposits'. Public deposits include the National Loans Fund, the Consolidated Fund and the account of the Paymaster General, which in turn includes the Exchange Equalisation Account.

(b) It is the **central note-issuing authority** in the UK – it is responsible for issuing bank notes in England.

(c) It is the **manager of the National Debt** – ie it deals with long-term and short-term borrowing by the central government and the repayment of central government debt.

(d) It is the manager of the Exchange Equalisation Account (ie the UK's **foreign currency reserves**).

(e) It acts as adviser to the government on **monetary policy** and, through its Monetary Policy Committee, manages interest rates in the light of the Government's inflation target.

(f) It acts as agent for the Government in carrying out its monetary policies. Since May 1997, it has had operational responsibility for **setting interest rates** at the level it considers appropriate in order to meet the Government's inflation target.

(g) It acts as a **banker to the commercial banks**, who keep accounts with the Bank of England.

(h) It acts as a **lender to the banking system**. When the banking system is short of money, the Bank of England will provide the money the banks need – at a suitable rate of interest.

Supervision of the banking system is now the responsibility of the Financial Services Authority – not of the Bank of England.

2.3 The central bank as lender of last resort

In the UK, the **short-term money market** provides a link between the banking system and the government (Bank of England). Normally, if one bank needs to borrow money it borrows it from another bank that has surplus funds at **LIBOR (London Inter-Bank Offered Rate)**. When such surplus funds are not available the Bank of England lends money to the banking system. The Bank thus acts as the **lender of last resort**.

(a) The Bank will supply cash to the banking system on days when the banks have a cash shortage. It does this by buying eligible bills and other short-term financial investments from approved financial institutions in exchange for cash.

(b) The Bank will remove excess cash from the banking system on days when the banks have a cash surplus. It does this by selling bills to institutions, so that the short-term money markets obtain interest-bearing bills in place of the cash that they do not want.

The process whereby this is done currently is known as **open market operations** by the Bank. This describes the buying and selling of eligible bills and other short-term assets between the Bank and the short-term money market.

2.4 Setting interest rates

Since 1997, the most important aspect of monetary policy in the UK has been the influence over interest rates exerted by the **Bank of England**, the **central bank** of the UK. The **Monetary Policy Committee (MPC)** of the Bank of England is charged with the responsibility of setting the **base rate** of interest with the aim of meeting the government's inflation target of 2% based on the **Consumer Prices Index (CPI)**, sometimes known by the name Harmonised Index of Consumer Prices (HICP).

If the inflation target is missed by more than 1 percentage point on either side – in other words, if the annual CPI inflation rate were to be more than 3% or less than 1% – the Governor of the Bank, as Chairman of the MPC, must write an open letter to the Chancellor explaining the reasons why inflation has increased or fallen to such an extent and what the Bank proposes to do to ensure inflation comes back to the target.

The MPC influences interest rates by deciding the short-term benchmark 'repo' rate at which the Bank of England deals in the money markets. This will tend to be followed by financial institutions generally in setting interest rates for different financial instruments. However, a government does not have an unlimited ability to have interest rates set how it wishes. It must take into account what rates the overall market will bear, so that the benchmark rate it chooses can be maintained.

The monthly minutes of the MPC are published. This arrangement is intended to remove the possibility of direct political influence over the interest rate decision.

The **UK inflation objective** was formalised in the 1998 Bank of England Act. That Act states that the Bank of England is expected 'to maintain price stability, and, subject to that, to support the economic policy of HM Government including its objectives for growth and employment' (Bank of England Act 1998).

3 Capital markets and money markets

Learning outcomes

1.2.1 International markets.
1.6.1 Primary markets – how investment markets introduce new funds to business and the government.
1.6.2 Secondary markets – how markets enable investors to adjust their investments to suit their needs.
1.7.9 Gilt yields.
1.7.10 Stock market indices and benchmarks.

3.1 Introduction

The following are types of market for dealing in capital.

(a) **Capital markets** are financial markets for raising and investing largely **long-term** capital.
(b) **Money markets** are financial markets for lending and borrowing largely **short-term** capital.

INVESTMENT AND RISK

What do we mean by **long-term**, as compared with **short-term** capital?

(a) By **short-term capital**, we mean capital that is lent or borrowed for a period which might range from as short as overnight up to about one year, and sometimes longer.

(b) By **long-term capital**, we mean capital invested or lent and borrowed for a period of about five years or more, but sometimes shorter.

(c) There is a **grey area** between long-term and short-term capital, which is lending and borrowing for a period from about 1-2 years up to about 5 years, which is not surprisingly referred to as **medium-term** capital.

Firms may obtain long-term or medium-term capital as **share capital** or as **loan capital**. Debentures, loan stock, bonds and commercial paper are all types of loan capital.

3.2 Stock markets

The **London Stock Exchange** is an organised capital market based in London which plays an important role in the functioning of the UK economy. It is the main capital market in the UK and operates as both a

(a) **Primary market** – a market where new funds are provided to issuers of new investments (eg. new share or bond issues). It makes it easier for large firms and the government to raise long-term capital, by providing a market place for borrowers and investors to come together.

(b) **Secondary market** – where currently existing investments may be traded. Secondary markets allow investors to purchase securities that have been issued previously. Such investors will often have had the benefit of being able to see how securities such as company shares have been trading. For the original investors who provide funds to enterprises in the primary market, the existence of secondary markets provides a means of exit, enabling the investor to sell the securities through the market. The Stock Exchange publicises the prices of quoted (or 'listed') securities, which are then reported in daily national newspapers such as the *Financial Times*. Investors can therefore keep an eye on the value of their stocks and shares, and make buying and selling decisions accordingly.

The Stock Exchange tries to enforce certain rules of conduct for its listed firms and for operators in the market, so that investors have the assurance that companies whose shares are traded on the Exchange and traders who operate there are reputable. Confidence in the Stock Exchange will make investors more willing to put their money into stocks and shares.

The **Alternative Investment Market** (AIM), which opened in 1995, is a market where smaller companies which cannot meet the more stringent requirements needed to obtain a full listing on the Stock Exchange can raise new capital by issuing shares. In this way, the AIM acts as a **primary market**.

Like the Stock Exchange main market, the AIM is also a **secondary market** in which investors can trade in shares already issued. The AIM is regulated by the Stock Exchange.

Stock market indices measure the rises and falls in baskets of stocks, and therefore act like a 'barometer' of market conditions and sentiment. Some important stock market indices are outlined in another Chapter of this Study Text.

Shares and other financial instruments may also be bought and sold outside the supervised and regulated official exchanges in **over-the-counter (OTC) markets**. OTC market prices are negotiated rather than set by auction, as is the case in most stock exchanges. In the USA, OTC market prices are reported via the National Association of Securities Dealers Automatic Quotation System (NASDAQ). Most OTC trading deals with shares that are not quoted on any public stock exchange.

3.3 Banks

Banks can be approached directly by firms and individuals for medium-term and long-term loans as well as short-term loans or overdrafts. The major clearing banks, many merchant banks and foreign banks operating in the UK are increasingly willing to lend medium-term capital, especially to well established companies.

3.4 Gilts

The gilt-edged market is a further major capital market in the UK, acting as a **primary market** in offering finance to the government. The **government** borrows over the medium and longer term by issuing **government stocks** (called 'gilt-edged stock' or **gilts**). Trade in second hand gilts (the **secondary market** in gilts) will continue until the debt eventually matures and the government redeems the stock.

The interest paid on a gilt relative to its market price is indicated by the **yield**: this is explained further in another Chapter of this Study Text. The yields on gilt-edged stocks indicate the market's view of the likely level of interest rates in the economy over the period until the gilt matures.

Gilts may be issued either by selling them direct to dealers, or by selling them to the Bank of England first, and then releasing them gradually ('on tap') to the market at a suitable time.

The primary gilts market is the market for the sale of new gilt issues. There is an active market in second-hand gilts with existing holders selling their holdings of gilts to other investors in the gilts market.

3.5 Providers of capital

The providers of capital include private individuals, such as those who buy stocks and shares on the Stock Exchange, and those who deposit money with banks, building societies and National Savings & Investments (NS&I), the government agency set up to borrow on behalf of the government, generally from individuals in the non-bank private sector of the economy.

There are also the important groups of **institutional investors** which specialise in providing capital and act as **financial intermediaries**, intermediating between suppliers and demanders of funds. Many financial services organisations now have diversified operations covering a range of the following areas of activity.

- (a) **Pension funds.** Pension funds invest the pension contributions of individuals who subscribe to a pension fund, and of organisations with a company pension fund.

- (b) **Insurance.** This includes life offices as well as general insurers. General insurance companies invest premiums paid on insurance policies by policy holders. Insurance companies, like pension funds, must do something with the premiums they receive, and in practice, they invest the money to earn a return.

- (c) **Investment trusts.** The business of investment trust companies is investing in the stocks and shares of other companies and the government. In other words, they trade in investments.

- (d) **Unit trusts.** Unit trusts are similar to investment trusts in the sense that they invest in stocks and shares of other companies. A unit trust comprises a portfolio – ie a holding of stocks or shares in a range of companies or gilts, perhaps with all the shares or stocks having a special characteristic, such as all shares in property companies or all shares in mining companies. The trust will then create a large number of small units of low nominal value, with each unit representing a stake in the total portfolio. These units are then sold to individual investors and investors will benefit from the income and capital gain on their units – ie their proportion of the portfolio.

- (e) **Venture capital companies.** Venture capital providers are organisations that specialise in raising funds for new business ventures, such as 'management buy-outs' (ie purchases of firms by their management staff). These organisations are therefore providing capital for fairly risky ventures. A venture capital

INVESTMENT AND RISK

organisation that has operated for many years in the UK is Investors in Industry plc, usually known as '3i'. In recent years, many more venture capital organisations have been set up, for example by large financial institutions such as pension funds.

The **role of financial intermediaries** in capital markets is illustrated in the diagram below.

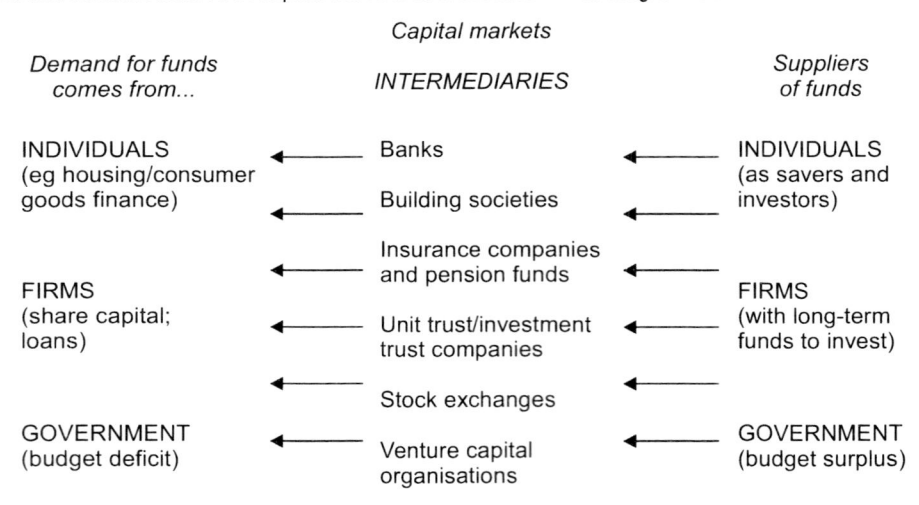

```
                           Capital markets
    Demand for funds                                    Suppliers
      comes from...         INTERMEDIARIES              of funds

    INDIVIDUALS      ←──── Banks                 ←──── INDIVIDUALS
    (eg housing/consumer                                (as savers and
    goods finance)   ←──── Building societies    ←──── investors)

                    ←──── Insurance companies   ←────
    FIRMS                  and pension funds            FIRMS
    (share capital;                                     (with long-term
    loans)          ←──── Unit trust/investment ←──── funds to invest)
                           trust companies

                    ←──── Stock exchanges       ←────
    GOVERNMENT                                          GOVERNMENT
    (budget deficit) ←──── Venture capital      ←──── (budget surplus)
                           organisations
```

3.6 Changes in capital markets

Recent years have seen very big changes in the capital markets of the world.

(a) **Globalisation of capital markets**

The capital markets of each country have become internationally integrated. Securities issued in one country can now be traded in capital markets around the world. For example, shares in many UK companies are traded in the USA. The shares are bought by US banks, which then issue ADRs (American depository receipts) which are a form in which foreign shares can be traded in US markets without a local listing.

(b) **Securitisation of debt**

Securitisation of debt means creating tradable securities which are backed by less liquid assets such as mortgages and other long term loans.

(c) **Risk management (and risk assessment)**

Various techniques have been developed for companies to manage their financial risk such as swaps and options. These 'derivative' financial instruments may allow transactions to take place 'off-balance sheet' and therefore not easily evident from the company's financial statements. The existence of such transactions may make it more difficult for banks and other would-be lenders to assess the financial risk of a company that is asking to borrow money.

(d) **Increased competition**

There is much fiercer competition than there used to be between financial institutions for business. For example, building societies have become direct competitors to the retail banks, and foreign banks have also competed in the UK with the big clearing banks. Banks have made shifts towards more fee-based activities (such as selling advice and selling insurance products for commission) and away from the traditional transaction-based activities (holding deposits, making loans).

Securitisation of debt involves disintermediation. **Financial disintermediation** is a process whereby ultimate borrowers and lenders by-pass the normal methods of financial intermediation (such as depositing money with and borrowing money from banks) and find other ways of lending or borrowing funds; or lend and borrow directly with each other, avoiding financial intermediation altogether. Securitisation of debt provides firms with a method of borrowing directly from non-banks. Although banks might act as managers of the debt issue, finding lenders who will buy the securitised debt, banks are not doing the lending themselves.

3.7 The money markets

The UK **money markets** are operated by the banks and other financial institutions. Although the money markets largely involve wholesale borrowing and lending by banks, some large companies and the government are also involved in money market operations. The money markets are essentially **shorter term debt markets**, with loans being made for a specified period, which may be as short as overnight, at a specified rate of interest.

The money markets operate both as a **primary market**, in which new financial claims are issued and as a **secondary market**, where previously issued financial claims are traded.

Amounts dealt in are relatively large, generally being above £50,000 and often in millions of pounds. Loans are transacted on extremely 'fine' terms - ie with small margins between lending and borrowing rates - reflecting the **economies of scale** involved. The emphasis is on liquidity: the efficiency of the money markets can make the financial claims dealt in virtually the equivalent of cash.

There are various markets.

(a) **The primary market** is the market where the Bank of England carries out open market operations in short-term financial instruments in order to ensure the liquidity of the banking system and to exert influence over interest rates.

(b) **The interbank market** is the market in which banks lend short-term funds to one another. The principal interest rate in this market is the London Inter-Bank Offer Rate or LIBOR, which is used by individual banks to establish their own base interest rates and interest rates for wholesale lending to large borrowers.

(c) **The Certificate of Deposit market** is a market for trading in Certificates of Deposit, a form of deposit which can be sold by the investor before maturity.

(d) **The local authority market** is a market in which local authorities borrow short-term funds from banks and other investors, by issuing and selling short-term 'debt instruments'.

(e) **The finance house market** covers the short-term loans raised from the money markets by finance houses (eg hire purchase finance companies).

(f) **The inter-company market** refers to direct short-term lending between companies, without any financial intermediary. This market is very small, and restricted to the treasury departments of large companies, and has largely been superseded by the sterling commercial paper market.

(g) **The sterling commercial paper market** is a market in which companies issue debt securities carrying interest, known as commercial paper (CP) with a maturity of up to one year, or medium term notes (MTNs) with a period of between one and five years.

A distinction is sometimes made between the **primary market** and all the other money markets which may be referred to collectively as the **parallel markets** or 'unofficial' markets.

4 International trade

Learning outcome

1.2.4 Political factors.

INVESTMENT AND RISK

4.1 Benefits of international trade

The output of goods and services overall among countries will increase if countries **specialise** in the production of goods and services in which they have a **comparative advantage**.

The **law of comparative advantage** (or comparative costs) states that two countries can gain from trade when each specialises in the industries in which it has lowest **opportunity costs**. Within a country, the opportunity cost for any category of product may be established in terms of the next most advantageous use of national resources. If two countries produce different goods most efficiently and can exchange them at an advantageous rate in terms of the comparative opportunity costs of importing and home production, then it will be beneficial for them to specialise and trade. Total production of each good will be higher than if they each produce both goods.

Trading between countries has been important for centuries. More efficient communications and transport in recent times have created conditions for increasing levels of international trade. Traditionally, services have generally had to be delivered at the point of use. Improved communications mean that it has become increasingly possible to trade in services between countries, as seen with the rapid expansion of outsourcing of services to offshore locations, as noted above.

The UK has historically been a net exporter of manufactured goods, with the result that the surplus foreign exchange earned allowed the economy to have a trade deficit (with more imports than exports) in the foods and raw materials sector.

In more recent times, the trade **deficits** in manufactures have been offset by oil exports, and by **surpluses** in the service sector and in earnings from assets owned overseas (for example, profits of overseas subsidiaries of UK companies).

The country's trading position with the rest of the world is recorded in the **balance of payments.** We discuss the balance of payments in the next chapter of this Study Text.

4.2 Barriers to international trade

In practice, many barriers to free trade exist because governments try to **protect** home industries against foreign competition.

Protectionism can be practised by a government in several ways.

- Tariffs or customs duties
- Import quotas
- Embargoes
- Hidden subsidies for exporters and domestic producers
- Import restrictions

Organisations and agreements that are significant in trying to promote free trade and to reduce protection are the World Trade Organisation, and various free trade agreements between groups of countries, including the **European Union**.

4.3 The World Trade Organisation

The **World Trade Organisation** (WTO) was formed in 1995 as successor to the General Agreement on Tariffs and Trade (GATT). The GATT was originally signed by 23 countries in 1947, with three aims.

(a) To reduce existing barriers to free trade

(b) To eliminate discrimination in international trade

(c) To prevent the growth of protection by getting member countries to consult with others before taking any protectionist measures

It has been estimated that the opening up of markets for agricultural and industrial goods following the 1993 GATT accord could have added around US$200-300 billion to world income.

4.4 The European Union

The **European Union** (EU) (formerly the European Community) is one of several international economic associations. The association was previously known as the European Community and the EEC, originally being formed in 1957 by the Treaty of Rome. The EU now consists of 27 nations, 12 of which joined since 2000.

The European Union has a **common market** combining different aspects, including **a free trade area** and a **customs union**.

(a) A **free trade area** exists when there is no restriction on the movement of goods and services between countries. This may be extended into a **customs union** when there is a free trade area between all member countries of the union, and in addition, there are common external tariffs applying to imports from non-member countries into any part of the union. In other words, the union promotes free trade among its members but acts as a protectionist bloc against the rest of the world.

(b) A **common market** encompasses the idea of a customs union but has a number of additional features. In addition to free trade among member countries there are also free markets in each of the **factors of production**. A British citizen has the freedom to work in any other country of the European Union, for example. A common market will also aim to achieve stronger links between member countries, for example by harmonising government economic policies and by establishing a closer political confederation.

4.5 The single European market

The EU set the end of 1992 as the target date for the removal of all existing physical, technical and fiscal barriers among member states, thus creating a large multinational European Single Market. This objective was embodied in the Single European Act of 1985. In practice, these changes have not occurred overnight, and many of them are still in progress.

Elimination of trade restrictions covers the following areas.

(a) **Physical barriers** (eg customs inspection) on good and services have been removed for most products. Companies have had to adjust to a new VAT regime as a consequence.

(b) **Technical standards** (eg for quality and safety) should be harmonised.

(c) Governments should not discriminate between EU companies in awarding **public works contracts**.

(d) **Telecommunications** should be subject to greater competition.

(e) It should be possible to provide **financial services** in any country.

(f) There should be **free movement of capital** within the community.

(g) **Professional qualifications** awarded in one member state should be recognised in the others.

(h) The EU is taking a co-ordinated stand on matters related to **consumer protection.**

There are many areas where harmonisation is a long way from being achieved. Here are some examples.

(a) **Company taxation**. Tax rates, which can affect the viability of investment plans, vary from country to country within the EU.

(b) **Indirect taxation** (eg Value Added Tax or VAT). While there have been moves to harmonisation, there are still differences between rates imposed by member states.

INVESTMENT AND RISK

(c) **Differences in prosperity**. There are considerable differences in prosperity between the wealthiest EU economies (such as Germany) and the poorest (eg some of the newly enrolled Eastern European members).

(d) **Differences in workforce skills**. Again, this can have a significant effect on investment decisions. The workforce in Germany is perhaps the most highly trained, but it is also the most highly paid.

(e) **Infrastructure**. Some countries are better provided with road and rail infrastructure than others. Where accessibility to a market is an important issue, infrastructure can mean significant variations in distribution costs.

4.6 Free movement of capital

Free trade is generally associated with the free movement of goods (and services) between countries. Another important aspect of international trade is the **free movement of capital**.

(a) If a UK company (or investor) wishes to set up a business in a different country, or to take over a company in another country, how easily can it transfer capital from the UK to the country in question, to pay for the investment?

(b) Similarly, if a Japanese company wishes to invest in the UK, how easily can it transfer funds out of Japan and into the UK to pay for the investment?

Some countries (including the UK, since the abolition of exchange controls in 1979) have allowed a fairly free flow of capital into and out of the country. Other countries have been more cautious, mainly for one of the following two reasons.

(a) The free inflow of foreign capital will make it easier for foreign companies to take over domestic companies. There is often a belief that certain key industries should be owned by residents of the country. Even in the UK, for example, there have been restrictions placed on the total foreign ownership of shares in companies such as British Aerospace and Rolls Royce.

(b) Less developed countries especially, but other more advanced economies too, are reluctant to allow the free flow of capital out of the country. After all, they need capital to come into the country to develop the domestic economy.

5 Globalisation

Learning outcome

1.2.2 Globalisation of trade and finance.

5.1 The process of globalisation

Companies are tending more and more to take a global view of business. The process of **globalisation** in various areas has been accelerated by improvements in communications, including the expansion and falling cost of air travel; the development of Internet-based systems; and improvements in telecommunications generally.

Production facilities for multinational operations may be located in particular countries for a variety of reasons.

(a) To give access to markets protected by tariffs
(b) To reduce transport costs
(c) To exploit national or regional differences in demand for goods
(d) To take advantage of low labour costs

Centralisation of production can bring important **economies of scale**. Economies of scale are reductions in costs resulting from larger-scale production. These must be balanced against transport costs and **barriers to trade**, such as tariffs (taxes on imports) and other restrictions imposed by one country against trade from another country.

The expansion of some industries and the contraction of others can reflect both **economic and technological progress** and the trend towards globalisation. **'Sunrise' industries** include information technology and genetics, whose importance is increasing worldwide. **'Sunset' industries** in the more developed Western economies include steel and shipbuilding whose prices have been undercut by more efficient producers in the Pacific Basin.

Capital markets of various countries have become internationally integrated – 'globalised'. The process of integration is facilitated by improved telecommunications and the deregulation of markets in many countries. Securities issued in one country can now be traded in capital markets around the world. This trend can only increase as stock exchanges are linked electronically.

5.2 Multinational enterprises

A **multinational** company is one that has production or service facilities in more than one country. Multinational enterprises range from medium-sized companies having only a few facilities (or subsidiaries or 'affiliates') abroad to giant companies having an annual turnover larger than the gross national product (GNP) of some smaller countries of the world. Indeed the largest – the US multinationals Ford and Exxon have each been reported to have a turnover larger than the GNPs of all but 14 countries of the world.

The size and significance of multinationals is increasing. Many companies in middle-income countries such as Singapore are now becoming multinationals, and the annual growth in output of existing multinationals is in the range 10-15%.

5.3 Foreign direct investment

For companies planning international investment activities (also known as **foreign direct investment** (FDI)), easy access to large amounts of funds denominated in foreign currencies can be very useful. Such funds are available in the eurocurrency markets – for debt denominated in different currencies – whose expansion has encouraged FDI.

FDI has been fuelled by global economic expansion and by the development of **'offshoring'** – the out-sourcing of services, such as telephone call centres and account servicing, to lower-cost overseas countries.

6 European Economic and Monetary Union

Learning outcome

1.2.3   European economic and monetary union.

6.1 The nature of EMU

There are a number of aspects of **European Economic and Monetary Union (EMU)** – a project involving member countries of the European Union – as follows.

(a) A **common currency** – the euro.

(b) A **European central bank**. The European Central Bank has several roles.

- Issuing the common currency
- Conducting monetary policy on behalf of the central government authorities

INVESTMENT AND RISK

- Acting as lender of last resort to all European banks
- Managing the exchange rate for the common currency

(c) **Centralised monetary policy,** applying across all of the countries adopting the common currency. This involves the surrender of control over aspects of economic policy and therefore the surrender of some political sovereignty by the government of each member state to the central government body of the union.

(d) **Economic integration.** This is a long-term process. The Single European Market concept has involved the removal of tariff and customs barriers between member States. The concept is intended also to cover labour markets and capital markets – to promote free movement of labour and capital. In practice, some barriers remain because of the different national structures and systems of member countries. The harmonisation of tax rates between different States is another aspect of economic integration that is far from being achieved.

6.2 EMU progress

May 1998 saw the meeting of those European Union countries wishing to join the **monetary union** at the outset. Italy, France, Ireland, Germany, Belgium, Luxembourg, the Netherlands, Finland, Spain, Portugal and Austria all signed up for the first phase of EMU starting on 1 January 1999. All of these countries abandoned their former 'legacy' currencies and are now within the '**Eurozone**' of countries using the euro as their main currency.

The **European Central Bank (ECB)**, which operates the Eurozone monetary policy, was established in 1998. Irrevocably locked exchange rates were fixed between the old currencies of participating countries.

The **UK** decided to opt out of monetary union but retains the right to join at a later stage. Gordon Brown, Britain's then **Chancellor of the Exchequer**, explained in the House of Commons that in reaching this decision, the Government Treasury department 'made a detailed assessment of five economic tests' believed to define whether a clear and unambiguous case could be made to support Britain joining a single currency.

- Whether there can be sustainable convergence between Britain and the economies of a single currency
- Whether there is sufficient flexibility to cope with economic change
- The effect on investment
- The impact on the financial services industry
- Whether it is good for employment

At the time of writing, there is no plan by the Government to repeat this assessment, which would be a precursor for a decision to join the euro, in the near future.

6.3 For and against monetary union

Arguments for and against monetary union are summarised in the Table below, with particular reference to the UK's position.

For	Against
Economic policy stability	**Confusion in the transition to monetary union**
• EMU members are required to keep to strict economic criteria.	• Introduction of a new currency and coinage could cause confusion to businesses and consumers.
• Politicians in member countries should tend to be less able to pursue short-term economic policies, for example just before an election, to gain political advantage.	• Firms might use it as an opportunity to push through price rises.

For	Against
Facilitation of trade • Will eliminate risk of currency fluctuations affecting trade and investment between EMU member countries. • Will eliminate need to hedge against such risks. • There will be savings in foreign exchange transaction costs for companies, as well as tourists. • Monetary union will enhance ease of trade with non EU countries. • Will encourage trade through transparency of prices	**Loss of national control over economic policy** • Under EMU, monetary policy would largely be in the hands of the relatively new European Central Bank, which (some say) has demonstrated greater interest in holding down inflation than in economic growth. • Individual countries' fiscal policies would also need to stay in line with European policy criteria. • The European economic policy framework puts great emphasis on price stability. • Restrictive monetary policies have sometimes resulted in disproportionate unemployment and output effects.
Lower interest rates • Will remove risk of inflation and depreciating currencies, reducing interest rates. • Will stabilise interest rates, possibly at a relatively low level.	**Consequences for the financial services industry** • Forecasts that the City of London might enter an immediate decline if the UK did not join have proved unfounded.
Seigneurage • Seigneurage is the benefit accruing from the right to issue currency. If the euro becomes a global reserve currency, non-EU nations will buy it to hold rather than for the purposes of trade. This will support the exchange rate and allow interest rates to be lower.	

INVESTMENT AND RISK

Key chapter points

- A government's economic policy aims may include sustainable economic growth, control of inflation within a target range, low unemployment, and a satisfactory balance of payments (international trade) position.

- **Fiscal policy** is the government's policy on taxation, borrowing and public (government) spending. **Monetary policy** is concerned with measures to change the amount of money in the economy (the money stock or money supply) and with measures to influence the price of money: ie, rates of interest.

- A **central bank** acts for a government, and typically has various functions, such as issuance of bank notes, management of government finances, dealing in the money markets to set interest rates, and acting as lender of last resort to the banking system.

- **Capital markets** are markets, including the Stock Exchange in which enterprises raise long-term capital, through issues of shares or debt (debentures or bonds). The government raises long-term funds through the gilts market, and also through National Savings & Investments. **Money markets** are markets serving short-term capital needs, from overnight periods upwards.

- In **primary markets**, new funds are made available to enterprises and to government. Instruments are subsequently traded in **secondary markets**.

- Countries benefit from trade when they can specialise in producing goods in which they have a **comparative advantage** in terms of the cost of production.

- The WTO and international trade agreement areas, such as the EU, serve to reduce some of the barriers to trade which individual countries might otherwise put up. The Single European Market concept involves the removal of physical, technical and fiscal barriers to trade within the EU, but the process of removing such barriers is not complete.

- International trade, production and capital markets are becoming increasingly globalised. Foreign direct investment (FDI) has been boosted recently by the rapid expansion of outsourcing of services to overseas countries.

- Introduction of the single European currency (the euro) in the 'Eurozone' countries has significant implications for how monetary policy is carried out within the single currency area. The euro forms a part of the longer-term project of economic as well as monetary union in Europe (EMU). The UK has remained outside the Eurozone, keeping its own currency for the time being.

Chapter Quiz

1 What are typical aims of a government's economic policy? .... (see para 1.1)
2 What is the full name of the PSNCR, and what does it represent? .... (1.3)
3 What is meant by the term 'lender of last resort'? .... (2.3)
4 How does the Bank of England influence interest rates? .... (2.4)
5 What is the UK's inflation target range? .... (2.4)
6 Distinguish between capital markets and money markets. .... (3.1)
7 Distinguish between primary markets and secondary markets. .... (3.2)
8 Outline the different aspects of European Economic and Monetary Union (EMU). .... (6.1)

chapter 3

Chapter topic list

1	National income	38
2	Economic growth and business cycles	41
3	Inflation and deflation	45
4	Interest rates	48
5	Money supply	50
6	Exchange rates and the balance of payments	54
	Key chapter points	61
	Chapter quiz	62

Economic analysis

INVESTMENT AND RISK

CHAPTER LEARNING OUTCOMES

1   **Understand** the macroeconomic factors that affect investment returns

    1.3   The role of government and central banks:

        1.3.2 Measuring money supply.
        1.3.3 Inflation.
        1.3.4 Deflation.
        1.3.5 Disinflation.
        1.3.6 Interest rates.

    1.4   Balance of payments

        1.4.1 Capital and current account.
        1.4.2 Exchange rates.
        1.4.3 The importance of the balance of payments.

    1.5   The economic and financial cycles

        1.5.1 Global influences.
        1.5.2 National income.
        1.5.3 The main stages of economic and stock market cycles.
        1.5.4 Longer term growth trends.

    1.7   The key economic indicators

        1.7.1 Gross Domestic Product (GDP).
        1.7.2 Retail Prices Index (RPI) and the Consumer Prices Index (CPI).
        1.7.4 Volume of fixed investment.
        1.7.5 Volume of consumer spending.
        1.7.6 Money stock.
        1.7.7 Foreign exchange rates.

1 National income

Learning outcomes

1.5.2 National income.
1.7.1 Gross Domestic Product (GDP).
1.7.4 Volume of fixed investment.
1.7.5 Volume of consumer spending.

1.1 The circular flow of income

Firms must pay households for the factors of production, and households must pay firms for goods. The income of firms is the sales revenue from the sales of goods and services.

This creates a **circular flow** of income and expenditure: income and output are different sides of the same coin.

```
                    Factor incomes paid by firms
                                (b)

                        Productive resources

        FIRMS                                    HOUSEHOLDS

                        Goods and services (output)
                                (c)
                                (a)
                    Expenditure on goods and services
```

Circular flow of income

(The diagram above assumes a 'closed' economy. A little later below, we add further elements to the model.)

1.2 Measuring economic activity

Economic activity can be measured in different ways, depending on which aspect of the circular flow is captured by the particular measure being used.

Three key measures of economic activity are:

- National income
- Gross national product (GNP)
- Gross domestic product (GDP)

UK **national income** is 'the sum of all incomes of residents in the UK which arise as a result of economic activity, that is from the production of goods and services. Such incomes, which include rent, employment income and profit, are known as factor incomes because they are earned by the so-called factors of production: land, labour and capital' *(Office for National Statistics)*.

National income is also called net national product. As noted above, the terms 'income' and 'product' are two different aspects of the same circular flow of income around the economy. The term 'net' means 'after deducting an amount for capital consumption or depreciation of fixed assets' from the gross figure.

Although technically national income has a particular definition, generally you will find all of the three measures given above (NI, GNP and GDP) loosely referred to as '**national income**'.

Calculating the national income serves several purposes:

- **Measuring** the **standard** of **living** in a country (national income per head)
- **Comparing** the **wealth** of different countries
- **Measuring** the **change** in **national wealth** and the standard of living
- **Ascertaining long-term trends**
- **Assisting central government** in its **economic planning**

INVESTMENT AND RISK

1.3 Gross domestic product (GDP)

National income is largely derived from economic activity within the country itself. Domestic economic activity is referred to as total domestic income or domestic product. It is measured gross. **Gross domestic product (GDP)** refers in the UK to the total value of income/production from economic activity within the UK.

1.4 Gross national product

'Some national income arises from overseas investments while some of the income generated within the UK is earned by non-residents. The difference between these items is net property income from abroad' (ONS).

1.5 GDP, GNP and national income

The relationship between GDP, GNP and national income is therefore as follows.

	GDP
plus	Net property income from abroad
equals	GNP
minus	Capital consumption
equals	National income (net)

1.6 Injections and withdrawals

As well as using total incomes in the circular flow as a measure for national income, we can use a method that measures total **expenditure**. In the diagram below, we add a number of **injections and withdrawals** into the circular flow, which arise from **saving** by consumers and **investment** flows into firms, from **imports** and **exports**, and from **government spending** and **taxation**.

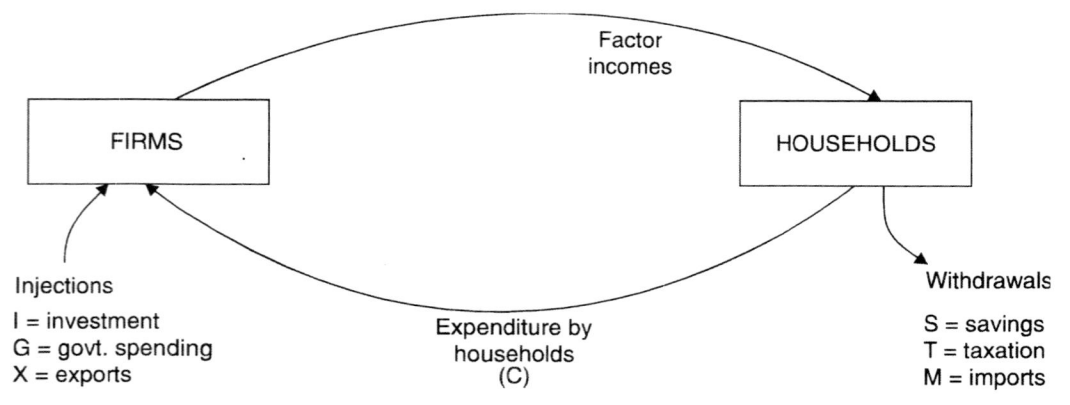

[Diagram: Circular flow between FIRMS and HOUSEHOLDS. Factor incomes flow from Firms to Households. Expenditure by households (C) flows from Households to Firms.

Injections (into Firms):
I = investment
G = govt. spending
X = exports

Withdrawals (from Households):
S = savings
T = taxation
M = imports]

Total spending, consists of **consumer spending**, government spending, **investment spending**, spending by foreigners on our goods and services minus spending by UK residents on foreign goods and services.

This can be symbolised as C + I + G − S − T + (X − M) (the circular flow of national income) where:

C = consumer expenditure
I = investment expenditure
G = government expenditure
S = savings
T = taxation
X = expenditure on our exports by foreigners
M = expenditure by us on imports

1.7 Consumption and investment

The **volume of consumer spending** is an economic indicator which can indicate the levels of consumer confidence. If consumer spending is growing more rapidly than economic output, this may result in inflationary pressures. The government might raise interest rates to make it less attractive to borrow money and this to dampen consumer spending.

Consumer spending is what creates **consumer demand** for goods and services. A government will want to keep the level of aggregate demand at a healthy level, but not so high as to create **inflationary conditions**, which can result if there is excess demand for the goods and services that the economy is producing.

Even when a household has zero income, it will still spend. This spending will be financed by earlier **savings** (and, in the real world, by **welfare receipts**). There is thus a constant, basic level of consumption. This is called **autonomous** consumption. When the household receives an income, some will be spent and some will be saved. The **proportion** which is spent is called the **marginal propensity to consume** (MPC) while the **proportion** which is saved is equal to the **marginal propensity to save** (MPS).

The **volume of fiscal investment** indicates how much business is spending on **fixed assets**, which are assets such as building and plant from which earnings are expected to be generated over the medium or long term. A strong level of investment indicates business confidence in the future, and investment is vital for the future well-being of the economy. If business confidence is low, entrepreneurs will not take the risk of investing in new production. If there is over-capacity, there may be less incentive for investments to be made.

1.8 Economic policy actions

If a government is planning its economic policy and wishes to increase the country's GDP and GNP, it might wish to turn its attention to any of these items, by:

- Trying to increase consumer spending, C
- Trying to increase private investment, I
- Deciding to increase government spending, G and/or I
- Trying to improve the balance of payments on overseas trade, (X – M)

2 Economic growth and business cycles

> **Learning outcomes**
>
> 1.5.1 Global influences.
> 1.5.3 The main stages of economic and stock market cycles.
> 1.5.4 Longer term growth trends.

2.1 National income and economic growth

As explained above, a figure can be put on the amount of economic activity or output in a national economy by aggregating all incomes, to give a total figure for **national income**. The bigger the national income in a country, the more income its individual inhabitants are earning on average. More income means more spending on the output of firms, and more spending means more output of goods and services and hence a rise in the standard of living, if the increase is not merely inflationary.

We have also noted earlier how growth in national income (**economic growth**) is an economic policy objective of most, if not all, governments.

INVESTMENT AND RISK

Most UK national income is derived from economic activity **within the UK**. Economic activity within the UK is referred to as total **domestic income** or **domestic product**. It is measured **gross,** ie before deducting an amount for capital consumption or depreciation of fixed assets, to give the **gross domestic product (GDP)**, referring to the total value of income/production from economic activity within the UK.

2.2 Business cycles

Business cycles or **trade cycles** are the continual sequence of rapid growth in national income, followed by a slow-down in growth and then a fall in national income. After a recession, growth typically starts again and, when national income has reached a peak, the cycle turns into recession once more. The business cycle in a typical developed economy now seems to last for around eight to ten years.

The usual **definition of a recession** is two or more successive quarters of falling GDP.

2.3 Phases of the business cycle

Four main typical phases of the business cycle can be identified.

	THE BUSINESS CYCLE
Depression	Heavy unemployment
	Low consumer demand
	Over-capacity (unused capacity) in production
	Prices stable, or even falling
	Business profits low
	Business confidence in the future low
Recovery	Investment picks up
	Employment rises
	Consumer spending rises
	Profits rise
	Business confidence grows
	Prices stable, or slowly rising
Boom	Consumer spending rising fast
	Output capacity reached: labour shortages occur
	Output can only be increased by new labour-saving investment
	Investment spending high
	Increases in demand now stimulate price rises
	Business profits high
Recession	Consumption falls off
	Many investments suddenly become unprofitable and new investment falls
	Production falls
	Employment falls
	Profits fall. Some businesses fail
	Recession can turn into severe depression

At point A in the diagram below, the economy is entering a **recession**. In the recession phase, consumer demand falls and many investment projects already undertaken begin to look unprofitable. Orders will be cut, stock levels will be reduced and business failures will occur as firms find themselves unable to sell their goods. Production and employment will fall. The general price level will tend to fall.

Business and consumer confidence are diminished and investment remains low, while the economic outlook appears to be poor. Eventually, in the absence of any stimulus to aggregate demand, a period of full **depression** may set in and the economy will reach point B.

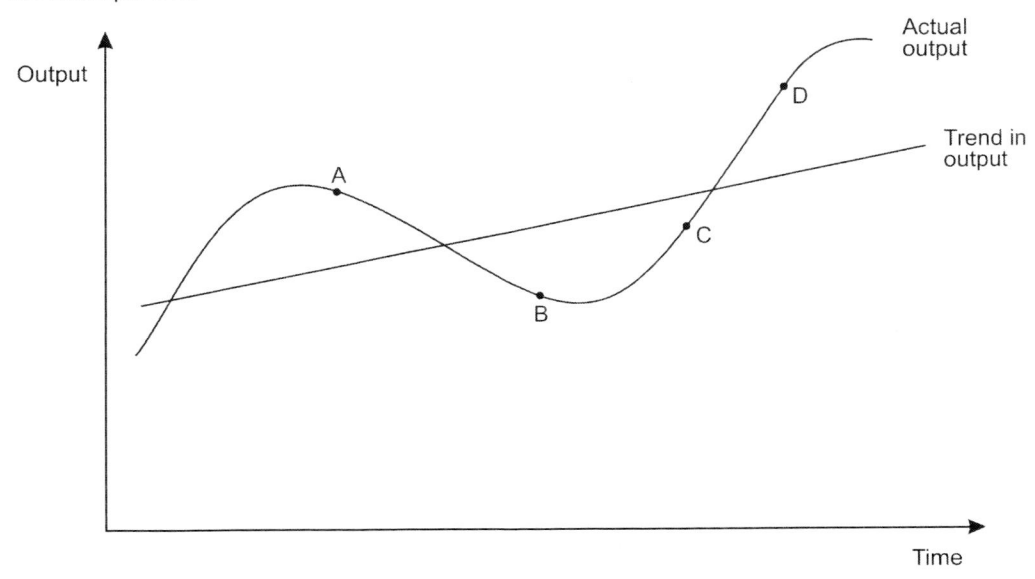

The business cycle

Recession can begin relatively quickly because of the speed with which the effects of declining demand will be felt by businesses suffering a loss in sales revenue. The knock-on effects of destocking and cutting back on investment exacerbate the situation and add momentum to the recession. Recovery can be slow to begin because of the effect of recession on levels of confidence.

At point C in the diagram, the economy has reached the **recovery** phase of the cycle. Once begun, the phase of recovery is likely to quicken as confidence returns. Output, employment and income will all begin to rise. Rising production, sales and profit levels will lead to optimistic business expectations, and new investment will be more readily undertaken. The rising level of demand can be met through increased production by bringing existing capacity into use and by hiring unemployed labour. The average price level will remain constant or begin to rise slowly.

In the recovery phase, decisions to purchase new materials and machinery may lead to benefits in efficiency from new technology. This can enhance the relative rate of economic growth in the recovery phase once it is under way.

As recovery proceeds, the output level climbs above its trend path, reaching point D, in the **boom** phase of the cycle. During the boom, capacity and labour will become fully utilised. This may cause bottlenecks in some industries which are unable to meet increases in demand, for example because they have no spare capacity or they lack certain categories of skilled labour, or they face shortages of key material inputs. Further rises in demand will, therefore, tend to be met by increases in prices rather than by increases in production. In general, business will be profitable, with few firms facing losses. Expectations of the future may be very optimistic and the level of investment expenditure high.

2.4 Consequences of business cycles

It can be argued that wide fluctuations in levels of economic activity are damaging to the overall economic well-being of society. The **inflation** and **speculation** that accompany boom periods may be inequitable in their impact on different sections of the population, while the bottom of the business cycle may bring high unemployment. Unemployment can bring poverty and uncertainty to people's lives, and governments must generally direct resources to alleviating the effects of joblessness.

INVESTMENT AND RISK

Governments generally seek to make adjustments in order to stabilise the economic system, trying to avoid the distortions of a widely fluctuating trade cycle. In practice, this is no easy task and, of course, business cycles persist.

Forecasting the pattern of the business cycle is very difficult in practice. The cycle is affected by such things as **oil prices** and **international political stability**, all of which are themselves difficult to predict.

Businesses must try to identify those measures which tend to give **advance warning** of movements in the business cycle such as **leading indicators** that include share prices, house building activity and interest rates.

2.5 Business cycles and investments

In a **recession** and at the start of a **recovery**, inflation and interest rates may be low or falling. In these conditions, lower yields will be required by investors in **fixed interest securities** and consequently investors will be prepared to pay higher prices for such securities. Higher interest rates in a boom period will tend to reduce the price of fixed income stocks.

The prices of **equities** (company **shares**) will tend to reflect market sentiment about prospects for the economy at the current stage of the business cycle. The main share price indices, such as the FTSE 100 Index in the UK and the S&P 500 Index in the USA, serve as 'barometers' of the market.

The levels of share prices are sharply influenced by changes in sentiment, which can occur rapidly. It will generally be changes in sentiment, perhaps triggered by news of an economic indicator being significantly lower or higher than was previously expected, that will cause significant stock market price movements. If there is a new expectation of an economic recovery, share prices may rise in anticipation.

Currently known news will generally already be reflected in share prices: if it were not, then investors would seek to take advantage of current prices, and this activity by investors would move prices until they did reflect the currently known news.

A situation of persistently rising share prices is often called a **bull market**. If the news on any likely recovery becomes unfavourable – for instance, if the recovery is expected to be delayed – then share prices may drop back again. If an economy is in a boom period, higher interest rates or new expectations of the boom coming to an end could reverse the general direction of share prices on to a downward path. A persistent downward trend in equities prices is often called a **bear market**.

In the long run, share prices will be influenced by the tendency for an economy to grow in output and for corporate earnings to grow.

2.6 International aspects

Rates of growth in the **rest of the world** will be important for any economy, such as the UK, that has a large foreign trade sector. If trading partners have slow growth, the amount of exports a country can sell to them will grow only slowly. This limits the country's own opportunities for investment and growth.

Different national economies may be at different stages of the business cycle at any one time. However, with increasing **globalisation of trade and investment**, there is a tendency for many different economies to follow a similar path together. In particular, the large size and economic wealth of the economy of the USA exerts a significant influence on the economies of other countries, particularly its major trading partners such as the UK.

The importance of the **USA** in the world economy means that investment markets, such as equity and bond markets, often react most closely to what is happening in the economy and markets of the USA. If there is an economic recovery in the USA, it is anticipated that this recovery will soon affect other economies, as US consumers and companies will demand more goods and services available on world markets. The stimulus to other countries will have knock-on effects in those countries as companies' earnings are boosted and employment rises.

3: ECONOMIC ANALYSIS

The linkage between the UK stock market and the US market has been summarised in the saying: 'When Wall Street sneezes, London catches a cold'.

2.7 World economic growth outlook

In its twice-yearly **World Economic Outlook** published in April 2010, the International Monetary Fund reported that the global economy has recovered better than expected from the financial crisis. World output is projected to grow by 4.25 per cent in 2010 as a whole and also in 2011. Achieving this will depend on policies to support the unemployed and to rebalance global demand.

3 Inflation and deflation

> **Learning outcomes**
>
> 1.3.3 Inflation.
> 1.3.4 Deflation.
> 1.3.5 Disinflation.
> 1.7.2 Retail Prices Index (RPI) and the Consumer Prices Index (CPI).

3.1 The nature of inflation

The price of something is the amount of money for which something of economic value is or might be exchanged. **Inflation** is the name given to a general increase in price levels.

Another way of describing a general rise in prices is as a decline in the **purchasing power of money**. Inflation is an important concern for investors, as well as for borrowers. However, just as there are many different prices, there are also many different things that a person might purchase with money. People spend money on goods for consumption, but they may also buy assets that are not for immediate consumption, such as a house. They may purchase investments, deferring consumption until a later date when the investment is sold or may provide an income.

3.2 Measuring inflation

Consumer price indices may be used for several purposes, for example as an indicator of inflationary pressures in the economy, as a benchmark for wage negotiations and to determine annual increases in government benefits payments. Countries commonly have more than one consumer price index because one composite index may be considered too wide a grouping for different purposes.

The **Retail Prices Index (RPI)** measures the percentage changes month by month in the average level of prices (including VAT and other duties) of the commodities and services, including housing and mortgage costs, purchased by the great majority of households in the UK. The items of expenditure within the RPI are intended to be a representative list of items, current prices for which are collected at regular intervals.

In December 2003, it was confirmed that the standardised European inflation measure, the Harmonised Index of Consumer Prices (HICP), is now used as the basis for the **UK's inflation target**. The UK HICP is called the **Consumer Prices Index (CPI)**. The CPI excludes most housing costs such as mortgages. However, pensions and benefits and index-linked gilts continue to be calculated on the same basis as previously, using the RPI.

If a prices index was 182.6 in October 2003 and rises to 185.1 in October 2004, what is the annual percentage rate of inflation to October 2004, to one decimal place?

185.1 / 182.6 = 1.0137
(1.0137 − 1) × 100 = 1.37%

After rounding, this gives an annual inflation rate of 1.4% to one decimal place.

Here are some past values for the **UK Retail Prices Index**.

October 1983	86.7
October 1993	141.8
October 2003	182.6

How has inflation eroded the purchasing power of money over the ten years and twenty years up to 2003?

£1 in October 2003 bought as much as £1 × 86.7/182.6 = 47.5p would have bought twenty years earlier.

£1 in October 2003 bought as much as £1 × 141.8/182.6 = 77.7p would have bought ten years earlier.

Savings of £1,000 held for the 20 years up to 2003 would need to have grown to £100 x 182.6/86.7 = £2,106 to preserve their purchasing power over the period.

3.3 Inflation, deflation and disinflation

Historically, there have been very few periods when inflation has not been present. High rates of inflation are generally considered to be harmful. However, **deflation** (falling prices, for a sustained period) is normally associated with low rates of growth and even recession. This is because falling prices could encourage companies to reduce output, as they will find that anticipated prices are less likely to cover their input costs. Reduced output may lead to rising unemployment, which will tend to depress demand and, in turn, production. The decline brought about may thus be self-perpetuating.

Disinflation refers to a situation in which there is a **reducing rate of inflation**. Prices are still rising, but at a reducing rate. If inflation is at too high a rate, a government will want a period of disinflation to bring it back to an acceptable range. Policymakers do not generally want to have a situation of deflation however, since this can produce the kind of problems we have mentioned above.

3.4 Why is inflation a problem?

An economic policy objective which now has a central place in the policy approaches of the governments of many developed countries is that of stable prices. It would seem that a healthy economy may require some inflation. This is implicitly recognised in the UK inflation target of 2% or less for the CPI (the same target as that of the European Central Bank, for the euro zone). Certainly, if an economy is to grow, the money supply must expand, and the presence of a low level of inflation can help to ensure that growth is not hampered by a shortage of liquid funds.

Inflation leads to a **redistribution of income and wealth** in ways that may be undesirable. Redistribution of wealth might take place from creditors (eg, lenders) to debtors (borrowers). This is because debts lose 'real' value with inflation. For example, if you owed £1,000, and prices then doubled, you would still owe £1,000, but the **real value** of your debt would have been halved. In general, in times of inflation those with economic power tend to gain at the expense of the weak, particularly those on fixed incomes such as many elderly people.

Also, there can be **balance of payments** effects. If a country has a higher rate of inflation than its major trading partners, its **exports** will become relatively expensive and **imports** relatively cheap. As a result, the balance of trade between imports and exports will suffer, affecting employment in exporting industries and in industries producing import-substitutes. Eventually, exchange rates between currencies will be affected.

Once the rate of inflation has begun to increase, there is a danger of **expectations** making it worse. This means, regardless of whether the factors that have caused inflation are still persistent or not, there will arise a generally held view of what inflation is likely to be, and so to protect future income, wages and prices will be raised now by the expected amount of future inflation. This can lead to the vicious circle known as the **wage-price spiral**, in which inflation becomes a relatively permanent feature because of people's expectations that it will occur.

3.5 Nominal returns and real returns

The quoted rate of interest or return on a deposit or other investment is sometimes called the **nominal rate of interest**.

If the return on deposits exceeds the rate of inflation, then there is a **positive real rate of return**. For example, if deposits earn 3.8% while the general rate of inflation is 2.3%, then the real rate of return is roughly 1.5%. £1,000 placed on deposit over one year will gain 1.5% in purchasing power during the year. Compared with one year earlier, 1.5% more in goods in services can be bought with the money.

If the rate of inflation exceeds the return on deposits, then there is a **negative real rate of return**. For example, if deposits earn 2.8% while inflation is 4.8%, there is a negative real rate of return of approximately 2%. £1,000 placed on deposit over one year will lose 2% of its purchasing power during the year. Significantly negative real rates of return can discourage saving, since the purchasing power of money will be eroded through time.

The true link between nominal returns, real return and inflation rates is

$$(1 + \text{Nominal return}) = (1 + \text{Real return}) \times (1 + \text{Inflation rate})$$

This can be approximated by

$$\text{Nominal rate} = \text{Real rate} + \text{Inflation rate}$$

which is what we have used in the above illustrations.

3.6 Inflation and deposits

Deposits, for example in retail bank and building society accounts, have generally yielded a positive rate of return in recent years while the rate of inflation has been low. During past periods of higher inflation, for example during the 1970s and 1980s, there were negative real rates of return.

Protection against erosion of purchasing power is provided by the **Index-Linked Savings Certificates** offered by the government agency **National Savings & Investments (NS&I)**.

3.7 Inflation and fixed interest securities

With fixed income **government securities ('gilts')** and fixed interest **corporate bonds** issued by companies, an investor receives the same income whatever the rate of inflation. If inflation rises, the purchasing power of the income will fall.

The prices of fixed interest securities will be influenced by expectations of inflation as well as by actual movements in inflation. If higher future inflation is expected, the prices of fixed interest securities will tend to fall, and *vice versa*.

Index-linked government securities can protect against inflation, if they are held to redemption. If held over a shorter term and sold before redemption, the degree of protection offered is less certain because the price of the gilt will fluctuate in the market.

3.8 Inflation and returns on equities

Over the longer term, shares in companies (**equities**) have generally provided returns **in excess of inflation**. Ultimately, equity returns depend upon **company earnings** (profits), which have tended to rise by more than the rate of inflation, as levels of economic activity and productivity have grown over time.

INVESTMENT AND RISK

At any time, it is **expectations of future earnings** can have as much effect on equity market sentiment as current or recently reported earnings. Expectations are subject to rapid changes in sentiment, and may be swayed one way or another by the flow of news on economic prospects and company prospects.

Rising company earnings are paid out in the form of dividends to shareholders or are retained in the business for future investment.

- Over the **long term**, the capital value of shares may rise, offering a return additional to the dividends received.
- Over **shorter periods**, the values of equities can fall or fluctuate quite dramatically, as sentiment changes. For this reason, equities are best seen as a long-term investment.

3.9 Inflation in prices and earnings

The earnings of those in jobs (**average earnings**) tend to increase by more than prices over the longer term. This is because of economic growth: more goods are produced over time, and people have an increased purchasing power arising from that extra production.

4 Interest rates

Learning outcome

1.3.6 Interest rates.

4.1 The role of interest rates in the economy

Credit is a scarce commodity, priced through **interest rates**. Interest is the payment made for the use of someone's money for a period: interest can be seen as the **price of money**.

There are many different interest rates in an economy. They include lenders' mortgage rates, banks' base rates and the rates at which banks lend to each other.

In general, interest rates in the economy tend to move up or down together.

(a) If some interest rates go up, for example bank base rates, it is quite likely that other interest rates will move up too, if they have not gone up already.

(b) Similarly, if some interest rates go down, other interest rates will move down too.

It is the general level of interest rates, but short-term interest rates in particular, that the government might try to influence.

4.2 Base interest rates

The most important **base rate** in the UK is the rate at which the **Bank of England** lends to other financial institutions: this is set by the Monetary Policy Committee in response to economic conditions. The retail banks usually follow this lead, although they are free not to do so.

LIBOR is the most widely used benchmark or reference rate for short term interest rates. LIBOR stands for the **London Interbank Offered Rate** and is the rate of interest at which banks borrow funds from other banks, in marketable size, in the London interbank market.

4.3 The term structure of interest rates

The **term structure of interest rates** refers to the different interest rates that there are for assets with different terms to maturity.

These various interest rates can be grouped into three broad classes, according to the length of time until the associated debts reach maturity.

- Short-term interest rates
- Medium-term interest rates
- Long-term interest rates

Longer term financial assets should in general offer a higher yield than short-term lending.

(a) The investor must be compensated for tying up his money in the asset for a longer period of time. If the government were to make two issues of 9% Treasury Stock on the same date, one with a term of five years and one with a term of 20 years (and if there were no expectations of changes in interest rates in the future) then the **liquidity preference** of investors would make them prefer the five year stock.

(b) The means of overcoming the liquidity preference of investors is to compensate them for the loss of liquidity; in other words, to offer a higher rate of interest on longer dated stock.

(c) There is a greater risk in lending longer term than shorter term for two reasons.

 (i) **Inflation**. The longer the term of the asset, the greater is the possibility that the rate of inflation will increase, so that the fixed rate of interest paid on the asset will be overtaken by interest yields on new lending now that inflation is higher.

 (ii) **Uncertain economic prospects**. The future state of the economy cannot be predicted with certainty. If an organisation wishes to borrow money now for, say, 15 years, there is no certainty about what might happen to that organisation during that time. It might thrive and prosper or it might run into economic difficulties for one reason or another.

 Investors will require a higher return to compensate them for the increased risk.

(d) Note, however, that two other factors also affect the cost of borrowing.

 (i) The risk associated with the perceived ability of the borrower to fulfil the terms of the loan
 (ii) Whether or not the loan is secured by a mortgage on an asset

4.4 Factors affecting interest rates

Interest rates on any one type of financial asset will vary over time. In other words, the general level of interest rates might go up or down. The general level of interest rates is affected by several factors.

(a) **The need for a real return**. It is generally accepted that investors will want to earn a 'real' rate of return on their investment, that is, a return which exceeds the rate of inflation. The suitable real rate of return will depend on factors such as investment risk.

(b) **Uncertainty about future rates of inflation**. When investors are uncertain about what future nominal and real interest rates will be, they are likely to require higher interest yields to persuade them to take the risk of investing, especially in the longer term.

(c) **Changes in the level of government borrowing**. When the demand for credit increases, interest rates will go up. A high level of borrowing by the government is likely to result in upward pressure on interest rates.

(d) **Higher demand for borrowing from individuals**. If individuals want to borrow more, for example because they feel confident about their level of future earnings, then interest rates will tend to rise.

- (e) **Monetary policy.** Governments may exercise influence or control over the level of interest rates in order to control inflation.
- (f) **Interest rates abroad.** An appropriate real rate of interest in one country will be influenced by external factors, such as interest rates in other countries and expectations about the exchange rate.

4.5 Nominal and real rates of interest

We discussed the relationship between **nominal** returns and **real** returns in the previous section of this Chapter.

Nominal rates of interest are rates expressed in money terms. For example, if interest paid per annum on a loan of £1,000 is £150, the rate of interest would be 15%. The nominal rate of interest might also be referred to as the **money rate of interest**, or the **actual money yield** on an investment.

Real rates of interest are the rates of return that investors get from their investment, adjusted for the rate of inflation. The real rate of interest is therefore a measure of the increase in the real wealth, expressed in terms of buying power, of the investor or lender. Real rates of interest are lower than nominal rates when there is price inflation. For example, if the nominal rate of interest is 12% per annum and the annual rate of inflation is 8% per annum, the real rate of interest (approximately 4%) is the interest earned after allowing for the return needed just to keep pace with inflation.

4.6 Effects of interest rates on investments

Returns on **bank deposits** are closely linked to other interest rates in the economy. If interest rates fall, keeping money on deposit will seem less attractive. However, this may reflect the fact that inflation has fallen. **Real interest rates** should be of more concern to the saver than nominal rates.

The relationship between the prices of **fixed interest securities** and interest rates is inverse. As interest rates rise, the prices of these securities fall. Suppose that a fixed interest security pays interest of 5% and is priced at £100. The yield is £5/£100 = 5%.

If interest rates now fall so that 4% is the expected return, then the holder of the security should now be able to obtain a price of around £125 for it. It still pays £5 and so at £125, it pays a yield at the new market rate of £5/£125 = 4%.

The **equity markets** generally favour lower interest rates because companies' profitability will generally be improved by lower borrowing costs for the company's debt and higher demand from consumers. Increased profits should feed through to higher dividend payments for shareholders. Accordingly, unexpected cuts in short-term interest rates are likely to cause a rise in share prices.

5 Money supply

Learning outcomes

1.3.2 Measuring money supply.
1.7.6 Money stock.

5.1 Narrow money and broad money

How much money is there in the economy? It is not always easy to decide whether a particular financial asset, for example a bank deposit, is money or not, and we can distinguish between **narrow money** and **broad money** when we try to measure the stock of money in the economy. (The **money stock** is an alternative term for the money supply.)

Financial assets must have a high degree of liquidity to be regarded as **narrow money**. A definition of narrow money is 'money balances which are readily available to finance current spending, that is to say for transactions purposes' *(Economic Progress Report).*

Broad money, in contrast, includes financial assets which are relatively liquid, but not as liquid as narrow money items. A financial asset which would be regarded as narrow money would also fall within the definition of broad money; but broad money, as its name implies, extends the range of assets which are regarded as money.

Broad money is 'money held for transactions purposes and money held as a form of saving. It provides an indicator of the private sector's holdings of relatively liquid assets – assets which could be converted with relative ease and without capital loss into spending on goods and services' *(Economic Progress Report).*

Narrow money can be defined in different ways, depending on how narrowly 'liquidity' is defined; similarly, broad money can be defined in a variety of ways. Even the broadest definition of money will exclude some financial assets. There will never be a clear dividing line between what is narrow money, what is broad money, and what is not money at all.

5.2 Monetary aggregates

Money supply measures are called **monetary aggregates**.

(a) M0 is the 'narrowest' definition of money, the great majority of which is made up of **notes and coin** in circulation outside the Bank of England. This is the formal definition:

M0 = notes and coins in circulation outside the Bank of England + Banks' operational deposits at the Bank of England

(b) M4 is a 'broad' definition of money, including deposits held for **savings** as well as **spending** purposes. The Bank of England also now publishes statistics for various 'liquid assets outside M4' for the benefit of those who are interested in a still broader definition of the money stock. The formal definition of M4 comprises:

M4 = Private sector holdings of Notes and coins
+ Banks' retail deposits
+ Building Society retail shares and deposits
+ Other interest bearing deposits (including Certificate of Deposits)

M4 itself contains some comparatively illiquid elements. For example, M4 contains deposits of any maturity with banks and building societies and certain paper and other capital market instruments of not more than five years' original maturity, although in practice the bulk of M4 is of under three months' residual maturity.

5.3 Monetary aggregates figures

To give you some idea of the relative sizes of each of these definitions of money, figures for the money stock in the UK in June 2001 are shown below. It is clear that physical notes and coin form a very small part of the larger aggregates.

			£ billion
M0	=	Notes and coin in circulation outside the Bank of England	32.8
	+	banks' operational deposits with the Bank of England	0.1
			32.9
M4	=	M4 private sector holdings of:	
		notes and coin	27.6
	+	banks' retail deposits	485.3
	+	building societies' shares and deposits	124.6
	+	other interest bearing deposits (including Certificates of Deposit)	281.3
			918.8

INVESTMENT AND RISK

> ### Exercise: Narrow money
>
> Which of the following best defines narrow money?
>
> A   Money balances that are readily available to finance current spending
> B   Money that is made from a valuable commodity such as gold or silver
> C   Notes and coins in circulation
> D   Interest bearing financial assets
>
> ### Solution
>
> A   B is a definition of commodity money, which is irrelevant to modern monetary theory. C is attractive but incorrect since it is an **incomplete** definition of UK M_0, which also includes banks operational deposits at the Bank of England and banks' and building societies' till money. D is part of broad money.

5.4 Controlling money supply growth

A government might take any of an number of broad approaches to controlling the growth of the broad money supply.

(a) To reduce or control government borrowing

(b) To finance as much government borrowing as possible by borrowing from the UK non-bank private sector, for example by encouraging National Savings in preference to issuing gilts

(c) To control the increase in bank lending

(d) To control external and foreign currency items, for example by keeping the balance of payments under control

As we saw in the previous Chapter, rather than imposing controls over lending, the current UK Government uses interest rate policy, implemented through the Monetary Policy Committee, as its main monetary policy tool.

5.5 Monetarist views of money supply and inflation

Monetarist economists have argued that **inflation** is caused by **increases in the supply of money**. There is a considerable debate as to whether increases in the money supply are a cause of inflation or whether increases in the money supply are a symptom of inflation. Monetarists have argued that since inflation is caused by an increase in the money supply, inflation can be brought under control by reducing the rate of growth of the money supply.

Monetarists argue that since money is a direct substitute for all other assets, an increase in the money supply, given a fairly stable velocity of circulation, will have a direct effect on demand for other assets because there will be more money to spend on those assets. If the total output of the economy is fixed, then an increase in the money supply will lead directly to higher prices.

This maybe referred to as the **quantitative theory of money** can be expressed through the **Fisher equation**

$$MV = PY$$

Where

- M = Money supply
- V = Velocity of circulation of money in the economy
- P = Price levels of goods traded
- Y = A real output in the economy, ie the number of transactions undertaken

Based on this, a rise in the money supply will lead to a rise in prices and probably also to a rise in money incomes. In the short run, monetarists argue that an increase in the money supply might cause some increase in real economic output and so an increase in employment. In the long run, however, all increases in the money supply will be reflected in higher prices unless there is longer term growth in the economy.

However, if the government controls the money supply without telling anyone what its planned targets of growth are, then people's **expectations** of inflation will run ahead of the growth in the money supply. Wage demands will remain at levels in keeping with these expectations. If the government succeeds in its aim of limiting the growth of the money supply, but wages rise at a faster rate, then higher wages will mean less real income and less real output. In other words, the economy will slump even further.

It is for this reason that the government must announce its targets for growth in the money supply.

(a) Most monetarists argue that the government must give a clear announcement of its targets for monetary growth so as to influence people's expectations of inflation.

(b) Some economists might argue that an **incomes policy** should be imposed by the government to prevent wage rises in excess of government targets.

Monetarists pointed to the high inflation of the mid-1970s as evidence in support of their views since very rapid monetary growth preceded the price inflation. However, later research suggested that soaring oil and commodity prices were the culprits. Falling commodity prices helped subsequently to reduce inflation.

5.6 Keynesian views of money supply

The economist **John Maynard Keynes** took a different view. He said that an increase in the money supply would lead to a fall in interest rates. The impact on the economy of the increase in the money supply then depends on the effect that the fall in interest rates produces.

According to the **Keynesian view**, both investment demand and consumer spending are **relatively insensitive** to interest rate changes, that is, they are relatively interest-inelastic. The **volume of investment** depends heavily, Keynes argued, on **technological changes, business confidence** as well as **expectations**. It follows that the increase in the money supply will have only a limited effect on aggregate demand and consequently relatively little effect on output and employment or on price levels.

Keynesians therefore argue that monetary policy to control the money supply would, have an effect on interest rates and changes in interest rates might in the longer term affect investment. In other respects, however, monetary policy would not really affect the economy and national income.

5.7 Monetary policy effects

We looked earlier at the **framework of UK monetary policy**, which is currently based on an explicit inflation target (of 2% or less for the Consumer Prices Index).

The Bank of England **reducing** interest rates is an **easing** of monetary policy.

(a) Loans will be cheaper, and so consumers may increase levels of debt and spend more. Demand will tend to rise and companies may have improved levels of sales. Companies will find it cheaper to borrow: their lower interest costs will boost bottom-line profits.

(b) Mortgage loans will be cheaper and so there will be upward pressure on property prices.

(c) Other asset values will also rise. Investors will be willing to pay higher prices for gilts (government stock) because they do not require such a high yield from them as before the interest rate reduction.

(d) Interest rates on cash deposits will fall. Those who are dependant on income from cash deposits will be worse off than before.

(e) Businesses will find it cheaper to borrow, and will find investment in expansion new business opportunities more attractive.

INVESTMENT AND RISK

The Bank of England **increasing** interest rates is a **tightening** of monetary policy.

(a) Loans will cost more, and demand from consumers, especially for less essential 'cyclical' goods and services, may fall. Companies will find it more expensive to borrow money and this could eat into profits, on top of any effect from reducing demand.

(b) Mortgage loans will cost more and so there will be a dampening effect on property prices.

(c) Asset prices generally will tend to fall. Investors will require a higher return than before and so they will pay less for fixed interest stocks such as gilts.

(d) Interest rates on cash deposits will rise, and those reliant on cash deposits for income will be better off.

(e) Businesses' borrowing costs will rise, and this may reduce company profits and act as a disincentive to make investments.

The interest rates on financial instruments with longer periods to maturity – such as the yield on long government stocks (**gilts**) – will be influenced by changing expectations in the markets of future levels of interest rates. The short-term rates set by the Bank of England do not change direction frequently. Consequently, the first rise in short-term rates for a period can be taken as a signal by the markets that more rises can be expected in the future. The Bank must be careful about the signals it gives to the markets, since the effect of expectations can be strong.

6 Exchange rates and the balance of payments

Learning outcomes

1.4.1 Capital and current account.
1.4.2 Exchange rates.
1.4.3 The importance of the balance of payments.
1.7.7 Foreign exchange rates.

6.1 What is an exchange rate?

An **exchange rate** is the price of one currency in terms of another. Dealers in currencies, such as banks, make their profit by buying currency at one exchange rate and selling it at a different rate. This means that there is a selling rate and a buying rate for deals between any two tradeable currencies. So, of course, no tradeable currency has only a single exchange rate.

Each currency has an exchange rate against every other tradeable currency. For a particular currency, in economic terms, the exchange rates with major currencies and with the nation's major trading partners are going to be important. For the UK pound sterling, exchange rates with the euro, the US dollar and the Japanese yen are key rates.

Below is a Table showing **exchange rates between major currencies** on a particular day. One pound sterling could buy (ignoring any spread between buying and selling prices to provide a profit for the intermediary) US$2.0188, €1.4278 or ¥231.4497.

	USD	GBP	EUR	JPY
USD	–	2.0188	1.4137	0.008722
GBP	0.4954	–	0.7004	0.004321
EUR	0.7073	1.4278	–	0.006169
JPY	114.6500	231.4497	162.1035	–

6.2 Currency trading

The **foreign exchange ('forex') markets** are worldwide and the main dealers are banks. The largest currency dealing centre is London, with a 31 per cent share of a huge **daily** worldwide market turnover of over $2,500 billion. Around 350 banks deal regularly in the London market. As well as currency flows involving companies and individuals buying goods and services in other countries, there are large investment flows, including speculative flows between currencies by financial institutions trading between each other with very fine (small) spreads between buying and selling prices.

6.3 Exchange rates and investment

Higher investment returns, including interest rates, in particular countries may attract flows of funds from other countries. An investor holding an **overseas investment**, denominated in another currency, is exposed also to changes in the exchange rates between that currency and the investor's home currency. Those changes could move in favour of or against the investor.

Exercise: Exchange rates

'Spyders' (Standard and Poor's Depository Receipts (SPY)) are an instrument denominated in US dollars that tracks the prices of shares in the S&P 500 Index.

A UK investor has a holding of Spyders. Over a particular month, the US dollar rises in value (appreciates) against sterling by 6%. The S&P 500 Index is virtually unchanged over the same month. What has been the effect on the value of the investment in Spyders, in sterling terms?

Solution

The price of Spyders will not have moved significantly in dollar terms. An investment denominated in dollars can now buy more pounds than a month earlier, and so the investment has appreciated in sterling terms.

6.4 Factors influencing exchange rates

A currency may have a fixed exchange rate meaning that its value is pegged to that of another currency. Alternatively a currency may have a floating exchange rate which is the case for the currencies of most major developed economies.

The exchange rate between two floating currencies is determined primarily by **supply and demand** in the foreign exchange markets. Demand comes from individuals, firms and governments who want to buy a currency and supply comes from those who want to sell it. The exchange rates of a currency are subject to a number of influences.

Levels of **inflation**, compared with the rate of inflation in other countries, have an influence. A country with a high level of inflation will tend to have a depreciating currency: if it did not, its exports would start to become uncompetitively priced in world markets. **Purchasing power parity (PPP)** theory predicts that, over the long run at least, exchange rates should move in line with prices so that an amount of money will buy the same goods and services, whichever currency it is changed into.

Real exchange rates can be calculated by adjusting exchange rates to take account of changes in relative prices levels between countries. How the adjustment is made would depend on the use to which the rates were to be put.

Interest rates compared with interest rates in other countries affect exchange rates. Higher interest rates will attract investment flows into a currency. Here it is the real level of interest that is important: a currency with high inflation as well as high interest rates is less attractive for investment than a currency with relatively low inflation and high interest rates.

INVESTMENT AND RISK

Levels of imports and exports will affect exchange rates. If a country imports much more than it exports, it must attract investment flows to balance its excess payments for imports. This may only happen up to a point. If the deficit persists, the currency may decline in value if investors become less willing to invest. As commented earlier, the USA currently runs a significant balance of trade deficit, and some commentators take the view that this may lead to a further decline in the value of the US dollar against other currencies.

Government policy on intervention can influence the exchange rate. Governments over some periods commit themselves, either publicly or without announcement, to maintaining a particular exchange rate or exchange rate range for their currencies. Governments may intervene by buying and selling currencies although most governments' currency reserves are too small to have much effect in this way. Another action that governments can take is to adjust interest rates to defend the desired exchange rate. In 1992, the UK Government sought to defend the value of the pound in order to keep it within its bands as specified in the European Exchange Rate Mechanism (ERM), a precursor to the single European currency (the euro). Interest rates in the UK were increased to 15% but a wave of selling by speculators forced the Government to abandon its attempt, and the pound was removed from the ERM.

Speculation can have an influence, particularly over a shorter-term period, and speculators may be particularly strong influence if a government is seeking to maintain a particular exchange rate, as in the ERM example just mentioned.

6.5 Foreign currency and international trade

Whenever there is international trade, there is generally a need for foreign currency for at least one of the parties to the transaction.

(a) If a UK exporter sells goods to a US buyer, and charges the buyer £20,000, the US buyer must somehow obtain the sterling in order to pay the UK supplier. The US buyer will do this by using some of his US dollars to buy the £20,000 sterling, probably from a bank in the USA.

(b) If a UK importer buys goods from Germany, he might be invoiced in euros, say €100,000. He must obtain this foreign currency to pay his debt, and he will do so by purchasing the euros from a UK bank in exchange for sterling.

(c) If a UK investor wishes to invest in US capital bonds, he would have to pay for them in US dollars, and so he would have to sell sterling to obtain the dollars.

Thus **capital outflows**, such as investing overseas, not just payments for imports, cause a demand to sell the domestic currency and buy foreign currencies. On the other hand, exports and capital inflows to a country cause a demand to buy the domestic currency in exchange for foreign currencies.

Exporters might want to sell foreign currency earnings to a bank in exchange for domestic currency, and importers may want to buy foreign currency from a bank in order to pay a foreign supplier.

6.6 Effects of a strengthening or a weakening currency

If the domestic currency strengthens (ie 'appreciates') in value against the currencies of a country's major trading partners, there will be the following effects.

(a) **Imports** will become cheaper. This can help companies that import raw materials although, if more goods, including consumer goods, are imported, the balance of trade may suffer.

(b) **Exports** will become more difficult for companies to sell at a profit. Exporters must either increase prices on world markets, which may mean that buyers go elsewhere, or they must hold their prices in foreign currency terms and thus receive less in the domestic currency. These effects may lead to the **share prices** of exporters suffering when the currency strengthens. Some larger companies may have 'hedged' against these effects, by using financial instruments that reduce the risks arising from currency fluctuations.

Exercise: Currencies

Work out for yourself what the economic effects will be if a currency weakens against the currencies of its main trading partners.

Solution

Imports become more expensive. This could improve the balance of trade by reducing import volumes, if the drop in volumes more than outweighs the higher prices paid for the imports. There could be an inflationary effect. Not only will direct imports cost more: companies importing raw materials will face higher input costs.

The competitiveness of exporting companies on world markets will be enhanced. They may be able to sell higher volumes, or they may be able to achieve higher profit from sales, for example if they can hold prices where they were before the depreciation of the currency, in domestic currency terms.

6.7 The balance of payments

The total pattern of all flows of funds into and out of a country is recorded in the country's **balance of payments**. The **balance of payments** is the statistical accounting record of all of a country's external transactions in a given period.

In balance of payments statistics, **current account** transactions are sub-divided into four parts.

- Trade in goods
- Trade in services
- Income
- Transfers

Before 1996, the term **visibles** was used in official statistics for trade in goods and the term **invisibles** was used for the rest. These terms have now been dropped in order to give more emphasis to the balances for trade in goods and services, although you may still find them mentioned.

Income is divided into two parts.

- Income from employment of UK residents by overseas firms
- Income from capital investment overseas

Transfers are also divided into two parts:

(a) Public sector payments to and receipts from overseas bodies such as the EU. Typically these are interest payments

(b) Non-government sector payments to and receipts from bodies such as the EU

The **capital account** balance is made up of public sector flows of **capital** into and out of the country, such as government loans to other countries.

The balance on the financial account is made up of flows of capital to and from the non-government sector, such as direct investment in overseas facilities; portfolio investment (in shares, bonds and so on); and speculative flows of currency. Movements on government foreign currency reserves are also included under this heading.

A **balancing item** appears in the balance of payments accounts because of errors and omissions in collecting statistics for the accounts (for example, sampling errors for items such as foreign investment and tourist expenditure and omissions from the data gathered about exports or imports).

The sum of the balance of payments accounts must always be **zero** (ignoring statistical errors in collecting the figures). This is for the same reason that a balance sheet must always balance: for every debit there must be a credit.

6.8 The UK balance of payments accounts

A UK balance of payment account at a particular point in time is summarised below.

UK balance of payments accounts

	£ billions
Current account	
Trade in goods	−26,767
Trade in services	11,538
Income	8,332
Transfers	−4,084
Current balance	−10,981
Capital account	776
Financial account	5,853
Net errors and omissions	4,352
	0

Given that the balance of payments in principle sums to zero, you may wonder what is meant by a surplus or deficit on the balance of payments. When journalists or economists speak of the balance of payments they are usually referring to the deficit or surplus on the **current account**, or possibly to the surplus or deficit on trade in goods only (this is also known as the **balance of trade**).

Exercise

'If the balance of payments always balances why do we hear about deficits and surpluses?'

Solution

The sum of the three balance of payments accounts must always be zero because every transaction in international trade has a double aspect. Just as accounting transactions are recorded by matching debit and credit entries, so too are international trade and financing transactions recorded by means of matching plus and minus transactions.

For example. if a UK exporter sells goods to a foreign buyer:

(a) The value of the export is a plus in the current account of the balance of payments

(b) The payment for the export results in a reduction in the deposits held by foreigners in UK banks (a minus in the assets and liabilities section)

Overall, all of the flows making up the balance of payments must balance, but if we take out flows such as investment flows and transfers between international institutions, we can calculate a **balance of trade**. The balance of trade includes all of a country's **imports** and **exports** of goods and services.

6.9 The balance of trade

The overall figure for the **balance of trade** or the **'current account'** shows us the difference between a country's imports and its exports of goods and services.

A problem arises for a country's balance of payments when the country has a deficit on current account (a **trade deficit**) year after year, although there can be problems too for a country which enjoys a continual current account **surplus**.

The problems of a **deficit** on the current account are probably the more obvious. When a country is continually in deficit, it is importing more goods and services that it is exporting. This leads to two possible consequences.

(a) The country may borrow more and more from abroad, to build up external liabilities which match the deficit on current account, for example encouraging foreign investors to lend more by purchasing the government's gilt-edged securities.

(b) The country may sell more and more of its assets. This has been happening recently in the USA, for example, where a large deficit on the US current account has been offset by large purchases of shares in US companies by foreign firms.

If a country has a **surplus** on its current account year after year, it might invest the surplus abroad or add it to official reserves. The balance of payments position would be strong. There is the problem, however, that if one country which is a major trading nation (such as Japan) has a continuous surplus on its balance of payments current account, other countries must be in continual deficit. These other countries can run down their official reserves, perhaps to nothing, and borrow as much as they can to meet the payments overseas, but eventually, they will run out of money entirely and be unable even to pay their debts. Political pressure might therefore build up within the importing countries to impose tariffs or import quotas.

6.10 How can a government rectify a current account deficit?

The government of a country with a balance of payments deficit will usually be expected to take measures to reduce or eliminate the deficit. A deficit on current account may be rectified by one or more of the following measures.

(a) A depreciation of the currency (called **devaluation** when deliberately instigated by the government, for example by changing the value of the currency within a controlled exchange rate system).

(b) Direct measures to restrict imports, such as tariffs or import quotas or exchange control regulations.

(c) Domestic deflation to reduce aggregate demand in the domestic economy.

The first two are **expenditure switching** policies, which transfer resources and expenditure away from imports and towards domestic products while the last is an **expenditure reducing** policy.

Problems with a trade deficit include the following.

(a) **Effect on growth**

Since a trade **deficit represents a leakage** of income from the national economy, there is a danger that **economic growth diminishes** unless internally generated growth can compensate for this.

(b) **Exchange rates**

A persistent trade deficit is likely to put **downward pressure** on the **exchange rate** as confidence in the currency is weakened and as demand for it, relative to other currencies in general, falls.

(c) **Domestic consequences**

A depreciating exchange rate will mean that the **price of imports** in domestic terms will be **rising**, putting pressure on **domestic inflation** with consequent knock-on effects for wage demands and unemployment.

Problems can emerge with persistent surpluses.

(a) **Overheating**

A trade surplus represents an injection into the national economy which may result in an **overheating** of the economy if domestic production is already at full capacity. Overheating will tend to reflect itself in **upward pressure on prices** as total demand for goods (domestic and foreign) exceeds total domestic supply.

(b) **Exchange rates**

Surpluses are likely to put **upward pressure** on the **exchange rate** which will push up the price of exported goods in foreign countries. This gives rise to the possibility that the surplus will decline.

INVESTMENT AND RISK

Where trade is out of balance, governments can take a number of measures, including the following, to restore the balance.

(a) **Transport restrictions**

Governments can discourage imports through **quotas**, controls or taxes (although this would doubtless lead to retaliatory action). Some argue that the imposition of product standards testing is a form of control. It might be illegal under EU rules or other treaty obligations (eg WTO).

(b) **Giving support to exporters**

This may take a number of forms such as export monopolies, advice (as provided by the government). Export credit insurance reduces the risk, and hence the return that might have to be earned.

(c) **Devaluing the currency**

Devaluation makes exports cheaper and increases their value.

(d) **General fiscal and monetary policy**

Economic policy can reduce the overall level of activity in the economy. While (a), (b) and (c) are **expenditure switching** policies, which transfer resources and expenditure away from imports and towards domestic products, this is an **expenditure reducing** policy.

(e) **Rising interest rates**

This will increase the value of the currency, to make imports cheaper.

(f) **Supply side measures**

In the long term, supply side measures on the 'supply side' – that is, to improve competition and the free up markets – can encourage exports.

Key chapter points

- Gross Domestic Product (GDP) is a measure of the total value of economic output within a country.

- Economic growth – growth in national output – is a central objective of governments. National output (or national income – another way of looking at the level of economic activity) is found to vary over a period of years in what is called the business cycle or the trade cycle.

- Stock market cycles move between bull markets and bear markets. Share prices reflect market sentiment, and changes in their general level usually reflect changes in the sentiment of market participants.

- The Retail Prices Index (RPI) and the new Consumer Prices Index (CPI) measure the general level of consumer prices. Unlike the RPI, the CPI excludes most housing costs. Inflation creates problems for economic decision makers, and for those on fixed incomes, and expectations of inflation can lead to a wage-price spiral which is difficult to stop.

- Disinflation describes a situation of falling inflation. Deflation is a term for negative inflation (falling prices). Deflation can be bad for economic welfare because companies may cut back on output if they anticipate prices falling, as they may not be able to cover their costs and make profits.

- Interest rates are the price of money or credit, and will vary for interest-bearing assets of different maturity dates.

- The money stock (or 'money supply') may be measured in narrow money or broad money measures. Monetarist economists have argued that inflation is caused by increases in the money supply. Keynesians see monetary control as less effective.

- In the previous Chapter and this one, we have seen how the UK government targets a range for the inflation rate, using interest rate changes as its main policy instrument. An earlier policy approach was to target a level of money supply growth, but money supply growth was found to be an unreliable guide to the level of consumer demand and inflation.

- Exchange rates are the prices of a currency in terms of other currencies. As with all markets, supply and demand factors determine prices. Purchasing power parity theory predicts that, over the long run, exchange rates should move into line with prices, so that an amount of money can buy the same goods and services in different currencies.

- The balance of payments records transactions between a national economy and the rest of the world, including investment flows, as well as trading transactions.

- When people talk of a balance of payments deficit, or surplus, they are generally referring to the balance of a country's trade between imports and exports of goods and services. The financial services sector helps to give the UK a surplus on its trade in services.

Chapter Quiz

1. What is the difference between GDP and GNP? .... (see para 1.5)
2. How is 'recession' usually defined? .... (2.2)
3. What is meant by a 'bear market'? .... (2.5)
4. Which inflation measure is used for the UK Government's inflation target? .... (3.2)
5. What is the difference between deflation and disinflation? .... (3.3)
6. Outline three factors influencing interest rates. .... (4.4)
7. Distinguish between 'narrow money' and 'broad money'. .... (5.1)
8. Outline the possible effects of a tightening of monetary policy. .... (5.7)
9. What is meant by 'purchasing power parity'? .... (6.4)
10. Distinguish between the current account and the capital account of the balance of payments. .... (6.7)

chapter 4

Taxation

Chapter topic list

1	Income tax	64
2	Capital gains tax	80
3	Stamp duty	88
	Key chapter points	90
	Chapter quiz	91

The topics covered in this chapter are also included in Approved Examination 1 *Introduction to UK Financial Services, Regulation and Ethics*. This chapter therefore repeats material from the chapter on Taxation in the CF1 Study Text. Even if you have already studied that Unit, you are advised to review this chapter, to ensure that you can recall the subject matter.

This chapter, like the other chapters in this Study Text, is based on the tax year **2010/11**.

Taxation is a complex subject, and is covered here to the depth required for your examination. There may be particular rules for special situations that are not covered here because they are beyond the requirements of the syllabus. Clients may require specialist tax advice.

INVESTMENT AND RISK

CHAPTER LEARNING OUTCOMES

2   **Understand** the basic principles of taxation applying to the investments of UK resident and domiciled individuals

   2.1   The key principles of income tax

   2.1.1   Liability to income tax.
   2.1.2   Allowances.
   2.1.3   Reliefs.
   2.1.4   Rates.
   2.1.5   Grossing up interest and dividends.
   2.1.6   Employed and self-employed income.
   2.1.7   Priorities for taxing different classes of income.

   2.2   The key principles of Capital Gains Tax

   2.2.1   Liability to CGT.
   2.2.2   Disposals.
   2.2.3   Death.
   2.2.4   Deductions.
   2.2.5   Losses.
   2.2.6   Main exemptions.
   2.2.7   Basic calculation of chargeable gains.
   2.2.8   Entrepreneur's relief.

   2.3   The main features of Stamp Duty Reserve Tax on securities

   - Corporate tax as at applied investments.

9   **Understand** tax planning strategies

   9.1   Basic income tax and capital gains tax computations – personal allowances, non-savings income, savings income, dividends, life assurance bond profits, chargeable gains.

   9.4   Rules and procedures relating to personal tax calculations.

   9.5   Tax calculations.

1 Income tax

1.1 Introduction to income tax

Learning outcome

2.1.1   Liability to Income Tax.

Who pays income tax?

Income tax is payable by all individuals and trusts **resident in the UK on their worldwide income**. Non-residents are only liable to income tax if they have a source of income derived in the UK.

Fiscal years

Income tax is calculated by reference to the **fiscal year**. This is also referred to as the income tax year or the year of assessment. The fiscal year runs from 6 April one year to 5 April the next year. The **fiscal year 2010/11 is the year ended 5 April 2011**.

Residence

An individual is resident in the UK in one of the following circumstances.

- He is present in the UK for **six months** (183 days) **or more** in the fiscal year in question.
- He is present in the UK for **periods averaging three or more months** in a year for **four** or more years.

It is possible to be resident in more than one country at a time.

There is also a tax classification of **'domicile'** that is initially based on your nationality at birth through it may be changed through emigration. If a person is **non-UK domiciled, but resident** for income and capital gains tax purposes, then they are taxed on the income and gains on their overseas assets when they are **remitted** back to the UK. The definition of 'remitted' is very broad, but, generally speaking, is when the resident gains control, eg putting proceeds of overseas investment into a UK bank account. In addition, such individuals are subject to an annual tax charge of £30,000 on unremitted income and gains.

Summary

Status	Tax Payable
UK resident and UK domiciled	Income tax on worldwide earned income
UK resident and non-UK domiciled	Income tax on earned UK income and overseas income remitted to UK
Non-UK resident	Income tax on UK earned income irrespective of domicile

Assessment of tax

Employees with simple tax affairs will not be asked to complete a Tax Return, as the PAYE deductions should be accurate. If an individual has more complicated tax affairs, he or she may need to complete a **self-assessment Tax Return**, to ensure that the correct tax liability is calculated. If there is income that has not been taxed, the individual must declare this to HMRC and complete a Tax Return.

If a paper Tax Return is issued, it must be completed and submitted by the **filing date**. This is:

(a) 31 October if the return was issued on or before 31 July

(b) For returns issued after 31 July, the earlier of
- 3 months after issue
- 31 January

The Tax Return includes a section for the taxpayer to compute his own tax payable (a **self assessment**), and this computation counts as an assessment to tax. The return and the balance of any tax payable are usually both due by 31 January following the end of the tax year.

A taxpayer may choose not to complete the section of the return in which he works out his tax payable (the **self assessment**). HMRC will then make the **computation** and prepare an assessment. This counts as a self assessment made by the taxpayer, so the rules in this section relating to self assessments still apply. However, HMRC will not guarantee to have the work done in time for the taxpayer to pay the correct amount by the due date, unless the return is submitted by the later of:

INVESTMENT AND RISK

(a) 30 September following the end of the tax year which the return covers
(b) Two months after it was issued

Payments on account

Some individuals – mainly the self-employed – will also need to make two payments on account. This will be the case if an individual

- Has a tax bill of £1,000 or more; and
- Paid less than 80% of their tax liability for the previous year by deduction at source (eg PAYE).

Each payment will normally equal **one half of the previous year's tax liability** (after taking off tax deducted at source and tax credits on dividends). The payments are due on **31 January** in the tax year and **31 July** following the tax year, with a balancing payment (or repayment) due by 31 January the following year.

Therefore, for an individual who had a net tax liability of £10,000 for fiscal year 2009/10, there will be two payments on account due for the 2010/11 fiscal year: £5,000 payable by 31 January 2011 and £5,000 payable by 31 July 2011. If the net liability for 2010/11 was subsequently calculated as £12,000, the balancing payment of £2,000 would then be due by 31 January 2012.

Penalties for non-compliance

Taxpayers filing tax returns late face maximum late filing penalties of £100 for returns up to six months late, then £200 if over six and up to twelve months late. Beyond twelve months, the maximum penalty is £200 plus 100% of the tax liability. A maximum penalty of £60 per day could be imposed if notice is given to the taxpayer.

Surcharges are imposed for tax paid late (but not payments on account by self-employed people). The surcharge starts at 5% for amounts more than 28 days late, increasing to 10% for payments more than six months late. Interest is charged on late payments on account.

Civil partnerships

As from **5 December 2005**, same-sex couples who obtain legal status as **'civil partners'** under the **Civil Partnership Act 2004** are treated **for all tax purposes** in the same way as a married couple. This treatment is not extended to common law partners.

1.2 Overview of income tax calculations

Learning outcome

9.4 Rules and procedures relating to personal tax calculations.

The flowchart below illustrates the stages in calculating an individual's income tax. Each stage is examined in more detail in the following sections.

Income Tax Calculation

1. Total all gross income for the fiscal year (exclude tax-free income from calculation)

⬇

2. Deduct any allowable deductions, e.g. personal allowance to establish taxable income

⬇

3. This taxable income is taxed at the relevant rate, depending on the source of the income, giving the investor's total tax liability for the year.

⬇

4. We must deduct any tax they have already paid in the year, leaving the investor's outstanding tax for the last year, which they must pay by 31 January at the latest.

1.3 Income tax calculation stage 1 – calculate total gross income

> **Learning outcome**
> 2.1.5 Grossing up interest and dividends.
> 2.1.6 Employed and self-employed income.

The first step in establishing the amount of income tax an individual or trust will pay is to calculate what income has been received or earned. We will need to exclude tax-free income and gross up income that has been received net.

Tax-free income

Some income is specifically tax free, free of both income tax and CGT. Such income should not be included in the tax calculation. The main examples of tax-free income are

- Premium Bond prizes.
- Interest earned on National Savings Certificates.
- Income from an Individual Savings Account (ISA).
- Gambling wins (including the National Lottery).
- Save As You Earn (SAYE) scheme interest.
- First £30,000 of a redundancy or other compensation payout.
- The proceeds of a qualifying life assurance policy.
- Life assurance bond withdrawals up to 5% p.a (cumulative) of the original premium, withdrawals above this level are taxable.

INVESTMENT AND RISK

Earnings from employment

The **earnings of employees** will include salaries, bonuses, commissions, fees, and taxable benefits in kind such as a company car, cheap loans and the cost of private medical insurance.

Earnings for duties performed in the UK are subject to the **Pay As You Earn (PAYE)** system, under which the employer deducts tax before paying the net amount to the employee. The HMRC (Her Majesty's Revenue & Customs, which includes what used to be known as the Inland Revenue) issues a **Tax Code** to indicate to the employer how much estimated tax should be deducted.

Benefits in kind

Pay is not the only benefit which may be provided by an employer for employees. One of the additional types of **benefit in kind** is the provision of a **company car**, most commonly provided for senior managers and sales representatives. The value of private use of the car, and of fuel if used privately, is taxable.

The taxable benefit is based on a percentage of the list price and the car's emissions level and varies between 9% and 35%.

In the case of **representatives**, a car is a necessary aid for them in their work. However they usually have the private use of a car when they are not using it on business and that private use is treated as a benefit in kind.

For senior managers, a company the car is less likely to be an essential part of their work and is more likely to be a **form of remuneration**.

Other taxable benefits in kind include the value of **meal vouchers** in excess of 15p per day and the cost of **private medical insurance**.

The position is complicated by the fact that different rules apply to employees in two **different groups**. The two groups are

- employees earning **£8,500 per annum or more** (referred to as higher paid employees) and directors of the company
- those who are earning less than £8,500 per annum ('excluded employees').

For directors and higher paid employees the employer must complete an HMRC **P11D form** giving details of all benefits and expenses payments.

Such **P11D employees** must pay tax on the value of benefits in kind whereas excluded employees are not liable for tax on many benefits. The deciding factor is whether or not an employee's pay and benefits in total reach the P11D level and the level of any benefits is included when making this assessment. An employee whose pay is £8,400 a year and who has benefits in kind valued at £200 per year is classified as a P11D employee.

Expenses of an employee must be incurred **wholly, exclusively and necessarily** for their work (for example, subscriptions to a professional association) for them to be allowable against the employee's tax liability.

Sole traders

A **self-employed** person running his or her own business, which is not formed as a limited company, is a **sole trader** even if the person employs other people.

Sole traders pay tax based on the **profit** for their **accounting year**. The accounting year will be the one which ends in the current tax year.

A sole trader is taxed on **business income minus allowable expenses**. Then, the process is the same as for an employed person: other income is added to earnings and deducting the personal allowance.

Even if the sole trader retains profits in the business and does not draw them out, they are taxable as earnings. The fact that the trader has chosen not to draw and spend them does not change their status as earnings.

The sole trader's tax for each tax year will be based on the profits made in the business year which ended in that same tax year. For example, if the trader's business year ends on 30 June, then the tax liability for the fiscal year 2010/11 will be based on the profit that the trader makes in the business year ending on 30 June 2010. This is known as the **current year basis**. Any other income received or earned, apart from tax-free income, will form the basis of any income tax computation.

Gross income

In order to calculate the amount of income tax that ought to be paid in a fiscal year (the **income tax liability**), it will be necessary to establish the **gross income** subject to tax. In many cases this will not be the amount of income actually received since many sources of income are received **net** of some income tax deduction.

The table below summarises how various sources of income are received.

Salary/Wages	Interest Income, eg Bank or Building Society Interest	UK Dividend Income
Received net of PAYE (Pay As You Earn) income tax at the appropriate rate for the individual.	Received **net of a 20% withholding tax**. Except for • Eurobond interest • Gilt interest ① • Most National Savings and Investments interest • Interest on deposits exceeding £50,000 ② • Interest paid to charities, pension funds or corporate investors ③ • Interest on offshore accounts (eg Isle of Man and Channel Islands)	Received **net of a 10% withholding tax** which cannot be reclaimed even by non-taxpayers

① Individuals, for their own convenience, may 'elect' to have their gilt interest paid net of 20% withholding tax.

② This must be a single deposit exceeding £50,000.

③ No income tax is deducted as these entities are non-taxpayers, or not subject to income tax in the case of companies. Non-taxpaying individuals may apply to have their bank or building society interest paid gross by signing a declaration.

Grossing up net income

If income is not received gross, this income must be grossed up first, before being totalled with other gross income.

How to gross up

The calculation to gross up will depend upon the source of the income, and how much tax has been withheld.

Source	Assumption of How Income is Received	To Gross Up
Bank account interest Building society account interest Corporate bond interest	Net of 20% tax	Net Interest × $\frac{100}{80}$
Dividend income (from shares, unit trusts, investment trusts, OEICs)	Net of 10% tax	Net Dividend × $\frac{100}{90}$

INVESTMENT AND RISK

Source	Assumption of How Income is Received	To Gross Up
Gilt interest Rents received	GROSS	**DO NOT GROSS UP** unless question states 'net gilt' interest, when you follow rules for bank interest
Salary	Net of PAYE tax	Add PAYE tax onto salary received

Example: Grossing up

Salary

Peter received a salary of £23,000 after PAYE of £8,100 had been deducted.

Gross income = £23,000 + £8,100 = **£31,100**

(Note that National Insurance contributions or other deductions from salary are not considered.)

Bank account interest

In the case of interest income, 20% tax will usually have been deducted from the income prior to receipt. The gross amount and the tax deducted can be calculated as illustrated in the following example.

Peter received bank interest income of £4,000.

Gross income: £4,000 × $\frac{100}{80}$ = **£5,000**

Tax deducted: £5,000 gross × 20% withholding tax = **£1,000**

Dividend income

A net dividend would be grossed up by multiplying by $\frac{100}{90}$ as the dividend would have suffered 10% withholding tax.

Peter received a net dividend of £900.

Gross income: £900 × $\frac{100}{90}$ = **£1,000**

Tax deducted: £1,000 × 10% withholding tax = **£100**

1.4 Income tax calculation stage 2 – allowable deductions and taxable income

Learning outcomes

2.1.2 Allowances.
2.1.3 Reliefs.

There are a number of allowable deductions an individual can make from gross income before tax is payable (see Tax Table). In addition, there are tax reliefs, whereby the individual is allowed to deduct an amount from their tax liability prior to calculating their final liability. These are either **allowances** or **charges on income**. The most important are outlined below. They both have the effect of reducing total tax payable by the investor.

Personal allowance

All UK residents, including children, are entitled to a **personal allowance** in each tax year which for 2010/11 is £6,475.

If a couple are living together and one of them does not have sufficient income to use up a personal allowance, the other can transfer assets to that person so that the income from those assets – previously taxable – will now no longer be taxable because it falls within the personal allowance. In order to do this, the **ownership** of assets must be totally transferred from one person to another: not everybody is willing to do that.

For individuals earning more than £100,000, their personal allowance is reduced by £1 for every £2 of income above this threshold.

Age allowances

There are higher personal allowances called **age allowances** for those in the age brackets 65 plus (£9,490 for 2010/11) and 75 plus (£9,640 for 2010/11).

If someone entitled to an age allowance has income over an annual sum known as the **income limit for age-related allowances**, the allowance is reduced gradually. The income limit is £22,900 for 2010/11 and the age allowance is reduced by £1 for every £2 of income in excess of the limit until it falls to the level of the normal personal allowance.

The following example will show the effect of additional income for someone whose income exceeds the income limit.

Example: Age allowance

A and B are aged 67 and single. A's income is at the income limit, while B's income is £200 higher than that. The effect of the income limit in each case is shown below.

Taxable income	A (£)	B (£)
Income (all pension)	22,900	23,100
Age allowance	(9,490)	(9,390)*
Taxable income	13,410	13,710

* £9,490 – £200/2

Tax	A		B	
	£	£	£	£
	13,410 × 20%	2,682	13,710 × 20%	2,742

Notice the difference in income and tax.

	Income £		Tax £
A	22,900		2,682
B	23,100		2,742
Additional income	200	Additional tax	60

Income of £200 in excess of the limit results in extra after-tax income of only: £200 – £60 = £140.

INVESTMENT AND RISK

Married couple/civil partnership allowance

The main **Married Couple's Allowance** was abolished from 6 April 2000, but the right to claim a couple's allowance remains for pensioners born before 6 April 1935. The amount of the allowance depends on whether at least one of the couple is aged 75 or over (at any time in the tax year). New marriages and civil partnerships meeting the age criteria will have an allowance based on the income of the highest earner.

The allowance is reduced by any excess over the income limit not used against the age allowance. The minimum amount available is £2,670 for 2010/11. The allowance available is then given as a reduction from tax payable at the rate of 10% (ie, the minimum amount of the reduction in 2010/11 is £267).

Blind person's allowance

A taxpayer who is registered with a local authority as a blind person gets a blind person's allowance (BPA) of £1,890 in 2010/11. The allowance is also given for the year before registration, if the taxpayer had obtained the proof of blindness needed for registration before the end of that earlier year.

Charges

A charge is a payment by a tax payer which is allowed as a deduction. An example is a payment to use a patent (patent royalty).

A charge is deducted from income **before** tax is calculated. This means that the borrower is effectively relieved from paying tax on that part of his income which is used to meet the charge, ie he obtains tax relief.

Donations to charity

A scheme of tax relief on gifts to charities by individuals applies to **'Gift Aid'** donations. A Gift Aid donation can be a 'one-off' gift or a regular gift to a charity. The taxpayer must make a Gift Aid declaration to the charity.

A Gift Aid donation is treated as though it was paid net of basic rate tax (20%). This amount can then be recovered by the charity. Higher rate relief is given to the taxpayer by extending his basic rate tax band by the grossed-up value of the gift.

Thus, if an individual who pays tax at the basic rate makes a gross charitable donation of £100, he can make a 'Gift Aid' declaration and so will pay (net) £80.

There is also income tax relief for gifts to charity of shares in quoted companies and land and buildings.

Pension contributions

Payments to a **personal pension scheme** (including a **stakeholder pension**) are paid net of basic rate tax to the pension provider. For example, if the scheme member contributes £1,000 to his personal pension scheme in 2010/11, he will pay £800 and the pension provider will reclaim £200 from HMRC. This addition from HMRC applies even if the scheme member is a non-taxpayer: someone can contribute up to £3,600 gross (£2,880 net) to a pension scheme even if they have no earnings.

If the scheme member is a higher rate taxpayer, he or she will receive higher rate relief by extending his basic rate tax band by the gross amount of the contribution (eg in the above example by £1,000). This is similar to the treatment for Gift Aid donations.

Contributions to **occupational pension schemes** by an employee are deductible from earnings for tax purposes.

Overseas tax relief

When a UK resident receives income from overseas, they will be liable to UK income tax. However, it is possible that the individual has already paid tax on that income to an overseas government, referred to as **withholding tax**. In order for this individual to avoid paying tax twice on the same source of income, there are **double taxation agreements** between many countries. If a double tax treaty does not exist, the UK Government will usually give relief unilaterally to avoid double taxation arising.

Basic principle for calculating income tax on overseas income

- If overseas tax paid on income is less than UK tax due, a UK resident owes HMRC the difference (ie can offset overseas tax against UK tax).
- If overseas tax paid is greater than UK tax due, a UK resident owes HMRC nothing, but he does not get a rebate.

Example: Double tax relief

Ms Forbes receives £1,500 gross overseas income. Overseas withholding tax is charged at 10%. Ms Forbes' income before overseas income is £50,000. Calculate the double tax relief available.

Solution

	(£)
Overseas tax paid £1,500 @ 10%	150
UK tax payable £1,500 @ 40%*	600

Therefore, the double tax relief available is £150, ie the lower of the UK tax payable or the overseas tax suffered. Therefore, Ms Forbes owes HMRC the difference, ie £450.

Each source of overseas income is dealt with separately and the amount of relief deducted before arriving at the individual's tax liability.

* To determine the relevant UK tax rate the gross overseas income is treated as being the top slice. Thus, in this example, with Ms Forbes receiving £50,000 of income before overseas income, the entirety of the overseas income would fall into the higher rate tax band.

Personal tax computation

An individual's income from all sources is brought together in a **personal tax computation**. We split income into **non-savings income, savings (excluding dividend) income and dividend income** as different rates are applied to the different sources (see Tax Tables). An income tax computation can be drawn up using three columns headed as follows.

Non-savings income £	Savings (excluding dividend income) £	Dividend Income £

Interest from cash deposits, government and corporate bonds, fixed income collective investments, and dividends from shares and equity collective investments are **'savings income'**. All other income is **non-savings income**, which may include (among other things) earned income, business profits and rental income.

In addition to different rates being applied to different sources of income, different rates are applied to different levels of income. Considering all potential sources, income may fall into one of four bands, the starting rate band covering the first £2,440 of income, the basic rate band covering the next £34,960 of income (up to a level of £37,400), a higher rate band for income above £37,400 and below £150,000, and the additional rate band for income above £150,000.

INVESTMENT AND RISK

Strictly speaking the starting rate band only applies to savings and dividend income and there is no starting rate band for non-savings income where the basic rate band covers the first £37,400 of income. However for the convenience of calculations, especially for low earners with several forms of income, it is, perhaps, easiest to assume that the starting rate band does still exist for non-savings income but that the rate for this band is the basic rate as we will illustrate below.

Statutory total income and taxable income

The total of an individual's income from all sources is the **statutory total income**. Once statutory total income has been calculated, personal allowances are deducted to arrive at **taxable income**.

Two allowances, the personal allowance and the blind person's allowance, are deducted from STI. The allowances come off non-savings income first, then off savings (excluding dividend) income and lastly off dividend income.

A taxable income computation can be set out as below.

Sue: taxable income for 2010/11

	Non-savings income £	Savings (excl dividend) income £	Dividend income £	Total £
Income from employment	36,000			36,000
Building society interest (× 100/80)		1,000		1,000
NS&I Savings Certificates interest		320		320
UK dividends (× 100/90)			1,000	1,000
Statutory total income (STI)	36,000	1,320	1,000	38,320
Less personal allowance	(6,475)			(6,475)
Taxable income	29,525	1,320	1,000	31,845

Note that the **National Savings & Investments** interest Sue receives is received **gross**. Building Society interest and UK dividends are received net and must, therefore, be grossed up for inclusion in the income tax computation.

1.5 Income tax calculation stage 3 – tax rates and tax liability

> **Learning outcomes**
>
> 2.1.4 Rates.
>
> 2.1.7 Priorities for taxing different classes of income.
>
> 9.1 Basic Income Tax and Capital Gains Tax computations – personal allowances, non-savings income, savings income, dividends, life assurance bond profits, chargeable gains.
>
> 9.5 Tax calculations.

Tax rates

The first step in calculating the income tax liability is to divide the total **taxable income** into three bands:

(a) **Starting rate band** – the first £2,440 of income
(b) **Basic rate band** – the next £34,960 of income
(c) **Higher rate** – the next £112,600 of income
(d) **Additional rate** – the remaining income

As already noted, the rate of tax applied to the income in each band depends on whether the income is non-savings income, savings (excluding dividend) income or dividend income.

4: TAXATION

There is only **one set of income tax bands** used for **all three types of income**. These bands must be allocated to income in the following order:

(a) **Non-savings income**
(b) **Savings** (excluding dividend) **income**
(c) **Dividend income**

Example: Personal tax computation

Zoë has total taxable income of £44,000. Of this £28,000 is non-savings income, £12,000 is interest and £4,000 is dividend income.

	Non-savings income £	Savings income £	Dividend Income £	Total £
Taxable income	28,000	12,000	4,000	44,000
Tax band allocation				
• Starting rate	2,440			2,440
• Basic rate	25,560	9,400		34,960
• Higher rate		2,600	4,000	6,600
	28,000	12,000	4,000	44,000

The sequence of events here is:

1. The first £2,440 of non-savings income is in the starting rate band. The remaining £25,560 of non-savings income is in the basic rate band. This leaves £9,400 (£34,960 – £25,560) of the basic rate band.

2. The first £9,400 of savings income consumes the remainder of the basic rate band, leaving £2,600 (£12,000 – £9,400) above the higher rate threshold.

3. As a result, all the dividend income is income above the higher rate threshold.

Some people find the easiest way to think about income tax is to imagine an empty measuring jug with markers up the side measuring two key points: £2,440 and £37,400 and £150,000.

In Zoë's case, we need to consider the three bands up to the higher rate, and not the additional rate.

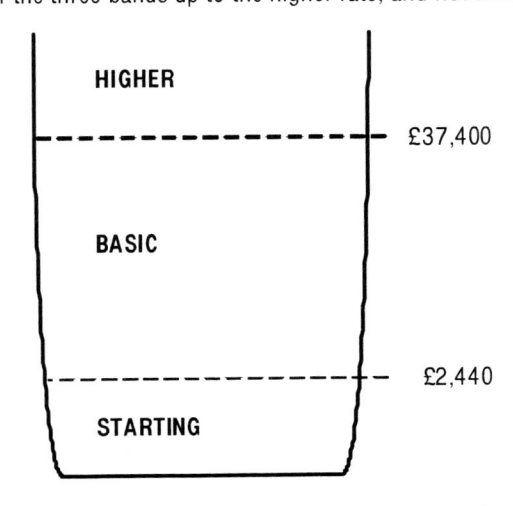

```
         HIGHER
    -----------------  £37,400

          BASIC


    -----------------  £2,440
         STARTING
```

Now we take our **taxable** income (after any deductions and allowances) and imagine that each source of income (salary, interest, dividends) is a different coloured sand and we 'pour' each type of income in the measuring jug. We have to do

INVESTMENT AND RISK

this in a specific order: salary first, then interest, then dividends, otherwise the calculation will not work. For Zoë this would look like

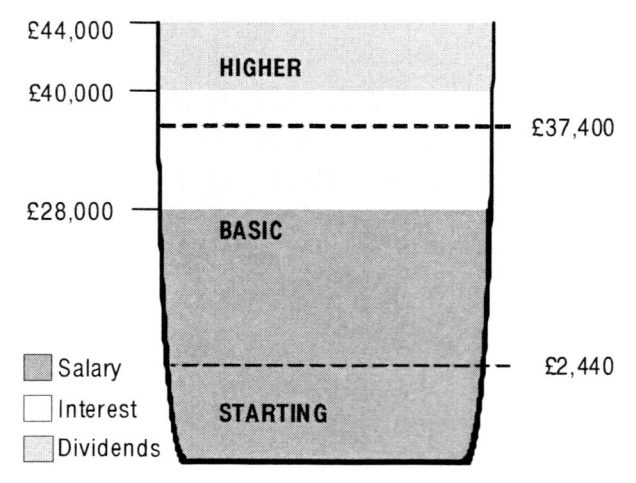

We now see that our total of £44,000 income can be split into five different categories, each being defined by the type of income it is, and the tax band it falls in.

To begin, we have £2,440 of salary in the starting band. The remaining £25,560 of salary is then in the basic band.

Then we look at the interest. Of the £12,000 total we still have room for £9,400 in the basic rate band (as the salary only took us up to £28,000). The remaining £2,600 is then in the higher band.

Finally, we have our dividend income, of which the whole £4,000 is in the higher band.

Computing the tax liability

The tax due on taxable income is then calculated in three steps using the appropriate rates for the income source (see Tax Tables).

Step 1: Deal with non-savings income first:

Non-savings income in the starting rate band is taxed at the basic rate of 20%. Next any non-savings income in the basic rate band is taxed at 20%, non-savings income above the higher rate threshold is taxed at 40%, and finally non-savings income above the additional rate threshold is taxed at 50%.

Step 2: Second, deal with savings (excl dividend) income:

Savings (excl dividend) income is dealt with after non-savings income. If any of the starting or basic rate bands remain **after taxing non-savings income** they can be used here. Savings (excluding dividend) income is taxed at 10% in the starting rate band. If savings (excluding dividend) income falls within the basic rate band it is taxed at 20%. Once income is above the higher rate threshold, it is taxed at 40% and then 50% at the additional rate.

Step 3: Third, compute tax on dividend income:

Lastly, tax dividend income. If dividend income falls within the starting or basic rate bands, it is taxed at 10% (never 20%). If, however, the dividend income exceeds the higher rate threshold, it is taxed at 32.5% first, and at 42.5% above the additional rate threshold of £150,000.

Continuing Zoë's income tax computation from the **Example** above, the tax liability is:

Income tax	£
Non-savings income	
£2,440 × 20%	488
£25,560 × 20%	5,112
£28,000	
Savings (excl. dividend) income	
£9,400 × 20%	1,880
£2,600 × 40%	1,040
£12,000	
Dividend income	
£4,000 × 32.5%	1,300
4,000	
Tax liability	9,820

1.6 Income tax calculation stage 4 – Outstanding tax liability

We have seen above how to calculate the income tax liability on non-savings, savings and dividend income. Once this is done there are two final steps to be made in order to compute the tax payable.

First, deduct the tax credit on dividends from the tax liability. Although deductible, this tax credit cannot be repaid if it exceeds the tax liability calculated so far.

Finally deduct the tax deducted at source from savings (excluding dividend) income and any PAYE. (PAYE is the tax deducted at source from an individual's earnings.) These amounts can be repaid to the extent that they exceed the income tax liability.

The resulting figure is the outstanding tax liability or tax payable which is the balance of the liability still to be settled in cash.

Continuing the example of Zoë, above, and assuming all interest was received net of 20% tax and PAYE of £7,000 had been deducted by her employees.

	£
Income liability	9,820
Less tax suffered	
PAYE	(7,000)
Tax credit on dividend (£4,000 × 10%)	(400)
Tax on interest (£12,000 × 20%)	(2,400)
Income tax payable	70

Below are some more examples of complete computations of income tax payable.

INVESTMENT AND RISK

> **Example: Further personal tax computations**
>
> (a) Kathy has a salary of £8,000 and receives net interest of £4,000.
>
> | | Non-savings £ | Interest £ | Total £ |
> |---|---|---|---|
> | **Income** | | | |
> | Earnings | 8,000 | | 8,000 |
> | Interest £4,000 × 100/80 | | 5,000 | 5,000 |
> | STI | 8,000 | 5,000 | 13,000 |
> | Less personal allowance | (6,475) | | (6,475) |
> | Taxable income | 1,525 | 5,000 | 6,525 |
> | **Tax band allocation** | | | |
> | Starting rate | 1,525 | 915 | 2,440 |
> | Basic rate | | 4,085 | 4,085 |
> | | 1,525 | 5,000 | 6,525 |
>
> | | £ |
> |---|---|
> | **Income tax** | |
> | Non-savings income | |
> | £1,525 × 20% | 305 |
> | Interest income | |
> | £915 × 10% | 91 |
> | £4,085 × 20% | 817 |
> | Tax liability | 1,213 |
> | Less tax paid on interest | (1,000) |
> | **Tax payable** | 213 |
>
> Some of the tax payable has probably already been paid on the salary under PAYE.
>
> The first £915 of interest income falls within the starting rate band so is taxed at 10% (not 20%). The tax paid on interest income is deducted from the tax liability. Remember that the interest deduction can result in excess tax being repaid, unlike with dividend tax credits which can only reduce the tax payable to £NIL.

(b) Jules has a salary of £20,000, business profits of £30,000, net dividends of £6,750 and building society interest of £3,000 net. He pays a copyright royalty of £2,000 and makes a gift aid donation of £800 (net).

	Non-savings £	Savings (excl dividend) £	Dividend £	Total £
Income				
Business profits	30,000			30,000
Earnings	20,000			20,000
Dividends £6,750 × 100/90			7,500	7,500
Building society interest £3,000 × 100/80	–	3,750	–	3,750
	50,000	3,750	7,500	61,250
Less charges	(2,000)	–	–	(2,000)
STI	48,000	3,750	7,500	59,250
Less personal allowance	(6,475)			(6,475)
Taxable income	41,525	3,750	7,500	52,775
Tax band allocation				
Starting rate	2,440			
Basic rate	34,960			
Higher rate	3,165	3,750	7,500	
Basic rate band extension for gift aid donation $800 \times \frac{100}{80}$	1,000			
	41,525	3,750	7,500	

	£
Income tax	
Non savings income	
£2,440 × 20%	488
£34,960 × 20%	6,992
£3,165 × 40%	1,266
	8,746
Savings (excl. dividend) income	
£3,750 × 40%	1,500
Dividend income	
£7,500 × 32.5%	2,438
Tax liability	12,684
Less tax credit on dividend income	(750)
Less tax suffered on building society interest	(750)
Tax payable	**11,184**

Copyright royalties are deducted as a charge on income (paid gross). The basic rate band is extended by the gross amount of the gift aid donation. Savings (excl. dividend) income and dividend income fall above the basic rate threshold so they are taxed at 40% and 32.5% respectively.

INVESTMENT AND RISK

2 Capital gains tax

2.1 Introduction to capital gains tax

> **Learning outcomes**
>
> 2.2.1 Liability to CGT.
> 2.2.2 Disposals.
> 2.2.3 Death.

Who pays capital gains tax?

Capital gains tax (CGT) is payable by **chargeable persons** on the **chargeable disposal** of a **chargeable asset** (ie the three criteria have to be met simultaneously) occurring in a given **fiscal year**.

Chargeable person

A chargeable person is an individual or trust who is **resident or ordinarily resident** in the UK.

'Ordinarily resident' is a medium-term view of residency. HMRC defines 'ordinarily resident' as being resident in the UK 'year after year'. It is, therefore, possible to be resident in the UK for, say, a single year without being ordinarily resident. More importantly, it is possible not to be resident in a particular year but to remain ordinarily resident, for example, if you usually live in the UK, but have gone abroad for a long holiday and do not set foot in the UK during that year.

Chargeable assets

For an individual, CGT must be applied to all assets unless they are specifically exempt. The key exemptions to be aware of are:

- The individual's **principal private residence**, ie his main home
- **NS&I Savings Certificates**
- **Gilts** (government stocks)
- **Qualifying corporate bonds** (see definition below)
- **Betting winnings**
- **NS&I Premium Bond prizes**
- **Qualifying life assurance policies** (if still owned by the original policyholder)
- **Livestock**, eg race horses
- Gains made in on an **ISA**
- **Wasting assets**, eg cars
- **Chattels** (tangible movable property) sold for £6,000 or less

Note that for these assets gains are not chargeable but losses are not allowable.

Chargeable assets include items such as foreign currency, antiques, shares and other investments including unit trusts and OEICs that invest in gilts and bonds.

A **qualifying corporate bond (QCB)** is a security (whether or not secured on assets) which:

(a) Represents a 'normal commercial loan'. This **excludes** any bonds which are **convertible** into shares (although bonds convertible into other bonds which would be QCBs are not excluded), or which carry the right to excessive interest or interest which depends on the results of the issuer's business

(b) Is expressed in sterling and for which no provision is made for conversion into or redemption in another currency

(c) Was acquired by the person now disposing of it after 13 March 1984, and

(d) Does not have a redemption value which depends on a published index of share prices on a stock exchange.

Permanent interest bearing shares issued by building societies which meet condition (b) above are QCBs.

Chargeable disposals

A **chargeable disposal** occurs when an asset is sold (in whole or in part), or given away, or if proceeds are received as a result of a liquidation of a company. The disposal can occur either in the UK or overseas, but is only treated as subject to CGT when made by a UK resident.

When an individual dies, the assets disposed of as a result of death are **not** subject to CGT. Unfortunately, this does not mean that tax is avoided – the government charges inheritance tax instead!

NB: Gifts between spouses are not liable to CGT.

2.2 Recent changes to the CGT regime

Major changes were introduced to the CGT regime from 6 April 2008 including the

- Withdrawal of taper relief
- Withdrawal of indexation allowance
- Introduction of Entrepreneurs' Relief
- Simplification of share matching rules

As a result, many of the historical complications of CGT have now been removed.

Taper relief

Taper relief was introduced from 6 April 1998 and could reduce the amount of the gain chargeable to CGT. The amount of relief available depended on whether the asset was classed as a business or non-business asset and also on the length of time an asset has been held since 1998.

For gains arising on or after 6 April 2008 taper relief is no longer available.

Indexation allowance

Indexation allowance was the precursor to taper relief and gave relief for the effect of inflation on the costs incurred on assets. Indexation was frozen as at 5 April 1998 with the introduction of taper relief. Before 6 April 2008, where an asset was held at 6 April 1998 and was disposed of, any gain would be eligible for both indexation allowance and taper relief.

For gains arising on or after 6 April 2008 indexation allowance is no longer available.

INVESTMENT AND RISK

2.3 Calculation of capital gains and losses

Learning outcomes

2.2.4 Deductions

2.2.5 Losses.

2.2.6 Main exemptions.

2.2.7 Basic calculation of chargeable gains.

2.2.8 Entrepreneurs' relief.

9.1 Basic Income Tax and Capital Gains Tax computations – personal allowances, non-savings income, savings income, dividends, life assurance bond profits, chargeable gains.

9.5 Tax calculations.

The basic computation

An individual pays capital gains tax (CGT) on his net chargeable gains (his gains minus his losses) for a tax year, less unrelieved losses brought forward from previous years and the annual exemption.

There is an **annual exemption** for each tax year (see Tax Tables). For 2010/11, it is £10,100. It is the last deduction to be made in the calculation of taxable gains.

Since 23 June 2010, CGT is charged at 28% for higher rate and additional rate taxpayers. Income and gains are added together to determine whether someone is in the higher or additional rate band. Other individuals have their gains taxed at 18%.

Losses

Allowable losses are deductible from chargeable gains in the tax year or accounting period in which they arise and any loss which cannot be set off in this manner is carried forward for relief in future periods. Losses **must** be used as soon as possible. Losses may not be set against income.

Example: Capital gains tax

In 2010/11, Jennifer has income of £90,000 plus the following gains and losses on disposals that were made after 22 June 2010. How much capital gains tax is payable?

	(£)
Chargeable gains	25,900
Allowable capital losses	8,000

The gains to be taxed are as follows.

	(£)
Gains	25,900
Less losses	(8,000)
	17,900
Less annual exemption	(10,100)
Taxable gains	7,800
@ CGT rate	×28%
CGT payable	2,184

Allowable losses brought forward are only set off to reduce current year chargeable gains less current year allowable losses to the annual exempt amount. No set-off is made if net chargeable gains for the current year do not exceed the annual exempt amount.

Examples: Capital gains tax losses

(a) George has chargeable gains for 2010/11 of £12,000 and allowable losses of £6,000. As the losses are **current year losses** they must be fully relieved against the £12,000 of gains to produce net gains of £6,000, despite the fact that net gains are below the annual exemption.

(b) Bob has gains of £15,000 for 2010/11 and allowable losses brought forward of £6,000. Bob restricts his loss relief to £4,900 so as to leave net gains of £(15,000 – 4,900) = £10,100, which will be exactly covered by his annual exemption for 2010/11. The remaining £1,100 of losses will be carried forward to 2011/12.

(c) Tom has chargeable gains of £5,000 for 2010/11 and losses brought forward from 2009/10 of £4,000. He will leapfrog 2010/11 and carry forward all of his losses to 2011/12. His gains of £5,000 are covered by his annual exemption for 2010/11.

Married couples and civil partnerships

A husband and wife are taxed as two separate people. The same applies to same-sex **civil partnerships**.

Each has an annual exemption, and losses of one of the couple cannot be set against gains of the other.

Disposals or gifts **between spouses** or **civil partners** who are living together give rise to **no gain and no loss**, whatever actual price (if any) was charged by the person transferring the asset to the other.

The basic CGT computation

A chargeable gain (or an allowable loss) is generally calculated as in the following example.

	£
Disposal consideration (or market value)	X
Less incidental costs of disposal	(X)
Less allowable costs	(X)
Capital gain	X

Incidental costs of disposal may include:

(a) Valuation fees (but not the cost of an appeal against the HMRC's valuation)
(b) Estate agency fees
(c) Advertising costs
(d) Legal costs

Allowable costs include:

(a) The original cost of acquisition
(b) Incidental costs of acquisition
(c) Capital expenditure incurred in enhancing the asset

Entrepreneurs' relief

Entrepreneurs' relief applies to gains arising on the disposal of:

- The whole, or part, of a trading business that is carried on by the individual, either alone or in partnership
- Shares in a trading company, or holding company of a trading group, provided that the individual owns at least 5% of the voting rights in the company and is an officer or employee of the company
- Assets used in a business that has ceased trade
- Asset used in a partnership
- Certain disposals by trustees

Since 23 June 2010, Entrepreneurs' Relief applies to the first £5,000,000 of any such gains (A lifetime limit of £2,000,000 applied in the period 6 April 2010 to 22 June 2010). The effect of the relief is to reduce the effective rate of CGT to 10% of this gain. Any gain in excess of £5,000,000 does not attract any relief and remains taxable at 18% or 28% depending on whether the individual is a basic rate taxpayer or higher..

The relief is applicable to individuals, rather than disposals. An individual will be able to make more than one claim for Entrepreneurs' Relief, up to a lifetime total of £5m of gains.

Rollover relief

A gain may be 'rolled over' (deferred) where it arises on the disposal of a business asset which is replaced. This is **rollover relief**. A claim cannot specify that only part of a gain is to be rolled over.

All the following conditions must be met.

(a) **The old asset sold and the new asset bought are both used only in the trade** or trades carried on **by the person claiming rollover relief**. Where part of a building is in non-trade use for all or a substantial part of the period of ownership, the building (and the land on which it stands) can be treated as two separate assets, the trade part (qualifying) and the non-trade part (non-qualifying). This split cannot be made for other assets.

(b) The old asset and the new asset both fall within one (but not necessarily the same one) of the following classes.

  (i) Land and buildings (including parts of buildings) occupied as well as used only for the purpose of the trade
  (ii) Fixed (that is, immovable) plant and machinery
  (iii) Ships, aircraft and hovercraft
  (iv) Goodwill
  (v) Satellites, space stations and spacecraft
  (vi) Milk quotas, potato quotas and ewe and suckler cow premium quotas
  (vii) Fish quota

(c) Reinvestment of the proceeds of the old asset takes place in a period beginning one year before and ending three years after the date of the disposal.

4: TAXATION

(d) **The new asset is brought into use in the trade on its acquisition** (not necessarily immediately, but not after any significant and unnecessary delay).

Calculation of CGT on shares

If the investor makes a capital gain on the realisation of a share it may be subject to capital gains tax, and this is how it will be calculated.

The basic calculation for **capital gains tax** is:

Profit = Proceeds (less sale expenses) less original investment cost

The profit thus calculated could become subject to capital gains tax if:

- The individual's gain is in excess of the annual exemption, or
- The gain is below the annual exemption but the investor has already made use of this in other transactions

There are methods of reducing the capital gain.

- The investor may have other capital losses including losses brought forward which could be offset.
- The investor may consider transferring the holding into a spouse's name prior to sale if the spouse has not used up his or her annual exemption.

Matching rules for sales of shares

Shares present special problems when computing gains or losses on disposal.

Matching rules determine which shares have been sold and so work out what the allowable cost on disposal should be.

Share disposals are matched with acquisitions in the following order.

(a) Same day acquisitions

(b) Acquisitions within the following 30 days

(c) Any shares in the s104 share pool. The s104 share pool for any particular share covers all purchases of that share prior to the disposal date. Though there may historically have been several purchases over many years contributing to the pool holding, each at different prices, the shares within the pool are treated as homogeneous or indistinguishable. Any disposals from the pool are taken out at the weighted average price of pool shares at the disposal date, as illustrated below.

Example: Share disposal

Catherine acquired the following shares in X plc.

	No. of shares	Price £
1.4.91	10,000	1.20
1.9.99	4,000	1.30
10.11.02	6,000	1.40
30.12.10	2,000	1.30

On 11.12.10 Catherine sells 12,000 shares at £1.35, calculate the chargeable gain on this disposal.

INVESTMENT AND RISK

> ## Solution
>
> Catherine will initially match the disposal with the 2,000 shares bought on 30.12.10 (bought in next 30 days). She will then match with 10,000 shares from the s104 share pool prior to disposal which is calculated as follows.
>
> **s104 share pool**
>
> | Acquisition date | Number | Price £ | Value £ | |
> |---|---|---|---|---|
> | 1.4.91 | 10,000 | 1.20 | 12,000 | |
> | 1.9.99 | 4,000 | 1.30 | 5,200 | |
> | 10.11.02 | 6,000 | 1.40 | 8,400 | |
> | s104 pool before disposal | 20,000 | | 25,600 | ⇒ Average price = 1.28 |
> | Disposal | (10,000) | 1.28 | (12,800) | |
> | s104 pool carried forward | 10,000 | 1.28 | (12,800) | |
>
> **Chargeable gain**
>
> | | £ | £ |
> |---|---|---|
> | Disposal proceeds | | 16,200 |
> | Cost | | |
> | – Next 30 days | 2,600 | |
> | – s104 pool | 12,800 | |
> | | | 15,400 |
> | Chargeable gain | | 800 |

The rule of matching share disposals with acquisitions within the following 30 days prevents a shareholder from carrying out '**bed and breakfasting**' of shares, as used to be possible several years ago. 'Bed and breakfasting' refers to selling and then repurchasing (typically the next day, hence the term 'bed and breakfasting') the same shares in order to 'crystallise' a capital loss, or a gain, to make efficient use of the individual's annual exemptions while keeping an investment in the same shares.

For someone wishing to crystallise a gain or loss but to retain similar investments, possible alternatives to 'bed and breakfasting' are:

- 'Bed and ISA': repurchase of sold shares within an Individual Savings Account, where they will be sheltered from CGT
- 'Bed and spouse': repurchase of the same shares as those sold, by the investor's spouse or civil partner
- Repurchase of shares similar to those sold, for example shares in the same sector, if such shares can be identified

Bonus issues of shares (scrip issues)

When a company issues **bonus shares,** all that happens is that the number of shares of the original holding is increased.

Since bonus shares are issued at no cost there is no need to adjust the original cost. Instead the numbers purchased at various times are increased by the bonus. The normal matching rules will then be applied.

Rights issues

The difference between a **bonus issue** and a **rights issue** is that, in a rights issue, the new shares are paid for and this results in an adjustment to the original cost. As with bonus issues, rights shares derived from shares in the s104 pool go into that holding. The number and cost of each of right issue is added to each holding as appropriate.

Collection of CGT

Gains, and (if the taxpayer chooses to compute the tax) the CGT, are shown on the individual's **tax return**. The taxpayer must pay that tax on 31 January following the tax year. There are no interim payments on account, as there are for income tax.

Taxable person

CGT and individuals

The rules outlined above describe the application of CGT to individual taxpayers who are resident or ordinarily resident in the UK.

CGT and trusts

Trusts terminology

Note the following terminology relating to trusts.

- When there is a **trust**, **trustees** deal with the **trust property** over which they have control for the benefit of other individuals, who are the **beneficiaries**.
- An individual who transfers assets into a trust during his lifetime is known as a **settlor** and such trusts are known as **settlements**. A settlor may also be a trustee and/or a beneficiary.
- **Life interest trusts** (or **interest in possession trusts**) are trusts in which beneficiaries (**life tenants**) are entitled to the enjoyment of the income during their lifetime after which further beneficiaries (**remaindermen**) may become entitled to the income and/or the capital.
- **Accumulation and maintenance (A&M) trusts** are trusts enabling a settlor to give property to young people with conditions attached preventing them from having access to income and/or capital at too young an age.

As a general rule the liability to tax on the gains accruing to the trust falls on the trustees, however:

- if the settlor (or immediate family) can or do benefit from the trust, they are liable on the gains of the trustees assuming they are resident or ordinarily resident in the UK.
- if the trust is a bare trust (see below), the trustees are ignored for CGT purposes, and the relevant beneficiaries are treated as if they had carried out the particular transactions themselves.

For CGT purposes a **bare trust** is one where the beneficiaries are 'absolutely entitled as against the trustee'. This generally is true where either:

- the trustee has no right to deal with the property except with the consent of the beneficiaries,
- the beneficiaries can take control of the property on giving due notice to the trustee.

The assessment of CGT for a trust is the same as for an individual with the exceptions that the annual exemption is half that allowed to individuals, ie £5,050 for 2010/11.

INVESTMENT AND RISK

CGT and charities

A **charity** is any body of persons or a trust which is established for charitable purposes only. The phrase charitable purposes covers:

- The relief of poverty
- The advancement of education
- The advancement of religion
- Certain, but not all, purposes beneficial to the community.

A charity is **exempt from capital gains tax** on any gains arising on the disposal of an asset **where the proceeds of the disposal are to be applied for charitable purposes**.

An issue arises when a trust is established for charitable purposes then, at some latter date, cease to be a charity but continues to hold any chargeable assets. In this situation the trustees are treated as though they sold, and immediately reacquired, the chargeable assets at their market value. Any gains on the deemed disposal is liable to CTG since the proceeds are not being applied for charitable purposes, rather they have been used to reacquire the asset.

3 Stamp duty

Learning outcome

2.3 The main features of Stamp Duty Reserve Tax on securities.

3.1 Stamp duty and stamp duty reserve tax (SDRT) on securities

When an asset is bought, the buyer may be liable to pay either stamp duty or stamp duty reserve tax (SDRT) on the purchase price. Where the asset is transferred using paper forms it will be liable to stamp duty, whereas assets that are electronically settled will be liable to SDRT (assuming a liability arises on that asset).

3.1.1 Stamp duty

For example, with regard to certificated UK shares, the tax is **payable by the buyer** and is charged at a rate of **0.5%** of the consideration **rounded up** to the **next £5**. The legislation refers to the rate as **£5 per £1,000 of the consideration or any part thereof**.

Note: Broker's fees are **not** included in the calculation of stamp duty.

Example

		(£)
Consideration (before broker's charges)	=	15,030.00
Stamp duty payable = 0.5% × £15,030	=	75.15
Rounded up	=	80.00

The buyer will send a stock transfer form and the share certificate to HM Revenue and Customs (HMRC) in order to pay the stamp duty, before passing the documents to the Registrar.

3.1.1 Stamp duty reserve tax (SDRT)

Stamp Duty Reserve Tax (SDRT) is a tax that complements the stamp duty provisions and is designed to cover transfers not envisaged by the original legislation (such as the uncertificated transfer of shares within CREST, part of Euroclear). The rate, by contrast, is a simple 0.5% of the consideration rounded up/down to the nearest penny.

> **Example**
>
> | | (£) |
> |---|---:|
> | Consideration (before broker's charges) = | 15,030.00 |
> | SDRT payable = 0.5% × £15,030 = | 75.15 |

As both taxes are based on the amount paid, they are also known as an 'ad valorem' tax. Note that they are only paid by the purchaser and not the seller.

The following table summarises the two taxes and the relevant exemptions.

	Stamp Duty	**Stamp Duty Reserve Tax**
Payable by the buyer of	Certificated shares	Uncertificated shares in dematerialised form
		Shares sold on the same day (so no entry appears on the register)
		New issues in renounceable form (such as rights letters)
		Share options
		Convertible loan stock
Rates*	0.5% consideration rounded up to next £5	0.5% consideration rounded to nearest penny
Persons exempt from either tax	Intermediaries*	
	Registered charities	
	Recipients of gifts	
Instruments exempt from either tax	Gilts	
	Sterling non-convertible UK loan stock/corporate bonds	
	Bearer stocks**	
	Foreign registered stocks	
	New issues of securities to the original owner	

*   London Stock Exchange members who are not fund managers are granted intermediary status.

**   Where shares are converted into bearer depository receipts (which are exempt from stamp duty or SDRT) HMRC make a one-off charge of **1.5%** on the conversion.

It should be noted that whilst transfers of units within a unit trust **are** subject to stamp duty, this is included within the price of a unit. Hence, the fund manager charges stamp duty **within the spread** of buying and selling prices.

3.2 Stamp duty land tax

Stamp duty land tax is an *ad valorem* tax payable by the buyer on the transfer of property or land. In contrast to stamp duty and SDRT, the rate of stamp duty land is dependent on the purchase price (see Tax Tables).

INVESTMENT AND RISK

Key chapter points

- Employed and self-employed individuals are liable to pay income tax. Some income is received in full with no tax deducted, while some income has tax deducted at source.
- All sources of income are aggregated in a personal tax computation. Some income is exempt from income tax and not included in the personal tax computation.
- All income in the personal tax computation must be included gross.
- Dividends are grossed up by multiplying by 100/90. Bank and Building Society interest is grossed up by multiplying by 100/80.
- Income is divided into non-savings income, savings (excluding dividend) income and dividend income.
- The personal allowance and blind person's allowance are deducted from Statutory Total Income to arrive at taxable income.
- There is one set of income tax bands which applies to all the income. Non-savings income is taxed first, then the savings (excluding dividends) income and finally dividend income.
- An individual pays CGT on his net taxable gains in a tax year. There is an annual exemption for each tax year.
- There needs to be three things for a capital gain to arise: chargeable person, chargeable disposal, chargeable asset. Disposals between spouses or civil partners are on a no gain/ no loss basis.
- Taxable gains are taxed separately from income.
- Capital losses are deducted against gains in the same tax year. Excess losses are carried forward. Brought forward losses cannot reduce taxable gains below the annual exempt amount.
- There are special rules for matching shares sold with shares purchased, being same day, next 30 days, s104 pool.
- Bonus and rights issues are attached to the holding to which they relate.
- Gilts and qualifying corporate bonds held by individuals are exempt from CGT.
- Stamp duty or SDRT is payable at 0.5% on the purchase of UK shares.

Chapter Quiz

1. What test applies for expenses of an employee to be allowable against tax? .... (see para 1.3)
2. On what period's profit is a self-employed person taxed in the current tax year? .... (1.3)
3. Who is entitled to age allowances? .... (1.4)
4. Distinguish statutory total income and taxable income. .... (1.4)
5. What is the CGT treatment of gains on UK government stock and qualifying corporate bonds? .... (2.1)
6. At what rates is CGT payable? .... (2.3)
7. What happens to capital losses which are not set off in the current tax year? .... (2.3)
8. What is the treatment for CGT purposes if shares are sold on one day and the same shares are repurchased on the next day? .... (2.3)
9. What is the stamp duty regime for CREST-registered shares? .... (3.1)

chapter 5

Chapter topic list

1	The role of cash deposits	94
2	UK deposit takers	97
3	Bank and building society accounts	98
4	Tax treatment of deposits	101
5	Cash ISAs	102
6	National Savings & Investments products	103
	Key chapter points	108
	Chapter quiz	109

Cash deposits

INVESTMENT AND RISK

Chapter Learning Outcomes

3   **Understand** the following asset classes, their main features and suitability for different consumer circumstances

    3.1   Cash deposits

        3.1.1   Main types of deposit account – instant access, notice and fixed rate.

        3.1.2   Characteristics and past performance – liquidity, rates of interest, real returns, institutions, statutory protection, risk factors, foreign currency deposits.

        3.1.3   Taxation of deposit interest – savings income, tax deducted at source, offshore accounts.

        3.1.4   ISAs.

        3.1.5   National Savings and Investments (NS&I) – deposit products including Guaranteed Equity Bonds.

    3.2   Government securities and corporate bonds

        3.2.7   National Savings and Investments – fixed-interest investments.

1 The role of cash deposits

Learning outcomes

3.1.2   Characteristics and past performance

- Liquidity.
- Rates of interest.
- Real returns.
- Statutory protection.
- Risk factors.
- Foreign currency deposits.

1.1 Key reasons for holding cash deposits

The key reasons for holding money as **cash deposits** are **security** and **liquidity.**

Accounts for holding cash deposits are generally characterised by a high level of security. **Capital** is very unlikely to be lost, at least in money terms. The purchasing power of capital held on deposit will, however, be eroded by **inflation**. Against this, there is the reward of any **interest** receivable, and the rate of interest may exceed inflation, resulting in a real rate of return for the investor.

An important advantage of cash deposits held in 'instant access' accounts is their liquidity. Every investor could have a need for cash at short notice, and so should plan to hold some cash on deposit to meet possible needs and emergencies.

Most people would be best advised to hold some cash deposits **before** they consider more **risky investments**.

A cash deposit account can serve as a vehicle for reaching a **savings target**, for example when saving for the cost of a major purchase, or for the **deposit** (part payment) on a **house purchase**.

1.2 Performance

Cash deposits generally earn for the investor a **return** in the form of **interest** paid regularly, but no **capital growth**. Interest is normally paid at a percentage rate on the capital invested, at rates of interest prevailing from day to day, or alternatively at rates fixed over certain periods.

We have already discussed the relationship between rates of interest and real rates of return. The performance of cash deposits as an investment can be measured as a **'real' rate of return** by comparing the interest rate with the rate of inflation.

Approximately:

Rate of interest – Rate of inflation = Real rate of return

For example, if annual interest is paid at 5%, and the rate of inflation is 2%, then the real rate of return is 3%. The purchasing power of the cash investment is increasing at 3% per year.

Interest rates on cash deposits will generally move approximately in tandem with rates of interest on borrowing: deposit takers obtain income from the difference between deposit rates and their lending rates. Interest rates generally will move in line with short-term **'base' rate of interest** set by the Bank of England's Monetary Policy Committee. This is set according to various economic conditions. If the economy appears to be 'overheating', with people finding credit and borrowing easy to obtain and afford, interest rates may be raised to discourage borrowing. Over the period since 1988, the base rate has varied between 15% and 3.5%.

Deposit taking institutions are in competition with one another and so the interest rates set on different deposit products will reflect these competitive market conditions.

The graph below gives a plot of **UK base rates** since 1990. The rates in 1990 were at a peak of 15% but, apart from a short lived increase in late 2002, have fallen significantly since then. Rates reached there a low point of 3.5% in the summer of 2003 but rose back slightly to 5.00% in summer 2008. In 2009, rates fell to 0.5% at the onset of the credit crunch and have remained at this level since.

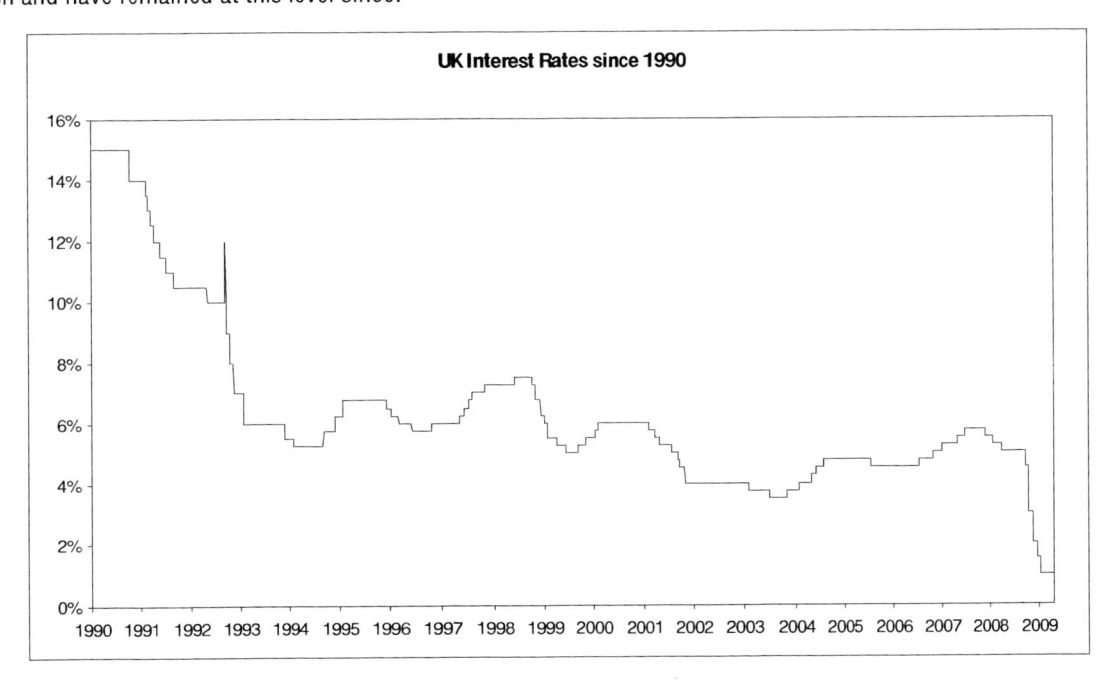

INVESTMENT AND RISK

1.3 Risks

Cash deposits involve:

(a) Very low **capital risk,** since capital will be lost only if the deposit taker defaults.

(b) **Inflation risk**, since inflation could exceed the interest payable. While an investor is locked in at fixed interest rates, inflation might race ahead due to unforeseen economic conditions, and the purchasing power of the investor's capital could fall.

(c) **Interest risk,** if the rate of interest paid is less than could otherwise be obtained on other low-risk investment products, or the investor is locked in at a fixed rate for fixed terms, when he might otherwise have been able to take advantage of rising interest rates available in the market.

With a deposit investment, the **capital** is secure in that the original capital is returned when the deposit is withdrawn, or the account matures, subject to any penalties which will have been made explicit in the terms and conditions of the account. Some degree of **capital risk** does however exist for the depositor. This is because there is a chance that the deposit taking institution fails, and therefore defaults and will not repay depositors' capital. This happened with the Bank of Credit and Commerce International, which collapsed in 1991.

If a UK deposit taker fails, the depositor will have recourse to the **Financial Services Compensation Scheme (FSCS),** which is administered by the Financial Services Authority (FSA).

1.4 Financial Services Compensation Scheme limits

The FSCS will pay compensation following default by a bank or building society of 100% of the first £50,000 deposited per depositor in each separately authorised institution.

These FSCS compensation limits:

- Apply only to UK sterling deposits held at a UK branch of the deposit taker
- Apply to each depositor with an institution, and not to each individual account with the institution
- Apply separately to each joint account holder: therefore, two joint account holders each could receive up to £50,000, for a joint account in which £100,000 was deposited

The **ceiling on compensation** available through the FSCS leads some investors to consider **spreading** their capital among a number of banks and building societies in order to reduce the overall risk.

The benefit of spreading the risk in this way should be weighed against the possible disadvantage of less interest being earned because of the investor missing out on higher rates offered for larger deposits.

1.5 EU Deposit Guarantee Schemes Directive

Under the EU Deposit Guarantee Schemes Directive, all member states of the EEA are required to establish a deposit guarantee scheme which gives a minimum level of protection for depositors of €20,000 per eligible depositor in the event of a bank failure.

A bank established in another EEA state should be a member of that state's compensation scheme, which is designed to protect depositors in that EEA country, and those with accounts at branches in other EEA countries.

1.6 Purposes of cash deposits

What roles might cash deposits play, when we come to consider an individual investor's portfolio?

(a) To provide **capital available on instant access** to pay for day-to-day living expenses. It is obviously an advantage if at least some of such funds can be held in an account which pays some interest and imposes no charges.

(b) To provide an **investment for the highly risk-averse client**. In this case, if there is a considerable amount of money to invest, it may be advisable to use a spread of accounts, instant access, notice and fixed term. The investor will need to ensure that he has invested sufficient in each account to secure advantageous terms.

(c) To provide an **investment for the client with a very small amount of capital** to invest. In this case it is important that the capital is secure and most probably that there is instant access to funds.

(d) To provide an **emergency fund of capital**, for example in case a client is made redundant, or major repairs are needed to a house or car.

(e) To **form the basis of a portfolio** for those who only want a small percentage of their capital exposed to risk. Investors who are only prepared to take a risk with, say, 10% of their capital may need to place the balance on deposit. Long notice periods or fixed terms may be acceptable to such clients for part of their portfolio.

(f) To provide an **account for non-taxpayers**, including children. They may need to use bank or building society accounts if the gross interest rate is attractive. On completion of the HMRC (Her Majesty's Revenue & Customs) form R85 by the non-taxpayer, interest will be paid gross.

(g) To provide a **short-term home for capital** that is earmarked for use in the near future, eg for the deposit to buy a house, pay school fees or take a major holiday. A notice period should be selected to fit the access requirement.

(h) To **provide a regular income.** A monthly interest account may be used for such an investor. A fixed rate monthly bond would be particularly useful for such a client.

(i) To provide **a means of regular savings.** Regular savings plans offered by banks and building societies are useful for small investors. There is typically no fixed term, with access to at least some of the capital without penalty.

(j) To provide a **temporary deposit for money awaiting investment in the equity market** because the timing for entry or re-entry is not currently deemed to be right.

2 UK deposit takers

Learning outcome

3.1.2 Characteristics and past performance:
- Institutions

2.1 Principal deposit takers

The principal UK deposit takers are:
- **Banks**
- **Building societies**

National Savings & Investments (NS&I) – a government agency, previously called 'National Savings' – also takes deposits but, as a government agency, has a different status in that it is not an authorised deposit taker.

Supervision of the prudential soundness of banks and building societies is the responsibility of the Financial Services Authority.

INVESTMENT AND RISK

2.2 Building societies

A **building society** is a mutual organisation, owned by its members. The members are the investment account holders and borrowers. Members of the Society have voting rights.

Some former building societies have 'demutualised' and turned themselves into banks, while others have been bought by banks. On **demutualisation** or acquisition of the Society, members may be entitled to a 'windfall' payment reflecting a share of the reserves of the organisation that have been built up over its life. However, most of the remaining building societies now require new account holders to waive their rights to such windfall payments, often by signing over the entitlement to charity. This is intended to prevent people opening accounts speculatively in the hope of gaining a windfall.

2.3 Banks

Banks are listed public limited companies, owned by their shareholders. The rights of account holders are limited to the terms and conditions of the account.

2.4 National Savings & Investments

Deposits held with **National Savings & Investments (NS&I)** are guaranteed by the government and therefore can be considered to be completely secure.

3 Bank and building society accounts

Learning outcome

3.1.1 Main types of deposit account – instant access, notice and fixed rate.

3.1 Current and savings account

Current accounts are bank accounts for day-to-day cash management. Current accounts offer instant access (see below) and offer the following facilities

- pay and receive cheques
- pay and receive automated bank transfers (standing orders, direct debits and direct credits)
- make cash withdrawal with a cash card
- internet and telephone banking
- overdraft facilities

The interest rate earned on cash deposits has, historically, been low and the rate charged on overdrafts has been quite high.

Historically, **savings accounts** did not offer such facilities and tended to require notice of withdrawal (see below) but did offer higher rates on cash deposits.

Now the distinction between current and savings accounts is becoming more blurred with some current accounts offering quite high deposit rates and some savings accounts offering many of the above facilities along with instant access.

3.2 Instant access

As the name implies, an **instant access account** allows the investor immediate access to funds. The investor will want to keep some funds available on instant access at minimum risk, for emergency purposes. At the time of writing, some deposit takers are offering up to 2.5% or more interest for instant access funds, before tax. This rate provides a very small real rate of return for a basic rate taxpayer.

Some accounts give instant access **subject to restrictions**. For example, an account might allow only two withdrawals per year.

3.3 Notice accounts

With a **notice account**, the investor must give, for example, 30, 60 or 90 days' notice of withdrawal unless he wishes to lose interest. There may be a higher rate of interest available to compensate for the requirement to give notice. However, the investor should be careful to weigh the advantage of any higher rate offered against the disadvantage of the loss of liquidity and the costs of penalties if the money needs to be withdrawn earlier than planned.

Example: Notice account

Alana has a sum of £10,000 to place on deposit. She can place it in an Instant Access account for which interest is paid annually at 3.5% (variable).

Alternatively, Alana can place the money in a Notice account, subject to 90 days' notice, and will then receive a rate of 4.0% (variable) annually. For immediate withdrawal, there will be a loss of 90 days' interest.

At the current rates:
- The Instant Access account will pay £350 annually, before tax.
- The Notice account will pay £400 annually, before tax.

If Alana needs to withdraw her funds in an emergency after one year, she will be lose interest before tax of:

£10,000 × 4.0% × 90/365 = £98.63

In that event, the total interest received on the Notice Account will be £400 − £98.63 = £301.37. This is lower than would have been received on the Instant Access account.

Check that you can see how it will take approximately two years for the Notice Account to begin to out-perform the Instant Access account, if the money is required without notice being given.

3.4 Monthly interest

Interest paid monthly will generally be slightly lower than on an instant or notice account which pays interest annually because of the increased frequency of payment of interest. When interest is credited month after month, then the interest itself will begin to earn interest as soon as it is credited.

Example: Monthly interest

An account pays interest at an annual rate of 3.6%. Interest is credited monthly.

3.6% / 12 = 0.3% will be paid monthly.

INVESTMENT AND RISK

> The annualised rate of interest is:
>
> $100 \times ((1 + 0.036/12)^{12} - 1) = 100 \times ((1.003)^{12} - 1)$
> $= 100 \times (1.0366 - 1)$
> $= 3.66\%$
>
> This shows that the account pays the same return as an annual interest account paying 3.66%.

3.5 Regular savings

Some accounts allow for **regular savings** to be made each month, possibly with some access to funds without penalty.

3.6 Time deposits or 'bonds'

Time deposits or **term accounts** offer investors terms that involve tying up the deposit for a fixed period, often at **fixed rates**. The period may range from seven days to several years, and there may be a fairly high minimum for such arrangements.

Time deposits may be offered as '**bonds**'. (Note that this is a different, and potentially confusing, use of the term 'bond', compared with the use of the same word for the asset class of gilts and other fixed interest securities. With time deposit 'bonds', there is no fluctuation in capital values, as there is with fixed interest securities.)

The bond offer may be open for a specified period, or the deposit taker may reserve the right to withdraw the offer at any time. The bond could run for a fixed term: 1, 2, 3, 4 or 5 years, with severely restricted access subject to a penalty, or no access at all.

Interest may be **tiered**. For example, a five year 'step-up bond' might offer a gross rate of interest of 3.0% in year one, 3.25% in year two, 3.50% in year three, rising to 4.0% in year four and a final 4.5% in year five.

3.7 Money market accounts

Some banks offer the facility to make **money market** deposits for periods ranging from overnight to five years. A bank can offer interest at a rate that is personal to the investor, based on current money market rates. One bank offers money market deposits either for a fixed term with fixed interest, or on a notice basis with variable interest.

A **call** account will allow the investor to access their money by the following day. This is close to the terms of an instant access account.

The principle of a fixed interest rate for a specified period is the same as for term deposits, but the use of the term 'money market deposit' usually implies that a tailored arrangement is made to meet a particular investor's needs.

Money market deposits can be appropriate for investors with a larger sum to invest – for example, proceeds from a house sale pending a later house purchase. There may be a **minimum investment** of £50,000 or more. With such an account the investor faces the additional risk of interest rate fluctuations.

3.8 Foreign currency accounts

Some UK banks offer accounts denominated in foreign currencies, such as the euro and the US dollar. Foreign currency accounts could be useful to someone with income or expenses in the foreign currency. With such an account the investor faces the additional risk of exchange rate fluctuation.

3.9 Offshore deposit accounts

Accounts at overseas branches of UK banks and building societies are open to UK residents and expatriates. The deposits can be held in **sterling** or **other currencies**, for example euros or US dollars. UK residents seeking an offshore deposit account will generally use a bank or building society in Jersey, Guernsey or the Isle of Man.

The range of accounts available may be designed for the needs of international clients particularly, including multi-currency accounts, although onshore accounts might be found to be more varied and more flexible for some individuals. The client can select an instant access, notice or fixed rate, fixed term account. The sterling interest rates offered generally reflect UK interest rates. The investor in an offshore deposit account will normally be able to conduct transactions by internet, post or bank credit transfer.

The **interest risk** for an offshore deposit held in sterling is the same as for one held onshore: for a variable rate account, interest rates may change. If the deposit is held in foreign currency, there is the additional risk of changes in exchange rates.

The other risk to consider is that of the security of the institution. Deposits might be held with a fully owned subsidiary of a major UK bank or building society. If the investment is deposited in the Isle of Man, Jersey or Guernsey compensation schemes are available which, like the UK Financial Services Compensation Scheme, secures 100% of the first £50,000 invested. Gibraltar has a Deposit Protection Scheme providing compensation of 90% of total deposits up to a maximum of £18,000 (or 20,000 euros if greater).

4 Tax treatment of deposits

> **Learning outcome**
>
> 3.1.3 Taxation of deposit interest – savings income, tax deducted at source, offshore accounts.

4.1 Income tax liability

4.1.1 Normal (onshore) accounts

For normal accounts, a UK resident will be subject to tax on bank and building society deposits in the tax year in which the interest is paid at one of the following savings income tax rates.

- 10% starting rate
- 20% basic rate
- 40% higher rate
- 50% additional rate

Interest on bank and building society accounts is generally **paid net** of 20% 'savings rate' income tax. You may find this referred to as **savings rate tax** in exam questions. The deposit taker pays the tax deducted to HMRC.

- **Non-taxpayers** can reclaim all tax deducted. (If someone expects their total income to be less than their personal allowance, they can submit **Form R85** to HMRC, so that the interest is received gross instead.)
- **Starting rate (10%) taxpayers** can reclaim a 10% refund, as their liability is 10%.
- **Basic rate (20%) taxpayers** have no more tax to pay since 20% was deducted at source.
- **Higher and additional rate (40%/50%) taxpayers** pay the additional tax due, through their annual tax assessment.

INVESTMENT AND RISK

> **Example: Taxation of interest**
>
> Suppose that each of a number of investors are each due £100 interest (gross) on their respective instant access accounts. £20 is deducted by the deposit taker and paid to HMRC, and so £80 net is credited to the depositor's account.
>
> - An investor who is a **non-taxpayer** can reclaim £20 from HMRC.
> - An investor who is a **lower rate taxpayer** can reclaim £10 from HMRC.
> - An investor who is a **basic rate taxpayer** has no more tax to pay or reclaim.
> - An investor who is a **higher rate taxpayer** must pay a further £20 to HMRC.
> - An investor who is a **higher rate taxpayer** must pay a further £30 to HMRC.

In the case of accounts with a minimum of **£50,000 held on fixed deposit** for a maximum of five years, interest can be paid **gross**.

If **money gifted by a parent** is invested in accounts held by a 16- or 17-year old earns income in excess of £100, then all of the income can be treated as the parent's income and would be taxable at the parent's highest rate of tax.

An investor who is **not ordinarily resident** in the UK can submit HMRC **Form R105** to the UK deposit taker, to apply to receive interest gross, although not all banks and building societies operate this scheme.

4.1.2 Offshore accounts

The **interest is paid gross** on all offshore accounts. UK residents must declare this income to HMRC and it will be normally be taxed at the same rates as UK savings income – 10%, 20%, 40% or 50%.

Offshore bank and building society accounts may be useful to an investor who is planning to move or retire abroad. If, in a particular tax year, the account holder is resident but not ordinarily resident in the UK, or not domiciled in the UK, interest will generally not be taxed if it is not remitted to the UK. The tax position in the investor's foreign country of residence will vary.

For other investors, there is little to be gained from receiving the interest gross except that paying the tax due will be deferred.

4.2 Capital gains tax position

As there is no **capital** appreciation on a deposit investment, there is no charge to **capital gains tax**.

5 Cash ISAs

> **Learning outcome**
>
> 3.1.4   ISAs.

For the tax year 2010/11 it is possible to invest £5,100 in a cash ISA. This will shield the interest received on the account from income tax for all taxpayers.

ISAs are covered in more detail in the tax wrappers section of this Study Book.

5.1 Providers

Cash ISAs are available from **National Savings & Investments (NS&I)**.

A large number of deposit taking institutions also provide cash ISAs and various financial institutions provide ISAs which may, or may not, include a cash component.

5.2 Investment limits and withdrawals

There is **no minimum investment level** or **notice period** other than any imposed by the provider.

The **£5,100 annual subscription limit** for a cash ISA refers to the **amount of money paid in**. If a withdrawal is made, subsequent payments into the ISA must still not exceed the £5,100 limit overall.

6 National Savings & Investments products

> **Learning outcomes**
> 3.1.5 National Savings and Investments – deposit products including Guaranteed Equity Bonds.
> 3.2.7 National Savings and Investments – fixed-interest investments.

6.1 Introduction

National Savings & Investments (NS&I) was formerly called 'National Savings'. NS&I products are offered by the government and, as such, are regarded as **'risk free'** investments. NS&I products are generally available through **Post Offices**.

6.2 Tax treatment

None of NS&I's products are subject to capital gains tax, but some products are subject to income tax.

6.3 NS&I product range

The NS&I product range can be divided into the following types, on which more detail is provided below.

- (a) Savings accounts
- (b) Income providing schemes
- (c) Growth schemes
- (d) Tax-free schemes, comprising:
    - (i) Savings Certificates
    - (ii) Cash ISAs
    - (iii) Children's Bonus Bonds
    - (iv) Premium Bonds

From time to time, NS&I also issues **Guaranteed Equity Bonds**, a product linked to stock market growth.

Interest rates and terms change fairly frequently, and up-to-date information can be found at the NS&I website – **www.nsandi.com**. (Follow the link to 'IFA Centre' and see the 'Quick Guide' for the latest summary.)

INVESTMENT AND RISK

6.4 Savings accounts

Feature	Easy Access Savings Account	Investment Account
General	Card and telephone-based account, can be held jointly. Available to children aged 11 or over.	Passbook account, can be held jointly. Available to children aged 7 or over.
Return	Tiered variable rates of interest.	Tiered variable rates of interest.
Investment limits	£100 – £2,000,000 per person	£20 – £1,000,000.
Access and penalties	Instant access up to £300 per day at Post Offices and ATMs. Larger withdrawals by post or telephone.	Instant access.
Tax treatment	Interest is paid gross but is liable to tax and must be declared.	Interest is paid gross but is liable to tax and must be declared.

6.5 Income providing schemes

Feature	Income Bonds	Guaranteed income bonds
General description	Provide an income. No fixed term of investment. Availability to children aged 7 or over	1-, 3- or 5-year bonds, giving a guaranteed rate of income. Capital is returned at maturity. Available to those aged 16 or over.
Return	The bond provides a monthly income. The rate is variable and is tiered according to the amount of the investment.	Guaranteed monthly income for term of bond.
Investment limits	£500 – £1,000,000 solely or jointly.	£500 – £1,000,000 per person.
Access and penalties	Easy access, no notice and no penalties for withdrawal. Funds normally received within 7 working days.	No penalty for repayment at full term. Otherwise 90-day penalty. Funds normally received within 7 working days.
Tax treatment	Interest is paid gross but liable to tax and must be declared.	Taxed at source at 20%. Non taxpayers and starting rate (10%) taxpayers can reclaim tax.

6.6 Growth schemes

Feature	Guaranteed Growth Bonds
General description	Offer fixed rates of interest for periods of 1, 3 or 5 years. Available to those aged 16 or over.
Return	Interest rates depend on term and amount invested. The interest is rolled up annually. A monthly income option is available at lower rates.
Investment limits	£500 – £1,000,000 per person.
Access and penalties	No penalty for repayment at full term. Otherwise 90-day penalty. Funds normally received within 7 working days.
Tax treatment	Taxed at source at 20%. Non taxpayers and starting rate (10%) taxpayers can reclaim tax.

6.7 Savings Certificates

Feature	Fixed Interest Savings Certificates	Index Linked Savings Certificates
General description	Open to individuals aged 7 or over who are resident in the UK for tax purposes. Guaranteed rate of interest rolled up at the end of a term. There are 5-year and 2-year fixed rate certificates. Currently (July 2010), there are no issues for sale.	Open to individuals aged 7 or over who are resident in the UK for tax purposes. Guaranteed rate of return based on inflation at the end of a term. There are 5-year and 3-year index-linked certificates. Currently (July 2010), there are no issues for sale.
Returns	A guaranteed rate of interest paid on encashment at end of term.	A guaranteed rate plus inflation paid on encashment.
Investment limits	£100 – £15,000 per issue plus no upper limit if reinvesting maturing certificates.	£100 – £15,000 per issue plus no upper limit if reinvesting maturing certificates.
Access and penalties	Access on 7 working days' notice. No interest is given if the bond is encashed in the first year except reinvested certificates.	No interest or inflation proofing is paid if encashed in first year unless the certificate is a reinvestment. After the first year, interest and inflation proofing paid for each full month invested. Payments normally received within 7 working days.
Tax treatment	Interest is tax free.	Interest is tax free.

6.8 Cash ISA and Children's Bonus Bonds

Feature	Direct ISA	Children's Bonus Bonds
General description	Open to individuals 16+ who are resident in the UK for tax purposes.	Can be opened by anyone who is 16+, for a child under 16.
Returns	Variable rate of interest.	Guaranteed rate of interest guaranteed for first 5 years. New rate quoted at each 5th anniversary until age 21.
Investment limits	£100 minimum, up to £5,100 per tax year.	£25 – £3,000 per issue, per child.
Access and penalties	Managed online or by phone. Repayments normally made within 7 working days.	No interest if encashed in first year, otherwise reduced interest if repaid before 5th anniversary. Payment normally received within 7 business days.
Tax treatment	Interest is tax free.	Interest is tax free, including gifts from parents.

INVESTMENT AND RISK

6.9 Premium Bonds

Feature	Premium Bonds
General description	Each £1 Bond gives a chance to win a prize each month. Can be bought by individuals 16+, or by parents, guardians and (great) grandparents for a child under 16.
Returns	A variable rate is paid out each month as prizes, from £50 prizes to two £1 million jackpots each month.
Purchase limits	£100, to £30,000 maximum holding.
Access and penalties	Repayment in 8 working days.
Tax treatment	Prizes are tax free.

6.10 NS&I Guaranteed Equity Bonds

NS&I's **Guaranteed Equity Bonds** offer returns linked to the growth in the FTSE 100 Index if the index rises increase but pays no dividends. If stock market prices decline, the capital invested remains secure. As such, though it offers security this NS&I product cannot be regarded as risk-free since the final value cannot be determined in advance.

Each **issue** of NS&I's guaranteed equity bonds is made available for a **limited period** only and currently (July 2010) there are no issues on sale. There is a minimum investment of £1,000 and a maximum of £1,000,000, or £2,000,000 for joint investments. The issue offers a return equivalent to a set percentage (eg 125% for 10th, 100% for 18th) of the growth in the FTSE 100 share price index over a 5-year period often with no upper limit though the 18th issue limits the return to 40%. If the FTSE 100 Index falls over the 5-year period, the investor's capital is returned with no growth. The level of the FTSE Index used when setting the return is the average over a 6-month period at the end of the 5-year period of the bond.

It is not possible to encash the bonds during their **5-year life**. The returns in excess of the capital invested are liable to UK income tax on maturity, at the rate then applying to savings income.

Investors **aged 18 or over** can hold NS&I's Guaranteed Equity Bonds, individually or jointly, or in trust for up to two individuals. The bonds can be held in trust for a child of any age.

On **death**, up to two **beneficiaries** of the estate can take over the bond. Otherwise, the personal representatives of the deceased may encash the bond but will receive a return of simple interest at 1% per annum only.

Exercise: NS&I Guaranteed Equity Bonds

A client tells you that she has heard about NS&I Guaranteed Equity Bonds (GEBs) offering a return of 125%. She comments that this seems to offer returns 25% better than a simple FTSE 100 index-tracking fund, if charges on the tracker are ignored.

What points would you make to the client?

Solution

There are a number of considerations to bear in mind.

The return offered on the GEBs excludes the effect of dividends, which would accrue to the FTSE 100 index-tracking fund.

If stock market growth is low or negative, the returns from a cash deposit account will be superior to that from the GEB. Because dividends accrue to an index tracking fund, such a fund may put-perform the GEB if there is a small decline in the stock market over the period.

Chapter Quiz

1. What are the risks involved in holding cash deposits? .... (see para 1.3)
2. What are the compensation limits for a depositor if a building society fails? .... (1.4)
3. What are the main legal differences between banks and building societies? .... (2.2, 2.3)
4. A client plans to open a building society account in order to take advantage of any windfall if the Society demutualises. What information and advice can you give? .... (2.2)
5. What is the effect of completing Form R85, and who should complete it? .... (4.1)
6. 'A UK resident holding cash in an offshore deposit accounts enjoys tax-free interest.' True or False? .... (4.1)
7. Up to what age can NS&I Children's Bonus Bonds be held? .... (6.8)

chapter 6

Government securities and corporate bonds

Chapter topic list

1	General features	112
2	Gilts	113
3	Corporate bonds	118
4	Local authority bonds	122
5	PIBS	123
6	Pricing bonds	124
7	Return measures – the yield and yield curves	128
8	The risks of holding a bond	132
	Key chapter points	135
	Chapter quiz	136

INVESTMENT AND RISK

Chapter Learning Outcomes

3   **Understand** the following asset classes, their main features and suitability for different consumer circumstances

   3.2   Government securities and corporate bonds

   3.2.1   Main characteristics of fixed interest investments – nominal value and market price, coupon, redemption date.

   3.2.2   Gilts – government guarantee, short, medium and long dated gilts, past performance, gilt strips, risk.

   3.2.3   Index-linked gilts – returns on income and capital, risk.

   3.2.4   Corporate bonds – borrowers' risk ratings and effects on yields, past performance.

   3.2.5   Other types of bonds – permanent interest bearing shares, zero coupon bonds, deep discounted bonds, convertible loan stock.

   3.2.6   Investment returns and risk – running yields, yields to redemption, capital returns, volatility, yield curves.

   3.2.8   Mechanics of dealing, including costs of purchases and sales.

   3.2.9   Taxation of government securities and corporate bonds – interest and capital gains/losses.

1 General features

Learning outcome

3.2.1   Main characteristics of fixed-interest investments – **nominal value and market price, coupon, redemption date.**

1.1 What are fixed interest securities?

Fixed interest or **'fixed income' securities** are securities that pay a pre-specified return, in the form of capital and income. Following US usage, such securities are also generally called **bonds**. Treasury bills, gilts, corporate bonds, loan stock, debentures and loan notes are names given to types of fixed income securities.

Bonds are loans, with the investor as the lender. The holder of the bond – that is, the investor – will be due to receive any interest payment (the coupon), and normally repayment of capital on maturity of the bond.

1.2 Issuers

The **issuers** of bonds include:

- **Government (Treasury bills and Government bonds** – called **gilts** in the UK)
- **Companies (corporate bonds)**
- Local authorities
- Supranational organisations such as the IMF

Treasury bills are very short-term government bonds. The term **corporate bonds** is used broadly to describe bonds issued by any entity other than the Government.

1.3 Features of fixed interest securities

Fixed interest securities generally have:

- A fixed **redemption value** which the issuer/borrower will repay to the holder of the bond on maturity (alternatively called the **face value**, **par value** or **nominal value**)
- A fixed annual rate of **interest** (the **coupon**) expressed as a percentage of the par value, note gilts and many other bonds pay two semi-annual sums
- A pre-specified **redemption** date (or maturity date)

Examples: Loan stocks

Issuer	Coupon	Maturity date
Lloyds TSB	9.625%	2023

In this example, for £1,000 nominal of the stock **Lloyds TSB 9.625% 2023**, Lloyds TSB plc will pay £48.12 interest every six months until 2023. (The dividend dates for this stock are 6 April and 6 October.)

This loan stock happens to mature on 6 April 2023, when holders will be repaid the face value.

Tesco 5.5% 2019 is another example of a corporate bond. This bond pays interest once yearly. On £1,000 nominal stock, Tesco plc pays interest of £55.00 on 13 December each year. The par value of £1,000 will be paid on 13 December 2019.

Bond **market prices** are quoted at the price for £100 nominal value of the stock. For example, a price of 96 means that £960 must be paid for £1,000 nominal of the stock.

A bond usually cannot be encashed (redeemed) before the specified maturity date. However, the holder of a bond can usually sell it in the stock market at any time, at whatever is the **market price** at the time. That is, the bond is **negotiable**.

The price at which the bond holder can sell will fluctuate according to supply and demand for the bond. Therefore, the holder cannot be sure of the price he would obtain by selling in the market before the bond matures. Note however that, if he holds the bond to maturity, the return is known.

A holding of a bond is normally described in terms of the **nominal value**: for example, a holding of £5,000 of a stock refers to stock with a nominal value of £5,000.

2 Gilts

Learning outcomes

3.2.2 Gilts – government guarantee, short-, medium- and long-dated gilts, past performance, gilt strips, risk.
3.2.3 Index-linked gilts – returns on income and capital, risk.

2.1 Introduction

UK Government securities are known as **gilts** or **gilt-edged securities.** Government securities are called gilt-edged because they were initially indeed gilt-edged documents, backed by a promise from the Government. The Government

INVESTMENT AND RISK

first borrowed from the City of London in the 16th century but the secondary market only became fully developed in the nineteenth century.

The issue of gilts helps the **government to fund its borrowings**, and in turn to replace the capital from maturing issues. The size of the gilt market depends on the government's borrowing needs. At some times the government is in a position to repay maturing issues without the need to borrow more. At such times, the gilt market reduces in size.

It is **guaranteed** that the Government will meet its obligations in respect of gilts. Therefore, there is no significant risk of gilts not being repaid in accordance with their terms. A **capital risk** is however involved in holding gilts which the holder may wish to sell prior to redemption, since the gilts will then need to be sold in the market, and market prices of gilts fluctuate.

Gilts are issued by the government at various times for different terms and rates of interest. Therefore the investor has a wide choice of securities to meet individual needs. We will now look at the various types of gilt available.

2.2 Characteristics of gilts

Historically, gilts were issued and managed by the Bank of England on behalf of the government; however, this role is now undertaken by the Debt Management Office (DMO).

Let us take a typical issue and examine the key features.

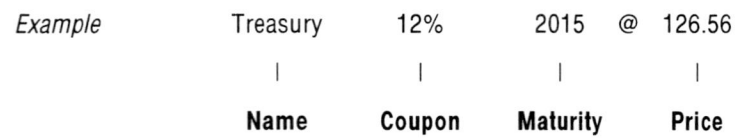

Example   Treasury   12%   2015   @   126.56
                  | | | |
                Name   **Coupon** **Maturity** **Price**

Name

Each stock bears a title. Treasury, Exchequer, Funding, Conversion, Consolidated (Consols), and War Loan are names used to indicate the government department that issued the debt. The names are irrelevant, since all debt is the government's debt and ranks equally.

Coupon

This is the rate of interest that will be paid each year based on the nominal value of the stock. In the UK, the convention is for this coupon to be paid on a semi-annual basis, in equal instalments. However, the 2½% consolidated stock pays on a quarterly basis.

The above stock pays a £6 coupon every six months (£12 each year). For an issue to be successful the coupon must appear to be at an attractive rate, this gilt was issued at a time when interest rates were much higher than at present.

Maturity

This is the date on which the government has agreed to repay the debt, which in this case is 2015.

Price

This is quoted in terms of the amount that an investor would have to pay in order to buy £100 nominal of the stock. Technically, an investor can buy as much as they want of a gilt, the market simply adopts this as a convention for the quote. The price is quoted in pounds and pence (decimal terms).

Quoted prices are clean prices, ie the price of the underlying capital only, excluding the right that may exist to the next coupon (accrued interest). The total price payable is the dirty price which is the clean price plus any accrued interest.

Normally gilts trade cum-div which means that the buyer will be paid the full next coupon. Gilts go ex-div seven business days before the coupon is paid (except the 3½% War Loan which goes ex-div ten business days before the coupon date).

Yield

In the *Financial Times*, both the Flat and Gross Redemption Yield (GRY) are published. By convention, the yield figures shown for gilts is twice the six-monthly yield, **not** the six-monthly yield compounded.

Registered/Bearer

Most gilts are **registered securities**: this means that the security is held in the name of the investor. If the word 'loan' appears in the title, it denotes a **bearer stock**. Such a stock is not registered in an individual's name and the only proof of ownership is the possession of the certificate.

2.3 Types of gilt

Gilts are classified in groups depending on their term to redemption. (As indicated below, the classifications used by the Government's **Debt Management Office (DMO)** differ from those you may find in the financial press.) Examples given are as at July 2010.

(a) **Shorts**: gilts with up to seven years to redemption according to the DMO classification (sometimes 'shorts' refers to gilts with up to five years to redemption, in the financial press).

   Example: Treasury 5¼ % 2012

(b) **Mediums**: gilts with between seven and fifteen years to redemption (five to fifteen years, in the financial press).

   Example: Treasury 5% 2018

(c) **Longs:** gilts with a period in excess of fifteen years to redemption.

   Example: Treasury 6% 2028

   During its life, a long-dated gilt will, of course, move through the categories, so the Treasury 6 pc 2028 will become a medium-dated gilt, and eventually a short-dated gilt.

(d) **Undated**. These gilts have no stated redemption date, but the Government promises to pay the interest indefinitely.

   Example: War Loan 3.5%

   War Loan is unlikely to be redeemed. The only situation in which the Government would repay this stock is if interest rates fell below 3.5% and they could refinance the borrowing at a lower coupon.

(e) **Gilts with a spread of redemption dates**. Some gilts have a spread of redemption dates.

   Where a **government stock** is **quoted with two dates**, this means that the Government (not the bond holder) has the option to redeem the stock at any time between the two dates.

   Example: Treasury 7¾% 2012/2015

   This designation states that the government can repay the gilt at any time between the years 2012 and 2015. They will only repay it if they can replace the borrowing with a new issue with an interest rate below 7¾%. If not, they will hold on until the last possible moment.

A further category of gilt is **index-linked gilts.**

INVESTMENT AND RISK

2.4 Index-linked gilts

The first **index-linked gilt** was issued in 1981. Originally, only pension funds could purchase them. However, from 1982 onwards index-linked gilts became available to all investors. Index-linked gilts have their income and redemption payments linked to the Retail Prices Index (RPI).

It is the RPI figure **three months before** each payment that is used in the calculation for index-linked gilts issued since June 2005. For index-linked gilts issued before June 2005 the figure used is the RPI eight months before the relevant cash flow date.

The indexation multiplies the coupon and capital payment by:

$$\frac{\text{RPI three/eight months before coupon or capital payment is due}}{\text{Base RPI for the stock } (= \text{RPI three/eight months before issue})}$$

Example: Index-linked 2½% Treasury 2020

We now look at how the index-linking works.

Suppose that an index-linked gilt is issued at a coupon of 2½% over a five year period. Over this period the RPI rises by 30%. Then, at redemption, the investor who has held the gilt since issue will receive a capital return of £130 for every £100 invested. The interest on the investment will also have risen by 30% to 3¼%.

An investor in index-linked gilts who holds then to their redemption date knows that protection against the effects of inflation is built in to the cash flows the investor will receive. If selling before redemption, there is the risk of volatility in the capital value, because market values will fluctuate because of changing interest rates and other economic conditions.

2.5 Gilt repo market

A **gilt repo** (**sale-repurchase** agreement) is an agreement whereby one party sells a government bond to a second party and then repurchases it from him at a specified later date at a given price. The given price is calculated taking into account the loss of interest on the money which has been paid for the security.

The seller of the repo is effectively obtaining a short-term loan, with the gilts as security. If the original seller does not repurchase the stock by the specified date, the purchaser can sell it to realise the cash. Because of this security, the rate obtained is very good. The seller continues to have exposure to the gilts market.

When the Bank of England makes a change to short-term interest rates, it generally does so through a change in its **repo rate** – the rate at which it deals in the repo market.

2.6 Gilt strips market

Before the introduction of **gilt strips** in 1997, the investor always purchased the right to a series of fixed coupon payments and a final redemption payment. With strips, it is possible for the individual coupon payments to be stripped away and traded separately.

For example, the DMO website shows that 2¼% Treasury 2014 was strippable from 17 April 2009. From that date, there were 10 coupon dates. Together with the redemption payment, this means that the stock was strippable into 11 different securities at that date:

- 10 strips, each entitling the holder to one of the interest payments
- One strip entitling the holder to the redemption payment on 7 March 2014

Gilt strips are classified as **zero coupon bonds**, as they each pay only a single amount on maturity. Before maturity, they can be traded. They will be priced at a discount to their maturity value.

2.7 Taxation of gilt strips

As zero coupon bonds, gilt strips are treated as **'relevant discounted securities'** by HMRC. The sale or redemption of such a bond is a disposal for **income tax purposes**, with any liability due in the year of disposal. For gilt strips, the profit or loss is dealt with on a 'mark to market' basis annually over the period of ownership. Income tax is therefore not deferred until disposal of the instruments. There is no charge to **capital gains tax**.

2.8 Influences on the prices of gilts

As in all markets, market prices of gilts are affected by **supply and demand**. If investors want to buy gilts, the prices will tend to rise (surplus **demand**). Similarly prices are likely to fall if a government is running a big deficit and issuing a large number of new gilts (surplus **supply**).

Short-dated gilts are very sensitive to changes in prevailing interest rates. We have already seen how, as interest rates rise and fall, the prices of fixed interest securities have an inverse relationship to the interest rate change, and the prices fall and rise. Suppose that the Government issues a 4% gilt with 6 years to redemption. Suppose that in the following year the Government wish to increase their borrowings by the issue of a further gilt but, because of prevailing market conditions, this time they need to pay an interest rate of 5% for a gilt with the same redemption date. Then the first issue must by now be less attractive and a new investor will wish to pay less than £100 for every £100 of the 4% stock issued earlier.

The price of **long-dated gilts** is not so directly influenced by short-term interest rate changes. The holders of long-dated gilts are concerned about possible changes in Government or economic policies and the effect that such factors may have on inflation rates. If investors believe there is likely to be a change in government and that a future government may not be able to control inflation, then the price of long-dated gilts may be depressed because of this.

Gilt prices may be affected by changes in **exchange rates**. If sterling is weak against other currencies, interest rates may have to rise, and again and gilt prices will be kept down.

Sometimes the state of the **equity market** can have a direct effect on gilt prices. In 1987, after the stock market 'crash', gilts offered higher returns than equities. Many investors switched into gilts and consequently gilt prices rose.

2.9 Buying and selling gilts

Gilts can be purchased:

- Through a stockbroker
- Through the Bank of England Brokerage Service
- Directly from the Debt Management Office, for new issues

A **stockbroker** will charge commission on the transaction, whether buying or selling. The commission might be, for example, 1% of the first £7,000 falling to 0.125% on the balance, possibly with a minimum commission. No **stamp duty** or **stamp duty reserve tax** is charged on buying or selling **corporate bonds** or **government bonds** and there is **no capital gains tax** chargeable on the sale of gilts or qualifying corporate bonds.

The stockbroker will get the best price for the client, and may give advice on selecting gilts to suit the circumstances of the investor.

If the client wanted to invest £10,000 in a gilt, the charges might be:

	£
1.0% on £7,000	70.00
0.125% on £3,000	3.75
Total cost	73.75

Gilt transactions are for cash settlement which means that the cheque is required the day following purchase.

INVESTMENT AND RISK

The private investor can purchase most but not all gilts via the **Bank of England Brokerage Service**. Application forms are available from Post Offices. The charge is 0.7% on the first £5,000 then 0.375%, with a £12.50 minimum on purchases (no minimum on sales). However, since this is a postal service, the deal cannot be executed on a specified day and the client does not know the price at which he is dealing. The Bank of England Brokerage Service does not provide advice to the investor.

2.10 New issues of gilts

The Debt Management Office (DMO) (an agency of the Treasury) is responsible for the long-term funding of the Government borrowing requirement and consequently is responsible for the issue of gilts.

The Government's favoured method of issue is **auction** – the same as that used for US Treasury bonds.

Professional investors known as **gilt edged market makers (GEMMs)** place bids. If the issue is oversubscribed, only the highest bids will be allocated stock. Bidders who are successful pay the price they have bid, and bidders therefore pay different prices.

Individuals can submit **non-competitive bids** for amounts up to £500,000 nominal value of stock. These are then accepted at the average acceptance price.

No commission is payable on stocks bought through DMO auctions.

In a '**reverse auction**', investors can offer their stock back to the Government who buy it back at the most favourable price, thus reducing their net borrowings. In this case, the Government is a net repurchaser of stock.

3 Corporate bonds

Learning outcomes

3.2.4 Corporate bonds – borrowers' risk ratings and effects on yields, past performance.

3.2.5 Other types of bonds – Permanent Interest Bearing Shares, zero coupon bonds, deep discounted bonds, convertible loan stock.

3.1 The market for corporate bonds

As we have seen, negotiable fixed interest securities can be issued by corporate entities as well as governments. The **corporate bond** market enables companies and other entities to borrow money at fixed rates of interest.

An investor considering purchasing corporate bonds may be concerned that the earnings of the company could be insufficient to pay the interest and repay the debt. There is, therefore, a higher risk than with a government security and investors will expect to receive a higher return in compensation. Large companies that are financially secure will not need to offer an interest rate much above that offered by the Government. Smaller companies will have to offer very attractive rates to persuade investors to take the risk.

As with other fixed interest securities, the investor in a corporate bond takes the **risk** that interest rates will rise while he is locked in. He can then sell the bond in the market but the price will have fallen as the yield has become less attractive.

Differences between corporate bonds and government stock (gilts)

- The corporate bond market is generally less liquid, at least for lower quality bonds. This can be a problem in adverse market conditions especially, when it may be difficult to sell stock.
- Corporate bond values can be affected by changes in the issuing company's creditworthiness.

6: GOVERNMENT SECURITIES AND CORPORATE BONDS

- As a result of the above factors, corporate bonds are generally higher-risk than government stock, and corporate bond yields are generally higher as a result.
- Prices of corporate bonds are generally more volatile than prices of government stock.
- The spreads between buying and selling prices are usually greater for corporate bonds, and may be as high as the range 7% to 9%.

3.2 Debentures or loan stock

Companies often need to borrow money. Sometimes this money is borrowed from banks, sometimes from investors by the issue of **debentures** or **loan stock**.

A **debenture** is a fixed interest security issued by a company for a fixed term. Where the term 'debenture' is used, there is usually some **security**. Some debentures are quoted on the London Stock Exchange and can be purchased and sold via a stockbroker.

The company issuing the loan will have to repay interest from profits and also find the capital to make repayment on redemption. There is a risk that they will not be able to do this, and an investor buying the stock should consider this risk.

3.3 Fixed and floating charges

The position of the lender on the winding up of a company, or if the borrowing company falls into arrears, will depend upon whether a loan is secured or unsecured. A loan may be secured by a **fixed charge** on assets such as land and buildings or a **floating charge** on current assets such as stock. If there is a default, secured assets can be seized and sold to repay the loan.

- A **fixed charge** is a charge over specific assets, which the company must not sell without the consent of the debenture holder.
- A **floating charge** is a general charge over assets that the company may trade in the normal course of its business. Clearly, such assets are likely to fluctuate and may not be so readily realisable as land and buildings.

A debenture holder with a fixed charge has a higher priority than a debenture holder with a floating charge, in the event of a winding up.

With **unsecured loan stock**, the lender ranks along with other creditors such as the company's trade suppliers on a winding-up.

- As with secured loans, there will be trustees to protect the interests of the stock holders, but the trustees do not hold assets.
- There will usually be restrictive covenants limiting the company's other borrowings, to protect the holders of the unsecured loan stock.
- Because of the higher risk, unsecured loans will generally have a higher yield than secured loans.

3.4 The trust deed

Trustees – generally, corporate trustees – are responsible for the operation of a debenture.

A **trust deed** protects the position of the lender in the event of the company winding up and generally, through **restrictive covenants**, limits the amount of other debt that the company can issue.

INVESTMENT AND RISK

The trust deed will cover:

- The terms of issue of the stock: interest, payment dates, redemption
- Assets on which the loan is secured
- Powers of trustees

The trust deed may also impose conditions on **financial ratios** to which the company must keep within, for example:

- Maximum debt as a proportion of shareholders' funds
- Interest payments to be covered by earnings by x times

3.5 Convertible loan stock

A **convertible loan stock** offers the investor a fixed interest rate (usually lower than a straight fixed interest security, to reflect the value of the conversion option), plus the option to convert into the company's ordinary shares at a later date on a pre-stated formula. Convertible stock is usually an **unsecured loan stock**.

There is a fixed rate of interest until the stock is converted. On conversion, the stock becomes ordinary shares, identical to shares purchased directly.

The investor can retain the original value of his capital. On repayment, corporate bonds simply repay the original investment, but the conversion option gives the chance of some capital appreciation. The option can be exercised if at an advantageous price and, if necessary, the shares sold immediately.

Let us look at how the conversion option works.

When the bond is issued the conversion terms will typically have been pitched above the share price at the time. So, if the share price was 75p, the conversion terms may have been that £1 of loan stock could be converted into one ordinary share. If, three years later, the price of the share is £1.50 then it makes sense to convert. However, during the period the price of the convertible stock will also have risen to reflect the attraction of the conversion option.

When purchasing a convertible loan stock, the investor should analyse the conversion premium. Those stocks offering high yields are likely to carry a high conversion premium and are in character more like an ordinary loan stock. Those stocks with a lower conversion premium are likely to have a lower yield and a more volatile price. These stocks are in most respects more like the share to which they can be converted.

Example: Conversion premium

A convertible loan stock has a convertible ratio of 10.2, ie for every £100 of loan stock given up 10.2 ordinary shares will be provided.

On the date of conversion the share is trading at 500p and the convertible at £80 the conversion price is £80/10.2 = 784p

$$\text{Conversion premium} = \frac{\text{Conversion price} - \text{current price of share}}{\text{Current price of share}}$$

$$= \frac{784 - 500}{500} = 56.8\%$$

3.6 Deep discounted and zero coupon bonds

A **deep discounted security** is a bond paying a very low interest rate that is issued at a large discount to the par (redemption) value. The return to the investor comes mostly from the discount below the par value.

Zero coupon bonds pay no interest at all. The return comes entirely as a gain at redemption. For example, a bond issued at 50p may be guaranteed to be repaid at 100p.

The price of a discounted security will get closer to the redemption value as time passes. As with other low coupon securities, the prices of deep discounted and zero coupon bonds will respond to changes in interest rates.

3.7 Taxation of deep discounted securities

For tax purposes, **'relevant discounted securities'** are bonds that are:

(a) Redeemable, and

(b) Have an issue price where the discount compared to the redemption price exceeds either:

   (i) 15%, or

   (ii) $1/2$% per annum for each year of the bonds life (eg a 10-year bond issued at < £95 and redeemable at £100).

Such bonds are not 'qualifying corporate bonds', due to their artificially low coupon, and there are special tax rules:

- Any gain on sale or on redemption is liable to income tax (not capital gains tax).
- A loss on disposal can be set against other income in the same tax year.

3.8 International bonds

The markets for corporate bonds are international, with many foreign entities issuing bonds on the London market. **Eurobonds** are fixed interest securities issued by governments or major companies in a currency other than that of the country or market in which they are issued. Do not be misled by the 'euro' part of the term, which does not refer to the 'euro' currency. Such bonds may be issued in various currencies. For example, **Eurodollar bonds** are denominated in US dollars.

Interest is paid annually and the stock is in bearer form (ie, the stock is not registered in a person's name; the certificate carries the right to interest, and coupons are attached for submitting to the registrar to claim interest.) Interest is paid annually. The smallest nominal amount of stock that can be purchased is generally high, and so many private investors will be precluded.

International bonds include the following:

- **Eurobond** – A fixed interest security issued either by a government or a major company in a currency other than that of the country or market in which it is issued (not just in 'euros').
- **Eurosterling** – Sterling deposits held by foreign institutions outside the UK.
- **Foreign bonds** – may be denominated in the currency of the country in which they are issued by a foreign corporate body.
- **Bulldog bonds** – bonds issued by foreign entities, offered in the UK and denominated in pounds sterling.
- **Yankee bonds** – US-dollar denominated bonds of non-US entities, issued in the USA. There are other nicknames, such as
- **Samurai bonds** – in the case of Japan
- **Matilda bonds** – in the case of Australia.

Investment in bonds of a different currency involves **risk** arising from **exchange rate** fluctuations which could significantly affect returns when measured in the investor's own currency.

INVESTMENT AND RISK

3.9 Floating rate notes (FRNs)

Floating rate notes (FRNs) are issued mainly by banks and financial companies. FRNs have a fixed redemption date and pay a coupon that is linked to a benchmark money market rate such as the London Inter Bank Offered (LIBOR), which is the rate of interest for short-term lending between banks. Interest is usually paid half-yearly of quarterly.

The interest rate for FRNs is typically set at the beginning of the interest period, as the average of the benchmark over a period of six months, and stated in terms of the number of hundredths of one per cent (**basis points**) above LIBOR.

For example, if LIBOR is 4.5%, then LIBOR plus 75 basis points means 5.25%: LIBOR with three quarters of one per cent added.

For private investors, FRNs are packaged over short terms with coupons rolled up and taxed as income at maturity.

FRNs are treated as **qualifying corporate bonds** for tax purposes and therefore the repayment at maturity is exempt from Capital Gains Tax (CGT).

Rates can generally be obtained for investments in excess of £250,000 for periods of between 12 and 24 months. As with other corporate bonds, the investor bears risk is based upon the security of the issuing company.

The price of FRNs should not fluctuate much from their nominal value.

- This is because changes in interest rates are reflected in the changing coupon, rather than in the capital value of the security.
- However, changes in the creditworthiness of the issuer could affect the price.

4 Local authority bonds

Learning outcome

3.2.5 Other types of bonds – Permanent Interest Bearing Shares, zero coupon bonds, deep discounted bonds, convertible loan stock.

4.1 General features

Some local authorities have issued fixed rate bonds as a means of borrowing money. Given Government restrictions on local authority finances, there are only a few such bonds available now and the market is small.

Yearling bonds are local authority bonds issued for one year and six days.

Local authority bonds available include **dated and undated bonds**.

Interest is paid half-yearly, net of 20% tax. With registration of the HMRC form R85, interest can be paid gross to a non-taxpayer.

4.2 Tax situation

As for gilts and qualifying corporate bonds, local authority bonds are exempt from **capital gains tax**.

Interest is taxable as **savings income**, in the way described in the first section of this Chapter.

4.3 Risks

There is a risk, as with all fixed interest investments, that interest rates will rise while the bond continues with a fixed rate of interest for the remainder of the term.

The bonds are secured by the assets of the local authority. There is potentially a very small risk, but local authority bonds will have slightly higher yields than an equivalent gilt to reflect the slightly higher risk.

5 PIBS

> **Learning outcome**
>
> 3.2.5 Other types of bonds – Permanent Interest Bearing Shares, zero coupon bonds, deep discounted bonds, convertible loan stock.

5.1 General features of PIBS

Permanent Interest Bearing Shares (PIBS) are issued by building societies. PIBS are a form of fixed interest stock and are traded on the London Stock Exchange. As with corporate bonds issued by companies, they fulfil a similar role to gilts but offer a higher return and carry a higher risk than gilts.

PIBS have the following features.

(a) Interest is paid (gross) at a fixed rate, half yearly. However there is no obligation on the building society to pay the interest in any one year. If they do not pay it they are under no obligation to roll it over to the next year (non-cumulative). It is highly unlikely that the building society would not pay the interest. This would only happen in a time of severe financial restraint.

(b) The share is **irredeemable**, and thus so has no redemption date. The only time it would be repaid by the issuing building society would be on liquidation, in which case the PIBS / PSBs holders would be the last creditors to be repaid.

(c) PIBS holders are members of the building society and will normally qualify for distributions on demutualisation.

5.2 Perpetual subordinated bonds (PSBs)

Where a building society has subsequently demutualised, PIBS are automatically converted into **perpetual subordinated bonds (PSBs)**. The name comes from the fact that they would be low down in the order for payment compared with other loans, if the issuer were to get into financial trouble.

5.3 PIBS and PSBs as investments

The PIBS/PSB market is fairly illiquid and an investor may find it difficult to trade when he wishes. The illiquidity of the market may result in relatively large spreads between buying and selling prices, adding to transaction costs. The market is relatively small, currently worth under £1 billion.

As with all fixed interest securities, if interest rates rise, the prices of PIBS/PSBs will fall as the fixed interest becomes less attractive.

PIBS have been of interest to some so-called 'carpetbaggers' who hold a minimum investment in the hope of a windfall on demutualisation of the building society, because PIBS holders have membership rights.

INVESTMENT AND RISK

Private investors can consider investing via a collective investment. The investor participates in a well spread portfolio of PIBS/PSBs. Income is often paid quarterly. There is typically a relatively high minimum investment (perhaps £20,000) and up-front charges of entry into the fund.

An ordinary investor in a building society is protected by the **Financial Services Compensation Scheme**, but PIBS/PSB holders are not.

5.4 Tax position

As noted above, interest from PIBS/PSBs is now paid **gross**. As for other fixed interest securities, the interest is taxable. Tax will be collected through the investor's tax assessment.

No capital gains tax is paid on sale because the shares are classified as qualifying corporate bonds.

5.5 Methods of purchase and sale

PIBS/PSBs can be purchased through a stockbroker.

The shares are bought and sold on the Stock Exchange and settlement takes about five days.

PIBS and PSBs can only be dealt in round amounts varying from 1,000 to 50,000 shares. Because the market for PIBS and PSBs is quite illiquid, the spreads between buying and selling prices can be large.

Although originally used primarily by institutional investors, the securities can be purchased by individuals.

6 Pricing bonds

> **Learning outcome**
>
> 3.2.8 Mechanics of dealing, including costs of purchases and sales.
> 3.2.9 Taxation of government securities and corporate bonds – interest and capital gains/losses.

6.1 Cash flows

It may help to think of an investment as a series of cash flows, starting with the initial money invested at a time called 'Year 0'.

The simplest type of bond is a **zero coupon bond**. Suppose that an investor buys a £100 zero coupon bond maturing in five years for a price of £76. The cash flows are as follows.

Time Year	Cash flow £
0 (now)	(76)
1	0
2	0
3	0
4	0
5	100

Most bonds are not zero coupon bonds. Most carry regular interest payments – the **coupon**.

6: GOVERNMENT SECURITIES AND CORPORATE BONDS

For example, suppose that a bond carries a 6% coupon and matures in four years' time. Suppose that the current **market price** is 95. Assuming annual coupon payments, the cash flows for the investment in a bond with £100 nominal value are as follows.

Time Year	Cash flow £
0 (now)	(95)
1	6
2	6
3	6
4	106

6.2 Bond prices and interest rates

If a bond with a nominal value of £100 has a market value of £100 it is said to be priced at par, however since bonds normally pay a fixed coupon their prices respond to changes in interest rates as follows

- If the coupon rate on the bond equates to prevailing interest rates it is offering a fair return and will, therefore, have a fair par value.
- If the coupon rate exceeds prevailing rates, the bond, if priced at par, would be offering an above market return. As a result it would be subject to buying pressure and its price would be bid up above par.
- If the coupon rate is below prevailing rates, the bond, if priced at par, would be offering an below market return. As a result it would be subject to selling pressure and its price would be bid down below par.

In conclusion, there is an inverse relationship between interest rates and bond prices. As rates rise prices fall, and as rates fall prices rise.

6.3 Quoted prices

Bond prices are quoted in the *Financial Times* and some other newspapers.

The prices quoted:

- Are the mid-point between buying and selling prices (called the **mid-market price**)
- Are **clean prices**, meaning that they take no account of **accrued interest** (explained below).

6.4 Clean prices and dirty prices

Interest payments are generally made to the holder who was registered **seven business days** before the interest payment date. After this date, the stock will be sold without interest (referred to as **ex interest** or **ex dividend**). The seller of the stock will receive the interest payment, generally for a full six months.

Sales at any time since the last interest payment up to this date are made **cum interest / cum dividend** (with dividend). In this case, the subsequent interest payment will be paid to the purchaser.

Accrued interest is the daily interest earned on the stock since the last interest payment date, which is paid and received at the time of a transaction in addition to the **clean price** of the stock, to give the **dirty price** that the buyer must pay.

INVESTMENT AND RISK

> ### Example: Pricing of bonds
>
> An investor pays £96 for a purchase of government stock with a coupon of 7%, ie it pays £3.50 every six months. He buys the stock sixty days after the last payment of interest and there are 183 days between the last payment and the next. He will pay the 'dirty price' as calculated below:
>
> Clean price   £96.00
> Interest   60/183 × £3.50 = £1.15
> Dirty price   £97.15

If a stock is sold **ex-interest/ex-dividend**, the buyer will be compensated for the fact that he receives no interest in respect of the time he has held the stock in the current interest period. Thus, the clean price will be adjusted **downwards** slightly to reflect this interest adjustment.

To summarise, if stock is sold:

Cum interest	Clean price *Plus* interest adjustment	= Dirty price paid
Ex interest	Clean price *Minus* interest adjustment	= Dirty price paid

6.5 Tax consequences of accrued interest

The **accrued income scheme** is designed to prevent taxable income being converted into capital gains (which are tax-free for individuals in respect of gilts and qualifying corporate bonds) by selling stocks cum-interest, when the interest is added in to the sale proceeds. The scheme ensures that the buyer and seller of stock will each be liable to income tax on the interest accruing during the period they each own the stock.

For stock sold **cum interest**:

- The purchaser receives the full six months' interest, but is taxed only on the interest accruing during the period of their ownership
- The seller is taxed on the interest accruing during the time they owned the stock, which was included in the selling price

For stock sold **ex interest**:

- The purchaser is deemed to have paid the clean price and to have received interest due between the purchase date and the interest due date. Tax is charged on this interest.
- The seller receives the full six months' interest payment but is not taxed on the interest adjustment compensated to the buyer

The accrued income scheme does not apply if an individual's total holdings of gilts and corporate bonds did not exceed £5,000 at any time in:

- The tax year in which the next interest due date falls **and**
- The previous tax year

6.6 The general income tax position

Interest received from fixed interest securities is taxed as **savings income**, in the tax year in which it is paid. Depending on the band in which the taxpayer's income falls, this means it will be taxed at:

- 0% for non-taxpayers
- 10% for starting rate taxpayers
- 20% for basic rate taxpayers
- 40% for higher rate taxpayers, or
- 50% for additional rate taxpayers

Interest on government stocks (gilts) is paid gross, unless:

- The investor elects to have 20% tax deducted at source, or
- Tax has been deducted at source for a gilt purchased before 6 April 1998 and the investor has not elected for gross payments

Interest on corporate bonds may be received gross, but some UK bond issues pay interest net of 20% tax.

Where 20% tax is deducted at source, non-taxpayers and starting rate taxpayers will be entitled to a refund. Higher and additional rate taxpayers will have additional tax to pay. Basic rate taxpayers have no additional tax to pay.

6.7 Capital gains tax: direct holdings

Individuals pay no capital gains tax (CGT) in respect of direct holdings of:

- Gilts
- Local authority bonds
- Qualifying corporate bonds

Qualifying corporate bonds comprise:

- All **company loan stock and debentures** (except loan stock convertible into shares) that are issued in sterling and bought by the investor after 13 March 1984
- **Permanent Interest Bearing Shares (PIBS)**

Therefore, gains are not taxed. Losses cannot be set against other taxable gains.

6.8 ISAs

For the tax year 2010/11 it is possible for any UK taxpayer over the age of 18 to invest £10,200 in a bond ISA. Since bonds are already exempt capital gains tax, the only advantage a bond ISAs offers is the shielding the coupon received from income tax for all taxpayers.

Bond ISAs can hold either or a combination of gilts and corporate bonds issued by a company incorporated anywhere in the world, though they must have a residual term of at least five years when first held by the ISA.

ISAs are covered in more detail in the tax wrappers section of this Study Text.

6.9 Indirect exposure to fixed interest

An investor can obtain the advantage of a fixed interest security by some indirect methods.

He can purchase a **guaranteed income bond** offered by an insurance company. Such a bond could pay a guaranteed income of, say, 5.0% net pa for three years with the return of the capital at the end of the period. The insurance company would have purchased fixed interest securities, possibly gilts, to enable them to offer such a guarantee.

Another indirect method of investment is the purchase of a **unit trust or OEIC fixed interest fund**. A professional fund manager will run a portfolio of fixed interest securities. Investors will be paying for this expertise in the management charges.

6.10 Capital gains tax: fixed interest funds holdings

Investors are liable to **capital gains tax** on holdings in **fixed interest funds** – unit trusts and Open Ended Investment Companies investing in fixed interest securities.

INVESTMENT AND RISK

7 Return measures – the yield and yield curves

Learning outcome

3.2.6 Investment returns and risk – running yields, yields to redemption, capital returns, volatility, yield curves.

7.1 Coupon and yield

The **coupon** on a fixed interest security is the **nominal rate of interest** per £100 of nominal stock.

Calculating bond **yields** allows the investor to relate the return to the amount he paid for the stock. You need to be able to define and to calculate:

- **Interest yield** (or '**running yield**')
- **Redemption yield** (both **gross** and **net**)

7.2 Gross interest yield

The interest yield is alternatively known as **income yield**, **flat yield** or **running yield**.

First, we will calculate the **gross interest yield** (ie, before tax).

$$\text{Gross interest yield} = \frac{\text{Coupon}}{\text{Clean price}} \times 100\%$$

If an exam question refers to the **running yield** or **interest yield**, without specifying whether this is **gross** or **net**, assume that it is referring to the **gross interest yield**.

Because the price of a bond is rarely exactly 100, the interest yield is almost always different from the nominal **coupon** interest rate.

7.3 Net interest yield

The **net interest yield** is the **gross interest yield** adjusted for income tax, at the rate incurred by the investor.

- For a **non-taxpayer**, Net interest yield = Gross interest yield
- For a **starting rate (10%) taxpayer**, Net interest yield = Gross interest yield × 0.9 (= Gross interest yield, less 10% tax)
- For a **basic rate taxpayer**, Net interest yield = Gross interest yield × 0.8 (= Gross interest yield, less 20% tax)
- For a **higher rate taxpayer**, Net interest yield = Gross interest yield × 0.6 (= Gross interest yield, less 40% tax)

Example: Interest yield

Treasury 8% 2015 is priced at £133.31, on a particular date.

The coupon is 8% but the **gross interest yield** is:

$$\text{Gross interest yield} = \frac{\text{Coupon}}{\text{Clean price}} \times 100\%$$

$$= \frac{8.0}{133.31} \times 100\% = 6.0\%$$

Net interest yield

- For a **non-taxpayer**: 6.0%
- For a **starting rate taxpayer**: 6.0% × 0.9 = 5.4%
- For a **basic rate taxpayer**: 6.0% × 0.8 = 4.8%
- For a **higher rate taxpayer**: 6.0% × 0.6 = 3.6%

7.4 Redemption yield

The **interest yield** does not tell the whole story for the investor. It does not reflect any capital gain or loss that will be incurred.

As the market in the security moves, its price will deviate from the 133.31 purchase price, and so the investor may incur a capital loss or gain if he re-sells the bond.

It is possible for the investor to hold until redemption, in which case we know that £100 will be received for every £100 nominal stock. This represents a capital loss compared with the purchase price of 133.31. The **redemption yield** reflects this capital loss, in addition to the interest payments that will be received.

For index linked gilts, the redemption yield is usually expressed as a real yield, ie the yield in excess of inflation. The difference between conventional redemption yields and redemption yields on index linked gilts of the same maturity will, therefore, reflect expectations of the rate of future annual inflation over the period to maturity.

7.5 Gross redemption yield

The **gross redemption yield** takes into account both the interest earned and the capital gain or loss annualised over the remaining term. The gross redemption yield for gilts is published daily in the *Financial Times*. Here are some examples.

- **Treasury 8% 2015 – yield to redemption 4.47%.** This figure indicates a capital loss if the stock is held to redemption because the yield to redemption is lower than the interest yield of 6.00% calculated above.
- **Treasury 4¼% 2032 – yield to redemption 4.67%.** This figure indicates a capital gain if the stock is held to redemption because the yield to redemption is higher than the coupon rate of 4.25%.

Calculation of the gross redemption yield assumes that interest payments are reinvested when received, and used to purchase more of the stock at the same gross redemption yield. The calculation requires the use of compound interest tables or a computer program.

A **formula** for calculating the gross yield to redemption **approximately** is:

$$\text{Redemption yield} = \text{Interest yield} +/- \frac{\text{Capital gain/(loss) to maturity/Number of years to maturity}}{\text{Clean price}} \times 100\%$$

Example: Gross redemption yield

On a particular date in 2003, the price of Treasury 8% 2015 was 133.31. As calculated earlier, the interest yield is therefore 6.0%.

A capital loss of £33.31 per £100 of nominal stock will be incurred over the 12 years to redemption.

$$\text{Gross redemption yield, approximately} = 6.0\% - \frac{33.31/12}{133.31} \times 100\%$$

INVESTMENT AND RISK

$$= 6.0\% - \frac{2.77}{133.31} \times 100\%$$

$$= 6.0\% - 2.1\% = 4.9\%$$

(This compares with the accurate figure of 4.74% published in the *Financial Times* at the same date.)

7.6 Net redemption yield

As recognised by the concept of redemption yield, the return from fixed interest securities arises from the coupon, adjusted for the capital gain or loss arising. The income from the coupon is taxable, while any capital gain is exempt from capital gains tax. This means that securities with the same gross redemption yield but different coupons will have different returns after tax, for a taxpaying investor.

The **net redemption yield** is the gross redemption yield, adjusted for tax.

We can calculate net redemption yield by adjusting the net interest yield by the difference between the gross redemption yield and the gross interest yield.

Net redemption yield = Net interest yield + Gain/(Loss) to redemption

Net redemption yield = Net interest yield + (Gross redemption yield − Gross interest yield)

Example: Net redemption yield

Above, we used the example of Treasury 8% 2015, when it was priced at 133.31.

We found that, for this stock:

Gross interest yield = 6.0%

Gross redemption yield = 4.9%, approximately

Loss to redemption + 6.0% − 4.9% = 1.1%

We also calculated the net interest yield for the different rates of tax paid by investors.

We can now calculate the net redemption yields, as shown in **bold** in the table below.

Treasury 8% 2015

	Interest yield	Redemption yield
Gross (no tax)	6.0%	4.9%
Net (10% tax)	5.4%	**4.3%**
Net (20% tax)	4.8%	**3.7%**
Net (40% tax)	3.6%	**2.5%**

You should be able to see that the difference between the gross and the net redemption yield is higher for stocks that are trading further away from their par value.

- **Lower coupon stocks** will be relatively more attractive to **higher rate taxpayers**, because income is a less significant element of the return.
- **Higher coupon stocks** will be relatively more attractive to **lower rate taxpayers**.

7.7 The normal yield curve

A graph of yields from different bonds (generally, gilts) shown against the time they have left to maturity is called a **yield curve**.

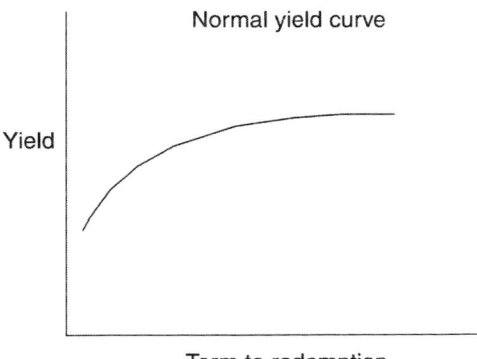

Normal yield curve (Yield vs Term to redemption)

(Note carefully that the yield curve does not show yields on securities at different points in time: it shows current yields on securities of different lengths of time to maturity.)

A **'normal' yield curve** has a positive (upward) slope, reflecting a situation in which securities with more time remaining to maturity have a slightly higher yield than shorter-dated securities. This reflects:

- **The time value of money.** Investors will generally require a higher yield for tying up capital for longer.
- **Greater uncertainty over longer future periods.** The further we look into the future, the more difficult it is to predict. A higher required yield for longer-dated bonds reflects this uncertainty.

Expectations of future higher interest rates can also give the yield curve a more positive upward slope than it would otherwise have. This is because one of the factors affecting the yield on longer-dated securities will be the interest rates expected during later parts of the period to redemption.

7.8 Flat yield curve

The yield curve may be approximately **flat**.

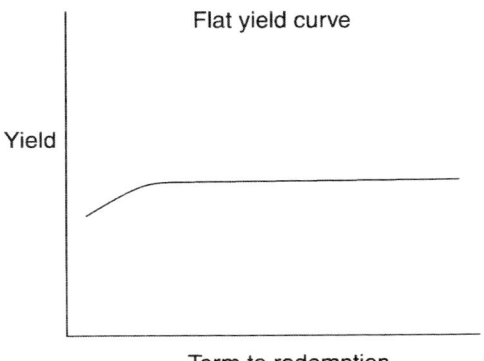

Flat yield curve (Yield vs Term to redemption)

A flat yield curve may reflect a relatively stable economic situation. Alternatively, the flattening off compared with the normal yield curve may reflect expectations of a gradual future decline in interest rates.

When short and long-term bonds are offering the same yields, those wishing to invest in bonds may wish to choose the bond with the least amount of risk. However, an investor's wish to have the certainty of holding bonds until maturity may put a high priority on choosing bonds with maturities matching dates when the investor wishes to realise funds.

7.9 Inverted yield curve

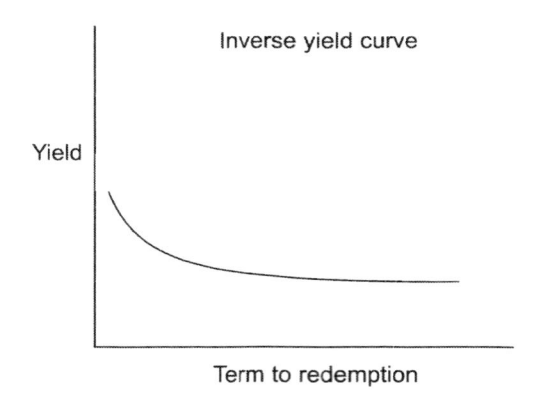

Inverse yield curve

Yield vs *Term to redemption* (downward sloping curve)

The yield curve may sometimes be inverted, with yields on longer-dated securities being lower than on shorter-dated securities.

An inverted yield curve may reflect:

- **Expectations that interest rates will fall** in the future
- Special **supply and demand conditions** in the market, for example a shortage of long-dated gilts

8 The risks of holding a bond

Learning outcome

3.2.6 Investment returns and risk – running yields, yields to redemption, capital returns, volatility, yield curves.

8.1 Introduction

An investor in a fixed income security is exposed to a number of different risks, and any complete assessment of a bond must include consideration of these factors. These bond risks include the following.

Interest rate risk

This is probably the most important risk because of the powerful relationship between interest rates and bond prices.

Inflation risk and real returns

Inflation risk is linked to interest rate risk, as interest rates rise to compensate bondholders for inflation or increases in required real rates of return.

Liquidity and marketability risk

This has to do with the ease with which an issue can be sold in the market. Smaller issues especially are subject to this risk. In certain markets, the volume of trading tends to concentrate into the 'benchmark' stocks, thereby rendering most other issues illiquid. Other bonds become subject to 'seasoning' as the initial liquidity dries up and the bonds are purchased by investors who wish to hold them to maturity.

Credit and default risk

Credit and default risk is the risk of the issuer defaulting on its obligations to pay coupons and repay the principal. The ratings by commercial rating companies can be used to help assess this risk.

Issue specific risk

There may be factors specific to the issue, which tend to either increase or decrease the risk, eg. issuer options such as the right to call for early redemption or possibly, holder options.

Fiscal risk

Fiscal risk represents risk that withholding taxes will be increased. For foreign bonds, there would also be the risk f the imposition of capital controls locking your money into the market.

Currency risk

For any investor purchasing overseas or international bonds, there is obviously also the risk of currency movements.

8.2 Interest rate risk

The **income (coupon)** from a bond remains the same through its life. However, during the life of the bond, there are factors that can make the bond more or less attractive to investors. These factors lead to the **price of bonds** changing.

We have seen how investments are subject to **systematic risks** arising from general market conditions and changes, such as:

- Economic prospects
- Government policy decisions
- Changes in inflation
- Changes in interest rates generally

If **interest rates rise**, the prices of bonds will generally **fall**. The reason for this can be seen if we appreciate that investors will **require** a particular level of return, depending upon rates of interest generally. If interest rates rise, investors' required rate of return rises. That means that they will be prepared to pay less for a particular bond with a fixed rate of interest than they were prepared to pay previously. If interest rates generally **fall**, then investors will be prepared to pay more for a fixed-rate bond than previously, and bond prices will tend **rise**.

This mechanism can be appreciated more clearly by thinking of **investors' required return** determining the **yield** they expect from bonds. Yield is a measure of the rate of income paid out as a proportion of the bond price. The rate of income does not change, but the bond price changes, and thus the yield changes.

Investors will generally require a higher return if the **expected rate of inflation rises.** Therefore, prices of fixed-rate bonds will tend to fall with rising expectations of inflation. However, **index-linked bonds** have a coupon that is linked to the inflation rate, with the result that the price of index-linked stock will tend to rise as higher inflation is expected.

Macro-economic factors, such as those discussed earlier in this Study Text, can lead to changes in interest rates and therefore to changes in bond prices, most particularly changes in inflation rates or in real rates of return.

8.3 Credit and default risk

Bond prices are influenced by the market's perception of the quality of bonds. A perception that a bond issuer might default on the bond will depress its value.

INVESTMENT AND RISK

Bonds issued by major **governments** (such as those of the USA and the UK) are often of the highest security and therefore the lowest risk. Governments can generally raise more money through taxation or they can increase the money supply (by 'printing money') rather than default on a bond. However, the perceived quality of the debt of different countries varies, affecting the price of government debt. In the recent past, capital and income defaults on the 'sovereign' (government) debt of some countries has been a problem.

Corporate bonds are generally perceived as more risky than the debt of major governments. Therefore, investors seek a higher rate of return from corporate bonds generally, and the price will typically be lower than for a government bond with a similar coupon and maturity date.

8.4 Credit ratings of bond issuers

Ratings are available that assess the **credit of bond issuers**. Such ratings can help to indicate the risk in holding the bonds of different issuers.

Changes in credit rating can have an effect on the prices of the issuer's debt in the market. In turn, this will affect the ability of organisations to raise new debt. If the creditworthiness of a company declines, the market will expect a higher yield from the debt. Therefore, it will be more expensive for the company to raise new debt.

Credit risk	Moody's	Standard & Poor's	Fitch	Classification
Prime	Aaa	AAA	AAA	Investment grade bonds
Excellent	Aa	AA	AA	
Upper medium	A	A	A	
Lower medium	Baa	BBB	BBB	
Speculative	Ba	BB	BB	Non-investment grade/junk bonds
Very speculative	B, Caa	B, CCC, CC, C	B, CCC, CC, C	
Default	Ca, C	D	DDD, DD, D	

Referring to the Table above, note the following points.

- **Prime ratings** are usually given to low-risk government debt and some major companies.
- Bonds from issuers with a rating of Baa or above from Moody's and BBB or above from S&P or Fitch are termed **investment grade** bonds, with a low risk of default. Yields are relatively low and the issuers can raise debt at low cost.
- Bonds with ratings below these levels ('speculative' and lower) carry a higher risk of default. These are **non-investment grade** bonds or **junk bonds**. Investors buying such bonds are generally speculating on there being a better outcome than the market predicts.

8.5 Volatility of bond prices

If there is a change in interest rate expectations, then bond prices generally all **move in the same direction**. However, certain characteristics will affect the **volatility** of the price of a bond.

We would expect greater volatility in:

- **'Junk' (non-investment grade) bonds,** because of their greater risk and speculative nature as compared with **investment grade bonds**
- **Lower coupon bonds**, because more of the return is attributable to the final redemption payment than for **higher coupon bonds**
- **Longer-dated bonds**, because current interest rate expectations have relatively less effect than for the shorter period to redemption of **shorter-dated bonds**

Key chapter points

- Fixed interest securities carry more risk than holding money in a deposit account because their capital value varies. Changes in interest rates and other economic factors can affect bond prices.

- The yield curve shows the yields on bonds having different periods to maturity.

- Fixed interest securities include those issued by governments (called gilts in the UK) and by companies and other corporate bodies (corporate bonds).

- Bonds from lower quality issuers (companies with poor credit ratings) will have higher yields than higher quality issuers (such as governments), reflecting the different levels of default risk.

- If held to redemption, the investment cash flows of fixed interest securities are known, assuming that the bond issuer does not default.

- Variations on bonds include Floating Rate Notes, linked to a benchmark interest rate, and zero coupon bonds, which pay no interest and are issued at a discount to their par value. There are also small markets in building society Permanent Interest Bearing Shares and in local authority bonds.

INVESTMENT AND RISK

Chapter Quiz

1. What RPI figure is used to determine the interest rate of an index linked gilt? ....(See paragraph 2.4)
2. What is a 'gilt strip'? ....(2.6)
3. What are the different types of security that may apply to corporate loan stock? ....(3.3)
4. How much stamp duty is chargeable on purchases of corporate bonds in the secondary market? ....(3.7)
5. How is the interest rate on Floating Rate Notes set? ....(3.9)
6. What are 'yearling bonds'? ....(4.1)
7. What are 'perpetual subordinated bonds'? ....(5.2)
8. Distinguish between the 'clean price' and the 'dirty price' for a gilt. ....(6.3 & 6.4)
9. Distinguish between a 'cum-interest price' and an 'ex-interest price'. ....(6.4)
10. What is the capital gains tax position of qualifying corporate bonds? ....(6.6)
11. What is the shape of a normal yield curve, and why is it this shape? ....(7.7)

chapter 7

Equities and derivatives

Chapter topic list

1	Equities as an investment	138
2	Dealing and taxation	141
3	Tax wrappers and tax incentives	144
4	Factors affecting share prices	145
5	Measuring company performance	150
6	Stock market indices	157
7	Derivatives and warrants	161
	Key chapter points	167
	Chapter quiz	168

INVESTMENT AND RISK

Chapter Learning Outcomes

3   **Understand** the following asset classes, their main features and suitability for different consumer circumstances

   3.3   Equities

   3.3.1   Main types of shares – ordinary and preference.

   3.3.2   Characteristics of equity-based investment – individual company performance, main factors that affect company profits and share values, size of company and market liquidity, sectors and markets.

   3.3.3   Investment ratios measuring performance and their limitations – price earnings ratio (PE), earnings per share, dividend yield, dividend cover, borrowing, net assets.

   3.3.4   Market behaviour – what makes markets fluctuate, fundamental analysis and market psychology.

   3.3.5   Past performance and volatility – growth and dividends.

   3.3.6   Stock market indices – main UK and overseas indices.

   3.3.7   Mechanics of dealing, including costs of purchase and sale.

   3.3.8   Taxation of dividends.

   3.3.9   Derivatives, futures and options, main features and uses.

   3.3.10 Employee share schemes and incentives.

   3.3.11 Alternative Investment Market shares and unlisted securities characteristics, past performance in terms of risk and returns.

   3.3.12 Mergers and acquisitions.

   3.3.13 Primary and secondary markets.

   3.3.14 Main components of company accounts that affect investment returns.

1 Equities as an investment

Learning outcomes

3.3.1   Main types of share – ordinary and preference.
3.3.13 Primary and secondary markets.

1.1 What are equities?

The term '**equities**' refers to the **shares** of companies. The **shareholders** of a company are its owners. The **directors** are the senior managers of the company and have the task of maximising the wealth of the ordinary shareholders.

1.2 Types of share

Ordinary shares

Ordinary shares are the most common type of share. As the owners of the company, ordinary shareholders are entitled to the post-tax profits of the company after **preference shareholders** (discussed below) have been paid their dividend. As already discussed, earnings are unlikely to be paid out in full each year: part, most or all of the earnings may be retained for re-investment in the business, for the benefit of shareholders in the future.

- Each ordinary share has a **nominal value**, such as 25p. The nominal value is not a reflection of the market value of the share. Ordinary shares are often described by the name of the company and the nominal value of the share. (Example: Tesco plc Ord. 5p)
- The purchase of an ordinary share in a company gives the investor the right to a dividend, if paid, and the right to receive a copy of the annual accounts.
- Companies listed on the London Stock Exchange must provide their shareholders with half-yearly results, which will indicate the size of the interim dividend.
- Each voting ordinary share generally carries one vote and the ordinary shareholder has a right to vote at the annual general meeting. The voting at the annual general meeting is normally to approve the accounts, to agree the dividend, to elect directors and to appoint auditors. The shareholders may also be asked to vote on other significant matters such as a change in share structure.
- On liquidation of a company, the ordinary shareholders are entitled to what remains after all creditors have been paid and other shareholders have been paid what they are due.

Deferred ordinary shares are now rare. They may give the shareholder greater voting rights, or rights to a higher dividend. In some cases, the shares do not qualify for a dividend until the company's profits have reached a prescribed level or until a particular date.

Shares may be designated as '**A shares**' or '**B shares**' for different reasons, to denote different rights attaching to each type of share. For example:

- Following the unification in 2005 of Royal Dutch and Shell Transport into one parent company, Royal Dutch Shell plc, the company has two classes of shares, called A shares and B shares. The A shares and the B shares have the same rights except regarding the source of dividend income: A shares have a Dutch source, while B shares are intended to have a UK source.
- B shares in Rolls-Royce Group plc are shares with limited voting rights that can, during defined periods, be redeemed for cash or, alternatively, can be converted into ordinary shares.

Non-voting shares are generally designated by the letter 'A' for a company that has them. Ordinary shares have preferential voting rights over the **A shares** although each type of share receives the same dividend. This type of structure has been used in family controlled companies as a means of raising more cash without losing control. The market value of A shares is usually lower than for the ordinary shares because of the lack of voting rights of the A shares. It is less usual now for a company to adopt this type of structure, which is frowned upon by some investors because of the restrictions to voting rights.

Partly paid shares. Partly paid shares became a common feature in the privatisation issues. The shares are paid for in instalments. Paying the instalment is a legal liability and not an option. If the holder does not wish to pay the instalment he can sell the share as 'partly paid' in the market before the obligation falls due. If he does not pay, his entitlement to the share is lost and he is only entitled to a return of his payments to date.

Treasury shares. With shareholders' authorisation to do so, some companies use their own cash resources to **buy back** their own shares in the market. These shares may be cancelled, or (within specified limits) may be retained by the company. Where a company holds its own shares 'in Treasury' in this way, without cancelling them, the shares are called **Treasury shares**.

INVESTMENT AND RISK

Preference shares

A company may or may not also have **preference shares** in its capital structure.

- A preference share pays a **fixed** rather than variable amount of **dividend**, normally **half-yearly**. Thus, preference shares are similar to **loan stock**.
- With loan stock, the interest must be paid even if the company is losing money. With **preference shares**, the dividend is only paid if there are enough post-tax profits to pay it.
- Preference shares do not usually carry voting rights unless the dividend payments fall into arrears.
- The **claims** of the preference shareholders ranks ahead of the ordinary shareholders in the event of a **liquidation**, but after the loan and debenture holders.

The **coupon** (dividend rate) on a preference share is quoted net of a **tax credit** of 10% that cannot be reclaimed by non-taxpayers. The tax position is as for ordinary shares (see above).

As with ordinary shares, gains on preference shares are subject to **capital gains tax**.

There are a number of types of preference share.

- **Participating preference shares.** The holder of this share stands a chance that if the company does well he will receive his fixed dividend plus an extra dividend, which will usually be a proportion of the ordinary dividend declared.
- **Cumulative preference shares.** A company might not pay a dividend on preference shares if there are insufficient post-tax profits. When the company is in a position to resume dividend payments, holders of cumulative preference shares will receive arrears of dividends. These arrears must be paid before the ordinary shareholders can receive their dividend. With **non-cumulative preference shares**, the right to any unpaid dividend is lost at the end of the financial year and no arrears are carried forward.
- **Redeemable preference shares.** Redeemable preference shares have a set redemption date or are redeemable at the company's option. This makes them similar to a loan stock.

Convertible preference shares offer a dividend plus the opportunity to convert to ordinary shares at pre-specified dates on pre-specified terms. Convertible preference shares will often have a higher market price than the ordinary share of the same company reflecting both the guaranteed dividend and the value of the option to convert. If it becomes very likely that conversion will take place, the price will move in line with those of the ordinary shares. If the investor does not convert by the last permissible date, he forfeits his right.

1.3 Exchange listings and quoted shares

Many smaller 'Limited' companies are private companies, which may be owner-managed and cannot offer their shares to the general public. The use of the term 'limited' indicates that shareholders have limited liability: if the company fails, shareholders can lose their entire investment in the company but the company's creditors cannot pursue the shareholders for any further money.

To offer shares for sale to the public, a company must be a 'plc' (**public limited company**).

- Such a company can seek a full **listing** on the **main market** of the London Stock Exchange (LSE), or
- It may join the less closely regulated **Alternative Investment Market (AIM)** that is also operated by the London Stock Exchange. Over 2,000 companies' shares have traded on the AIM.

Companies whose shares are traded on the LSE are generally known as **quoted companies**. Listed shares are those which have been admitted to the Official List by the **UK Listing Authority** (UKLA) a division of the Financial Services Authority. Joining the Main Market of the LSE involves a two stage processes.

7: EQUITIES AND DERIVATIVES

- The UKLA is responsible for the approval of prospectuses and the admission of companies to the Official List.
- The LSE is responsible for the admission to trading of companies to the Main Market.

A share that has satisfied the UKLA listing rules but has not yet satisfied the LSE admission to trading will not be able to be traded on the full market. Such **unquoted shares** will have very low liquidity since they cannot be freely traded and therefore represent a higher risk investment.

For companies with a listing, the LSE acts as both a

- Primary market – a market where companies issue new shares in order to raise finance
- Secondary market – where existing shares can be traded

2 Dealing and taxation

Learning outcomes

3.3.7 Mechanics of dealing, including costs of purchase and sales.
3.3.8 Taxation of dividends.

Equities are **bought and sold** by private investors, by large institutions such as life assurance companies and pension funds, and by foreign investors. The investor buys ordinary shares for two main reasons:

- To receive dividends from the company's earnings stream (**income**)
- To gain from increases in the price of the share (**capital gain**)

The **buying (offer) price** of a share will generally be higher than the price at which an investor can **sell (bid price)**. The difference **(spread)** earns an income for **market makers**, who deal in the stock and maintain **market liquidity**.

2.1 Equities as part of a portfolio

Direct holdings of ordinary shares could be appropriate in a **portfolio** for an investor who obtains advice on an ongoing basis or who wishes to spend the time researching has own investments. Over the short term, capital values (as reflected by share prices) can fluctuate greatly, although dividend payments are more stable than capital values. Over the long term – for example, over most five-year periods – the share market has been found to out-perform the general rate of inflation, fixed interest securities and deposit funds.

Investors with smaller amounts to invest and who do not wish to build their own portfolio can gain exposure to equity markets through **pooled investments** such as unit trusts, open ended investment companies (OEICs) or investment trusts.

Ordinary shares should only be considered if the client is well aware of the risks associated with individual company share ownership. The investor must be aware that there is no guarantee of dividends or of return of capital. Particularly with more speculative investments, it is possible that the whole investment in a particular share will be lost. **Diversification** into different shares can help to reduce the risk of substantial losses arising from the failure of individual equity investments.

An investor should always have other assets that can be realised more easily. Although equities may be sold relatively quickly, the price might be unfavourable at the time funds are required.

It is often said that an investor ought not to invest money in shares that he or she cannot afford to lose.

2.2 Buying and selling shares

Equities are bought and sold through a stockbroker. The broker can deal for the client in one of three ways.

- **Execution only dealing service**. In this case the stockbroker simply carries out the client's instructions.
- **Advisory or non-discretionary service**. In this case the stockbroker makes recommendation but the client makes the final decision.
- **Discretionary service**. In this case, the stockbroker will have authority to buy and sell without reference to the client. A carefully worded agreement will lay down the parameters for transactions, for example, the amount of risk the client wishes to take or the types of securities he wishes to consider.

If the stockbroker is acting on an **execution only** basis, this means that the client has agreed that he chooses not to receive advice on his investments. Investors making their own investment decisions will give instructions to the broker to buy and sell shares and the broker will generally use either the **Stock Exchange Electronic Trading Service (SETS)** or the **Stock Exchange Trading Service – quotes and crosses (SETSqx)**.

Liquid shares (as defined in the Financial Instruments Directive, MiFID – see regulations later in this Study Book) are traded on **SETS** which is an **order-driven** system; SETSqx is used for trading non-liquid stocks. Investors submit orders to the SETS system via LSE member firms. The information is transmitted electronically and orders are automatically executed where possible. SETS sends out information (orders, transactions, other messages) via a broadcast public feed.

The market comprises **marketmakers** and **brokers**. There are a generally a number of marketmakers quoting bid and offer prices for a particular share. The marketmakers are in competition with each other for business, and the broker will choose the best price offered when executing his client's order (the principle of **best execution**). Some brokers are allowed to act in dual capacity as market maker and broker, and many large banks operate in this dual capacity.

The settlement system now used for shares in most larger companies is called **CREST** (Certificateless Registration of Electronic Stock and Share Transfers). It is advantageous for investors who deal regularly to become members of CREST via a nominee account with a broker. Dealing through such a company could result in achieving better prices than via a paper transaction (which is still permitted), swift settlement of trades and no requirements for signed transfer forms or share certificates. The fastest settlement is currently three-day settlement. **'T + 3'** means that money must be paid for a trade within three business days after the deal is struck.

2.3 Costs of investing in shares

The costs of investing in shares can be broken down as follows.

(a) **Purchase cost**. The purchase cost includes a **spread** which is the difference between the bid and offer price of the share. The spread, from which marketmakers makes their profits, could be 0.5% for a liquid share or 5% or more for a less easily traded share.

(b) **Broker's commission**. A typical charge would be say 1.5% on a deal up to £7,000 with a minimum charge of £25. Execution only services, including online brokers, are generally cheaper than this, ranging from around £10 per deal upwards.

(c) **Stamp duty and SDRT**. As stated earlier in this Study Book, 0.5% Stamp Duty Reserve Tax (SDRT) is payable on the value of purchases of UK equities settled through CREST, rounded up to the nearest 1 penny. 0.5% Stamp Duty is payable on purchases of UK equities not settled through CREST, rounded up to the nearest £5. Stamp duty on stock registered in Ireland is charged at 0.1%.

(d) **Panel of Takeovers and Mergers Levy**. The PTM levy is a flat £1 on either sales or purchases in excess of £10,000.

Below is an example of the possible cost of the purchase and sale of shares to the value of £10,001.

Cost of purchase

	£
Shares	10,001
Brokerage commission 1.5%	150
Stamp duty at 0.5%	50
PTM levy	1
Total cost	10,202

Cost of sale

	£
Shares	10,001
Brokerage commission 1.5%	150
PTM levy	1
Total cost	10,152

2.4 Taxation of dividends

Dividends are paid with a **10% tax credit**.

- The tax credit generally cannot be re-claimed, even by a non-taxpayer.
- There is no further tax to pay for a basic rate or starting rate (10%) taxpayer.
- A higher (or additional) rate taxpayer has a liability to pay an additional 22.5% (32.5%) tax on the gross dividend. (However, there would be no further liability if the shares are held in an **ISA**.)

The **tax credit** can be calculated as: **Dividend received × 10/90**

The position for a dividend received of £100 for different types of taxpayer is summarised in the table below.

	Non-taxpayer	Starting rate taxpayer	Basic rate taxpayer	Higher rate taxpayer
	£	£	£	£
Dividend	100.00	100.00	100.00	100.00
Tax credit	11.11	11.11	11.11	11.11
Additional tax due	Nil	Nil	Nil	25.00
Total tax suffered	11.11	11.11	11.11	36.11*
Net income	100.00	100.00	100.00	75.00

* Note that the effective tax rate on dividends for higher rate taxpayers is (36.11/111.11) × 100 = **32.5%**.

2.5 Capital gains tax

If the investor makes a capital gain on the realisation of a share it may be subject to capital gains tax.

The basic calculation for **capital gains tax** is:

Profit = Proceeds (less sale expenses) less original investment

The profit thus calculated could become subject to capital gains tax if:

- The individual's gain is in excess of the annual exemption, or

INVESTMENT AND RISK

- The gain is below the annual exemption but the investor has already made use of this in other transactions

There are methods of reducing the capital gain.

- The investor may have other capital losses including losses brought forward which could be offset.
- The investor may consider transferring the holding into a spouse's name prior to sale if the spouse has not used up their annual exemption.

2.6 Stamp duty and stamp duty reserve tax

Depending on how the deal is settled, share purchases will be subject to either stamp duty or stamp duty reserve tax at 0.5% of the value of the transaction. Stamp duty reserve tax is payable on electronically settled trades (the vast majority), whereas stamp duty is payable on physical trades.

3 Tax wrappers and tax incentives

Learning outcome

3.3.10 Employee share schemes and incentives.

3.1 Equity ISAs

For the tax year 2010/11 it is possible for any UK taxpayer over the age of 18 to invest £10,200 in an equity ISA. An equity ISA shields any dividends received and capital gains from tax. However, since any dividends are received net of basic rate tax, this does not offer any income tax advantage to a lower or basic rate taxpayer since no extra tax would have been payable by them outside the ISA.

Equity ISAs can hold shares listed on a recognised stock exchange but cannot hold shares that are only listed on AIM.

ISAs are covered in more detail in the tax wrappers section of this Study Text.

3.2 Enterprise investment scheme

The Enterprise Investment Scheme (EIS) is designed to help unlisted trading companies raise finance through offering tax incentives to individuals who are unconnected with that company and who buy shares in the company.

EISs are covered in more detail in the tax wrappers section of this Study Text.

3.3 Employee share scheme

Employee share schemes are designed to encourage broader share ownership among employees of a business and certain schemes offer tax incentives to employees who buy shares or options in the company.

Employee share schemes are covered in more detail in the tax wrappers section of this Study Text.

4 Factors affecting share prices

> **Learning outcomes**
>
> 3.3.2 Characteristics of equity-based investment
> - Individual company performance.
> - Main factors that affect company profits and share values.
> - Size of company and market liquidity.
> - Sectors and markets.
>
> 3.3.4 Market behaviour – what makes markets fluctuate, fundamental analysis and market psychology.
>
> 3.3.5 Past performance and volatility – growth and dividends.
>
> 3.3.11 Alternative Investment Market shares and unlisted securities – tax characteristics, past performance in terms of risk and returns.
>
> 3.3.12 Mergers and acquisitions.

4.1 Past performance of equities

The **real (inflation-adjusted) returns** achieved by equities over the long term can seem impressive. £100 invested in 1899 in a broad portfolio of equities, with income reinvested, would have grown to £750,000 by the end of 2008. Over the long term, global equity returns can be expected to be in the order of 5-6% above the rate of inflation. The ability of equities to produce these returns above inflation reflects the fact that **economic growth** produces growth in companies' earnings, which benefit shareholders.

Consider also though, that the same £100 from 1899 mentioned above would have grown to £1,200,000 when stock markets peaked in 1999. The risk of equity investment is highlighted if we note that an investment of £10,000 made at the market peak in 1999 would have lost almost 40% of its value by the end of 2008. The value would have fallen to approximately £6,000. That investment then needs to grow by 67% for the investor to get back to their starting position of £10,000: this could take many years.

This illustration underlines the possible downside effects on an investor's capital from the volatility of share prices. There have been periods in which sharp falls in stock markets have occurred – for example, in the USA in 1929, in the UK in 1973-74, in Japan after 1989 and internationally in 2008/09.

These potential returns and risks have been even greater for the less liquid **AIM Shares** and probably even greater still for **unquoted shares** though the data is difficult to derive for these.

4.2 The value of a share

Investment theory tells us that the **value of a share** to the investor is the **net present value** (that is, the value adjusted to current day terms) of all the anticipated **future dividend payments** arising from the share. If future growth in earnings and consequently dividends is anticipated, this will be reflected in the share value. Because the future is extremely difficult to predict and because our perceptions of the future will change when the information we have at any time, the perceived value of a share can fluctuate with sometimes great volatility. Clearly, when a company goes into **liquidation** it will have zero value on that basis.

INVESTMENT AND RISK

4.3 Dividends and re-investment

A company's **earnings** (profits) can be used either to **pay dividends,** or to **re-invest** within the business. Some companies do not pay dividends, for example because they have not yet made profits, or because they choose instead to retain their earnings and to re-invest them in order to generate **growth**.

To take one example, the American corporation Microsoft, which has been a highly profitable company for many years, has only fairly recently started to pay any dividend at all. The company's shares are currently worth around $242 billion. How then does such a company command a high stock market valuation, if the value of a share is the net present value of its future dividends? The answer is that such a company has the prospect of paying out significant dividends at some stage in the future. Its re-investment of earnings enhances its ability to generate future dividends.

As a consequence, investors tend to have to choose between low dividends and high growth or high dividends and low growth.

4.4 Liquidity

Liquidity refers to the markets ability to trade shares without significantly affecting prices which is very much influenced by market capitalisation. A highly liquid stock will be able to sustain large trading volumes before any noticeable price movement occurs, whereas stocks with low liquidity will find that even small trades result in price changes.

4.5 Supply and demand in share markets

As with all markets, the main determinants of the prices of shares are the **supply** of and **demand** for those shares. The prices of equities move continually during Stock Exchange trading hours.

Share prices can change as a result of information becoming available to investors about various matters, including:

- The earnings prospects and asset values of individual companies
- The membership of the Board
- Adverse factors affecting companies, such as legal action against it, or action by a bank to call in loans
- Industry and economy surveys, for example about levels of retail sales, or productivity
- Macro-economic developments, for example: the expected level of interest rates, or where an economy appears to be located in the business cycle
- Changes in government policy, for example on taxation and monetary policy
- Movements in other stock markets around the world, such as the USA and Japan
- Global economic and political developments

4.6 Investor information

Investors follow the public statements made by the company through the London Stock Exchange's **Regulatory News Service (RNS)**. RNS statements cover matters such as results announcements, major developments, and purchases or sales of the company's shares by its directors. If the company warns that profits will be lower than anticipated (a **profit warning**), there is usually a sharp drop in the share price.

Many companies aim to present a stable and steadily rising pattern of **dividend payments** from year to year. Sharp changes from the usual pattern may be taken by investors as a **signal** of a change in the company's fortunes, which may cause a shift in the share price. An unexpected cut in the level of dividends could depress investor sentiment and the share price may fall.

Because of increasing interdependence of national economies through trade (**globalisation**), share prices can be heavily affected by economic news from around the world, particularly from the world's largest economy, that of the USA.

Trading in shares by anyone with **insider information** about the shares that has not been made public is illegal.

4.7 Company management

Investors will look for evidence of the **quality of a company's management**, although such evidence can be difficult to obtain in practice. Do the directors have the competence and motivation to drive the business forward in the interests of the shareholders, making any changes necessary to adapt to future developments? Changes in Board membership can affect investors' assessment of a company's prospects and the share price may move as a result. If a director resigns, investors will be interested in the reason for the resignation. If new directors are appointed, their experience and past track record will be of interest.

4.8 The business cycle

The **business cycle** is a periodic pattern of faster and then slower or negative economic growth. **Cyclical shares** are shares that are particularly affected by the business cycle because the demand for those companies' products oscillates over the years of the business cycle.

- **Cyclical shares** include, for example, car manufacture and housebuilding, as the performances of such companies tend to rise quickly when the economy is on an upswing and fall sharply when the economy drops.

- A share would be described as **counter-cyclical** if its price tends to move conversely to a cyclical share. This could include shares in companies that produce items people need regardless of the state of the economy, such as food and prescription drugs. Such shares are sometimes called **defensive shares.**

4.9 Interest rates

Some companies' shares are affected more by **interest rates** than others. For example, because house purchase decisions are influenced by mortgage rates, house building companies will be particularly sensitive to interest rate changes. If people are moving house less as a result of interest rate increases, businesses such as DIY and carpeting may also face a downturn in demand and therefore earnings.

In general, an increase in short-term interest rates will tend to exert downward pressure on equity prices. This is because companies' borrowing costs will increase while consumer demand will be reduced by a higher cost of credit. Lower demand for goods and services will tend to reduce companies' sales revenue and profits.

4.10 Investor sentiment and market psychology

Share prices are also affected by **changing investor sentiment** and the speculative motive of investors.

A **bear market** is one in which prices persist on a downward trend: Market sentiment then tends to be pessimistic. In a **bull market**, there is much optimism comes to the fore, and prices are on a rising trend.

Speculative motives can drive share prices spiralling higher. Investors may buy particular shares in the hope of taking advantage of a rising trend in prices. Investors may tend to move with a **herd mentality**. As more investors buy, prices are driven higher still and this may encourage still further buying. A process in which prices are bid higher cannot continue indefinitely if the **fundamental factors** do not justify the prices. Eventually the 'bubble' may burst when prices fall back and there is a sudden change in sentiment. The fall in prices can then be as steep as the original rise and those who bought at the highest prices will suffer losses. This herd mentality can result in significant volatility for the shares affected.

4.11 Fundamental analysis and technical analysis

What do we mean by 'fundamental factors'? There are two very different forms of analysis used in stock selection: **fundamental analysis** and **technical analysis** ('**FA**' and '**TA**').

Fundamental analysis looks at the underlying financial position of the company. It looks, for example, at earnings, cash flow, cash reserves, dividend levels, sales and stock. FA looks at the economic and financial fundamentals of the company and the way it is run, the size of the order book and features of the market in which it operates. Analysts using this approach hope to find companies that have either been undervalued or have a potential to increase in value through growth. They also hope that in time this will be realised by other investors and the value of the company will rise.

Investors seeking hidden value are often termed **value investors**, while those seeking exceptional growth prospects are termed **growth investors**.

In contrast to fundamental analysis, **technical analysis** (also called '**chartism**') is an approach which looks at patterns of past and recent share price movements in order to come to a view on whether to buy or sell a stock at the present time. While the emphasis of FA is on analysing the underlying financial condition and prospects of companies, TA pays more attention to market psychology and market sentiment. An underlying implication of TA is that future share prices will be influenced by past share price patterns.

Technical analysts use a variety of graphs to make assumptions about a particular share such as whether the price is increasing, decreasing and where the 'price resistance' and 'support levels' are. For each of these charts there are various ways of interpreting the information. For example, with a line chart, the TA investor might be looking for formations such as 'head and shoulders', or 'double tops'. In addition to looking at price movements, technical analysts can study volume of trade and the momentum (rate) of movements.

If any of the above systems worked with a high degree of accuracy then it should be possible to make regular profits. However, paradoxically, if such profits are exploited widely by investors, then the anomalies which the method seeks to exploit should tend to disappear. It is an implication of the **efficient markets hypothesis** that all existing information is already reflected in share prices and that it is therefore impractical to make returns higher than those of the market in general, for the same level of risk.

Most investors who are proponents of the TA approach do not use it alone, but will often apply principles of fundamental analysis as well. In the next Section of the Chapter, we describe some of the ratios and measures that can be used in analysing company fundamentals.

4.12 Mergers and acquisitions

In investment theory, a company's principal objective is to **increase its shareholders' wealth**. In practice, company directors may be pursuing other objectives, such as increasing market share or the size of the company's operations.

Growth in a company may occur in two ways.

- **Organic growth** occurs when a company manages to increase its sales, for example by winning new customers.
- Alternatively, growth may occur through mergers and acquisitions. Mergers and acquisitions are sometimes called '**takeovers**'.

A **merger** occurs when two companies agree to combine as a single company, with integrated control. There is usually an exchange of shares to effect the merger, and this has no capital gains consequences as no disposal has taken place.

With an **acquisition**, the acquiring company is the new owner of the combined businesses. One company 'takes over' another. The offer made may be in cash only, or a combination of cash, shares and possibly fixed interest stock. Cash received will be treated as a disposal for capital gains tax purposes. An exchange of shares for fixed interest stock avoids crystallising a disposal for capital gains tax purposes.

In the quest for increasing shareholder value, companies may carry out mergers and acquisitions to take advantage of **cost savings** and other '**synergies**' resulting from forming a larger unit. In some cases, a company may seek to improve its competitive advantage by buying up competitor companies.

When an acquisition is announced, the share price of the acquiring company often falls. This tendency suggests that shareholders are often sceptical about whether an acquisition will actually add shareholder value in the way that the company directors hope it will.

The acquiring company will often have to pay a **premium** above the share price of the company being acquired, to induce the shareholders of that company to sell their shares. Belief that a company will be a takeover target can push up its share price, in anticipation of the premium which may be paid.

4.13 Defending against a takeover

Whether a company is vulnerable to takeover depends on who controls the majority of shares in issue and on the **voting rights** of shares. For the minority of companies with two classes of shares, one with voting rights and one without, control of the company can be with shareholders who do not hold a majority of shares but do hold a majority of votes.

- **Private companies** can defend themselves relatively easy against takeover because their shares tend to be closely held.
- **Public companies** are more susceptible because a predator can build up a shareholding by buying shares in the market.

A 3% interest in a public company is a '**notifiable interest**'.

- The shareholder must notify the fact (plus any increase or decrease of a whole percentage point above or below 3%) to the company.
- The company will then inform the **Regulatory News Service (RNS)** of the Stock Exchange, which will make it public.

4.14 Takeover rules

The **City Code on Takeovers and Mergers** lays down strict rules on the conduct and timing of a takeover bid.

Where control of a company is acquired by a person, or persons acting in concert, a general offer to all other shareholders is normally required.

Rule 9 of the City Code provides that if a person, or a group acting in concert, acquires shares taking their holding to 30% or more of the voting rights of a company, the acquirer must make a mandatory cash offer for the rest of the shares.

The **Companies Act** provides a procedure for mandatory acquisition of the shares of minority shareholders following a takeover offer. If the bidder secures 90% acceptances to the offer (excluding shares held by the bidder), it will have the right to compulsorily acquire the remaining shares.

During a takeover offer, the offeror, the offeree company, and their advisers may not provide **information** to a restricted number of shareholders only: information must be made available to all shareholders. All shareholders of the same class of an offeree company must be treated similarly by an offeror.

Parties to an offer must do all they can to prevent creation of a **false market** in the shares of the companies concerned. They must take care that statements are not made which could mislead the market.

INVESTMENT AND RISK

Directors of the offeror and the offeree company must always, in advising their shareholders, act **only in their capacity as directors** and not have regard to their personal or family interests. The directors must consider the interests of all **shareholders** taken as a whole, and those of **employees** and **creditors**.

5 Measuring company performance

Learning outcomes

3.3.3 Investment ratios, measuring performance and their limitations – price earnings ratio (PE), earnings per share, dividend yield, dividend cover, borrowing, net assets.

3.3.14 Main components of company accounts that affect investment returns.

5.1 Companies' financial statements

The companies issuing shares on the UK and other stock markets vary widely in various aspects, including their size, the structure of their funding from debt or equity, their business activities, their business strategy and the geographical spread of their activities. **Company law** and **accounting standards** are designed to standardise the figures a company must publish in its **financial statements** as far as is practicable. Companies are required to make various disclosures to enable the prospective investor, as well as other stakeholders in the business such as its creditors, to enable them to assess the soundness of the business. The financial statements include figures from which can be calculated key **ratios** like the ones we explain in this section.

The Companies Act makes it a legal requirement for a company to provide a **'true and fair'** set of accounts, and the Accounting Rules, set by the Accounting Standards Board, clarify the contents of the various sections of the accounts.

The **annual financial statements for a listed company** will contain the following sections, which can be used to gain information about a company from the investment perspective.

- A Chairman's statement
- A directors' report
- An income statement
- A statement of total recognised gains and losses
- A balance sheet
- A cash flow statement
- An auditors' report
- Notes to the accounts

The **income statement** records the company's trading for a **past accounting period**. It shows whether a company is managing to sell its goods or services for more than the cost of producing/providing them over the period covered. These figures do need careful interpretation as a profitable company can still run out of money, for example, if it is investing heavily in capital goods such as land or buildings while lacking the cash to pay for it.

The **balance sheet** summarises a company's **assets and liabilities** at the end of accounting year, subject to various assumptions provided in the notes.

The **cash flow statement** is a summary of cash movements in and out of the company. Without adequate cash flow, there could be problems with a company continuing in business, as suppliers will not get paid, employees cannot be paid and the marketing, selling and distribution costs cannot be met. With a reasonable level of cash flow the company can expand; without it, it may contract. Even companies with a healthy balance sheet can have problems when the cash flow is not positive.

Notes to the accounts describe the company's **accounting policies** and make various other disclosures. Careful examination can occasionally reveal factors that may easily be missed by looking at the accounts themselves.

5.2 Uses and limitations of investment ratios

As we saw earlier, **fundamental analysis** is a process of analysing company performance in order to assess the value and future prospects of shares in companies. This approach contrasts with that of **'chartists'**, who analyse the patterns of fluctuations in a share's price or in a share price index (showing trends in share prices overall) up to the present in order to form a view of how the price or index will move in the future.

An investor in equities will often want to assess the **prospects** and the **risk** of an investment in the shares of a company. The calculation of a number of **investment ratios** using figures from the financial statements can help in making the investment decision. Clearly the investor will want to assess whether a share is worth buying at the current **share price**. Some of the investment ratios are linked to the share price and so will change as the share price changes from day to day.

Investment managers and fund managers will monitor investment ratios in making investment decisions for the pooled funds they manage for clients. **Analysts** also carry out such analyses in issuing **buy**, **sell** or **hold** recommendations on a particular share. A hold recommendation is not as strong as a buy, and suggests that if an investor already holds the shares, then he should continue to hold it. Analysts may also suggest a **target** price which they expect a share to achieve.

Investment ratios allow the investor to:

- Assess trends in a company's performance over a number of years
- Compare ratios with those of other similar companies or sector averages

Limitations of investment ratios include the following.

- They use historical data, which may not be a guide to the future or to the potential of an investment.
- Differences in accounting policies in different companies may reduce the value of comparisons between companies.
- Accounting policies may change over time, making comparisons between different periods problematic.
- In spite of accounting standards and the statutory requirement for the financial statements to be audited, there is the possibility that management may use 'creative accounting' to manipulate how results are reported.
- Substantial inflation can make it difficult to discern genuine trends through time in data, although in today's low inflation environment in most developed countries, this is now less of a problem than it used to be.

In this section, we look at how the following ratios are calculated:

- **Earnings per share**
- **Price to earnings (P/E) ratio**
- **Dividend yield**
- **Dividend cover**
- **Loan capital gearing**
- **Net asset value per share**

We shall use the accounts of a fictitious company, SV plc, for the years ending 31 December 2009 and 31 December 2008, to illustrate the calculation of ratios.

INVESTMENT AND RISK

Example: Accounts of SV plc

Income statement account for the year ending 31 December

	2009 £'000	2008 £'000
Turnover	1,500	1,290
Operating costs	1,290	1,113
Net operating profit	210	177
Interest payable	(25)	(21)
Profit on ordinary activities before taxation	185	156
Tax on profit on ordinary activities	(60)	(47)
Profit on ordinary activities after taxation	125	109
Preference dividends	(14)	(14)
Profit for the financial year	111	95
Dividends to ordinary shareholders	(55)	(47)
Profit retained for the financial year	56	48

Additional notes:

Operating costs comprise:

	2009 £'000	2008 £'000
Cost of sales	780	616
Distribution costs	325	336
Administration expenses	130	120
Other sales overheads	55	41
Total	1,290	1,113

SV plc
Balance sheets as at 31 December

	2009 £'000	2008 £'000
Fixed assets		
Intangible assets	320	310
Tangible assets	430	390
	750	700
Current assets		
Stock	98	96
Debtors	138	125
Cash at bank and in hand	20	17
	256	238
Current liabilities		
Creditors: amounts due within one year		
Borrowings	(97)	(99)
Other	(140)	(129)
	(237)	(228)
Net current assets/(liabilities)	19	10
Total assets less current liabilities	769	710
Creditors due after one year		
Loan stock	(105)	(112)
Other borrowings	(28)	(18)
	(133)	(130)
Total	636	580

	2009 £'000	2008 £'000
Capital and reserves		
Called up share capital:		
Ordinary shares 10p	200	200
Preference shares	100	100
Share premium account	152	152
Profit and loss account	184	128
	636	580

Note: There are £100,000 of preference shares in issue.

5.3 Earnings per share

As its name implies, the **earnings per share** or **EPS** shows the **profit** in pence earned by the company per share.

You should be able to appreciate that a change in the share price from one day to the next will not affect the EPS.

A listed company is required to set out EPS figures in its financial statements.

$$EPS = \frac{\text{Profit attributable to ordinary shareholders}}{\text{Number of shares in issue}}$$

The **profit** figure to use in the EPS formula is the company's historical profit for the period (usually, one year) after tax, minority interests, extraordinary items and preference dividends.

For SV plc:

	2009 £	2008 £
Profit after taxation	125,000	109,000
Preference dividends	(14,000)	(14,000)
Profit attributable to ordinary shareholders	111,000	95,000

The balance sheet of SV plc shows that it has share capital of £200,000 made up of ordinary shares with a nominal value of 10p. Therefore the number of shares in issue is £200,000/10p = 2,000,000.

So, SV plc's EPS is:

	2009	2008
EPS	$\frac{£111,000}{2,000,000} = £0.0555$, or 5.55 pence	$\frac{£95,000}{2,000,000} = £0.0475$ or 4.75p

The company has earned a profit of 5.55 pence during the year for each ordinary share.

If a company is making losses, the EPS becomes negative and is referred to as the **loss per share**.

5.4 Price/earnings (P/E) ratio

We did not need to know the price of the share in the market to calculate the EPS.

The **price/earnings (P/E) ratio** relates the earnings per share to the **share price**. P/E is a commonly used measure of value.

INVESTMENT AND RISK

$$\text{P/E ratio} = \frac{\text{Today's market price for the share}}{\text{Earnings per share}}$$

The current price of a share can be found from various on-line sources, or from the *Financial Times*. Suppose that shares in SV plc are trading at 84 pence each.

Then, for SV:

	2009	2008
P/E ratio	$\dfrac{84p}{5.55p} = 15.1$	$\dfrac{78p}{4.75p} = 16.4$

The P/E ratio shows the **multiple** of earnings you will currently have to pay to buy the share. The ratio therefore measures how expensive a share is relative to its earnings for the most recent period. Shares in SV plc are trading at around 15 times its earnings this year against 16 times last year.

The P/E ratio can be calculated for particular **industry sectors**. This enables comparison of a share with its sector. Different P/E ratios are typical of different sectors, partly reflecting different perceived growth prospects and risks of investing in different sectors. A company's P/E should usually be assessed in the context of the P/Es of similar companies.

If a company is making losses, the P/E would be negative and as such is not a very useful figure. If a company is only making a small level of earnings, the P/E will be high, and may be in the hundreds. P/Es at such very high levels are not a very useful indicator, since a small change in earnings could change the P/E greatly.

Companies trading on very high P/Es often do so because significant **growth in earnings** is anticipated in the future. Such shares are sometimes called **growth shares**. Alternatively, a company might be rated by investors on the **value of its assets**, even if its earnings are low or even negative, if investors anticipate that these assets (for example, freehold buildings) could be sold off in the foreseeable future.

However, a high P/E ratio might mean that the company's shares are simply over-priced, perhaps because of over-optimism by investors. **Value investors** are particularly interested in shares with low P/E ratios, because this could indicate that the share is currently under-valued, perhaps because it just has not been noticed widely by investors or is currently ignored by institutional investors. Such investors buy in the hope that the share could become more widely noticed by others in the future and therefore bought more widely. Then, the share price should rise, leading to the P/E rising to more realistic levels. The value investor who bought it before this re-rating will have benefited from a capital gain as the price rose.

The P/E ratio can be calculated for all the constituent shares on a particular **stock market** or in a **share index**, such as the FTSE All-Share Index or the FTSE 100 Index. The *Financial Times* publishes these statistics daily as well as a breakdown by sector (FTSE sector indices). For example, on 26 July 2010, the P/E ratio for the FTSE 100 was 16.01. For technology hardware and equipment companies' shares in the All-Share Index, which might be bought for their growth prospects, the average P/E was 39.31. For life insurance companies, the average P/E was 9.80.

Relatively high P/E ratios for the market as a whole suggest investor optimism that earnings will grow in the foreseeable future to justify a higher multiple of current earnings being paid for shares. If an economic recession is anticipated or if there is general investor pessimism, earnings may be expected to fall and the current P/E ratios may fall to single digit figures for many companies.

5.5 Dividend yield

The **dividend yield** measures the net dividend per ordinary share as a percentage of the ordinary share price.

$$\text{Dividend yield} = \frac{\text{Dividend per share}}{\text{Market price for the share}} \times 100$$

The dividend yield for SVC plc is calculated as follows.

	2009	2008
Dividend yield	$\frac{£55,000/2,000,000}{84p} \times 100\% = 3.27\%$	$\frac{£47,000/2,000,000}{78p} \times 100\% = 3.01\%$

Dividends are a distribution of earnings but, as we saw earlier, some earnings may be retained for re-investment in the business, leaving only part of earnings to be distributed as dividends. As we also saw earlier, some companies may no dividends at all.

Getting the dividend policy right is a **balancing act** for many companies. The payment of a **reasonable dividend** is important to many investors, but maintaining the level of that dividend is also important. If the company pays out too much to support the dividend in a bad profit year then it cannot retain the profits to fund future growth. Companies generally choose to pay a level of dividends that they hope to be able to maintain and perhaps increase in future, if circumstances allow.

You should be able to see that, if a company's share price falls, then the yield will increase.

The *Financial Times* publishes total **yield figures for major share indices**. For the 100 largest UK companies in the FTSE 100 Index, the overall average yield was 3.32% in July 2010. For the Alternative Investment Market index, the average yield was 0.74%. The AIM includes many smaller and newer companies which do not yet have an established record of earnings from which dividends could be paid. When share indices rise, the yield for the index will fall unless dividends have risen over the same period.

5.6 Dividend cover

Dividend cover shows how many times over the **dividend** could be paid out of available profits.

$$\text{Dividend cover} = \frac{\text{Profit attributable to ordinary shareholders}}{\text{Dividends paid}}$$

The greater the **dividend cover**, the greater the reassurance for the investor that **dividend payments** can continue. Companies with lower levels of dividend cover may have to reduce dividends if profits decline. Dividend cover is particularly important for investors seeking income.

As for the EPS calculation above, profit attributable to ordinary shareholders is derived from profit after tax, minority interests, extraordinary items and preference dividends.

For SV plc:

	2009	2008
Dividend cover	$\frac{111,000}{55,000} = 2.36\times$	$\frac{95,000}{47,000} = 2.02\times$

Dividends are **covered** 2.36 times by earnings this year against 2.02 times last year.

If the dividend cover is less than one, this means that the dividend is being paid partly out of reserves, after consuming all the profits. Then, the current rate of dividends cannot continue indefinitely unless profits rise.

INVESTMENT AND RISK

5.7 Gearing

Gearing is a measure of the amount of a company's debt, and it can be calculated in different ways. It can be calculated as the proportion of **long-term borrowings** to the **total capital employed**.

$$\text{Gearing} = \frac{\text{Long-term debt}}{\text{Total capital employed}} \times 100\%$$

Long-term borrowings include preference shares, loan stock, debentures, bank loans and any overdrafts or other borrowings repayable after more than one year. 'Current' liabilities as shown on the balance sheet are repayable within one year. **Total capital employed** comprises **Total assets less current liabilities.**

From the balance sheet of SV plc and including preference shares within long-term debt, we have:

	2009	2008
Gearing	$\frac{£133,000 + £100,000 *}{£769,000} \times 100\% = 30.3\%$	$\frac{£130,000 + £104,000}{£710,000} \times 100\% = 32.4\%$

* Borrowings due after one year + preference shares

We can alternatively calculate gearing as the ratio of long-term debt to **ordinary shareholders' funds**, which we calculate by deducting preference share capital from the total of capital and reserves. This measure of gearing helps to indicate the amount of **financial risk** to which the ordinary (equity) shareholders are exposed.

$$\text{Gearing} = \frac{\text{Long-term debt}}{\text{Ordinary shareholders' funds}} \times 100\%$$

For SV plc, using this form of the gearing ratio we have:

	2009	2008
Gearing	$\frac{£133,000 + £100,000}{£636,000 - £100,000} \times 100\% = 43.5\%$	$\frac{£130,000 + £100,000}{£580,000 - £104,000} \times 100\% = 47.9\%$

If a company has relatively **low gearing**, by either measure, then it is mainly being financed by equity. A **highly geared** company is relying heavily on borrowings for its capital.

A company with high borrowings is vulnerable to:

- Possible difficulties in paying interest and repaying debt if operating profits fall
- Rises in interest rates which will increase the cost of variable rate finance and could also affect demand for the company's products or services in many sectors

5.8 Net asset value per share

The **net asset value per share** is the book value of tangible assets (as measured by the accounts) attributable to one ordinary share. (Intangible assets would include the value of such things as brands or 'goodwill' purchased when a business is bought by the company.)

$$\text{Net asset value (NAV) per share} = \frac{\text{Net assets attributable to ordinary shareholders}}{\text{Number of ordinary shares in issue}}$$

The net assets attributable to ordinary shareholders is the capital employed in the company excluding claims having priority over the ordinary shares, such as loans and preference shares.

For SV plc:

	2009	2008
NAV per share	$\dfrac{£636{,}000 - £100{,}000}{2{,}000{,}000} = 26.8$ pence	$\dfrac{£580{,}000 - £100{,}000}{2{,}000{,}000} = 24.0$ pence

The NAV per share gives some indication of how much a shareholder would receive if the company were liquidated and sold all of its assets while meeting all its liabilities. However, in practice, assets may not be saleable for the same values as those shown in the balance sheet.

NAV is a particularly appropriate measure for shareholdings in investment companies and property companies, whose assets can be realised relatively easily.

For other types of companies, the excess of the share price over the NAV per share provides an indication of the amount that the investor would be paying for the 'goodwill' and earnings prospects of the business in excess of the book value of its assets.

Exercise: SV plc

Look back at the figures earlier in the section to assess how much a buyer of shares in SV plc is paying for the 'goodwill' in the business.

6 Stock market indices

Learning outcome

3.3.6 Stock market indices – main UK and overseas indices.

6.1 Introduction

When evaluating the performance of **individual securities** or **whole portfolios** against the **market**, there is usually an appropriate **index** to use as a basis of comparison.

Finding the best index to provide a valid basis for comparison can be a problem. Indices can cover different types of securities in different countries, with different levels of market capitalisation.

Note that stock market indices take no account of **dealing costs** (broker's commission, stamp duty and the marketmaker's spread between buying and selling prices) and any **capital gains tax** that an investor may suffer.

Various types of security have **benchmarks** published by various interested parties. Some other forms of investment also have their own indices, such as the Nationwide or the Halifax House Price Indices, which reflect prices of residential property nationally and by area of the UK.

Below, we describe the important indices for equity markets. From a UK perspective, we will be interested in indices covering both the domestic market and other important overseas markets.

6.2 UK indices

FTSE indices are the most widely used for the UK stock market. The **FTSE** Group originated as a joint venture of the Financial Times and the London Stock Exchange.

INVESTMENT AND RISK

FTSE produces a large number of different equities indices, the best known of which are the **FTSE UK Series**, which includes the important **FTSE 100 Index** (the 'Footsie') and the **FTSE All-Share Index.** The FTSE Group also has other indices covering index-linked and fixed-interest securities markets. These are very useful where the portfolio has an asset allocation outside equities.

The number of companies included in various indices at the time of writing is indicated in the Table below.

UK share indices	
• FTSE All-Share (628)	• FTSE TechMARK All-Share
• FTSE 100	• FTSE TechMARK 100
• FTSE 250	• FTSE Fledgling (166)
• FTSE 350	• FTSE All-Small (438)
• FTSE Small Cap (272)	• FTSE AIM All-Share (856)

6.3 Calculation of FTSE indices

The FTSE indices are generally **arithmetical weighted** indices. The weights are the market capitalisation of each company: (shares in issue × share price). The larger the company, the greater is its weighting in the index. Thus, a movement of 1% in the share price of one of the larger companies in the index will have a greater effect on the index than will a 1% movement in the share price of a smaller constituent company.

The weights applied are adjusted to reflect the **free float** of the shares of each company. The free float is the proportion of shares that are available to trade on the stock market. If the free float is less than 75% of the total number of shares, then the weighting is adjusted accordingly. In cases where a large proportion of a company's shares are owned by directors, or by another group company, adjusting for the free float means that the index will reflect more closely the actual supply of stock in the market.

The index is calculated as:

- **The sum of** the market values (or capitalisations) of the companies in the index, after any free float adjustment
- **Divided by** the market values at the base date for the index
- **Multiplied by** the base number, eg 1000

The FTSE indices do not assume reinvestment of dividend income. In other words, they are **price indices** and not **total return indices**. This contrasts, for example, with the **DAX 30** Index (Germany), which includes reinvested income.

When comparing fund performance with an index, it is vital to take account of this distinction between **price indices** and **total return indices**. For example, if a tracker fund did not pay out dividends, its performance should be compared with an index that has been adjusted to reflect total returns, by including reinvestment of dividend income. Fund managers often use the FTSE Indices calculated on a total return basis for this purpose.

Some indices are calculated on both a price basis and a total return basis, although the important **Dow** (USA) and **Nikkei** (Japan) indices are calculated on a price basis only.

6.4 FTSE 100 Index

The **FTSE 100 Index** (the **'Footsie'**) is the best-known UK index and is the index most often quoted as the 'barometer' for the share market. The FTSE 100 contains shares of the 100 UK companies with the largest market capitalisation. The index is an arithmetic weighted index, and is re-weighted every day. During the trading day, it is calculated in real time.

Constituent **reviews** of the companies in the index are carried out **quarterly**. Additions and deletions are performed strictly in accordance with a set of rules supervised by an independent **Steering Committee**.

The **base date** of the index was 1 January 1984, when the base number was 1,000.0.

An index based on 100 companies may not initially seem very comprehensive but, given the size of the companies included, the FTSE 100 Index represents approximately 80% of the total capitalisation of the UK equity market.

6.5 FTSE All-Share Index

The **FTSE All-Share Index** is made up of approximately 700 shares representing around 98% to 99% of the total capitalisation of the UK equity market. As with other indices, there is a version that **excludes investment trusts**.

The FTSE All-Share is an aggregation of the FTSE 100, FTSE 250 and FTSE Small Cap indices.

Like the FTSE 100, the FTSE All-Share is calculated in real time. Constituent companies are reviewed annually in December.

The All-Share Index is less affected by price movements in individual shares than the FTSE 100 Index and this makes it a useful index for a **tracker fund**. As a benchmark, the All-Share provides the widest representation of a diversified UK share portfolio.

The All-Share Index is divided into **38 sectors** covering the various sectors in which UK companies operate.

6.6 FTSE 250 Index

The **FTSE 250 Index** is comprised of the **next 250 companies after the FTSE 100 companies** by market capitalisation. The FTSE 250 is a real time index, representing approximately 18% of the total UK market capitalisation. The constituent companies are reviewed quarterly. A version of the FTSE 250 excluding investment trusts is published.

6.7 FTSE 350 Index

The **FTSE 350 Index** is a combination of the **FTSE-100** and the **FTSE-250** and so covers the **UK's top 350 companies** by market capitalisation.

There are three variations on this index, one of which is the index **excluding investment trusts**. The other two variants are on the basis of yield. The constituent companies are ranked according to dividend yield and divided in two to produce separate **higher yield** and **lower yield** indices.

6.8 FTSE Small Cap Index

The **FTSE Small Cap Index** is comprised of companies with the smallest capitalisation of the capital and industry segments of the All-Share Index. This index represents approximately 2% of the total UK market capitalisation. Again, there is a variant that excludes investment trusts.

The Small Cap index is calculated in real time, and a review of constituent companies is now held quarterly.

6.9 FTSE Fledgling Index

The **FTSE Fledgling Index** is made up of around 200 companies that are smaller in size than those in the FTSE Small Cap Index. The Fledgling Index represents approximately 1% of UK market capitalisation. There is a version of the Fledgling Index that excludes investment trusts.

INVESTMENT AND RISK

The Fledgling Index is calculated at the end of each trading day, and a review of constituent companies is held annually in December.

6.10 Other FTSE UK indices

The **FTSE All-Small Index** combines the Small Cap and Fledgling indices, is calculated at the daily close of business and is reviewed annually in December.

The **FTSE AIM Index Series** covers **companies** on the **Alternative Investment Market**, a less strictly regulated market than the 'main market'. AIM companies may be relatively small, may have a relatively short trading record, and investments in AIM company shares generally carry more risk than investments in listed companies.

The FTSE AIM Series comprises the following real-time indices:

- FTSE AIM UK 50 Index (largest 50 eligible UK companies)
- FTSE AIM 100 Index (largest 100 eligible companies)
- FTSE AIM All-Share Index (revised & renamed FTSE AIM Index)

The **FT 30**, also known as the **FT Ordinary Share Index**, is the oldest UK share index. It was established in 1935 by the Financial Times with a base value of 100 and reflects the share prices of 30 of the largest companies in the UK. The FT 30 is an unweighted index with each share counting equally rather than in proportion to its market capitalisation. It is calculated as a geometric mean. Rather than qualifying on the basis of size, companies are included in the FT 30 by discretion of the committee that compiles the index, so as to reflect a wide range of sectors in the economy. The FT-30 is rarely quoted nowadays as a barometer of the market, although but it could be of some use to economists as its constituents widely represent different industrial, commercial and service sectors.

The **FTSE TMT Index** is compiled to reflect the performance of companies in the technology, media and telecommunications (TMT) sectors. In order to minimise the risk arising from concentration, exposure to individual large constituents, a tiering system is used.

TechMARK is a sector comprising businesses at the cutting edge of technological innovation. The **FTSE techMARK All-Share Index** includes all TechMARK companies that are in the FTSE All-Share Index. The top 100 of these shares make up the **FTSE techMARK 100 Index**. There is a **FTSE techMARK mediscience Index** including pharmaceutical, biotechnology and medical equipment and supplies companies.

FTSE4Good is a series of indices reflecting the performance of companies that pass certain ethical criteria. These indices are covered further in Chapter 14 of this Study Text.

6.11 US indices

Because of the large size of the US economy and because other world stock markets seem often to take their lead from the US markets, US stock market indices are widely monitored by investors throughout the world.

Dow Jones and Co publish four of the main indices in the US, the best known of which is the Dow Jones Industrial Average. It also produces indices relating to US bonds, transportation stocks and utilities.

The **Dow Jones Industrial Average (DJIA or 'the Dow')** is globally the best known of all share price indices. It was first calculated on 12 stocks in January 1897, but now contains 30 stocks, chosen by Dow Jones and the *Wall Street Journal*, which are designed to represent a balanced selection of **blue chips**. In recent years, the constituents have gradually been altered, to reflect the shift in the US economy away from traditional manufacturing towards computers and service industries.

The **Dow** is **price-weighted**, so a move in the share price of a company with relatively modest market capitalisation can have as great an influence on the day's price movements as a comparable move in the price of a large one. With the Dow, this factor is reduced by the selection of very large companies, and by the tendency for US companies to manage

7: EQUITIES AND DERIVATIVES

the nominal value of their shares to ensure market prices that fall into a roughly comparable range, between $30 and $100. The original base number was 100 and the index is calculated in real time.

Standard and Poor's (S&P) produce a range of indices covering a wide range of US securities, the most widely known of which is the **S&P 500**.

The **S&P 500 index** is a weighted, composite index covering 500 shares listed on the New York Stock Exchange. The shares represent some 80% of the total market capitalisation and, as such, are very representative of the US market. The index is seen globally as a broad indicator of the US equities market.

There are also important indices covering the technology-weighted NASDAQ: the **NASDAQ Composite Index** and the **NASDAQ 100 Index**.

6.12 Japan

The **Nikkei 225**, once known as the **Nikkei-Dow index**, is an index of shares on the Tokyo stock exchange and is published by Nihon Keizai Shimbun, Tokyo. Like the Dow-Jones Industrial Average, on which it was modelled, it is a **price-weighted index**. Movement in the share price of a small company may have as great an influence on the day's price movements as a comparable move in the price of a large one. With the **Nikkei**, this effect is heightened by the presence in the index of a number of traditional manufacturing firms, many of which are now considerably less important than they used to be.

The Tokyo authorities have, for some time, attempted to encourage global markets to look at other, broader, more modern indices weighted according to market capitalisation, such as the **TOPIX** and the **Nikkei 350**, but global attention still tends to focus on the **Nikkei 225**.

6.13 Other international indices

There are indices for market prices for various countries and regions of the world. There is daily coverage of many such indices in the *Financial Times*.

The **FTSE All-World Index** covers equity markets globally, covering over 2,000 stocks in 49 countries. For European markets overall, the **FTSE Eurotop 300** is a euro-denominated index covering the 300 largest stocks on major European stock markets and the **FTSE Eurobloc 100** index covers the most traded stocks in the **euro** zone.

In **France**, the **CAC 40 index** is the main real-time indicator, but is a subset of the **SBF-120 index**. The **SBF 120** is, in turn, a subset of the **SBF 250**, which has replaced the old **CAC General index.**

The **DAX 30 ('the DAX')** is the principal real-time share index for 30 major stocks in **Germany**. The **DAX** is a **total return index**, meaning that it measures the price movements of its constituents plus dividends paid to shareholders.

The **Hang Seng Index** covers a selection of Hong Kong equities.

7 Derivatives and warrants

Learning outcome

3.3.9 Derivatives – futures and options, main features and uses.

INVESTMENT AND RISK

7.1 Introduction

Derivatives are instruments based on the underlying assets such as bonds and ordinary shares which enable investors to reduce risk or enhance returns on these investments. They include **futures**, **options** and **contracts for differences (CFDs)**, and you should have some knowledge of these types of derivative.

Derivatives are often only thought of in terms of trying to boost **returns** but at the expense of increasing **risk**. However, derivatives can be used to reduce ('**hedge**') risk as well as to enhance returns.

We also look in this section at **warrants** and **covered warrants**. Warrants are similar in principle to options.

7.2 Futures

A **futures contract** involves an agreement between two parties to exchange a specified item at a specified price on a specified future date.

A futures contract can be a contract to buy or sell commodities, currencies, debt instruments or indices. Financial futures are traded on NYSE Liffe.

Futures contract are traded on an exchange with the contract terms clearly specified by the rules of the exchange. The first futures market was established in the nineteenth century, in Chicago. Futures based on the prices of agricultural commodities allow farmers to be sure of the profit they will receive from the commodities, months in advance of the commodities being produced.

The contracts are of a **standardised size**, with **standardised delivery dates**. This means that it may not be possible to match the exact exposure one requires over the exact period for which it is required. For example, a requirement to buy €950,000 using a currency future must be dealt with by buying 8 contracts, since the contract size is €125,000 (€950,000/€125,000 = 7.6, which is 8 contracts to the nearest whole number).

Futures are traded on **margin,** meaning that the trader only has to spend a small amount of money, far below the value of the underlying security, to be exposed to the price rise or fall of that security.

Participants in the futures markets may either be speculators, who are prepared to take risks in the hope that the market moves in their favour, or parties seeking to hedge risks – that is, to be more sure of the financial position they will be in, when the futures contract expires.

Stock index futures contracts are based on the value of an index. For these futures the gains or losses are determined by movements in the index. Managers can use futures to protect portfolios. For example, if the manager thinks the market will fall he can sell index futures. If the market does fall, the value of his portfolio will have fallen but he can offset this by the profit from the contract. He has protected himself from the fall, without having to sell securities in the portfolio directly.

We now look at an example of how this would work.

Example: Index futures

Index futures are quoted in index points which are multiplied by the index multiplier (in the case of the FTSE 100, £10 per index point). The value of a futures position is:

Number of contracts × Index multiplier × Index level

Suppose that a manager runs a portfolio of £15m. He believes the market will fall from its current index level of 6,000. He wishes to protect his portfolio, so he sells 250 contracts. That is:

250 × £10 × 6,000 = £15m

> If the market falls by 250 points the fund will receive:
>
> 250 × £10 × 250 = £625,000.
>
> So long as the underlying portfolio is invested mainly in FTSE stock, this profit should roughly mirror the loss in the value of the portfolio and so the situation has been hedged.

Note that, as with other types of futures, stock index futures are settled in cash not the physical delivery of the stock.

7.3 Options

An **option** provides its buyer with the right, but not the obligation, typically to buy or to sell a commodity, currency or security, at a set price (the exercise price) over a specified time period.

Options in commodity futures, options in share indices, currencies, bonds and equities are traded on NYSE Liffe. There are option contracts, with a series of exercise dates, in individual shares of leading UK companies, and in the FTSE 100 Index and the FTSE 250 Index.

In a similar way to an insurance contract, the option buyer pays a non-refundable amount (**premium**) to another party who takes the risk of a claim being made. The maximum that the option buyer can lose is the premium paid.

Payment of a premium is one **difference between options and futures**: there is no initial payment for a futures contract. Another difference is that an option need not be exercised: it confers a right but **not** an obligation. A future will run to delivery, or be closed beforehand.

Complex strategies are possible using options of different kinds and in different combinations, but basically there are two types of options:

- Calls
- Puts

The owner of a **call option** has the option to **buy** a particular commodity or security at a certain price in the future. Such an option could be purchased if the buyer takes the view that the price is going to rise.

> **Example: Call options**
>
> **November - XYZ plc (current share price 254)**
>
> | | January | April | July |
> | --- | --- | --- | --- |
> | 240 | 25 | 35 | 42 |
> | 260 | 14 | 24 | 31 |
> | 280 | 7 | 15 | 23 |
>
> The chart above indicates that an investor could purchase the April 260 call option for a cost of 24p per share. One option contract would then give him the right to purchase 1,000 shares at 260p at any time between the date of purchase and April.
>
> If the price rises to (say) 300p, the investor may **exercise** his option and then sell the shares into the market at a profit.
>
> His profit will be 300p – 260p – option premium of 24p = 16p per share.
>
> Alternatively, he could **sell** his option in the market. The option will be worth the difference between the market price and the option price = 40p per share. From this he must deduct his premium, so the net result is the same whichever course of action he takes.

INVESTMENT AND RISK

The owner of a **put option** has the option to sell a particular commodity or security at a specified price in the future. Such an option could be purchased if the buyer takes the view that prices are going to fall, or alternatively to protect a profit on an investment.

Below is an example of put option prices using the example of the same share as in the call option **Example** above.

Example: Put options

November - XYZ plc (current share price 254)

	January	April	July
240	6	10	12
260	14	18	20
280	27	29	30

In this example, if the investor thought the share price was likely to fall below 240 then he can purchase the put option April 240 for a premium of 10p per share. If the price does fall to say 200p then the investor can exercise the option and sell the shares to the writer of the option at 240p. If, on the other hand, the price of the share in April is 250p then the investor will not exercise the put option. He has lost his premium but has still protected his holding against further large price falls.

Note that every option involves payment of a premium even if the option is not exercised.

Note also that an option can be used to take a **speculative** position – in the hope of making a profit from prices movements – or as a **hedge** – when a position is taken contrary to a risk exposure that an investor has.

Writing a call or put. The party receiving the premium in an option contract is the writer of the contract. Sometimes it can be advantageous for an investor to be the writer of the option. **Writing a call** could be useful in a scenario when a stock should be held but it is unlikely that the share price will move much in the coming months.

Example: Writing options

Suppose that ABC plc shares are currently (in April) trading at 1000p, and that the investor could sell July 1050p call options at a premium of 35p per share. This creates an immediate return of 3.5% for three months. If the price remains static as predicted, the investor retains the premium. If the share price rises above 1050p, the investor must sell but he has his sale price of 1050p per share plus the 35p premium = 1085p per share.

In this case, the call is covered, ie the investor holds this stock. If he does not and the call is exercised, he may have to buy in stock at a high market price and could suffer a considerable loss.

If **writing a put**, the writer will not want the price to fall significantly. If it does, he must supply stock which will be at a loss. However, he will retain the premium.

There is trade in the various standardised **traded options** available themselves and these can be bought and sold on an exchange at any time. On the other hand, an **'over-the-counter (OTC) option'** or **'negotiated option'** is tailor-made by a financial institution for a particular client and will not be readily tradable.

An **American-style option** is one that can be exercised at any time up to expiry.

A **European-style option** can only be exercised on expiry.

7.4 Warrants

Similarly to share options, **warrants** confer the right of the holder to purchase a fixed number of shares at a specified price (the **strike price**) on a fixed date or dates. Warrants are a security rather than a separate class of share and are transferable (that is, they can be sold in the market).

Warrants give the holder no right to income: they only produce capital growth, and this is dependent on the price of the underlying share reaching the strike price at the expiry date when the warrants can be exercised. Where it does not, the warrants expire worthless. Because of this, they are high-risk investments.

7.5 Covered warrants

Covered warrants are a relatively recent innovation. These are warrants based on an underlying share or index which are issued by a financial institution rather than by the company itself. The warrant is called 'covered' because the issuing institution will hold the underlying asset, to cover its exposure.

Call warrants give a right to buy at a specified price within a specified time period, while **put** warrants give a right to sell at a specified price within a specified time period.

A call warrant may be purchased as a bet on the price of the underlying asset rising, while a put warrant may be bought as a bet on the price falling.

For example, suppose that the ordinary shares of X plc trade at 120p currently (at 15 June). An investor who believes the price will rise may be able to buy a call warrant to buy at 150p by, say, 30 September. This warrant might be priced at, say 5p for each share. If the X plc share price rises to 160p, the warrant can be excised for a profit in since 160p – 150p = 10p proceeds, compared with the cost of 5p. If the share price does not reach 150p by 30 September, the warrant will be worthless on expiry. Therefore, warrants are risky investments although, if the 'bet' is correct, significant profits can be earned due to the 'gearing' effect of warrants.

A put warrant to sell X plc at 100p by 30 September could be exercised if the share price of X plc falls below 100p. The profit on exercise will depend on how far below 100p the price falls, less the initial warrant cost.

Covered warrants can be sold on in the market before being exercised, in which case part of their value will be the **time value** attributable to the hope that the warrant can eventually be exercised at a profit.

Covered warrants have even been available for house price indices, as well as share prices and indices.

7.6 Contracts for difference

Along with futures and options, **Contracts For Difference (CFDs)** come under the FSA's definition of '**derivatives**'. CFDs are a relatively new type of contract and are offered by many companies which also offer **spread betting**. CFDs can often be purchased through the internet. It has been estimated that CFD trading in the UK now accounts for approximately 30% of all London equity trading.

CFDs are different from traditional **cash-traded** instruments (such as equities, bonds, commodities and currencies) in that they do not confer ownership of the underlying asset. Investors can take positions on the price of a great number of different instruments. Many of the companies offering CFDs offer contracts in thousands of UK, US, European and Far Eastern shares.

The price of the CFD tracks the price of the underlying asset, and so the holder of a CFD benefits, or loses, from the **price movement** in the stock, bond, currency, commodity or index etc. But the CFD holder does not take ownership of the underlying asset.

CFDs are **margin-traded**, meaning that the investor does not have to deposit the full value of the underlying asset with the CFD provider. Thus, an investor or fund manager can use CFDs to buy exposure to market movements using only a fraction of the capital they would require in the cash market. The investor then has a geared position relative to the capital deposited.

CFDs allow the investor to benefit from downward movements in a share or other price if they choose. This has the effect of adopting a position of '**short selling**' the stock. This flexibility, and the possibility of **margin trading**, means that CFDs can be used flexibly either for hedging or speculation.

To understand **how CFDs work**, it is helpful to consider how the company offering the CFD is able to pay an investor whose CFD has resulted in a price movement that is favourable for the investor. When a company offering CFDs sells a contract, it may seek to 'hedge' its own liability to pay out for price movements in the stock concerned by buying a matching quantity of the stock in the market. However, if the company has customers adopting long and short positions, these will in effect cancel each other out, and so the degree to which the company has to hedge will be reduced.

The costs of CFDs comprise a cost built into the **spread** of the CFD price, together with a **funding charge**.

7.7 Tax and gearing

Derivatives have the advantage that there is **no stamp duty** to pay, although the holder will be liable to **capital gains tax**.

Because of the possibility of adopting a **geared** exposure, investors should be cautious and only enter into contracts if they are fully aware of the possible consequences.

Key chapter points

- Equities are ordinary shares and the shares of companies listed on the Stock Exchange are usually easily tradable. Many people participate in equity investment through pooled investment schemes such as unit trusts, OEICs and investment trusts.

- Ordinary shares and preference shares differ in their dividend rights, in the rights they give over control of the company and in their priority of entitlement to assets on a liquidation.

- There are risks in holding shares: much or even all of the investor's capital might be lost. Diversification can help to reduce the risk, but equities are not suitable for all investors.

- Investors in equities usually hope for capital growth in the value of their shares and may also receive income in the form of dividends.

- Shares prices fluctuate continuously through Stock Exchange trading hours and reflect the supply and demand for the shares.

- Share prices are influenced my wider factors such as economic conditions and general investor sentiment as well as by specific factors relating to the particular company.

- Fundamental analysis is concerned with identifying underlying factors that indicate the strength of performance by a company. Investment ratios help in understanding and evaluating a company's shares as an investment.

- Ratios for similar companies can be compared and it may be possible to identify shares that are currently under-valued. Ratios can also help in identifying trends in a company's performance through time.

- Key UK share price indices are the FTSE 100 Index ('the Footsie') and the FTSE All-Share Index.

- The DJIA ('the Dow'), the S&P 500 and the NASDAQ indices are keenly watched barometers of the US market. The Nikkei 225 index covers the stock market of Japan, another important stock market.

- Futures and options are derivatives which allow various sophisticated investment and risk-hedging strategies to be implemented.

INVESTMENT AND RISK

Chapter Quiz

1. What can a public limited company (plc) do that a private limited company (Ltd) cannot do? .... (see para 1.3)
2. Outline the main features of the London Stock Exchange and AIM .... (1.3)
3. What are convertible preference shares? .... (1.2)
4. Identify the different elements in the cost of a direct investment in shares. .... (2.3)
5. List five factors affecting the supply and demand for shares. .... (4)
6. What is meant by the term 'fundamental analysis'? .... (4.11)
7. What are the two ways in which a company may grow? .... (4.12)
8. What is the relationship between earnings per share and the P/E ratio? .... (5.4)
9. What might a low P/E ratio indicate? .... (5.4)
10. How is dividend cover calculated? .... (5.6)
11. What does the NAV per share indicate? .... (5.8)
12. List five major UK share price indices. .... (6.2)
13. What is the difference between a price index and a total return index? .... (6.3)
14. Give examples of two major indices of prices on US stock markets. .... (6.11)
15. Define a futures contract. .... (7.2)
16. What is the difference between a call option and a put option? .... (7.3)
17. What is a covered warrant? .... (7.5)

chapter 8

Property

Chapter topic list

1	Investment in property	170
2	Residential property	173
3	Commercial property	177
4	Indirect investment in property	179
5	Appraisal	182
	Key chapter points	184
	Chapter quiz	185

INVESTMENT AND RISK

Chapter Learning Outcomes

3   **Understand** the following asset classes, their main features and suitability for different consumer circumstances.

   3.4   Property

   3.4.1   Characteristics of commercial and residential property investment – returns from rent and capital growth, supply and demand, risks, quality of tenants, occupancy levels, liquidity, depreciation, maintenance costs.

   3.4.2   Past performance – differences between commercial and residential property (buy to let), key determinants of past investment returns, volatility, income and capital returns.

   3.4.3   Borrowing – its effect on risk and returns.

   3.4.4   Transaction costs – commissions, fees and Stamp Duty Land Tax.

   3.4.5   Taxation issues – taxation of rental income, interest relief, Capital Gains Tax.

   3.4.6   Indirect property investment vehicles – unit trusts/OEICs, property shares, life assurance property bonds, offshore funds, Real Estate Investment Trusts (REITs).

1 Investment in property

Learning outcome

3.4.1   Characteristics of commercial and residential property investment

- Supply and demand.
- Risks.
- Quality of tenants.
- Occupancy levels.
- Liquidity.
- Depreciation.
- Maintenance costs.

3.4.2   Past performance – differences between commercial and residential property (buy-to-let), key determinants of past investment returns, volatility, income and capital returns.

3.4.3   Borrowing – its effect on risk and returns.

3.4.4   Transaction costs – commissions, fees and Stamp Duty Land Tax.

1.1 Property markets

The UK has a relatively high level of **owner-occupation** of **residential property**. Home ownership has been promoted by tax incentives, including exemption from capital gains tax for the taxpayer's own principal private residence.

The rented sector has seen the rise of '**buy-to-let**' ownership of property by many new private landlords during the 1990s and early 2000s. More easily obtainable mortgage finance for buy-to-let and rising house prices have fuelled the buy-to-let boom. By 2003, almost 5% of total mortgages outstanding were buy-to-let loans, up from under 1% five years earlier. The expansion in buy-to-let could make residential property values more volatile, as buy-to-let landlords may be more likely sellers than owner-occupiers in a housing market downturn.

The market in **commercial property** – retail, offices and industrial units – has tended in the past to be dominated by investment by insurance companies and pension funds. These institutions may act as property developer and, once the property is built, the landlord. More recently, more private investors have been making direct investment in commercial property. Some have made investments via Self-Invested Personal Pension Plans (SIPPs).

Commercial property is typically let on **long leases**. In the past this could be as long as 99 years. Now it is likely to be a maximum of 25 years, with three or five year rent reviews. **Factories and warehouses** tend to produce the highest yields in the property sector and shops typically produce the lowest yields.

The value of commercial property is generally assessed as a **multiple** of the rental income. For example, a property might be purchased at 18 years multiple of the rent. The owner of the property obviously hopes that the rental income from his property will increase. A property price set at a high multiple may reflect expectations of strong future rental growth.

1.2 Gearing of property investments

Given their substantial size and the fact that a lender can usually be given security in the form of a legal charge on the property, property investments are often made with help from borrowed funds. That is, the investment is **'geared'**.

The **gearing effect** of borrowing for property purchase can be severe if prices start to fall, and **negative equity** can even result in some cases where the loan is a high percentage of the property value.

Example: Effect of house price falls

An investor obtains a mortgage of £80,000 and pays £20,000 of her own money to buy a property for £100,000.

The investor then has equity of £20,000 in the property.

Interest rates rise and prices in the local property market fall by 10%.

If the investor wishes to sell, the price will be around £90,000.

Ignoring the original purchase costs and the selling costs, and loan capital repayments, the investor will have £10,000 after repaying the loan of £80,000. Her equity has fallen by 50% from the original £20,000 investment.

1.3 Long-term returns

Research shows that, over the long run, investment in property has provided real returns ahead of the returns on cash and gilts and slightly below that of equities. The annualised return for **commercial property** was 11.6% over the 30-year period to the end of 2001 (IPD estimates). Returns from equities were 13.5% over the same period. The commercial property market has undergone 'crashes' from time to time: between 1989 and 1992, following a period of significant levels of speculative development in London, some office rent levels halved. Property yields are currently looking attractive on income grounds relative to the low yields from government bonds.

The **residential property** market tends to move in cycles different from those of the commercial property market, and it is influenced by economic factors such as disposable incomes and interest rates. A major slump in the residential market followed substantial rises in interest rates in the years following 1989. A shortage of building land and planning restrictions contributes to rising prices in some areas, particularly the South of England.

In early 2007, many commentators believed that residential property was significantly over-valued in the market, and that a correction is likely at some stage. The credit crunch that arose in late 2007 has resulted in significant falls in the value of residential property and some commentators now consider it overvalued. Over the long run, a fairly stable relationship between real incomes and house prices can be expected: this implies that, as the economy grows, positive long-term real returns are likely. Over shorter periods, expectations and buyer psychology play a part: a widespread

INVESTMENT AND RISK

belief that property prices will continue to rise can become a self-fulfilling prophecy over shorter-term periods as buyers pile in to the market.

1.4 Advantages of property ownership

There are various **advantages** in owning **residential property**.

1. **Security** – Many investors participate in residential property ownership by owning the home in which they live. One of the attractions of **owner-occupation** is psychological: most owner-occupiers like the security of a permanent home they own, even if it is subject to a mortgage.

2. **Capital appreciation** – Over the long term, UK residential and commercial property values have out-stripped general price inflation, although the property market is susceptible to cyclical fluctuations.

3. **Income generation** – If for some reason the owner cannot live in a residential property for a period, for example when working abroad, the property can be let and used to create an income. Similarly, if a client owns a holiday home, this can be let for part of the year. The rental income will, hopefully, offset general running expenses.

4. **Income stream** – Tenants in property must continue to pay their rent even if they are unemployed (residential) or making trading losses (commercial). This characteristic of the **rental income stream** is more like that from fixed interest securities than from shares (equities). This insulates the landlord from some cyclical economic changes, provided the property does not fall vacant.

5. **Increasing income** – Property can produce an **increasing rental income** if good tenants can be found and maintained and no capital values rise.

6. **Buy-to-let** – 'Buy-to-let' investment – discussed further below – offers the prospect of rental yield plus a potential capital gain.

7. **Collateral** – Residential property can be used as collateral security for a loan or mortgage. This borrowing capacity is more easily available on property than on many other assets.

8. **Diversification** – Including property as an asset class provides diversification for the investor who also has investments in other asset classes such as fixed interest securities, equities and different property classes. The **capital value** of commercial property does not follow the residential property market.

9. **Downsizing** – It is possible to use a property as part of an investor's retirement fund. He or she can decide to sell a large house, moving to a smaller one on retirement and using the surplus funds to invest and create income.

1.5 Disadvantages of property ownership

Disadvantages include the following.

1. **Lack of liquidity** – One of the main disadvantages of owning property is its lack of **liquidity**. The property can only be sold if a buyer can be found.

2. **Indivisibility** – Properties must usually be **purchased as a whole**. Because there are relatively few property sales and the sums involved are usually large, property can be difficult to research as an investment area.

3. **Investment scales** – **Diversification** into different properties in different areas will only be possible for a portfolio of substantial value.

8: PROPERTY

4   **Transaction costs** – As well as agents' and legal costs, purchases of property are subject to stamp duty land tax. Taken together and depending on the purchase price, these costs may add up to several percentage points to the cost of a purchase.

5   **Time** – Often the sale of a property can be protracted and the vendor may be incurring expenses during this period.

6   **Maintenance costs/depreciation** – Property naturally deteriorates or depreciates over time and the costs of maintaining a property investment are significantly higher than for other asset classes such as shares or bonds.

7   **Management costs** – Property can be **expensive to manage**. The buildings have to be kept up to a high standard if suitable tenants are to be found and retained. The owner will have the expense of an agent who will be in charge of the day-to-day running of the property and finding and vetting suitable tenants. Other professional advisers will need to be employed from time to time such as surveyors and lawyers to draw up suitable leases and contracts.

8   **Slumps** – From time to time, there will be **slumps** in the property market and these may be protracted.

9   **Quality of tenants** – If a property is leased out, there may be times when a suitable tenant cannot be found. In addition there are charges involved in letting property. A letting agent may be needed to vet suitable tenants, collect rents and oversee the upkeep of the property.

10 **Occupancy levels** – Occupancy levels can never be guaranteed and if it is unoccupied (a **void period**) maintenance costs will be incurred but no income generated to cover them rendering the investment a drain on income rather than a source.

2 Residential property

Learning outcomes

3.4.1 Characteristics of commercial and residential property investment.

- Supply and demand.
- Risks.
- Quality of tenants.
- Occupancy levels.
- Liquidity.
- Depreciation.
- Maintenance costs.

3.4.4 Transaction costs – commissions, fees and Stamp Duty Land Tax.

3.4.5 Taxation issues – taxation of rental income, interest relief, Capital Gains Tax..

2.1 Tax position: income

Profits from renting out property are treated as earned income for tax purposes.

- This will be taxed at the taxpayer's marginal rate of 20%, 40% or 50%.
- Each tax year's profit is taxed in that tax year.
- Mortgage interest on the property being let counts as a deductible expense to set against the letting income.

- Other costs are also deductible, including maintenance costs, 10% wear and tear allowance or costs of replacing furniture, fixtures and fittings, estate agent's commission and management expenses, but not improvement expenditure.

Landlords energy saving allowance. Landlords qualify for an income tax deduction of up to **£1,500 per building** when they install **loft or cavity wall insulation, draught-proofing or hot water system insulation** in a dwelling which they let.

If the landlord is **non-UK resident**, the tenant or letting agent is required to deduct basic rate tax from the property income before remitting rent to the landlord. A landlord may however apply to HMRC to come within the self assessment regime, in order to be permitted to receive gross payments of rent.

If the investor owns **furnished holiday accommodation** which is let out on a frequent basis (at least 70 days in a 12 month period) he may, if he satisfies the following criteria, be able to treat the letting **as a trade**. In this case be may obtain other reliefs and allowances.

- The property must be situated in the UK.
- The property must be run on a commercial basis.
- The property must be furnished.
- The property must be available to let for not less than 140 days per fiscal year.
- The property must not normally be occupied by the same person/people for more than 31 days for at least seven months within a twelve-month period.

2.2 Tax position: capital gains

If a house is the investor's **principal private residence**, the sale of the property will be exempt from **capital gains tax (CGT)**. If not, gains will be subject to CGT.

2.3 Stamp duty land tax on residential property

Stamp duty land tax (SDLT) is a form of tax payable on buying property, and is charged on the purchase consideration (price) of **residential property** at the rates set out below (**2010/11**). The tax is rounded up to the next multiple of £5.

Consideration	Rate
Up to £125,000 (£150,000 in Disadvantaged Areas)*	Nil
£125,001* – £250,000 (£150,001 – £250,000 in Disadvantaged Areas)	1%
£250,001 – £500,000	3%
£500,001 +	4%

*A first time buyer's threshold of £250,000 applies from 25 March 2010 until 24 March 2012. Above this value the tax is as for other buyers.

No SDLT is chargeable for transfers on divorce or for transfers to charities if the land is to be used for charitable purposes.

2.4 Letting part of a home

If an individual lets a room or rooms in his or her **main residence** as **furnished living accommodation**, then a special tax exemption called the **rent a room scheme** may apply.

The limit on the exemption is gross rents (before any expenses or capital allowances) of £4,250 per year (2010/11). This limit is halved if any other person (including the first person's spouse) also received income from renting accommodation in the property while the property was the first person's main residence.

If gross rents (plus balancing charges arising because of capital allowances in earlier years) are not more than the limit, the rents (and balancing charges) are wholly exempt from income tax and expenses and capital allowances are ignored. However, the taxpayer may claim to ignore the exemption, for example to generate a loss by taking into account both rent and expenses.

If gross rents exceed the limit, the taxpayer will be taxed in the ordinary way, ignoring the rent a room scheme, unless he elects for the 'alternative basis'. If he so elects, he will be taxable on gross receipts plus balancing charges less £4,250 (or £2,125 if the limit is halved) with no deductions for expenses or capital allowances.

An election to ignore the exemption or an election for the alternative basis must be made by the 31 January which is nearly two years from the end of the tax year concerned. An election to ignore the exemption applies only for the tax year for which it is made, but an election for the alternative basis remains in force until it is withdrawn or until a year in which gross rents do not exceed the limit.

2.5 Buy-to-let

Introduction

Buy to let refers to the purchase of property – usually residential property purchased by individuals – with the purpose of letting it.

Various lenders are prepared to grant **mortgages** to 'buy to let' purchasers, typically requiring the purchaser to provide, say, 20 per cent of the capital required for the purchase. The lender may base the size of the loan on expected rents.

The letting may be **managed** by **letting agents**, who will generally take a percentage of the rent as their fees. If agents are not used, the 'buy to let' investor must be prepared to devote part of their own time to managing the tenancy and dealing with tenants, repairs and so on. This commitment is likely to require the investor to live reasonably close to the property.

As already mentioned, rental income will be taxed at the taxpayer's marginal rate of tax (10%, 20%, 40% or 50%). Deductions against tax on rents received may be claimed for the interest on loans (mortgages) to buy or improve the property, and costs of maintenance, such as insurance, cleaning, gardening, agent's commission and other reasonable management expenses (but not the capital cost of improvements).

For property let furnished, the initial cost of furniture, fittings and fixtures is not allowable, but the actual cost of subsequent **replacement** may be claimed; alternatively, a **wear and tear allowance** of 10% of rents received may be claimed.

A gain on eventual disposal of a property that is not the taxpayer's principal private residence is liable to **capital gains tax**. The base cost will be the cost of acquisition plus subsequent improvement expenditure that has not been allowed for tax.

Some **void periods** when no rent is received must be expected. These occur between tenancies, or when a tenant does not pay rent. Landlords are protected by the law but enforcement could involve instructing a solicitor, adding to costs.

Factors in choosing a property

As with other investments, the choice of a residential property to purchase needs some consideration.

A **location** in which there will be a **plentiful supply of good tenants** for the type of property being purchased may be different from the favoured locations for owner-occupied property. Major cities usually have a steady demand of tenants, whether from college students, young working adults or temporary visitors to the city.

INVESTMENT AND RISK

Over-supply of rental properties affects some areas where 'buy to let' investments are common. To avoid areas of over-supply, local knowledge can be acquired, for example by talking with local residents or estate agents and checking on the supply of property 'to let' boards or on local newspaper advertising.

Some locations will attract **higher rental yields**, for example areas where rental property is in relatively short supply.

Location will also be important when an investor considers the eventual sale of the property. Most investors will be looking for prospective **capital growth** as well as yield, and may judge some areas to be more likely to produce such growth than others.

The **age and condition of the property** can greatly affect the work and expense involved in maintaining it. Newer properties needing less maintenance can be particularly attractive to 'buy to let' investors.

Diversification

As with other types of investment, the 'buy to let' investor should consider the extent to which **diversification** could reduce risks. In the case of residential property, diversification is possible for an investor with multiple properties. Such an investor might spread properties owned across a range of areas and property types, in order to reduce risks from void periods and local changes. However, maintaining properties in different areas may increase management costs.

Capital growth

Because the UK has a relatively high proportion of **owner-occupiers**, it is this sector that has the greatest influence on prices. Over the longer term, it has been found that property prices have risen in line with growth in average incomes, and have therefore tended to exceed general price inflation.

A shortage of building land and planning restrictions also contribute to rising prices in some areas, particularly the South of England.

In mid-2008, house prices underwent a correction, prices having fallen across the year.

The **gearing effect** of borrowing for house purchase can be severe if prices start to fall, and **negative equity** could result, particularly if the loan is a high percentage of the property value.

Example: Effect of house price falls

An investor obtains a mortgage of £80,000 and pays £20,000 of her own money to buy a property for £100,000.

The investor then has equity of £20,000 in the property.

Interest rates rise and prices in the local property market fall by 10%.

If the investor wishes to sell, the price will be around £90,000.

Ignoring the original purchase costs and the selling costs, and loan capital repayments, the investor will have £10,000 after repaying the loan of £80,000. Her equity has fallen by 50% from the original £20,000 investment.

Tenure

'Buy to let' investors should let properties under **assured shorthold tenancies**, which were introduced under the Housing Act in 1988. Before that, the Rent Acts had controlled rent levels and had restricted the freedom of landlords to re-possess properties.

Assured shorthold tenancies are typically for twelve months or more, but they can now be of any length. Such tenancies give the landlord the right to re-possess the property at the end of the period if he does not wish to renew the agreement.

For an assured shorthold tenancy:

- The tenant must be an individual
- The dwelling must be let as separate accommodation, and
- The dwelling must be the tenant's main or principal home

Tenancies that do not qualify as assured shorthold tenancies will generally be **'common law'** or **contractual** tenancies.

Advantages of buy-to-let

'Buy to let' schemes became popular in the late 1990s, mainly because of:

- Rising property values
- Readily available funds from lenders, with 'buy to let' mortgages being specifically marketed

With 'buy to let' investments:

- For a relatively small capital outlay, the investor can gain exposure to housing market gains
- As well as any capital gain, rents are earned to produce a yield and will offset interest costs

Disadvantages of buy-to-let

Disadvantages include the following.

- In areas of weak housing demand or over-supply, properties may be **vacant** for long periods.
- If house prices fall, losses may be suffered. The **gearing effect** of **borrowing** to finance the investment will amplify the effect of losses on the investor's equity.
- It may take some **time to sell** property in order to realise the value of the investment.
- **Transaction costs** are significant, including legal costs, stamp duty land tax payable on purchase, plus estate agents' costs usually payable on sale.
- **Capital gains** are liable to be taxed. Unlike the case with a portfolio of shares, it is not usually feasible to sell part of a property in order to take advantage of the annual capital gains tax exemption.

3 Commercial property

Learning outcomes

3.4.1 Characteristics of commercial and residential property investment.

- Supply and demand.
- Risks.
- Quality of tenants.
- Occupancy levels.
- Liquidity.
- Depreciation.
- Maintenance costs.

3.4.4 Transaction costs – commissions, fees and Stamp Duty Land Tax.

3.4.5 Taxation issues – taxation of rental income, interest relief, Capital Gains Tax.

INVESTMENT AND RISK

3.1 The commercial property market

Much of the **commercial property** in the UK is the property of large institutions such as insurance companies and pension funds. These institutions may act as property developer and, once the property is built, the landlord. However, an **individual investor** may also purchase or own commercial property units. Although not as widespread as 'buy to let' investment in residential property, investment in commercial property has become increasingly popular among private investors in recent years.

Commercial property is of three main types:

- Retail (shops and stores)
- Office buildings
- Industrial factories and warehouses

Commercial property is typically let on **long leases**. In the past, these could be as long as 99 years. Now, a lease is likely to be a maximum of 25 years, with three or five year rent reviews.

Factories and warehouses tend to produce the highest yields in the property sector and shops typically produce the lowest yields.

A number of the leading estate agents in the UK produce **indices** of the movement in rental and capital values of commercial property. There is also an index produced by Investment Property Databank (IPD). This organisation monitors the performance of commercial properties owned by the large institutions.

The value of commercial property is normally calculated as a **multiple** of the rental income. For example, a property might be purchased at 18 years multiple of the rent. The owner of the property obviously hopes that the rental income from his property will increase. A property price set at a high multiple may reflect expectations of strong future rental growth.

Commercial property tends to follow a **cyclical pattern**, often opposing to the performance of equities (shares). The recent low yields on fixed interest securities such as gilts have made the higher yields available in commercial property more attractive.

3.2 Tax position: income

As for residential property, **rents** constitute taxable profits, which are computed for tax years and are taxed at the taxpayer's marginal rate of tax. Each tax year's profit is taxed in that year.

Rent for furniture supplied with premises is taxed as part of the rent for the premises, unless there is a separate trade of renting furniture.

Mortgage interest on the property being let will be as a deductible expense to set against the letting income.

For a **non-UK resident** landlord, the tenant or letting agent must deduct basic rate tax from the rent, unless the landlord has arranged with the HMRC to receive rent gross.

3.3 Tax position: capital gains

As for residential property, gains on disposal of commercial property will come under the **CGT** rules.

3.4 Stamp duty land tax on commercial property

Stamp duty land tax (SDLT) is charged on the purchase consideration (price) of **non-residential property** at the rates set out below. (For non-residential property, the Nil rate threshold is set at £150,000 instead of the £125,000 threshold that applies to residential property, but the rates are otherwise the same.)

The **2010/11** rates shown below apply whether or not the commercial property is in a designated **Disadvantaged Area**.

Consideration	Rate
Up to £150,000	Nil
£150,001 – £250,000	1%
£250,001 – £500,000	3%
£500,001 +	4%

The tax is rounded up to the next multiple of £5.

4 Indirect investment in property

Learning outcome

3.4.6 Indirect property investment vehicles – unit trusts/OEICs, property shares, life assurance property bonds, offshore funds, Real Estate Investment Trusts (REITs).

4.1 Property shares

If a client wants an exposure to property but does not have sufficient capital to purchase a property, he may buy shares in **companies that own or develop properties**.

A company that holds properties over the medium or long term is likely to have a steady income from rents paid. A development company makes much of its return from profits on sale, and so earnings may fluctuate from time to time.

A property company can diversify by holding many properties, and the shareholder gains the benefit of that diversification in lower risk as compared with owning one or two properties.

For information on the performance of property shares, the investor can refer to the property sub-index of the FT-SE Actuaries indices. The investor should be aware that the prices of property shares tend to be more volatile than the actual property values.

The price of the shares will move with supply and demand, and may diverge from **underlying asset values**. **Gearing** (borrowing) by the company can increase the share price volatility.

The share price can be affected by **systematic** factors affecting the stock market as a whole, as well as factors specific to the company or the property sector.

Compared with direct investment in property, a significant advantage of this means of investing in property is **liquidity**. The investor can realise his investment in a listed property company easily through a stockbroker, since there are market makers who must quote prices for all listed stocks.

4.2 Property unit trusts and OEICs

Originally, **unit trusts** were prohibited from directly investing in property and could only invest indirectly via property shares. This has now changed and unit trust and Open Ended Investment Company (**OEIC**) managers can invest directly into commercial property. At the launch of such a fund, the manager must be confident that he will attract sufficient funds to make adequate property purchases to establish a well spread portfolio.

There are however restrictions on the proportion of the fund that can be invested in leases with less than 60 years to run, or in unoccupied property. There are also restrictions on holding mortgaged property, which limit gearing. No more than 15% in value of the fund assets can be invested in a single property.

INVESTMENT AND RISK

Additionally, there are unit trusts and OEICs that invest in **property company shares**.

As with unit trusts and OEICs generally, the investment will be redeemed at net asset value. However, if many investors choose to sell at one time, the unit trust or OEIC may need to invoke its right to postpone encashment of units/shares until property can be sold. This possible restriction in **accessibility** makes property funds potentially less liquid.

As for all unit trusts, OEICs and investment trusts, there is no capital gains tax within the fund, but investors are subject to capital gains tax on gains when they sell the units or shares.

4.3 Property investment trusts

Property investment trusts are pooled investments but are only permitted to invest in shares and securities of property companies, not in property directly. They are permitted to borrow, which increases the risk for the investor, as well as the possible return.

The share price of the trust will fluctuate with supply and demand for the shares of the trust, and may be at a discount or a premium to the net asset value.

4.4 Real Estate Investment Trusts (REITs)

Real Estate Investment Trusts (REITs) are **'tax-transparent' property investment vehicles** which were first formed in the USA, where the name 'REITs' originated. Other countries, including Japan, the Netherlands and France, now have their own versions of **REITs**. The UK introduced its own version of REITs from **1 January 2007**.

Tax-transparent property investment vehicles, such as REITs, distribute nearly all of their taxable income to investors. Provided they do this, the vehicles are granted exemption from capital gains tax and from corporate taxes. Investors pay tax on the dividends and capital growth at their own marginal tax rates, thus avoiding the double taxation that would otherwise affect investors in UK property companies.

In order to qualify as a REIT a company will need to meet certain conditions. The key features are:

- The company must be a UK resident, closed-ended company listed on a recognised stock exchange (which means the main market and does not include AIM).
- The shares in the company must not be closely held, which means that no one person (individual or corporate) should hold more than 10% of the shares.
- The property letting business, which will be tax exempt, must be effectively ring-fenced from any other activities and should comprise of at least 75% of the overall company, with regard to both its assets and its total income.
- A minimum of 90% of the UK-REIT's profits from the ring-fenced letting business must be distributed to investors.
- The UK-REIT will be required to withhold basic rate tax on the distribution of profits paid to investors.
- The distributions are taxed as property income at the holder's marginal rate.
- The company will be subject to an interest-cover test on the ring-fenced part of its business, a measure of the affordability of any loans.
- Other distributions will be taxed in the same way as normal dividends.
- The ratio of interest on loans to fund the tax-exempt property business to rental income must be less than 1.25 : 1.

It is possible to hold REITs within **ISAs** and **Child Trust Funds**.

UK **property companies** are able to choose to **convert** to become REITs. The conversion charge for companies wishing to become REITs in the UK is 2% of the market value of the properties concerned. The charge can be spread in instalments (0.5%; 0.53%; 0.56%; 0.6%) over four years.

4.5 Enterprise Zone property

Expenditure on industrial and commercial buildings in an **Enterprise Zone** qualifies as 100% deduction against the investor's income. The investor can make a direct investment or via a unit trust. The advantage of the unit trust is a lower initial investment and a spread of properties. Nevertheless there is typically a high risk within the fund. An individual who invests in such a unit trust is treated as if he has incurred a proportion of the trust's expenditure on enterprise zone property and he will qualify for industrial buildings allowances. These allowances can be set against other income for tax purposes.

4.6 Insurance company property funds/property bonds

Life insurance companies have funds that invest specifically in commercial property. An investor can choose regular premium or single premium investment plans (which may be termed '**life assurance property bonds**').

The value of units is directly linked to the net asset values of the properties held. The fund is not permitted to borrow.

Although these funds are more liquid than direct investments in property, the fund retains a rarely invoked right to postpone encashment of units if necessary. This could be necessary if many investors wish to encash units at a particular time, necessitating the sale of properties – a process than could take some time.

Income and capital gains are subject to tax within the fund at 20%. This cannot be reclaimed by non-taxpayers and higher rate tax payers will pay additional tax.

4.7 Limited liability partnerships

A limited liability partnership is a form of unincorporated business. One of the major differences between a company and a partnership is the legal ownership of the business assets and the related tax consequences.

In a company, the company legally owns the business assets, not the shareholders – the shareholders simply benefit from and are taxed on any dividends paid out and any gains realised from share price movements.

In a partnership, the partners do legally own the business assets. For example, in a partnership with two equal partners, each legally owns half of the business assets and is taxed directly on any income and gains generated from those assets.

This tax-transparent structure of the limited partnership makes it an attractive vehicle for institutional investors, such as pension funds or insurance companies, which are partially or wholly tax-exempt. It enables them to invest jointly with tax-paying entities, such as property companies, without losing their tax advantages.

4.8 Offshore property funds

Many UK investment managers now operate **offshore property trusts**, for example in Guernsey.

These trusts are **closed-ended**, meaning that, as with conventional investment trusts, new shares are not created or cancelled when investors buy or sell. These stocks are relatively high-yielding and have proved attractive to many retail and institutional investors over recent years, when many investors have sought to reduce their exposure to equities.

Because the trusts are registered offshore and are not subject to UK tax, they can pay out dividends that are close to the underlying yield on UK commercial property, with the tax liability depending upon the tax status of the investor.

INVESTMENT AND RISK

These funds are very similar to **REITs**. Many trade at a premium to the net asset value of the underlying investments. Onshore (ie, UK) property companies have, in contrast, often traded at a discount to NAV, partly because of the unfavourable tax structure existing before 1 January 2007, the date of introduction of REITs in the UK.

Unauthorised Property Unit Trusts

There are a number of unauthorised property unit trusts that have been set up to allow tax-exempt pension funds to take a stake in a diversified property portfolio. The funds are tax exempt both in terms of capital gains and income tax, though the allocation of their units is strictly limited to investors with similar tax exemptions.

The main disadvantages of such funds is the lack of flexibility in making withdrawals, particularly on a substantial scale. This problem arises as a result of the difficulty in selling any underlying assets to finance such a substantial withdrawal.

4.9 Advantages of pooled property investments

- The investor is 'buying' expert property management.
- The investor can buy into a large well spread fund. This can be spread according to type, eg office, warehousing, retail and geographically, with reduced risk because of this diversification.
- Although there is some illiquidity in the pooled finds, particularly in the property fund and the Enterprise Zone schemes, liquidity is greater than with direct investment.
- A relatively small amount of money can be invested in a pooled fund. A substantial sum would need to be committed to the purchase of even a modest commercial property.

4.10 Disadvantages of pooled property investments

- The investor does not have direct control over the properties.
- It may be difficult to realise capital quickly particularly from a property bond or Enterprise Zone scheme.
- The Enterprise Zone schemes are illiquid and high risk.

5 Appraisal

Learning outcome

3.4.1 Characteristics of commercial and residential property investment.
- Returns from rent and capital growth.

The **rental yield** from a property investment can be calculated as:

$$\text{Rental yield} = \frac{\text{Gross rent} - \text{Expenses}}{\text{Cost of property, including Buying costs}}$$

Gross rent should be adjusted by excluding estimated **void periods**, which can generally only be estimated if we want to calculate the yield for a future period.

Expenses will include agents' charges, buildings insurance (and contents insurance, if furnished) and the cost of renewals of furnishings and appliances. Total expenses could be estimated at 20% or 25% of the gross rent.

Buying costs include legal fees, the cost of surveys or valuation, stamp duty land tax and the initial cost of furnishings. Agent's fees might be incurred on the transaction if an agent has been employed to search for the property, but usually only the seller incurs agent's fees.

Note that the costs of loan interest have not been included in 'expenses'. The rental yield measures the rent after expenses as a proportion of the capital cost of the investment. The rental yield income can be compared with the rate that the investor is paying for a loan to purchase the property.

Example: Rental yield

A house is divided into two flats, each of which is expected to be rented for £480 per complete month. Void periods are expected for 10% of the time of ownership. The house was purchased for £180,000, excluding stamp duty land tax. Other purchase costs were £1,200. Agent's expenses will be charged at 15% of the gross rent and further expenses are estimated at 5% of the gross rent.

What is the rental yield?

Gross rent, excluding void periods = £480 × 12 months × 2 flats × 90% = £10,368.

Adjusting for expenses: £10,368 × 80% = £8,294.

$$\text{Rental yield} = \frac{£8,294}{£180,000 + £1,800 + £1,200}$$

$$= \frac{£8,294}{£183,000} = 4.5\%$$

'Buy to let' investors might typically hope for a rental yield of around 5% to 8%. However, typical yields will vary beyond this range, depending on the housing and rental market in the area.

Key chapter points

- 'Buy to let' is a form of direct investment in residential property. Returns can vary widely between different regions and at different times.
- Properties should be selected with care. All costs and possible void periods should be fully evaluated.
- Most 'buy to let' investors hope for capital gains, but gearing means that a downturn in the market could affect equity severely.
- Commercial property forms a different market and some exposure may be considered by investors seeking to diversify across various asset classes.
- Indirect or pooled investment in property allows relatively small sums to be invested in a diversified portfolio of properties, and there is much more liquidity than with direct investment.
- The date of introduction of REITs – Real Estate Investment Trusts – in the UK is 1 January 2007. REITs enjoy exemption from tax on income and gains from property. REIT distributions will be paid net of tax at 20%. REITs are eligible for inclusion in ISAs and CTFs.

Chapter Quiz

1. What is the main tax consequence of a house being an owner-occupier's principal private residence? .... (see para 2.2)
2. What are the alternative ways in which deductions can be made against tax for furnishings in a rental property? .... (2.4)
3. What form of tenancy should a 'buy to let' investor normally offer to tenants? .... (2.5)
4. How is rental yield calculated? .... (5)
5. What is meant by a 'multiple' in the context of commercial property? .... (3.1)
6. What is a 'void period'? .... (2.5)
7. What is the limit above which stamp duty land tax is charged on a purchase of commercial property? .... (3.4)
8. What is a 'REIT'? Outline the current position regarding such investment vehicles in the UK. .... (4.4)

Chapter 9

Chapter topic list

1	Commodities	188
2	Collectibles	190
	Key chapter points	192
	Chapter quiz	193

Commodities and Alternative Investments

INVESTMENT AND RISK

Chapter Learning Outcomes

10 **Understand** how other issues affect investment planning.

   10.5   Alternative investments (gold, art, antiques), commodities, alternative energy.

1 Commodities

Learning outcome

10.5   Alternative investments (gold, art, antiques), commodities and alternative energy.

1.1 Introduction

Commodities for investment purposes are essentially raw materials that can be bought and sold easily in large quantities on organised markets. They fall into one of three categories.

- **Energy commodities**: oil, natural gas, coal
- **Hard commodities**: metals (gold, copper, lead, tin, etc.) and diamonds.
- **Soft commodities**: mostly foodstuffs, such as cocoa, coffee, soya, sugar, etc.

The prices of these commodities are, as for all assets, driven by the influences of supply and demand and can, therefore, be significantly affected by factors such as

- Good/poor harvests;
- Exceptionally good/bad weather;
- Political unrest in the producing country.

As a result, commodities have the following general characteristics

- They generally produce no income
- Values can change dramatically in response to economic change, natural disasters and other economic shocks
- Commodities may be expensive to store and may be subject to deterioration over time

In relations to the second of these points, natural disasters and other economic shocks often lead to a shortage of supply in essential commodities, leading to significant price rises. Commodities can therefore, be viewed as a hedge against such events.

Investors can buy and sell commodities in two ways.

1.1.1 Cash market

Trade on the cash market is for immediate delivery, known as trading **physicals** or **actuals**, with the price paid being the **spot price**. Payment must be made immediately and charges are made for storage and insurance. There is a standard contract size, 25 tonnes for copper for example, to aid the smooth running of the market.

1.1.2 Futures market

Trade on the futures market is for delivery at an agreed future price at an agreed future date. There are rules about how far in advance such futures contracts can be arranged (up to three months for copper for example). The advantages of dealing in futures are the absence of storage costs and the effect of gearing – only a small margin being required to gain exposure to a large asset value.

1.2 Investment in commodities

1.2.1 Direct investment

Physicals

An investor can buy and sell commodities directly through a commodity broker, or invest in a commodities fund. Dealing in physical commodities is not a practical proposition for most investors because of the minimum quantities that must be traded and the risk of deterioration in quality. The cash market is primarily for users of that raw material/agricultural product, rather than the investor.

For non-deteriorating commodities such as metals, however, it is possible and practical to take a direct holding in the commodity, which will be stored in a London Metal Exchange (LME) approved warehouse. The investor should consider the storage costs, etc. involved with this option.

Futures

Futures do, however, provide a useful investment vehicle for the purposes of diversifying and hedging as we discuss in the section on futures and options.

Advantages of direct investment

Direct investment offers the following advantages over indirect investment.

- Commodity consumers will want to be able to acquire the commodity possibly in advance of needing it if prices are favourable.
- There will be lower risks (counterparty risk, political risk).

1.2.2 Indirect investment

Shares of commodity companies

One approach to indirect investment would be to acquire shares in a commodity producing company, eg mines. As commodity prices rise, we could anticipate that the company's revenue, and correspondingly, the share price will rise. The extent of this relationship, however, also depends on how the costs may fluctuate.

Although all producers will face the same selling price, they will not all face the same cost pressures and hence, though we may expect share prices to move with the underlying commodity prices, the correlation will not be perfect.

Commodity funds

The choice for most investors is a sterling commodities fund. Authorised unit trusts are not allowed to invest in commodities; hence, if the investor wishes to have a professionally managed fund, he must look offshore. A variety of funds deal in commodities, differing in their areas of specialisation, permitted levels of gearing and ability to go short. Most funds use both the cash and futures markets, hence the fund performance may not exactly correspond to the underlying commodities.

These funds are of interest to an investor who is interested in real assets as a hedge against inflation and is also looking more towards capital growth than income.

INVESTMENT AND RISK

In addition to these more normal funds, exposure may be gained to commodities through certain hedge funds, and through Exchange Traded Commodities (ETCs), a variation of ETFs where a number of competing products have been issued.

Like ETFs, ETCs are asset-backed open-ended investments that track the performance of the underlying commodity/index. They are traded and settled like shares and have the support of a market maker to ensure liquidity and are available on single commodities (eg gold) or on commodity indices (eg energy or precious metals).

Advantages of indirect investment

The advantages of indirect investment are as follows.

- The shares will probably pay a dividend unlike any direct investment.
- Lower holding/storage costs.
- Lower minimal dealing size.

2 Collectibles

Learning outcome

10.5 Alternative investments (gold, art, antiques), commodities and alternative energy.

2.1 Introduction

Below are some types of investment that could be called '**collectibles**'.

Works of art	Wine
Antiques	Limited edition books
Coins	Diamonds
Stamps	Gold items
Vintage cars	

Collectibles have the following general features.

- They generally produce **no income**.
- They can be **difficult to value**, particularly for unique items.
- **Values can change** with changes in fashion or, for commodities like gold, with inflation.
- Collectibles are **expensive to keep** because they are vulnerable to atmospheric change, burglary and so on. There can be additional costs of custodianship, possibly in a bank, and heavy insurance premiums.
- The **cost of buying and selling** collectibles can be high, with dealers' margins or commissions being substantial.
- Collectibles may have low **marketability**. An item may be difficult to sell in a hurry and the price raised may be a great disappointment.
- **Specialist knowledge** is required in the selection of the item.
- The less knowledgeable **investor may be vulnerable** to the unscrupulous expert.

2.2 Collectibles in a portfolio

Investment advisers will not often be called upon to recommend an alternative investment. The client will normally already have an interest in whatever the collectible item may be. The pleasure provided by the activity of collecting items will often be an important aspect.

Collectibles may be of particular use to a higher rate taxpayer who has no intention of disposing of the items during his lifetime. As the artefacts generate no income, the collector will suffer no tax whilst he holds them. There will be no CGT on death. Inheritance tax will be avoided if the item is given for national purposes or the public good. Collectables also provide a good hedge against inflation.

2.3 Tax position

Normally no income is generated for the individual investor, and so consequently there will be no **income tax**. A charge to **CGT** is likely to arise on the disposal of most collectible items if the gain is in excess of the annual exemption.

The investor must beware of being treated by the HMRC as trading. If he is treated in this way any gains will be subject to income tax.

Antiques and paintings, being chattels, are exempt from capital gains tax if the sale proceeds do not exceed £6,000. If the proceeds do exceed £6,000 marginal relief is allowed. In this situation the chargeable gain would be the lower of

- $5/3 \times$ (sale proceeds − £6,000)
- Actual chargeable gain using normal CGT rules

As a result, when the sale proceeds are above £15,000 the mainstream CGT rules will produce a lower bill.

If the collectible item is a motor car suitable for private use, the gain on the sale will be exempt from capital gains tax.

Key chapter points

- Commodities are essentially raw materials that can be easily bought and sold in large quantities on organised markets.
- Collectibles, such as art or antiques, can be a part of a portfolio of investments, and this will usually be where the investor has a particular interest in the items collected.

Chapter Quiz

1. Identify five features of collectibles which are relevant to the investor. ....(See para 2.1)

chapter 10

OEICs and unit trusts

Chapter topic list

1	Collective investments	196
2	Unit trusts	198
3	OEICs and ICVCs	206
4	Unit trusts and OEIC classifications	209
5	FSA rules	217
6	Offshore funds	220
7	Structured investment funds	224
	Key chapter points	225
	Chapter quiz	226

INVESTMENT AND RISK

CHAPTER LEARNING OUTCOMES

4 **Understand** the following packaged products, their main features and suitability for different consumer circumstances.

    4.1   OEICs and unit trusts

        4.1.1   Structure of OEICs (investment companies with variable capital – ICVCs) and unit trusts the common characteristics of funds and the main differences, relative merits of direct investment and investment in funds.

        4.1.2   Range of funds – different UK fund classifications, hedge funds, limited issue funds, tracker funds.

        4.1.3   Charges and pricing – initial and annual charging structures, single and bid/offer pricing, dilution levies.

        4.1.4   Taxation onshore and offshore – taxation within the funds, taxation of UK individuals and trustee investors.

        4.1.5   Recognition by the FSA of offshore funds.

        4.1.6   Structured investment funds – equity index-based and equity-based growth and income funds.

        4.1.7   Relative merits of direct investment versus investment in funds.

        4.1.8   The process of buying and selling OEICs and unit trusts.

        4.1.9   Fund supermarkets and wraps.

    4.5   Multi managers – manager of managers and fund of funds,

    4.7   Exchange Traded Funds.

1 Collective investments

Learning outcome

4.1.7 Relative merits of direct investment versus investment in funds.

1.1 Introduction

A **collective** or **pooled** investment is a scheme by which the money of a large number of investors can be pooled to purchase shares or other securities. By participating in a collective investment, investors can participate in a pool of investments that would be more difficult to own directly as an individual.

1.2 Advantages and disadvantages of collective investments

There are advantages and disadvantages of collective investment, as compared with direct investment.

Advantages of collective investments

- An individual can invest relatively small amounts, perhaps on a regular basis.

- The pooling of investments enables the fund to make purchases of securities at lower cost than would be possible for an individual.
- The time involved in directly managing one's own portfolio is saved.
- The funds are managed by professional fund managers. A fund manager with a good past performance record may be able to repeat the performance in the future.
- A wide diversification between different shares and sectors can be achieved: this can be impractical and costly in dealing charges for a small portfolio held by an individual.
- Risk is reduced by exposure to a widely diversified spread of investments in the underlying portfolio.
- Specialisation in particular sectors is possible.
- The investor can gain exposure to foreign stocks, which can be costly and inconvenient for an individual who holds shares directly.
- Different funds provide for different investment objectives, such as income or growth, or a combination of both.

Disadvantages of collective investments

- The individual can only choose baskets of investments selected by fund managers, not by himself, and this will not suit all investors.
- Although the individual does not have to pick individual securities, he still has to choose the fund manager, and different managers' performance can vary widely.
- Although 'star' fund managers can have a successful track record with a fund, such 'star' managers may switch jobs, making future management of the fund less certain.
- Larger collective funds find it more difficult to invest in shares of companies with a relatively small capitalization, because of the small quantities of stock available.
- Successful collective funds investing in smaller companies can become a victim of their own success if more funds are brought in, as a greater fund size can make it more difficult for such a fund to follow their successful strategy.

1.3 Types of collective investment

The following are types of **collective investment:**

- Unit trusts
- Open Ended Investment Companies (OEICs)
- Offshore funds
- Exchange Traded Funds (ETFs)
- Hedge funds
- Closed end funds, including investment trusts, and split capital investment trusts
- Venture capital trusts
- Private equity funds
- Structured investment funds

Unit trusts and OEICs are often referred to using the general term '**funds**'. An OEIC is alternatively called an **Investment Company with Variable Capital (ICVCs).**

INVESTMENT AND RISK

1.4 Open-ended and closed-ended funds

Unit trusts are normally **open-ended** funds. This means that the trust can create new units when new investors subscribe and it can cancel units when investors cash in their holdings.

This makes unit trusts and OEICs different from **investment trusts**, which are **closed-ended**: new investors buy investment trust shares from existing holders of the shares who wish to sell.

Open-ended funds	Closed-ended funds
• The price closely reflects the underlying net asset value (NAV) of the investment.	• The investments must be purchased from another investor. The price is subject to supply and demand and may not reflect the underlying value (NAV). High demand increases the price; low demand reduces the price. • Where the price is greater than the underlying value of the investment, it is said to be at a 'premium' to NAV, where it is below it is at a 'discount' to NAV.
• New investors can bring in new money, allowing the fund managers to invest in new opportunities.	• There is no new money coming in: fund managers must sell assets in order to make investments.
• When investors sell, assets must be sold to release cash to pay them possibly disrupting set policies and strategies.	• When investors sell, there is no need to sell assets as the total amount of money invested remains; the same set policies and strategies can be maintained.
• Unit trusts, OEICs and life assurance investments are open-ended, as are many offshore investment funds.	• Investment trusts and some offshore funds are closed-ended.

1.5 ISAs

Unit trusts, OEICs and investment trust shares (non-AIM) can be held in the tax-advantaged wrapper of an **Individual Savings Account (ISA)**.

2 Unit trusts

Learning outcomes

4.1.1 Structure of OEICs (investment companies with variable capital – ICVCs) and unit trusts – the common characteristics of funds and the main differences.

4.1.3 Charges and pricing – initial and annual charging structures, single and bid/offer pricing, dilution levies.

4.1.4 Taxation onshore and offshore
- Taxation within the funds.
- Taxation of UK individuals and trustee investors.

4.1.8 The process of buying and selling OEICs and unit trusts.

10: OEICs AND UNIT TRUSTS

2.1 Characteristics of unit trusts

2.1.1 Introduction

A **unit trust** is a professionally managed **collective investment** fund.

- Investors can buy **units**, each of which represents a specified fraction of the trust.
- The trust holds a **portfolio** of securities.
- The assets of the trust are held by **trustees** and are invested by **managers**.
- The investor incurs **annual management charges** and possibly also an **initial charge**.

An authorised unit trust (AUT) must be constituted by a **trust deed** made between the manager and the trustee and is authorised by the FSA.

The basic principle with AUTs is that there is a single type of undivided unit. This is modified where there are both **income units** (paying a distribution to unitholders) and **accumulation units** (rolling up income into the capital value of the units).

Unit trusts have been available in the UK since the 1930s. Taking unit trusts together with **Open Ended Investment Companies (OEICs),** funds under management now exceed £200 billion.

If the fund manager wishes to **market** the unit trust in **other member states of the EU**, he may apply for certification under **UCITS** (Undertakings for Collective Investment in Transferable Securities).

2.1.2 The role of trustees

Trustees of a unit trust must be FSA-authorised and **fully independent** of the trust manager.

Trustees are required to have **capital** in excess of £4 million and, for this reason, will normally be a **large financial institution** such as a bank or insurance company. The primary duty of the trustees is to protect the interests of the unit holders.

The trustees must:

- **Safeguard the assets** of the trust (all purchases will be in the name of the trustees).
- Ensure that the manager is **acting in accordance** with the trust deed and is not in breach of rules set out by their regulators
- Establish and maintain a **register** of unit holders listing their names and addresses and details of the numbers and types of units held, in particular
    - Issue certificates of ownership to unit holders.
    - Cancel certificates of ownership when they are redeemed.
    - Arranging for income to be distributed to unit holders.
- Ensuring that any **advertising is fair and not misleading** and complies with regulatory requirements.
- **Replace the manager** if they believe that he is not acting in the investor's best interest, or if required to do so because of the manager not being able to continue (for example by insolvency)
- Carry out the **proposals of a vote** by the majority of the unit holders (for example to remove the fund manager)

The **investor** in a unit trust owns the underlying value of shares based on the proportion of the units held. He is effectively the beneficiary of the trust.

The **trust deed** of each unit trust must clearly state its **investment objectives**, so that investors can determine the suitability of each trust. The limits and allowable investment areas for a unit trust fund are also laid out in the trust deed together with the investment objectives.

INVESTMENT AND RISK

2.1.3 The role of the manager

The manager must also be **authorised** by the FSA and his role covers:

- **Marketing** the unit trust
- **Managing** the assets in accordance with the trust deed
- **Pricing** – calculating bid and offer prices for the trust
- **Selling/buying** units in the trust to/from investors
- **Maintaining a record** of units for inspection by the trustees
- **Supplying other information** relating to the investments under the unit trust as requested
- **Informing the FSA** of any breaches of regulations while it is running the trust

Fund managers can perform these tasks themselves, or may **subcontract** them to a third party.

The fund manager must comply with **investment restrictions** applying to all unit trusts that are set out by the FSA and are described later.

2.2 Dealing in units

2.2.1 Introduction

As noted earlier, a unit trust is an open-ended fund. The size of the fund and the number of units in issue changes as units are either created by the managers to meet purchases by the public, or are liquidated (cancelled) as a result of sales of units back to the managers. Unit trusts are not usually quoted on the London Stock Exchange and the market in units is made by the managers themselves.

2.2.2 Buying units

When an investor decides to invest in a unit trust, he contacts the managers either directly or through his bank, broker/dealer or other agent. The price charged is that ruling on the day the order is received. The managers issue a **contract note** showing the number of units he has purchased, the price and the total amount payable. No additional commission or transfer stamp duty is payable as these are built into the price.

2.2.3 Selling units

When an investor is selling units, either directly or through his bank, broker/dealer or other agent, it is the manager who buys them. Again, the price for the units is that ruling on the day the order is received and a **contract note** is issued showing the price and total proceeds. The investor must sign an endorsement on the back of the **certificate** giving up rights of ownership of the units and send this to the managers, who then send a cheque for the proceeds to the investor.

2.2.4 Share exchange

Some fund groups offer the facility to use existing shares to fully or partly invest into unit trusts or OEICs. The fund manager can do this by purchasing the shares from the investor for inclusion into one or more of his own funds or sale if they are not required. In these circumstances, they will normally buy the shares at the purchase price rather than the sale price, giving the investor a better return. Alternatively, the manager can purchase the shares from the investor and sell them via their own dealer, usually with less commission being charged.

10: OEICs AND UNIT TRUSTS

2.2.5 Creations and liquidations

The managers are making a market in their units and at the end of each day they may have a position in their units in the same way that stock exchange market makers have a position in the stocks in which they deal. The managers may have sold more units than they have bought or *vice versa* – it would be an unusual day in which sales and purchases were equal.

If they have sold more units than have been sold back to them, they must create more units to meet their sales (unless they have stock of units). If they have bought back more units than they have sold, they must decide either to hold the excess on their books to meet sales in the future or to liquidate (cancel) units.

Creations and liquidations of units represent transactions between the manager and the trustee. To create units the manager prepares a calculation showing the cost of the units to be created and lodges this with the trustee. They must then pay the trustee the total cost, usually within four business days. This transaction increases the number of units in issue.

To liquidate units, a similar calculation is prepared and lodged with the trustee. The trustee reduces the number of units in issue accordingly when he has received endorsed certificates to the total number of units to be liquidated and pays the manager the proceeds from the fund to enable him to settle with the unit holders.

2.2.6 Certificates

It is an important part of the trustee's duty to ensure that at no time are there certificates in issue for more units than those for which he holds assets in the fund. So, when units are created, he issues no certificates until he has received the money for the creation from the manager. When units are liquidated he does not pay the managers until endorsed certificates are lodged with him. When units are bought and resold by the manager he does not issue certificates to the new holders until he has endorsed certificates from other holders to an equivalent number of units. This protects the investor against the possibility of fraud by the manager when dealing in their units with the public.

At any time, the number of units issued may be less than the number for which the trustee holds assets.

2.2.7 The manager's box

Trust managers can keep units repurchased from unit holders to enable them to supply units to purchasers without creating new units. This will increase liquidity in the investment and will help the manager avoid having to create and cancel shares every day. It also saves considerable money on the acquisition and disposal costs of the underlying assets, as units are recycled rather than being created and destroyed. The trust manager can use this to make profits on the units sold via the box. In the right circumstances, the manager can effectively keep the full spread, representing a useful additional income stream that is not visible as a charge to the customer.

Once very significant in unit trusts, holding a large box is now not so common because of regulations introduced to reduce the scope of this practice.

2.3 Unit trust pricing

2.3.1 Introduction

The idea underlying pricing is that whole of the fund and the income it generates belong to the unit holders in proportion to their holdings. At any time the value of a unit is the value of the investments and cash held, together with the income in hand and receivable, divided by the number of units issued.

A demand for units in a particular trust does not result in a rise in price unlike direct investments. It simply means that more cash is available for investment in the shares selected by the investment manager. Only fluctuations in the prices of the underlying investments cause the price of units to move.

The value of a unit is, therefore, calculated as

INVESTMENT AND RISK

$$\text{Value} = \frac{\text{Investments} + \text{Cash held} + \text{Income received or receivable}}{\text{Number of units in issue}}$$

However, there are potentially four different prices for us to consider.

- Creation price.
- Liquidation price.
- Offer price.
- Bid price.

Along with a number of other pricing details.

2.3.2 Creation price

The creation price is the price the manager must pay to the trustee in order to create a new unit. It is calculated as the lowest market dealing offer price of the securities in the fund plus accrued income, stamp duty and commission. It therefore represents the amount it would cost to invest in the portfolio held by the fund.

2.3.3 Liquidation price

The liquidation or cancellation price is the price the manager receives from the trustee on cancelling units. It is calculated as the highest market dealing bid price of the securities in the fund plus accrued interest less commission, and represents the net proceeds available if the portfolio were to be disposed of.

2.3.4 Offer price

This represents the price at which units are offered for sale by the manager to the investor. The maximum offer price is the creation price plus the manager's initial charge (typically 5% to 6%).

2.3.5 Bid price

The bid price represents the price at which the manager is willing to repurchase units from the unit holders. The liquidation price less any exit charge represents the minimum bid price.

The method of calculation for **maximum buying (offer) price** and **minimum selling (bid) price** is laid down by the FSA.

FSA formula for calculation of maximum offer price	FSA formula for calculation of minimum bid price (cancellation price)
Take the total cost of buying the underlying securities of the trust (at current market buying prices)	Take the total cost of selling the underlying securities of the trust (at current market selling prices)
Add stockbroker dealing commission and stamp duty etc.	Deduct stockbroker dealing commission
Add in uninvested cash and accrued income since the last distribution	Add in uninvested cash and accrued income since the last distribution
Divide the total by the number of units in issue (to give the **creation price**)	Divide the total by the number of units in issue
Add any initial charges	Deduct any exit charges applicable
Round to four significant figures	Round to four significant figures

2.3.6 Offer and bid basis pricing

Introduction

For most unit trusts, the difference between the offer and bid price will be in the range of 6%-10% and is called the full spread. However the typical spread actually experienced by the market is in the range of 5%-7% and the managers have the right to move the spread offered within the full spread.

Offer basis pricing

If the market is moving **upwards**, it is likely that investors will be **buying**. In these circumstances, managers can move the **spread** to the **top of the range**. This effectively means that the **offer price** being paid will be the **creation price** and increases the price for buyers. However, it also **increases** the price for **sellers of units** who will get a price of 5-7% **below the creation price** and considerably higher than normal. When this happens, prices are said to be on an '**offer**' basis.

Bid basis pricing

If the market is moving **downwards**, it is likely that investors will be **selling**. In these circumstances, managers can move the **spread** to the **bottom of the range**. This effectively means that the **buying price** being paid will be the **cancellation price** and **reduces** the price for sellers. However, it also **reduces** the price for buyers of units who will get a price of 5-7% **above the cancellation price** and considerably lower than normal. When this happens, prices are said to be on a '**bid**' basis.

2.3.7 The valuation point

The calculation of **buying** and **selling prices** will take place at the **valuation point**, which is at a particular time each day. The valuation point must be shown in the trust literature. A company can choose any time but most use mid-day.

The creation of units must take place within 24hrs of the valuation point

2.3.8 Historic pricing and forward pricing

Prices can be set on a **historic** or **forward pricing** basis.

- Where the price the investor pays is based on the **previous valuation point**, the pricing is described as **historic**. All units purchased up to the valuation point on the following day will be at the same, previous price.

- Where the investor pays a price based on the **next valuation point**, it is called **forward pricing**. All units purchased up to next valuation point will be at that price.

Each system has merits. With **historic pricing** the investor knows the price he will pay for units, but the value of the underlying securities may not be reflected in the price paid. This is good if prices have moved up, but bad if they have moved down. Investors find future pricing confusing, as it is not possible to determine in advance the price they will pay, but the price will be **more reflective** of the **underlying value** of the securities.

On a **historic pricing** basis, the manager creates units at the valuation point according to the amount of sales expected up to the next valuation point. If sales exceed expected levels, the manager must either move to forward pricing or risk loss of money for the fund if there is an unfavourable price movement.

On a **forward pricing** basis, the manager must create units at the valuation point sufficient to cover transactions since the last valuation point.

Under the FSA's **COLL** rules covered later, the manager must create units within **24 hours** of the valuation point.

INVESTMENT AND RISK

A manager using the historic pricing basis must move to a forward pricing basis if the value of the fund is believed to have changed by **2% or more** since the last valuation and if the investor requests forward pricing.

2.3.9 Single pricing

Some fund managers use **single pricing**, in which case there is the same price quoted for buying and selling units, with any charges being separately disclosed.

2.4 Charges

2.4.1 Introduction

The **charges** on a unit trust must be explicit in the trust deed and documentation. They should give details of the current charges and the extent to which managers can change them.

Charges need to be made to cover the following **costs**.

- Managing the fund
- Administration of the fund
- Marketing
- Regulation and compliance costs
- General administration
- Direct marketing costs
- Commissions for intermediaries

These charges can be taken in one or more of three ways, via an **initial charge**, an **exit charge** or through **annual management charges**.

2.4.2 Initial charges

The **initial charge** is added to the **buying price**. So, the buyer suffers both the bid/offer spread, and the initial charge. Managers might charge 3.0-6.5% on **equities**, and less on **fixed interest funds** (1-4%). Other funds with lower charges include **index tracker funds** and **cash/money market funds**, where the lower price reflects the lower burden of management. Where an initial charge is small or non-existent, there may be a further charge on exit.

Fund managers may offer discounts on the usual initial charge, particularly for direct sales or sales through '**fund supermarkets**'.

2.4.3 Exit charges

As an alternative to initial charges, a few trusts apply **exit charges**. These charges are typically invoked where the investor sells the investment within a set period of time, eg five years.

The **exit charge** levied will typically be on a **sliding scale**, for example varying from 5% if the investment is encashed in the first year and reducing by 1% for each subsequent year. After the fifth year, the exit charge will be zero, but the annual management charge will have been higher and the managers will have covered the cost of the initial charge. If the investment continues, they will still be getting their management charge at a higher rate.

2.4.4 Annual charges

An **annual charge** of around 0.5–1.5% of the underlying fund will generally be made to cover the ongoing cost of the investment management of the trust. In some cases part of the annual management charge is paid to intermediaries as **renewal commission**, typically at a rate of 0.5% per annum. The cost will vary with the level of management required on a fund. **Offshore funds** require more management and costs are likely to be **higher**. **Tracker funds** require less management and costs will be **lower**. Some funds will have several tiers of management and will allow access to a wide range of investment managers via a single management company. In this case, each tier of management will need to recoup its costs and, in these cases, annual management costs will be higher.

Management charges can be taken from income or capital, but historically has been taken from income. The main reason for this is that the charges could be offset against taxable income.

FSA rules permit **performance-related charges**. These may be based on growth of the fund, or out-performance of the fund's standard benchmark. The basis of the charges must be disclosed in the fund prospectus and key features document.

2.5 Fund distributions

2.5.1 Introduction

Distributions from unit trusts (and OEICs) are treated in the same manner as the underlying investments. That is distributions made by an equity fund are treated as dividends and paid net of 10% withholding tax, whereas distributions from bond and money market funds are treated as interest payments and are paid net of 20% tax.

2.5.2 Income equalisation payments

Between distributions of income from a unit trust (or an OEIC – covered below), the unit price includes the value of any income received by its underlying assets since the previous distribution when buying such units, investors are effectively buying the right to this income.

On the first distribution of income after the purchase of units, the trust will pay out to the new unit holder the income which has accrued between the date of purchase of the units and the distribution date. In addition as the unit holder has paid for income accrued before he purchased the units this amount will be refunded to him as a capital payment.

The total amount received by the unit holder should therefore be the same as the full dividend received by the original unit holders but the distinction between income and capital repayment is important for the investor's personal tax purpose.

This refund of capital, known as **income equalisation**, is not part of taxable income but should be deducted from the base cost for capital gains tax purposes. The equalisation payment is treated as a **discount** on the **purchase price** of the units. This discount **reduces** the **acquisition cost** and effectively **increases** any **capital gains** that could result on disposal, potentially giving rise to a higher CGT charge.

2.6 Taxation of unit trusts

2.6.1 Authorised unit trusts

In order to be **marketed** to the public, a **unit trust** must be authorised by the FSA. Authorised unit trusts are **exempt from tax on gains** made within the fund, giving them an advantage, for instance, over life funds.

For a trust that has less than 60% of its funds in interest bearing securities, any income (other than dividend income from UK companies, which is not taxable) is taxed to corporation tax at **20%**. Foreign withholding tax on dividends will be offset against the tax charge, subject to double taxation treaties.

Management expenses can be offset against income from **non-UK equities.**

Unit trusts do not pay tax on gains from options or futures.

From **1 April 2006**, **Qualified Investor Scheme (QIS)** investors are made subject to a special annual income tax charge on movements in the capital value of their holding if they own more than 10% of the value of a QIS fund. This measure

INVESTMENT AND RISK

is intended to prevent QIS investors from taking advantage of a tax treatment intended for pooled investors, whilst possibly retaining some of the control that is a feature of direct investment.

The tax treatment of fund **distributions** parallels the tax treatment of direct holdings of equities and bonds.

Under the 'bond fund test', if the trust holds 60% or more of its investments in **interest bearing securities**, the income is deemed to be interest and the distribution is made net of 20% tax, which can be reclaimed by non-taxpayers. 10% taxpayers can reclaim 10%, while basic rate taxpayers have no further liability. Higher rate taxpayers (and discretionary trusts) must pay additional tax at 20% of the gross amount.

For **equity unit trusts**, the distribution is made with a 10% tax credit, whether to **individuals** or **trustee** investors.

The tax treatment for different types of **individual taxpayer** is then as for dividends from shares held directly. The tax credit cannot be reclaimed by non-taxpayers. The tax credit satisfies the tax liability for a basic or lower (10%) rate taxpayer, but higher rate taxpayers (and discretionary trusts) will be liable to an additional 22.5% on the grossed-up figure. Additional rate tax payers will be liable to an additional 32.5%.

From **6 April 2007**, funds have been able to pay interest distributions **gross** (ie, without deduction of tax) to **non-taxpayers** and those whose income falls below their personal allowance and other reliefs, in the same way as banks and building societies can pay interest gross, saving such investors the need to reclaim the tax deducted.

The investor is liable to **capital gains tax** on disposals of unit trust investments.

There is **no stamp duty** or **stamp duty reserve tax** to pay on purchases of UK unit trusts.

2.6.2 Unauthorised unit trusts

Unauthorised unit trusts are used for specific applications such as **Enterprise Zone property** holdings, where they are not marketed directly to the public, and are subject to income tax and CGT within the fund. Investors are liable to any additional income tax and CGT on disposal.

There is an **exempt** type of **unauthorised unit trust** that may be used as investments for pensions and registered charities. **Exempt unit trusts** are free of CGT on disposals within the fund and are subject to income tax rather than corporation tax.

3 OEICs and ICVCs

Learning outcomes

4.1.1 Structure of OEICs (investment companies with variable capital – ICVCs) and unit trusts – the common characteristics of funds and the main differences.

4.1.3 Charges and pricing – initial and annual charging structures, single and bid/offer pricing, dilution levies.

4.1.4 Taxation onshore and offshore
- Taxation within the funds.
- Taxation of UK individuals and trustee investors.

4.1.8 The process of buying and selling OEICs and unit trusts.

3.1 The OEIC framework

Open Ended Investment Companies (OEICs) are managed, pooled investment vehicles in the form of companies. They invest in securities with the objective of producing a profit for investors. Unlike unit trusts, the OEIC structure is recognised throughout Europe. The possible prospect of UK participation in economic and monetary union (EMU) and the single European Market helped to drive the UK to adopt this form of pooled investment, in addition to the unit trust. Regulations made under the European Communities Act brought OEICs into existence in the UK in 1997.

These regulations provided for the incorporation in the UK of OEICs that fall within the scope of the **UCITS (Undertaking for Collective Investment in Transferable Securities)** Directive (see later). This means they can invest only in **transferable securities** (for example, listed securities, other collective investment schemes, certificates of deposit). UCITS must be open ended. UCITS certification allows the fund to be marketed throughout the European Economic Area (EEA).

If it is marketed in the UK, an OEIC must be **authorised** by the Financial Services Authority (FSA).

With the implementation of the Financial Services and Markets Act 2000 (FSMA 2000), the range of UK authorised OEICs was extended to be similar to that of unit trusts, including money market funds and property funds for example, and (as we have seen) OEICs are now alternatively termed **Investment Companies with Variable Capital (ICVCs)**. Authorisation as an ICVC defines the regulations (ie, the Treasury's ICVC Regulations, as well as further FSA regulations) with which the fund must comply.

Unit trusts and OEICs are **Authorised Investment Funds (AIFs)**, and are often collectively referred to as **funds**.

Both OEICs and unit trusts are types of **open-ended collective investments**. However, with a unit trust, the units held provide beneficial ownership of the underlying trust assets. A share in an OEIC entitles the holder to a share in the profits of the OEIC, but the value of the share will be determined by the value of the underlying investments. For example, if the underlying investments are valued at £125,000,000 and there are 100,000,000 shares in issue, the net asset value of each share is £1.25.

The holder of a share in an OEIC can sell back the share to the company in any period specified in the prospectus.

3.2 The structure of OEICs

Unlike unit trusts, **OEICs** have a **corporate structure**. The objective of the company is to make a profit for shareholders by investing in the shares of other companies. The open-ended nature of an OEIC means that it is priced based on asset values like a unit trust.

Where a unit trust has a manager, an OEIC has an **Authorised Corporate Director (ACD)**, who **may be the only Director**. The responsibilities of the **ACD** include the following.

- Day-to-day management of the fund
- Pricing of the fund
- Management of the investments
- Dealing in the underlying securities
- Preparation of accounts
- Compliance with OEIC regulatory requirements

In order to ensure that the **ACD** acts in the interests of **investor protection**, there is a **separate, independent depository**. The responsibility of the **depository** is similar to that of a trustee for a unit trust and covers the following.

- Overseeing the management of the investment company
- Protecting the interests of the investor
- Valuation and pricing of OEIC shares
- Dealing in shares for the OEIC
- The payment of income distributions
- Generally overseeing the ACD
- Ensuring that the ACD is acting in accordance with his investment powers
- Ensuring the ACD is acting in accordance with his borrowing powers

INVESTMENT AND RISK

The ACD and the depository must be regulated by the FSA, and approved as **'authorised persons'**. FSA rules cover the sales and marketing of OEICs, and there are cancellation rules.

The following requirements apply to OEICs.

- There must be an **Annual General Meeting**.
- **Unaudited interim and audited final reports** must be made to the holders of shares each year, complying with the **Statement of Recommended Practice for authorised funds**.
- **Short form accounts** may be prepared but full financial statements must be provided on request.

3.3 Pricing, buying and selling

The shares in the OEIC express the entitlement of the shareholders to the underlying fund which, like a unit trust, is valued of a Net Asset Value basis. With equities, there are a limited number of shares available in each company and an individual must sell the share before another can buy. Because an OEIC is open-ended, the number of shares in issue can be **increased** or **reduced** to satisfy the demands of the investors.

Historically OEICs were all **single priced instruments**, therefore there was no bid/offer spread with OEICs. The buying price reflects the value of the underlying shares, with any initial charge reflecting dealing costs and management expenses being disclosed separately. Under FSA rules, OEICs have been permitted to use dual pricing since October 2008, though few do.

Within an OEIC the **costs of creation** of the fund may be met by the fund.

A further charge, known as a **dilution levy**, may be made at the discretion of the ACD. The **dilution levy** may be added to the single price, or deducted from the redemption price. The purpose of such a levy is to protect the interests of the shareholders in general and may be charged if the fund is in decline or is experiencing **exceptionally high levels of net sales or redemptions** relative to its size. This levy, if charged, is paid into the fund and not to the managers.

When the investor wishes to **sell** the **OEIC**, the **ACD** will **buy** it. The money value on sale will be based on the **single price** less a **deduction** for the **dealing charges**. The price may be further reduced by any **dilution levy**.

The **ACD** may choose to **run a box**. Shares sold back to the ACD will be **kept** and **reissued** to investors, reducing the need for creation and cancellation of shares.

The **register of shareholders** must be **updated daily** and include all shareholdings of the ACD and those held in the box (if there is one) as well as those of the investors.

3.4 Taxation and OEICs

3.4.1 Taxation of the fund

OEICs themselves face a tax regime similar to that faced by **unit trusts**. Interest, rent and foreign dividends not taxed at source is subject to a 20% corporation tax charge. UK interest and dividends received net will suffer no further tax. Capital gains within an OEIC are exempt from CGT.

Where an OEIC is based **offshore**, the distributions will **not be taxed** internally. This will provide a **benefit** to non-taxpaying investors, and a cashflow benefit to tax paying investors.

3.4.2 Taxation of the investor

Income tax

Distributions (dividends) paid to investors in an OEIC are taxable in the same way as the distributions from unit trusts.

10: OEICs AND UNIT TRUSTS

- Equity fund dividends are paid with a **tax credit** of 10% that satisfies the **tax liability** for basic and lower rate taxpayers. **Higher rate taxpayers** are liable to an additional 22.5%. **Additional rate taxpayers** are liable to an additional 32.5%.

- Fixed interest funds pay interest with 20% tax deducted, which satisfies the liability for basic rate taxpayers. Higher rate taxpayers and discretionary trusts must pay 20% more and starting rate taxpayers can reclaim 10%. Additional rate taxpayers must pay 30% more.

Non taxpayers may **reclaim** tax on interest distributions, but not equity distributions.

Capital gains tax

For investors' OEIC holdings outside a tax-advantaged wrapper such as an ISA, **capital gains tax** will be chargeable on disposals.

Stamp duty

There is no UK stamp duty to pay on purchases of OEICs.

3.5 Advantages of OEICs for the investor

As for unit trusts, the general advantages of collective investment outlined at the beginning of this Chapter apply to OEICs. Like unit trusts, there is a wide range of types of fund available.

The introduction of OEICs was expected to lead to a **reduction in costs for the investor** and **transparency of charges**. At the same time, there is **no dilution** in **investor protection**.

The charges with **OEICs** may be lower than for unit trusts, particularly in respect of **cost of entry (setting up)** and **exit (encashing the investment)** due to single pricing. Annual management costs are not set out as a separate charge as with unit trusts. It is still possible to quantify the costs by looking at the **total expense ratio (TER)** of the company. Figures for this are available in the public domain, allowing investors to make valid comparisons between investment managers. There is further discussion of TERs in the next Chapter, in the context of investment trusts.

For the investment industry, an advantage of OEICs is that they are **widely recognised throughout Europe**.

4 Unit trust and OEIC classifications

Learning outcomes

- 4.5 Multi managers – manager of managers and fund of funds.
- 4.7 Exchange Traded Funds.
- 4.1.2 Range of funds – different UK fund classifications, hedge funds, limited issue funds, tracker funds.
- 4.1.9 Fund supermarkets and wraps.

4.1 IMA categories

The **Investment Management Association (IMA)** publishes sector definitions to classify unit trusts and OEICs. The groups correspond to different investment objectives.

- Immediate income
- Growing income
- Capital protection

INVESTMENT AND RISK

- Capital growth/total return
- Specialist funds

UK fund classifications

Income funds		Growth funds		Specialist funds
Immediate income	**Growing income**	**Capital protection**	**Capital growth/total return**	
UK Gilts UK Index Linked Gilts £ Corporate Bond Global Bonds £ Equity & Bond Income £ High yield £ Strategic bond	UK Equity Income UK Equity Income and Growth	Money Market Protected/Guaranteed Funds	UK All Companies UK Smaller Companies Japan Japanese Smaller Companies Asia Pacific including Japan Asia Pacific excluding Japan North America North American Smaller Companies Europe including UK Europe excluding UK European Smaller Companies Cautious Managed Balanced Managed Active Managed Global Growth Global Emerging Markets UK zeros	Specialist Technology & Telecommunications Personal Pensions Absolute returns Property

The detailed IMA sector definitions are set out below. The percentage limits given in these definitions could form the basis of exam questions.

Funds: IMA classifications

Funds principally targeting income – immediate income

UK gilts. Funds which invest at least 95% of their assets in Sterling denominated (or hedged back to Sterling) triple AAA rated, government backed securities, with at least 80% invested in UK government securities (Gilts).

UK index linked gilts. Funds which invest at least 95% of their assets in Sterling denominated (or hedged back to Sterling) triple AAA rated government backed index linked securities, with at least 80% invested in UK Index Linked Gilts.

£ corporate bond. Funds which invest at least 80% of their assets in Sterling-denominated (or hedged back to Sterling), Triple BBB minus or above bonds as measured by either Standard & Poor or equivalent. This excludes convertibles, preference shares and permanent interest bearing shares (PIBS)

£ strategic bond. Funds which invest at least 80% of their assets in Sterling denominated (or hedged back to Sterling) fixed interest securities. This includes convertibles, preference shares and permanent interest bearing shares (PIBs). At any point in time the asset allocation of these funds could theoretically place the fund in one of the other Fixed Interest sectors. The funds will remain in this sector on these occasions since it is the Manager's stated intention to retain the right to invest across the Sterling fixed interest credit risk spectrum.

£ high yield. Funds which invest at least 80% of their assets in Sterling denominated (or hedged back to Sterling) fixed interest securities and at least 50% of their assets in below BBB minus fixed interest securities (as measured by Standard and Poors or an equivalent external rating agency), including convertibles, preference shares and permanent interest bearing shares (PIBs).

Global bonds. Funds which invest at least 80% of their assets in fixed interest stocks. All funds which contain more than 80% fixed interest investments are to be classified under this heading regardless of the fact that they may have more than 80% in a particular geographic sector, unless that geographic area is the UK, when the fund should be classified under the relevant UK heading.

UK equity & bond income. Funds which invest at least 80% of their assets in the UK, between 20% and 80% in UK fixed interest securities and between 20% and 80% in UK equities. These funds aim to have a yield of 120% or over of the FTSE All Share Index.

Funds principally targeting income – growing income

UK equity income. Funds which invest at least 80% of their assets in UK equities and which aim to achieve a historic yield on the distributable income in excess of 110% of the yield of the FT All Share Index.

UK equity income and growth. Funds which invest at least 80% of their assets in UK equities, aim to have a historic yield on the distributable income in excess of 90% of the yield of the FTSE All Share Index at the fund's year end and which aim to produce a combination of both income and growth.

Funds principally targeting capital – capital growth/total return

UK zeros. Funds investing at least 80% of their assets in Sterling denominated (or hedged back to Sterling), and at least 80% of their assets in zero dividend preference shares or equivalent instruments (ie not income producing). This excludes preference shares which produce an income.

UK all companies. Funds which invest at least 80% of their assets in UK equities which have a primary objective of achieving capital growth.

UK smaller companies. Funds which invest at least 80% of their assets in UK equities of companies which form the bottom 10% by market capitalisation.

Japan. Funds which invest at least 80% of their assets in Japanese equities.

Japanese smaller companies. Funds which invest at least 80% of their assets in Japanese equities of companies which form the bottom 30% by market capitalisation.

Asia Pacific including Japan. Funds which invest at least 80% of their assets in Asia Pacific equities including a Japanese content. The Japanese content must make up less than 80% of assets.

Asia Pacific excluding Japan. Funds which invest at least 80% of their assets in Asia Pacific equities and exclude Japanese securities.

North America. Funds which invest at least 80% of their assets in North American equities.

North American smaller companies. Funds which invest a least 80% of their assets in North American equities of companies which form the bottom 20% by market capitalisation.

Europe including UK. Funds which invest at least 80% of their assets in European equities. They may include UK equities, but these must not exceed 80% of the fund's assets.

Europe excluding UK. Funds which invest at least 80% of their assets in European equities and exclude UK securities.

European smaller companies. Funds which invest at least 80% of their assets in European equities of companies which form the bottom 20% by market capitalisation in the European market. They may include UK equities, but these must not exceed 80% or the fund's assets. ('Europe' includes all countries in the MSCI/FTSE pan European indices.)

Cautious managed. Funds investing in a range of assets with the maximum equity exposure restricted to 60% of the fund and with at least 30% invested in fixed interest and cash. There is no specific requirement to hold a minimum % of non UK equity within the equity limits. Assets must be at least 50% in Sterling/Euro and equities are deemed to include convertibles.

Balanced managed. Funds would offer investment in a range of assets, with the maximum equity exposure restricted to 85% of the Fund. At least 10% must be held in non-UK equities. Assets must be at least 50% in Sterling/Euro and equities are deemed to include convertibles.

Active managed. Funds would offer investment in a range of assets, with the Manager being able to invest up to 100% in equities at their discretion. At least 10% must be held in non-UK equities. There is no minimum Sterling/Euro balance and equities are deemed to include convertibles. At any one time the asset allocation of these funds may hold a high proportion of non-equity assets such that the asset allocation would by default place the fund in either the Balanced or Cautious sector. These funds would remain in this sector on these occasions since it is the Manager's stated intention to retain the right to invest up to 100% in equities.

Global growth. Funds which invest at least 80% of their assets in equities (but not more than 80% in UK assets) and which have the prime objective of achieving growth of capital.

Global emerging markets. Funds which invest 80% or more of their assets directly or indirectly in emerging markets as defined by the World Bank, without geographical restriction. Indirect investment eg China shares listed in Hong Kong, should not exceed 50% of the portfolio.

Note: The above sectors also require funds to be broadly diversified within the relevant country/region/asset class. Funds that concentrate solely on a specialist theme, sector or single market size (or a single country in a multi-currency region) would be incorporated in the Specialist sector (see below).

Funds principally targeting capital protection

Money market. Funds which invest at least 95% of their assets in money market instruments (ie cash and near cash, such as bank deposits, certificates of deposit, very short term fixed interest securities or floating rate notes). These funds may be either "money market funds" as defined by SIB, or "securities funds" as long as they satisfy the criterion of concentrating on money market instruments.

Protected/guaranteed funds. Funds, other than money market funds which principally aim to provide a return of a set amount of capital back to the investor (either explicitly guaranteed or via an investment strategy highly likely to achieve this objective) plus some market upside.

Specialist sectors

Specialist. Funds that have an investment universe that is not accommodated by the mainstream sectors. Performance ranking of funds within the sector as a whole is inappropriate, given the diverse nature of its constituents.

Technology & telecommunications. Funds which invest at least 80% of their assets in technology and telecommunications sectors as defined by major index providers.

Personal pensions. Funds which are only available for use in a personal pension plan or FSAVC scheme.

Property. Funds which predominantly invest in property. In order to invest "predominantly" in property, funds should either:

- invest at least 60% of their assets directly in property; or
- invest at least 80% of their assets in property securities; or

when their direct property holdings fall below the 60% threshold for a period of more than 6 months, invest sufficient of the balance of their assets in property securities to ensure that at least 80% of the fund is invested in property, whereupon it becomes a hybrid fund

Absolute returns. Funds aimed at delivering positive returns in all market conditions.

10: OEICs AND UNIT TRUSTS

The IMA classifications above are based on broad criteria. For example, within particular categories such as UK All Companies, there will be some funds focusing on mainstream **'blue chip'** stocks, some funds investing in **recovery stocks** and some funds concentrating on **special situations** such as companies that are rich in cash relative to their share price.

Within the specified IMA categories of funds are the following types of fund for which there is not a separate classification:

- **Index-tracking funds**, which mechanically 'shadow' a particular share index such as the FTSE 100 Index rather than being actively managed by fund managers (see below)
- **Ethical funds**, which fall mainly within the UK All Companies and Global Specialist sectors. (Ethical investing is discussed in a later chapter.)

Although unit trusts and OEICs are often thought of particularly as providing exposure to **equity** markets, note from the classifications given above that there are the following types of fund available as well.

- **Bonds funds**, investing in fixed interest securities including government bonds, corporate bonds and convertibles.
- **Cash funds**, which enable the investor to have the advantage of wholesale rates on cash deposits. An investor might use a cash fund to hold money before it is switched into other funds.

4.2 Tracker funds

An **index tracker fund** is based on a simple concept. The tracker fund aims to match the performance of a particular index, such as the FTSE 100 Share Index, thus giving the investor an opportunity to benefit from positive movements in the overall market.

Tracking involves investing in the shares that make up the index, in the proportions in which those shares make up the index. Investors should note however that some quoted indices, such as the FTSE 100 Index are **price indices** rather than **total return indices**. A price index ignores dividends paid, while a total return index includes reinvested income (dividends). Data is often available on both bases for a particular index.

A tracker will not be able to match the total return from a **total return index** consistently, because of:

- Variations arising from **tracking errors** (see below)
- **Transaction costs** arising from buying and selling the shares held in the fund (spread and dealing commission)
- **Charges** levied by the manager of the tracker, to cover the manager's costs and profit

Management costs for tracker funds should be relatively low. The fund only requires **passive management** because there is no need for research to be undertaken as with an **actively managed** fund.

The **active** fund manager will analyse the investments and sectors in which a fund invests, and will base decisions about whether to buy or sell on this analysis. With **passive** index-tracking fund management, the criterion for inclusion of a particular stock in the fund portfolio is simply that a share forms part of the index.

Tracker funds can occur in various forms, including unit trusts, OEICs/ICVCs, investment trusts and **exchange traded funds (ETFs)**.

4.3 Exchange traded funds

Exchange traded funds (ETFs) are a relatively new type of open ended fund which has proved very popular in the USA.

ETFs are available to track general share price indices (eg, the FTSE 100 Index in the UK, or the S&P 500 Index in the USA) or indices for market sectors (eg, pharmaceuticals, or energy stocks).

INVESTMENT AND RISK

The fact that ETFs have prices quoted in real time throughout trading hours sets them apart from other types of index-tracking fund.

Relatively **low charges** and the fact that **no stamp duty** is applied to purchases are attractions of ETFs, though they are subject to income tax and capital gains tax like normal shares.

In theory, the price of an ETF should closely follow the underlying index, although in practice the price may diverge from the net asset value by perhaps 1%.

4.4 Tracking methods

There are different ways in which a tracker fund can operate.

- **Full replication** is an approach whereby the fund attempts to mirror the index by holding shares in exactly the same proportions as in the index itself.

- **Stratified sampling** involves choosing investments that are representative of the index. For example, if a sector makes up 16% of the index, then 16% of shares in that sector will be held, even though the proportions of individual companies in the index may not be matched. The expectation is that with stratified sampling, overall the '**tracking error**' or departure from the index will be relatively low. The amount of trading of shares required should be lower than for full replication, since the fund will not need to track every change in capitalisation of a share. This should reduce transaction costs and therefore will help to avoid such costs eroding overall performance.

- **Optimisation** is a computer-based modelling technique which aims to approximate to the index through a complex statistical analysis based on past performance.

The **constituent companies in indices** such as the FTSE 100 Index are reviewed from time to time, and some companies will usually drop out while others will join.

The large amounts of funds invested in tracker funds could have a distorting effect on the market, for example if many tracker funds buy a particular share at the point when it is included in the index. Undoubtedly, **inclusion** in an index can be beneficial to the price of a share, while **exclusion** may be a factor causing a share to receive less attention from investors and to fall out of favour. However, because many funds do not follow a policy of full replication, and because a change in demand for a share will be anticipated by the market once it is known that the share is a likely candidate for inclusion in or exclusion from an index, there is unlikely to be a sudden change in the prices of shares at the point when the inclusion or exclusion is announced.

4.5 'Guaranteed' funds

Before 2001 rule changes, the word 'guaranteed' or other terms implying a degree of capital security were not allowed to be used in fund names. Now, funds are permitted to label themselves as 'guaranteed' if there is a separate full money back guarantee. Details of any guarantee must be disclosed in 'consumer facing material'.

4.6 Multi-manager schemes

Multi-manager schemes are increasingly popular and are now offered by most fund management groups. These schemes can give clients access to the investment management expertise of a number of investment houses within the framework of a single unit-linked life assurance or pension investment. The schemes often allow switches at low cost between funds, giving access to hundreds of different fund, sector and management options.

The switching feature of multi-manager arrangements is an advantage to the investor who is concerned about under-performance, since he or she can easily and cheaply switch to another manager. An investor may also want to switch easily between funds if his or her risk profile has changed. This type of flexibility is not available where a life office offers only its own funds, and can be a useful marketing tool.

4.6.1 Funds of funds

With **funds of funds**, a number of funds are packaged together within an overall 'umbrella' fund. These may operate in two ways.

- A number of sub-funds (eg, for equities, bonds or specific currencies) in which investors can spread their investments may be set up within the structure of the fund itself.
- Alternatively, the fund may offer a 'menu' of third party funds from which investors can make a selection. This can give investors pooled access to funds to which they would not be able to access individually.

A fund of funds is said to be '**fettered**' if it only invests in the funds of a particular management group. A fettered fund of funds might apply no annual charge on top of the fees charged for the underlying fund.

Management groups may be able to negotiate lower charges on the funds they use, but investors should find out about the overall charging level.

4.6.2 Manager of managers schemes

With a **manager of managers fund**, instead of choosing funds run by other fund managers as part of their collective fund, the fund manager passes sums of money to other managers directly to manage for them. These other managers are given strict investment objectives and can be replaced if they do not achieve them. These schemes still represent a two-tier management system and are therefore costly.

Funds of funds structures shelter investments from **capital gains tax**, since a switch between funds does not crystallise a capital gains tax liability.

4.7 Fund supermarkets

Fund supermarkets are a concept in internet-based financial services (**e-commerce**). Funds supermarkets offer funds from various different providers, particularly for holding in an **Individual Savings Account (ISA)**.

A full online fund supermarket may provide:

(a) The ability to **'mix and match'** funds from different providers within a single ISA or other account without incurring the extra charges normally associated with self-select ISAs. However, only **unit trusts** and **open-ended investment company** investments can be held, so that investors wanting a selection of individual shares or investment trusts will still need to choose a self-select ISA

(b) The facility to **deal online** by credit card or debit card in real time without the need to download and print an application form

(c) The facility to **track and manage** the account online

(d) The ability to switch between funds within the service at minimal cost

Discount brokers operating on an **execution only** basis are sometimes referred to as fund supermarkets, but they do not normally offer the same mix and match facility and switches.

Discounts may be offered on funds' initial charges, and the fund supermarket may hope to generate revenue from ongoing trail commissions from customers who use their service. Fund supermarkets hope to win customers by offering the convenience of **consolidating** the availability of different funds through a single agency.

INVESTMENT AND RISK

With funds supermarket **consolidation services**, it is possible to invest with several different fund managers and have all transactions summarised on a single statement, electronic or paper. Distributions can be aggregated and paid by a single cheque and in many cases, regular withdrawals of capital from the whole portfolio can be automated to 'simulate' an 'income'. As well as having a wide choice of funds it is possible to switch between funds at low cost and avoid a high proportion of the initial charge.

Most fund supermarkets specialise in unit trusts and OEICs, but there are similar services for onshore and offshore life assurance funds and also pension funds.

When choosing which fund supermarket to use, there are a number of factors to take into account:

- The number of fund managers accessible
- The number of funds accessible
- Costs involved in switching funds
- Whether access is available on a regular premium basis
- Any minimum investment
- How income is taken from the funds. Some funds allow a programmed series of monthly withdrawals to allow a larger and more regular income (particularly effective to make use of the annual CGT exemption)
- Additional services available (such as data and information or access to make switches and make new contributions via internet)

4.8 Wrap accounts

A further development is the introduction of **'wrap' accounts**. These allow a wider range of assets to be held including:

- Unit trusts/OEICs – based on a 'supermarket'-type arrangement
- ISAs
- Pension investments from a SIPP or SSAS
- Life Assurance Bonds
- Child Trust Funds
- Shares, held in a nominee account

A single annual management fee will typically be charged.

The holdings are all shown in a single account, which can usually be accessed online. The investor can view the value of his or her assets and asset allocation, based on up-to-the-minute data.

The ability to analyse all these assets from a single source allows easy management of funds under a range of different arrangements as part on a single portfolio.

4.9 Investment risks

The risk of loss from an investment in collective funds will depend largely on:

- The categories of assets in which it invests, and
- The success (or otherwise) of the investment strategy of the fund

Bond funds carry a lower risk than **equity funds** because of the lower risks of fixed interest securities as a **category of asset** that we have discussed earlier in this Study Text.

Although **diversification** within funds reduces risk, an **investment strategy** such as specialisation within particular sectors can increase risk and broadly speaking, the level of risk should be viewed as similar to the risk of a portfolio of similar assets held directly. Various funds based on **technology and internet stocks** were marketed heavily at around the time of the **'dot com boom'** of 1999 and 2000, only to suffer heavy losses in capital value when the boom turned into a crash. With the benefit of hindsight, it can be seen that many investors in these funds entered the sector at precisely the wrong time.

5 FSA rules

Learning outcome

4.1.5 Recognition by the FSA of offshore funds.

5.1 The COLL Sourcebook

The regulations covering authorised unit trusts (AUTs) and OEICs/ICVCs are found in the Collective Investment Schemes Sourcebook named '**COLL**' which came into force on **13 February 2007**.

5.2 Types of authorised fund

The FSA recognises two different types of scheme available to retail investors

- **UCITS schemes** – schemes that conform to the UCITS Directive and can be marketed throughout the European Economic Area (EEA)
- **Non-UCITS retail schemes** – authorised funds capable of being marketed to retail investors but which do not fall within the scope of UCITS, perhaps as a result of the assets held. Such schemes can only be marketed in the UK

In order to ensure the protection of retail investors, the FSA impose investment limits for these schemes.

In addition to the two retail schemes, the FSA recognises a third type of scheme, the **Qualified Investor Scheme (QIS)**, that is only available to more experienced investors. No investment limits are considered necessary for QISs.

5.3 Types of security

The FSA recognises two different types of security, approved securities and non-approved securities.

Approved securities consist of securities that are listed on an eligible market within an EEA state, ie

- Transferable securities
    - Shares
    - Debentures
    - Government and public securities
    - Warrants
    - Certificates representing certain securities (eg depository receipts)
- Approved money market instruments
- Collective investments
- Derivatives
- Deposits

Any other securities, eg unlisted securities, are non-approved.

INVESTMENT AND RISK

5.4 Investment limits

Authorised fund managers of AUTs and ICVCs must ensure that, taking account of the investment objectives and policy of the authorised fund as stated in the most recently published prospectus of the fund, the scheme property of the authorised fund aims to provide a prudent spread of risk. This is achieved by setting

- **Aggregate spread limits** – limits on the proportion of the fund that may be invested in certain classes of investments
- **Individual spread limits** – limits on the proportion of the fund that may be invested in the approved securities of one body/issuer
- **Concentration limits** – limits on the maximum proportion of the securities issued by any one body that may be held by the fund

Aggregate spread limits

The following aggregate limits are placed on the proportion at the total fund value that can be placed in the various fund investments.

		UCITS schemes	Non-UCITS retail schemes
Transferable securities	– approved	100%	100%
	– non approved	10%	20%
Other funds	– regulated	100%	100%
	– non regulated	0%	20%
Money market instruments and deposits		100%	100%
OTC derivatives		100%	100%
Gold		0%	10%
Real property		0%	100%
Fund borrowing		10% (Temporarily)	10% (Permanently)

Individual spread limits – diversification

In addition to these aggregate limits, the FSA impose the following spread limits. For non-tracking funds, the maximum proportion of the fund that can be exposed to any one body (excluding government and public securities) is as follows.

	UCITS schemes	Non-UCITS retail schemes
Deposits	20%	20%
Transferable securities **or** money market instruments issued by a single body	10% in each of up to 4 securities, 5% thereafter	10%
Covered bonds, ie bonds issued by EEA financial institutions	25% provided < 80% in covered bonds in total	25%
Transferable securities **and** money market instruments	20%	20%

Aggregate of two or more of Transferable securities **or** money market instruments Deposits OTC derivatives	20% (subject to * above)	20%
Government and public securities where they represent <35% of the fund > 35% of the fund	No limit 30% in any one issue + minimum six issues held in fund	No limit 30% in any one issue + minimum six issues held in fund
Other funds Provided that the other fund's own exposure to further other funds is limited to	20% 10%	35% 15%
OTC derivatives	5% (increased to 10% if the counterparty is an approved bank)	10%
Real property	N/A	15%

For tracking funds, both UCITS and non-UCITS schemes can invest up to 20% in any one particular share, and up to 35% where justified by exceptional conditions.

Concentration limits

UCITS schemes must comply with the following concentration limits related to the proportion of the issue of any one investment that they may hold

	UCITS schemes
Non-voting shares	0%
Shares issued by one company	10%
Debt issued by one company	10%
Money market instruments issued by one body	10%
Units in a collective investment	25%

5.5 Use of derivatives - Efficient portfolio management

Transactions in derivatives, stock lending and writing of options are permitted for all funds except for feeder funds. Such transactions must satisfy two general conditions; that they are economically appropriate and covered by assets or cash. Transactions are entered into for one of three aims.

INVESTMENT AND RISK

- Reducing risk.
- Reducing cost.
- Generating capital/income with no risk.

The first two aims allow a manager to carry out asset allocation through the use of derivative overlays. The third aim allows for arbitrage and writing options.

5.6 Redemptions

Under FSA rules, redemption of non-UCITS retail schemes and QISs may, on proper disclosure to the investor, be deferred to the next valuation point if redemptions exceed 10% of the value of the fund. In addition, for property funds and schemes offering a guaranteed return, redemptions may be limited for up to six months.

5.7 FSA cancellation rules

To comply with **FSA cancellation rules,** firms giving advice on unit trusts and OEICs must allow investors who have received advice 14 days in which to cancel their investment. The cancellation period does not apply for sales made at a distance rather than face-to-face. More detail on cancellation rules is given later in this Study Text.

If customers who are eligible choose to cancel their units and the market has fallen, they will receive the **offer price** on the date of cancellation. This could be less than their original investment. If the market has risen they will not benefit from the rise and will only be refunded their original investment.

If a firm does not give to a **retail customer** information about his cancellation rights, the contract remains cancellable for up to two years and the retail customer will be not liable for any shortfall.

5.8 Limited issue funds

Under FSA rule changes introduced in 2001, unit trusts and OEICs are allowed to cap the number of units in issue. The introduction of such **limited issue funds** is intended to allow funds to be managed more efficiently, particularly in less liquid markets such as **smaller companies** and some **emerging markets**. For example, a fund investing in smaller capitalisation equities which becomes very popular may become a victim of its own success: if a large level of investment flows in to the fund, it may be impractical to invest such levels of funds in small companies. The limited issue funds rules also help funds to structure products that offer some form of downside protection.

6 Offshore funds

Learning outcomes

4.1.4 Taxation onshore and offshore

- Taxation within the funds.
- Taxation of UK individuals and trustee investors.

4.1.5 Recognition by the FSA of offshore funds.

6.1 Introduction

The term **'offshore fund'** refers to funds run outside the UK, usually in low tax areas. These include the Channel Islands, the Isle of Man, the Cayman Islands, Hong Kong and Bermuda. In recent years, Luxembourg and Dublin have become more significant also, as 'tax havens' within the European Union.

Many offshore funds are run by companies associated with large UK unit trust groups and most of the countries involved now have their own regulatory framework. Certain offshore funds receive recognition under sections 264, 270 and 272 of the **Financial Services and Markets Act 2000** (FSMA 2000).

Since 1979 when UK exchange controls were abolished, it has become relatively easy for the UK resident to invest his money abroad in equities, bonds or pooled investments such as bonds, UCITS (Undertakings for Collective Investments in Transferable Securities) and OEICs.

There may be income and capital gains tax advantages for **UK expatriates who are non-UK resident** and for **non-UK domiciled UK residents**. For non-UK domiciled persons, there may be inheritance tax advantages. However, investment in offshore funds may be not be as advantageous for **UK residents** as they think, particularly from a tax point of view.

In most cases, the tax benefit is limited to a possible **deferral of tax payments** resulting from income being paid gross.

There can be tax disadvantages, particularly if the offshore fund invests in UK shares.

S 238(1) of FSMA 2000 prohibits any authorised person from promoting any collective investment scheme in the UK unless it is an authorised unit trust, an authorised OIEC, or a recognised scheme. The Financial Services Authority recognises the following **offshore pooled investments**.

(a) Funds categorised as **Undertakings for Collective Investments in Transferable Securities (UCITS)** are constituted in other European Economic Area member states. These funds are automatically recognised by the Financial Services Authority and can be marketed freely in the UK.

(b) **Funds authorised in designated territories**, that is non-EU territories such as the Channel Islands, Bermuda and the Isle of Man. These funds may not be automatically recognised by the FSA. However, the FSA recognises that certain countries in which investments are based offer a similar regulatory authority and investor protection to that afforded to the UK investor onshore. These regulatory authorities are as follows.

Bermuda	Bermuda Monetary Authority
Guernsey	Financial Services Commission
Isle of Man	Financial Supervision Commission
Jersey	Financial Services Department

(c) **Individually recognised overseas schemes funds**. The FSA also provides for the recognition of overseas schemes on an individual basis.

Non-regulated and non-recognised funds are subject to severe marketing restrictions in the UK. Prospectuses and details can only be forwarded to investment professionals such as stockbrokers and Independent Financial Advisers (IFAs).

6.2 Offshore OEICs

OEICs (Investment Companies with Variable Capital – **ICVCs**) are the most common form of pooled investment in Europe. OEICs are based on the European type of ICVC known as Société d'Investissement à Capital Variable (**SICAV**). Unit trusts, in contrast, are more like what are known in Europe as Fonds Commun de Placement (**FCP**).

- The attraction of the OEIC is that it can issue any number of types of shares. As we saw earlier, an OEIC is 'open-ended', because the total amount invested in the scheme can be increased.

INVESTMENT AND RISK

- The ability to offer a wide number of types of shares led to the concept of umbrella funds. In this type of fund, there are many types of share under one management (the umbrella). Each type of share can invest in a different international sector.

- There is a wider range of funds offered to the investor through an offshore OEIC than an onshore unit or investment trust. The funds include UK Equity, International Equity, International Emerging Markets, International Managed, America, Europe, Japan, Latin America, India, Korea, Hong Kong, Australia, Commodities and Currency funds (in all the major currencies) and Fixed Interest funds (in all the leading currencies: eg yen, sterling, euro, US$).

6.3 UCITS

UCITS are not a separate type of investment, but a classification for existing investments such as unit trusts that can be marketed throughout the European Economic Area.

UCITS were created as a result of the UCITS Directive introduced by the Council for the European Communities on 20 December 1985 (updated by UCITS II and III). The idea of the Directive was that it would introduce a framework under which a fund management group could market a fund domiciled within one member state to investors resident in another member state.

Under the framework, a manager of a mutual fund certified as a UCITS in its country of domicile may not be refused permission to market the fund in another member state provided it complies with local marketing requirements.

The Directive covers:

- Funds situated in the territory of a EU member state
- Publicly offered funds
- Funds investing in transferable securities (usually shares and bonds listed on a stock exchange or traded on a regulated market)
- Funds whose units can be redeemed at the request of the holder

The Directive does not cover **closed-ended funds** (such as UK investment trusts) and UCITS funds cannot hold **commodities** or **property**.

A fund is authorised by the regulatory authority of its domicile and it is granted a UCITS certificate. Application is then made to the regulatory authority of other member states in which the provider wishes to market the fund. After two months the fund may be marketed.

6.4 Underlying funds of overseas pooled investments

There are a wide number of funds available to the investor in an offshore umbrella fund and it is possible to invest in any of the major currencies. The following types of funds are often used by investors.

(a) **Equity funds**. The equity funds most commonly used are overseas funds such as North America, Japan and the Far East. Offshore funds often offer a better choice of individual country funds such as Korea or India. Withholding taxes imposed by many countries on dividends mean that growth may be given priority over income.

(b) **Fixed interest**. Many UK investors, particularly non-taxpayers, may find offshore fixed interest funds attractive. The funds can be denominated in various currencies. The funds invest in bond markets across the world in both government and corporate stocks. Most bonds can be purchased by the fund to secure a yield free of tax. The investor can receive a high yield paid gross.

(c) **Currencies**. The funds give the international investor a method of investing in professionally managed currency funds at relatively low costs. In many instances an umbrella fund is used with many sub-shares being issued for all the different currencies. There is no corresponding sector among the unit trusts.

10: OEICs AND UNIT TRUSTS

6.5 Taxation of offshore funds

In general terms there will be no tax paid by an offshore fund. However, there may be withholding tax which may not be reclaimable by the fund. In addition, a fund may be subject to a small amount of local tax. Jersey funds are subject to a flat yearly corporation tax and Luxembourg funds to a tax on the asset value each year. The expenses of an offshore fund cannot be offset against its income.

6.6 Taxation of the individual

The taxation of the individual will depend upon the status of the fund whether it has **distributor** or **non-distributor** status.

(a) **Distributor status.** Distributor funds are those which are certified annually by HMRC as pursuing a policy of distribution of income. A fund will obtain this status if it distributes at least 85% of its net income after expenses. There is a concession for funds where the gross income in a year is very low and where the cost of distributing that income would be disproportionate to its value. The *de minimis* rule is set at 1% of the average value of the fund's assets. These funds are allowed to be certified as having distributor status.

The distributions paid from such funds are paid gross. A UK resident will have to declare this income and pay tax as follows.

(i) A non-taxpayer will have no liability to tax on the distribution.
(ii) A basic or lower rate taxpayer will pay 10% tax on the distribution.
(iii) A higher rate taxpayer will have to pay 32.5% on the distribution.
(iv) An additional rate taxpayer will have to pay 42.5% on the distribution.

On encashment of the holding or transferring between classes of participating shares, should a capital gain arise, the investor may be liable to capital gains tax depending on his circumstances. The profits could become subject to capital gains tax if:

(i) The gain is in excess of the annual CGT exemption
(ii) The gain is below the annual exemption but the investor has already made use of this in other transactions whether on or offshore

There are of course methods of reducing the capital gain.

(i) The investor may have other capital losses which can be offset.
(ii) The investor may consider transferring the holding into a spouse's name prior to sale if he or she has not used up the annual CGT exemption.

(b) **Non-distributor status.** This category of fund is often referred to as a **roll-up fund**. In this instance, all income is accumulated in the fund. If a fund is not certified with distributor status, on receipt of a distribution or on total encashment a charge to income tax arises. A charge to **income tax** on a gain rather than **capital gains tax** can be a **disadvantage**. As the charge is to income tax, there will be no annual CGT exemption to deduct and no indexation allowance or tapering allowance.

Those not resident in the UK will pay no UK income tax or capital gains tax on an offshore holding but of course they may be subject to tax charges in their new place of residence.

6.7 Uses of offshore funds

Offshore pooled investments may be useful for those who require a wider choice of funds than is available onshore. Offshore funds are particularly attractive to investors who wish to use **currency funds** or **hedge funds**.

INVESTMENT AND RISK

A fixed interest fund with **distributor** status may be useful for a non-taxpayer. His money will be invested in a fixed interest fund which is rolling up tax-free and he will receive a gross dividend.

A **non-distributor** fund, the taxpayer would pay no tax while his income was rolling up. If a higher rate taxpayer can take encashment when he will be basic rate taxpayer later, this might work to his advantage.

The non-distributor fund may be useful for a UK resident who is anticipating retiring abroad. He can roll up his investment tax-free and encash it when he is no longer a UK resident and subject to UK tax. He should however check on the tax treatment of his investment in the country in which he is then resident.

7 Structured investment funds

Learning outcome

4.1.6 Structured investment funds – equity index-based and equity-based growth and income funds.

Structured products are available that link repayment of capital to the investor by a pre-determined formula to the performance on an index such as the FTSE 100 Index (most commonly), or to other factors or combinations of factors.

Some funds make use of derivatives in order to make a guarantee of a return of capital to the investor (which might be in the range 85% to 100% of the original investment, for example). A **fixed period** often applies to the investment. Returns may be specified in a proportion of the rise of an index. Many share price indices, including the normally quoted version of the FTSE 100 Index, do not reflect dividends paid out by companies. In making comparisons of the investment performance of structured products based on an index, this should be taken into account.

Such structured funds may be located **offshore** (ie, outside the UK mainland).

Key chapter points

- Unit trusts and OEICs are open-ended collective investments, and so their price closely reflects the underlying net asset value. OEICs are Investment Companies with Variable Capital (ICVCs).

- Unit trusts and OEICs are sometimes referred to as Authorised Investment Funds (AIFs).

- Unit trust and OEIC investments carry the risks of their underlying investment class – for example, equities or bonds – but provide a vehicle for diversification within asset classes and sectors.

- The IMA classification system is used for unit trust and OEIC funds.

- There is currently a period of transition from the FSA's CIS rules for collective investment schemes and new COLL rules which will apply to all authorised unit trusts and OEICs by 13 February 2007.

- The COLL rules provide for two types of fund for retail investors: UCITS schemes – similar to existing schemes – and non-UCITS schemes – with less stringent rules. QISs – qualified investor schemes – are for institutions and expert private investors.

- There are FSA rules covering the extent of diversification of funds and maximum holdings by the fund in individual companies and securities.

- Maximum bid and minimum offer prices are set by FSA rules. Single pricing is operated by some unit trusts, and by OEICs, with any charges being disclosed separately.

- The valuation point is different for funds using historic pricing compared with those using forward pricing.

- Income from equity funds is taxed in the same way as dividends. Income from funds investing in bonds is taxed as interest. Disposals are chargeable to CGT.

- The OEIC/ICVC framework allows a fund to be marketed throughout the EEA.

- While a unit trust has a Manager and Trustees, the OEIC has an Authorised Corporate Director and a separate independent Depository. The manager / ACD runs the fund according to its objectives, dealing with marketing, investment and administration. The trustee / depository checks that rules are being followed and holds the assets on behalf of investors.

- The tax benefits of offshore funds to a UK-resident and domiciled investor are mainly limited to the deferral of payment of tax. Non-UK domiciled investors, or non-UK residents who are UK-domiciled, may benefit from the fact that income suffers UK tax only when it is remitted to the UK.

Chapter Quiz

1. What is meant by a fund being termed 'open-ended'? .... (see para 1.4)
2. What is the difference between income units and accumulation units in a unit trust? .... (2.1.1)
3. Outline the duties of the trustee of a unit trust. .... (2.1.2)
4. What is 'offer basis pricing'? .... (2.3.6)
5. In what circumstances must a fund manager who uses historic pricing switch to providing quotes on a forward pricing basis? .... (2.3.8)
6. In what situation does an income equalisation payment arise? .... (2.5.2)
7. How much capital gains tax must a unit trust or OEIC pay? .... (2.6.1, 3.4)
8. What is an Authorised Corporate Director and what is the ACD's role? .... (3.2)
9. What is the 'dilution levy' in respect of an OEIC? .... (3.3)
10. Identify the five main overall categories of funds in the IMA's classification system. .... (4.1)
11. Distinguish active fund management and passive fund management. .... (4.2)
12. Distinguish between funds of funds and manager of managers schemes. .... (4.6)
13. What is the significance of UCITS certification? .... (5.2)
14. What minimum percentage of a securities fund must be invested in approved securities? .... (5.3)
15. What are the FSA rules on diversification of funds? .... (5.4)
16. What, if any, are the tax advantages of offshore funds as an investment for different categories of investor? .... (6.1)
17. What do you understand by the abbreviations ICVC, SICAV and FCP? .... (6.2)

chapter 11

Investment trusts

Chapter topic list

1	The investment trust framework	228
2	Buying and selling	233
3	NAV and investment performance	235
4	Split capital investment trusts	239
5	Warrants and other share classes	243
6	Investment trusts and taxation	244
7	Comparison of fund types	245
Key chapter points		247
Chapter quiz		248

Chapter Learning Outcomes

4 **Understand** the following packaged products, their main features and suitability for different consumer circumstances

    4.2 Investment trusts

        4.2.1 Basic structure and characteristics – closed ended structure, differences between closed and other funds, range of investment trusts.

        4.2.2 Main different classes of shares – ordinary, income, zero dividend, capital.

        4.2.3 Dealing.

        4.2.4 Pricing, net asset value (NAV).

        4.2.5 Premiums and discounts.

        4.2.6 Gearing – advantages and drawbacks in terms of risk and flexibility.

        4.2.7 Past performance of investment trusts – risk and returns.

        4.2.8 Taxation – dividends and capital gains of investment trusts and for the investors who own them.

        4.2.9 Warrants.

1 The investment trust framework

Learning outcome

4.2.1 Basic structure and characteristics – closed ended structure, differences between closed ad other funds, range of investment trusts.

1.1 History

Investment trusts have a long history in the UK. The Foreign and Colonial Investment Trust was the first to be founded in 1868 with the aim of 'giving the investor of moderate means the same advantage as the large capitalist'. The investment trust provided a way for the small investor to have some exposure to investments in overseas stocks that it would have been impractical for the investor to buy individually. By mid-2003, there were 371 trusts in total, with total assets in the region of £50 billion.

1.2 What is an investment trust?

Investment trusts are a form of **collective investment**, pooling the funds of many investors and spreading their investments across a diversified range of securities.

Investment trusts are managed by professional **fund managers** who select and manage the stocks in the trust's portfolio. Investment trusts are generally accessible to the individual investor, although shares in investment trusts are also widely held by institutional investors such as pension funds.

Investment trusts are **public limited companies** (plcs) listed on the London Stock Exchange. Whereas other companies may make their profit from manufacturing or providing goods and services, an investment trust makes its profit solely from investments. The investor who buys shares in the investment trust hopes for **dividends** and **capital growth** in the value of the shares.

1.3 Comparison with unit trusts and OEICs

Investment trusts have wider investment freedom than unit trusts and OEICs/ICVCs. Investments trusts can:

- Invest in unquoted private companies as well as quoted companies
- Provide venture capital to new companies or companies requiring new funds for expansion

The corporate structure of an investment trust gives it a further advantage over unit trusts and OEICs because it can raise money more freely to help it to achieve its objectives. Unit trusts' and OEICs' powers to borrow are more limited. The ability to **borrow** allows an investment trust to 'gear up' returns for the investor. However, this **gearing** increases the volatility of returns.

Investment trusts are **closed-ended** investments. The number of shares in issue is not affected by the day-to-day purchases and sales by investors.

An advantage of the closed-ended capital structure is that it allows the managers to take a **long-term view** of the investments of the trust. With an open-ended scheme such as a unit trust or an OEIC, if there are more sales of units or shares by investors than purchases, the number of units is reducing and the fund must pay out cash. As a result, the managers may need to sell investments even though it may not be the best time to do so from a long-term viewpoint.

The **price of shares** of the investment trust **rises** and **falls** according to **demand** for and **supply** of the shares of the investment trust, and not directly in line with the values of the company's assets, ie **the underlying investments**. In this way, investment trust prices can have greater **volatility** than unit trusts and OEICs, whose unit prices are directly related to the market values of the underlying investments.

Because prices are **dependent on supply and demand**, the price of the shares can be **lower** than the **net asset value (NAV)** of the share. This can allow investors seeking income to **buy** investment trusts at a **discount**, while the **income** produced by the portfolio is based on the market value of the underlying investments. The income yield is therefore enhanced.

Charges incurred on investment trust holdings can be compared with the alternatives. Some **unit trusts and OEICs** have **initial charges** of around 5%. Initial charges may be much lower than this (at around 0.25%) for some investment trust savings schemes. However, there may be charges on selling investment trust holdings.

1.4 Open-ended and closed-ended funds

Unit trusts are normally **open-ended** funds. This means that the trust can create new units when new investors subscribe and it can cancel units when investors cash in their holdings. This makes unit trusts and OEICs different from **investment trusts**, which are **closed-ended**: new investors buy investment trust shares from existing holders of the shares who wish to sell. The table below compares the differing characteristics of open-ended and closed-ended funds.

Open-ended funds	Closed-ended funds
• The price closely reflects the underlying net asset value (NAV) of the investment.	• The investments must be purchased from another investor. The price is subject to supply and demand and may not reflect the underlying value (NAV). High demand increases the price; low demand reduces the price. • Where the price is greater than the underlying value of the investment, it is said to be at a 'premium' to NAV, where it is below it is at a 'discount' to NAV.

INVESTMENT AND RISK

Open-ended funds	Closed-ended funds
• New investors can bring in new money, allowing the fund managers to invest in new opportunities.	• There is no new money coming in: fund managers must sell assets in order to make investments.
• When investors sell, assets must be sold to release cash to pay them possibly disrupting set policies and strategies.	• When investors sell, there is no need to sell assets as the total amount of money invested remains; the same set policies and strategies can be maintained.
• Unit trusts, OEICs and life assurance investments are open-ended, as are many offshore investment funds.	• Investment trusts and some offshore funds are closed-ended.

1.5 AIC and classification of investment trusts

The **Association of Investment Companies (AIC)** represents investment trusts, Venture Capital Trusts and closed-ended AIM investment companies.

The AIC classifies investment trusts into a number of sectors and a number of specialist sectors. The classification of each trust is based on a combination of the regional or industry focus of the portfolio and the investment objective of the trust. The AIC classifications for investment trust companies are shown in the box below.

Investment trusts: AIC classifications

General sectors

Global Growth. Companies whose objective is to produce a total return to shareholders from capital growth and some dividend income. They will have less than 80% of their assets in any one geographical area.

Global Growth & Income. Companies whose objective is to produce a total return to shareholders from capital and dividend growth and which typically have a yield on the underlying portfolio ranging between a 100% and a 175% of that of the FTSE All-World Index. They will have less than 80% of their assets in any one geographical area.

Global High Income. Companies which invest in equities and fixed interest securities, whose objective is to provide dividend growth to shareholders. They will typically have a yield on the underlying portfolio above 150% of that of the FTSE All-World Index. They will have less than 80% of their assets in any one geographical area.

Global Smaller Companies. Companies which invest at least 80% of their assets in smaller company securities. They will have less than 80% of their assets in any one geographical area.

UK Growth. Companies which invest in UK securities and aim produce a total return to shareholders from capital growth and some dividend income. They will have at least 80% of their assets in UK securities.

UK Growth & Income. Companies which invest in UK securities and aim to produce a total return to shareholders from capital and dividend growth and which typically have a yield on the underlying portfolio between 100% and 175% of that of the FTSE All-Share Index. They will have at least 80% of their assets in UK securities.

UK Smaller Companies. Companies which invest at least 80% of their assets in UK smaller company securities.

UK High Income. Companies which invest at least 80% of their assets in UK equities and fixed interest securities in the UK, whose objective is to produce dividend growth to shareholders. They will typically have a yield on the underlying portfolio above 150% of that of the FTSE All-Share Index.

North America. Companies which have at least 80% of their assets in North American securities.

North American Smaller Companies. Companies which have at least 80% of their assets invested in North American smaller company securities.

Asia Pacific - Including Japan. Companies which have at least 80% of their assets in Asia Pacific securities, which includes a Japanese content of over 20%.

Asia Pacific - Excluding Japan. Companies which have at least 80% of their assets in Asia Pacific securities, which includes a Japanese content of less than 20%.

Japan. Companies which have at least 80% of their assets in Japanese securities.

Japanese Smaller Companies. Companies which have at least 80% of their assets invested in Japanese smaller company securities.

Europe. Companies which have at least 80% of their assets in European securities.

European Smaller Companies. Companies which have at least 80% of their assets invested in European smaller company securities.

European Emerging Markets. Companies which have at least 80% of their assets in European emerging market securities.

Global Emerging Markets. Companies which have at least 80% of their assets in global emerging market securities.

Latin America. Companies which have least 80% of their assets in Latin American securities.

Hedge Funds. Companies whose policy is to invest in a portfolio of Hedge Funds and/or employ a range of direct hedging investment strategies.

Private Equity. Companies which have a significant portion of the company's portfolio invested in the securities of unquoted companies.

Country Specialists. Companies whose policy is to invest in one or two countries. Companies are classified into Europe Asia Pacific and Other sectors.

Property Sectors

Property Securities. Companies whose policy is to principally invest in property securities.

Property Direct – UK. Companies whose policy is to invest in property in the UK

Property Direct – Europe. Companies whose policy is to invest in property in Europe.

Property Direct - Asia Pacific. Companies whose policy is to invest in property in Asia Pacific.

Property Specialist. Companies whose policy is to invest in a specialist sector of the property market.

Specialist Sectors

Biotechnology/Life Sciences. Companies whose policy is to invest in biotechnology and/or life sciences securities.

Canadian Income Trusts. Companies whose policy is to invest in Canadian income trusts.

Commodities & Natural Resources. Companies whose policy is to invest in a commodities and natural resource securities.

Endowment Policies. Companies whose policy is to invest in with-profits endowment policies or life assurance policies.

Environmental. Companies whose policy is to invest in environmental and alternative energy securities.

Financials. Companies whose policy is to invest in the financial services securities.

Forestry & Timber. Companies whose policy is to invest in forestry and timber related investments and securities.

Infrastructure. Companies whose policy is to invest in infrastructure investments.

Liquidity Funds. Companies whose policy is to invest in funds.

Litigation. Companies whose policy is to invest in litigation and arbitration cases, claims and disputes.

Securitised Debt. Companies whose policy is to invest in securitised debt instruments.

Small Media, Communication & IT Companies. Companies whose policy is to invest in small media, communication & IT companies' securities.

Technology, Media, Telecommunications. Companies whose policy is to invest in technology, media, telecommunication securities.

Utilities. Companies whose policy is to invest in utility and utility related securities.

Zero Dividend. Companies whose policy is to invest in Zero Dividend Preference shares or equivalent instruments (non-income producing).

VCT Sectors

Venture Capital Trusts (VCT). VCTs are a form of closed-ended fund that were introduced by the 1995 Finance Act to help provide finance for small UK businesses to develop. By adhering to the VCTs rules of investing in unquoted and AIM/OFEX listed companies VCTs are able to offer tax benefits to investors. Pre-qualifying VCTs are those that are not required to hold 70% in qualifying investments. A VCT must hold at least 70% by value of its investments in qualifying holdings by the end of the company's accounting period beginning no more than 3 years after launch.

VCT Generalist. Companies whose policy is to invest in a range of qualifying investments in different sectors.

VCT AIM Quoted. Companies whose policy is to invest in a range of qualifying companies listed, or about to be listed, on AIM or on any other exchange where the securities are treated as unquoted.

VCT Specialists sectors

Environmental. Companies whose policy is to invest in environmental and alternative energy companies.

Healthcare & Biotechnology. Companies whose policy is to invest in healthcare and biotechnology companies.

Media, Leisure & Events. Companies whose policy is to invest in media, leisure and events companies.

Technology. Companies whose policy is to invest in technology companies

1.6 Management

As a company, an investment trust has a **Board of Directors**. The **objective** of a company is to **invest** the money of the shareholders, so decisions on **investment strategy** are very important. These decisions might be made by the directors (in a **self-managed trust**), or may be delegated to an external fund management company. In all decisions, the directors of the company should act for the **benefit** of the shareholders.

Decisions made by the management of the company are open to scrutiny by shareholders, who may act if they are **not satisfied** with the performance. One sanction for shareholders is to **sell** their holding, which could affect the share price. If the share price falls significantly, the company could become a takeover target for other trusts or 'asset strippers' who may buy the shares in order to press for it being wound up.

Special resolutions, and those passed at the annual general meeting, will be subject to a vote by the shareholders. This will include **election of directors** and **appointment of professional advisers**. Some investment trusts also buy in other specialist services such as investment or registration services and the appointment of these will be subject to a shareholder vote.

1.7 Regulatory aspects

An **investment trust** is a listed company, governed by the Companies Act and Stock Exchange regulations. As with other companies, it is bound by the rules set out in its Memorandum and Articles of Association, which are set up when the company is formed. An investment trust is not a trust in the legal sense of that term.

The trust is also subject to the rules of the **Financial Services Authority**, the overall regulator of the financial services industry.

The following principles set down by the FSA apply to a company that seeks to apply for a listing as an investment trust.

- The investment managers must have adequate experience
- An adequate spread of investment risk must be maintained
- The investment trust must not control, seek to control or actively manage companies in which it invests
- The investment trust must not deal in investments to a significant extent
- The Board of the investment trust must be free to act independently of its management
- The investment trust must seek **approval by HMRC** (under s842, Income and Corporation Taxes Act 1988 (ICTA 1988))

Conditions that must be met for HMRC approval are covered later in this Chapter.

The trust itself does not have direct dealings with the public. If the management company offers the shares of the trust for sale to the public through a savings scheme, then the company must be authorised by the FSA to carry on investment business under the **Financial Services and Markets Act 2000**.

2 Buying and selling

Learning outcome

4.2.3 Dealing.

2.1 Prices

The quotation of the price of investment trust shares is similar to that for equities generally, and a dealer will give two prices.

- The higher price is the **offer price**, at which an investor can buy the shares
- The lower price is the **bid price**, at which a holder of the shares can sell

In a price quote in a newspaper or web site, a single price may be given: this will typically be the **mid-market price**, between the offer and bid prices.

The difference between the offer price and the bid price is the **spread**. The spread for less liquid shares will generally be wider than for more frequently traded and liquid stocks.

2.2 Dealing

Shares in investment trusts can be bought through a **stockbroker**, who is likely to charge the same level of commission as for other equities. If the investor's agreement with the broker is **execution only** (without advice), then commission might be as low as 0.5%, or £10 per deal. Stamp duty will be payable at 0.5% of the purchase consideration.

If the broker is providing an **advisory service**, then commission will be higher, for example 1.5% or 2% of the purchase consideration. Some brokers provide **discretionary investment trust management services** for individuals with larger sums to invest. The broker will select trusts that meet the investor's investment objectives and will charge an annual management fee in addition to dealing charges.

An investor can usually **deal through the investment trust managers** instead of through a broker, and may incur lower charges by doing so.

INVESTMENT AND RISK

Small investors who do not have an account with a broker may prefer to deal through the managers. However, the managers may only deal on a daily basis, while a broker will be able to quote an up-to-the-minute price and a deal can be made instantly by telephone.

2.3 Savings and investment schemes

The major trust management groups also operate **regular savings schemes**, through which an investor can make monthly investments.

- 'Drip-feeding' an investment through such a scheme takes advantage of **pound cost averaging**: with regular fixed investments, fewer units are bought when the units are relatively expensive, while fewer units are bought when unit prices are lower.
- Typically, such schemes will have a minimum investment of £25 or £50 per month.
- **Charges** are typically in the range 0.25% to 1% of the initial investment. Dealing may be at no extra charge.
- **Dividend reinvestment** (in further shares) may be available as an option for investors who do not require income.
- **Financial advisers** may be paid **commission** through such schemes. Investors may agree for up to 3% to be deducted from lump sum investments to pay an adviser.
- A low cost **share exchange service** is offered by some investment trust groups, enabling investors to realise their existing equity investments and to be given investment trust shares in return.

2.4 ISA wrappers

Investment trust managers generally offer the facility for investment to be made through a stocks and shares Individual Savings Account (ISA).

The manager may make an additional flat rate or percentage charge for providing the ISA wrapper.

All **HMRC (s842) approved investment trusts** can now be held in an ISA.

The main appeal of ISA wrappers for investment trusts (and other equity investments) is to:

- Those who have a liability to pay **capital gains tax** because they have gains in excess of the annual allowance, and
- **Higher rate taxpayers**, who have to pay further tax on dividends they receive outside a tax-advantaged wrapper.

2.5 Charges

Firstly, there are **internal charges** applied within the fund. These include funds' annual management charges, which generally range between 0.25% and 1.5% of the fund's total value.

Certain other costs, such as auditors' fees, custody fees, directors' remuneration, secretarial costs and marketing costs, may be charged in addition. They will normally be charged against the income of the trust, or in some cases against capital. Such charges will normally be disclosed in the investment trust company's annual report and accounts.

These various management expenses incurred within the fund over a year are totalled to give a **Total Expense Ratio (TER)**. TERs for funds are calculated by a research company called Fitzrovia International plc. Fitzrovia aims to calculate TERs on a consistent basis to allow comparison across investment trusts and other funds. The TERs of investment trusts are often lower than those of unit trusts and OEICs, many of which fall in the range 1% to 1.5%.

There has been a growing trend for collective investment funds to introduce **performance-related fees** for fund managers. The basic principle is to reward outperformance against a selected benchmark, as specified by the Board of Directors.

There are various internal charges that are not reflected in the TER. The TER does not include the following costs included in the expenses section of the annual accounts: performance fees, restructuring costs and various other costs related to the investment transactions that the fund enters into. These transaction-related costs include stamp duty and brokers' commissions. Bank interest incurred, losses or gains on currency and the spreads incurred between buying and selling prices of investments made by the trust will also not be reflected in the TER.

There are also charges that are **external** to the fund which the investor may incur.

(a) The **spread** is the difference between buying and selling prices, as set by marketmakers.

(b) **Dealing charges,** including **commission** and 0.5% **stamp duty**, are payable to the broker carrying out the transaction.

(c) **Product wrapper charges,** usually administration charges, may be charged by the manager of a 'wrapper' such as an ISA used to hold the investment in the collective fund.

(d) **Charges for advice** may be incurred in addition if the investor takes financial advice. An Independent Financial Adviser (IFA) may charge a fee for advice. An up-front **initial commission** may be paid to an IFA, and there may also be a periodic **trail commission** payable to the adviser. Some advisers may agree to rebate part or all of commission received against fees for advice.

2.6 Disclosures

Firms providing investment trust savings schemes and ISAs for investment trust investments must provide a **Key Features Document (KFD)** to the customer.

The Key Features Document gives general information about the investment trust and also must include a table illustrating the effect of charges and expenses over periods of 1, 5 and 10 years. The table must assume a standard investment growth rate of 6% for investment trust savings schemes and a rate of 7% for ISA schemes. (The rate is higher for ISAs to reflect broadly the effect of the differences in tax treatment.)

Using standard growth rates enables the investor to compare the products of different product providers of investment trust schemes. The investor can also make comparisons with other types of product, such as unit trusts, OEICs and insurance-based contracts, for which similar information must be made available by product providers.

3 NAV and investment performance

> **Learning outcomes**
> 4.2.4 Pricing and net asset value (NAV).
> 4.2.5 Premiums and discounts.
> 4.2.6 Gearing – advantages and drawbacks in terms of risk and flexibility.
> 4.2.7 Performance of investment trusts – risk and returns.

3.1 Aspects of performance

An investment trust share is similar to any other equity, except that the specific objective of the company is to invest rather than to transact other forms of business. The **past performance** of the trust can be measured against standard

INVESTMENT AND RISK

benchmarks of performance such as **market indices** most closely covering the market sector in which the trust invests. Outperformance of market indices over a period of years can indicate skilled and successful investment management.

Aspects of investment trusts influencing the assessment of performance are:

- Dividend growth and gross yield (calculated in the same way as for other shares)
- Net asset value (NAV)
- Levels of discount/premium to NAV
- Gearing

3.2 Net asset value

The **net asset value (NAV)** is the **net worth** of the company expressed in terms of the value of company assets per share.

The calculation of **net asset value** is one of the most important pieces of information for determining the value of an investment trust. It is essentially the **net worth** of an investment trust company's equity capital, usually expressed in pence per share and is calculated by totalling:

(a) The value of the trust's listed investments at mid-market prices
(b) The value of its unlisted investments at directors' valuation
(c) Cash and other net current assets

The company's liabilities are deducted from this figure, including any issued preference capital at their nominal value. The resulting figure is the **asset value** or **shareholders' funds** of the company. Dividing by the number of shares gives the **net asset value** per share. The **valuation** may be carried out monthly, weekly or daily.

The **net asset value** of an investment trust with assets worth £9 million, with liabilities of £3 million and 12 million ordinary shares would be 50p per share, ie (£9 million – £3 million) *divided* by £12 million. However, this figure is an **undiluted figure**. It does not make any allowances for any **warrants** in issue (which we discuss later in this Chapter).

In order to allow for the effects of **warrant holders** taking up their subscription, the subscription price is added as an asset and the new shares created are added to the total number of shares. The calculation for **diluted NAV** is therefore:

$$\text{Diluted NAV} = \frac{\text{Net assets (assets less liabilities) plus warrant subscriptions}}{\text{Shares in issue plus new shares in respect of warrants}}$$

3.3 Premium/discount to NAV

The share price at a particular time may be **greater** or **less** than the **NAV**. For example:

- If the NAV is 100 pence and the share price is 86 pence, then the shares are trading at a **discount** of 14%.
- If the NAV is 100 pence and the share price is 108 pence, then the shares are trading at a **premium** of 8%.

The *Financial Times* publishes figures for the **discount or premium to NAV** along with the share prices of investment trusts.

If shares in an investment trusts are trading at a **premium to NAV**, this may reflect investors believing strongly in the management of the company and in their ability to make the **assets grow**.

It is unusual for an investment trust to remain at a premium for an extended period of time. An investor who buys investment trust shares when they are a premium risks the possibility that the premium may be reduced or may switch to a discount, in the future.

Most investment trusts operate at a **discount to NAV**. The level of premium or discount relates to the **demand for shares** and any factor that can influence demand will affect it. For example, if investment in the Far East becomes unpopular because of forecasts of economic weakness in that region, share prices may fall and, if the values of the underlying assets have not fallen so much, the level of **discount to NAV** may increase.

The existence of a discount may be favoured by investors seeking income. If an investment trust has £1 million of assets and 900,000 shares in issue at a market price of 100p, an investor could be seen as buying £1.11 worth of assets per share. If we assume a yield of 4%, then an investment trust investor will get 4.44p per share as a distribution (ignoring charges). An investor in an equivalent unit trust would only receive 4p.

The fact that a discount to net assets is common presents a problem in the initial **launch** of an investment trust, when the trust must raise enough money from new investors to make the trust viable. If investors foresee that a discount is likely, they will need some additional incentive to invest at the launch. Some investment trust companies arrange the capital structure of the company in order to ensure that the investment trust shares are marketable. One common way of doing this is to issue **warrants**, with for example one warrant being given away with every five shares issued – this is sometimes referred to as a '**sweetener**'. Another way is to split the capital of the company into several **different classes of share** each of which produce a different form of investment return.

3.4 Gearing

Gearing is a measure of the extent of borrowing by an investment trust and can be calculated as:

$$\text{Gearing} = \frac{\text{Borrowings}}{\text{Capital and reserves}} \times 100$$

For example, if an investment trust has £100 million of total assets and £14 million of borrowings, shareholders' funds (capital and reserves) are £86 million. If the trust's total assets increase or fall by 10% to £110 million or £90 million respectively, and borrowings remain the same at £14 million, the shareholders' funds will have grown to £96 million or fallen to £76 million. This represents an increase or decrease in shareholders' funds of 11.6%, which in both cases is 16% more than the 10% increase or decrease in total assets.

We can say that the shareholders' funds are 16% geared ((14/86) × 100%), or we can express this as a **gearing ratio** of 116 ((100/86) × 100%).

The **gearing ratio** is expressed as a ratio of total assets to shareholders' funds multiplied by 100.

A gearing ratio of 100 means that there is no gearing. Generally, the higher the gearing factor, the more sensitive an investment trust's shares will be to the movements up and down in the value of the investment portfolio.

When investment managers **borrow**:

- There is an increase in the value of the assets purchased with the borrowed money
- Interest becomes payable on the loan

Where the growth in asset value exceeds the interest, which is likely in a **rising market**, the extra profits benefit the shareholders as a possible increase in **dividend** and/or **NAV**. Where this is not the case, which is likely in a falling market, the gearing causes an erosion of value. Overall, **gearing** increases the **volatility** of the share. The more highly geared a share is, the greater the movements will be relative to the market.

The loans may be in the form of **long or short-term bank lending**. The investment trust may also issue **debentures**, **unsecured loan stock** or **convertible loan stock**.

Example: Gearing

Aston Investment Trust has shareholders' funds of £10 million and loans of £2 million. The gearing of this company is £2 million/£10 million or 0.2. Gearing can be expressed in percentage terms, ie 20%, or as a gearing ratio of 120.

If Aston uses the borrowing to increase its holdings in shares and markets move up, the net asset value of the company is increased by the growth on the borrowing less the interest.

INVESTMENT AND RISK

> If Aston pays interest on its loan at a rate of 8% over a year and the value of the underlying investments increases by 20% over the same period, by what percentage will the NAV increase?
>
> ## Solution
>
> The gross value of the investments will be £12 million in total (the assets plus the borrowing). The assets will increase by 20% or £2.4 million, less the interest payable of 8% × £2 million = £160,000. The total NAV will be £14.24 million, less the borrowing of £2 million, an increase in value of £12.24 million/£10 million = 22.4%.
>
> Suppose that Aston's underlying assets lose value by 20%.
>
> (a) The value of the shares invested will be £12 million in total (assets plus borrowing).
>
> (b) The assets will decrease by 20% or £2.4 million, plus the interest payable of 8% × £2 million = £160,000.
>
> (c) The total NAV after the fall will be £12 million less £2.4 million, less £160,000 = £9.44 million, less the borrowing of £2 million.
>
> This gives a decrease in value from £10 million to £7.44 million, ie a 25.6% decrease.

3.5 Buybacks of shares

If the discount to NAV becomes very wide, investment trust managers may decide to **buy back** some of the shares, thus reducing the excess supply and possibly narrowing the discount.

As for other companies, a buyback by an investment trust of its own shares requires the permission of shareholders.

The following **FSA rules** apply to share buybacks.

- The approval of shareholders on one occasion can be to buy back up to 14.99% of the shares only. (Further approval would be needed to buy back more shares.)
- The trust must not pay more than 5% above the market price to buy back its own shares.
- The share buyback must be financed out of the investment capital of the trust.

Investment trusts are allowed to hold shares bought back (consisting of up to 10% of capital) '**in treasury**', rather than cancelling them. The shares could then be sold again at a later date. This mechanism can offer the trust a way of balancing supply and demand for its shares at different times.

3.6 Winding up of an investment trust

Some investment trusts are set up with a **limited life.** Provision is made for shareholders to vote on whether to wind up the trust at the end of the specified period. As with all companies, the shareholders can in theory vote to wind up an investment trust at any time.

A reason for setting a limited life is to avoid a persistent wide discount developing. As the planned winding up date draws closer, the discount should narrow as investors are anticipating the sale of the net assets of the trust and distribution of the proceeds.

If a trust is wound up, shareholders will receive the NAV for their shares, after paying any prior charges and winding-up expenses.

4 Split capital investment trusts

> **Learning outcome**
>
> 4.2.2 Main different classes of share
> - Ordinary.
> - Income.
> - Zero dividend.
> - Capital.
>
> 4.2.6 Gearing – advantages and drawbacks in terms of risk and flexibility.
>
> 4.2.7 Pass performance of investment trusts – risk and returns.

4.1 Overview

A **split capital investment trust** is like other investment trusts in that it has a single portfolio of investments. A split capital trust however involves a number of different classes of share, with holders of the different classes having different entitlements to returns of capital or income from the trust.

A split capital trust has a limited life. The period of time remaining to the planned winding up of the trust is usually very significant in how the prices of the different classes of share move.

Split capital investment trusts allow trust managers to tailor returns to appeal to different investors with different strategies, circumstances and attitudes. For example, if a **low risk** but **rising income** is required, **stepped preference shares** might be suitable. If an increasing income is required but high risk is acceptable, an **income share** might be more appropriate.

The **capital value** of all classes of share will vary up until the trust is wound up. At that stage, the amount of capital returned will depend on the class of share and the order of priority in which the trust is wound up.

An investment trust may be split into different classes of share as set out below.

Class of share	Income return	Capital return at redemption
Income ordinary	High/rising	Predetermined
Capital ordinary	None (with some minor exceptions)	Remaining surplus
Preference/stepped preference	Predetermined	Predetermined
Zero dividend preference	None	Predetermined

Source: AIC

4.2 Income shares

There are different types of **income share**. A financial adviser must be very clear about the terms of the different types of share, as some can result in substantial loss of capital.

Income shares pay regular dividends from surplus income on trust assets and have a predetermined maturity value, known as the redemption price (typically, the same as the issue price of £1). The redemption price is paid subject to there being sufficient assets remaining after debts and other preferred classes of share have been paid. The market price of these shares fluctuates above and below the redemption price, depending on dividend prospects and time to maturity.

Some income shares pay high income but have only a nominal redemption value, say 1p. Such shares may be attractive to an investor who has capital gains on other investments that can be set off against the capital loss.

INVESTMENT AND RISK

4.3 Income and residual capital shares

Income and residual capital shares (also known as **ordinary income shares** or **highly geared ordinary income shares**) offer a high and rising income plus all the surplus assets of the trust at the winding-up date after other prior-ranking classes of shares have been repaid. They have no predetermined redemption value and are last in the order of priority.

If issued by a trust in **combination** with a **zero dividend preference share**, holders of such shares are entitled to all the income generated by the trust. If issued by a trust with a **stepped preference share**, the holders receive all excess revenue after the predetermined dividend payment to the other class of share has been made.

Income and residual capital shares offer the potential for **high dividends** and **capital returns**, although their high gearing does make them a relatively **high-risk investment**.

4.4 Capital shares

Capital shares do not pay dividends. Holders receive all of the capital remaining when the preference and income shareholders have been paid their maturity values. The absence of guarantees means that capital shares are inherently risky. When the trust matures, the capital shareholders are last in line; if there is nothing left, they could come away empty-handed. There is the potential for impressive growth, or significant losses, through **gearing**.

> **Example: Capital shares**
>
> Greatwood Investment Trust has 500,000 income shares (£1 at redemption) and 500,000 capital shares. It has an asset value of £500,000 with ten years to run to redemption. If the fund grows at an average 10%, the fund will be worth £1,296,871 at redemption. The income shares will be repaid at £1 each or £500,000. This leaves £796,871 for the capital share investors (£1.59 per share).
>
> If the growth rate were 11%, the fund would be £1,419,710. This would give the capital shareholders (£1,419,710 – £500,000) = £919,710 (£1.84 per share). Thus, small increases in growth rate give large increases in capital returns.
>
> At what rate of growth would capital shareholders in Greatwood receive nothing at wind up?
>
> **Solution**
>
> If the fund produced exactly £500,000, the capital shareholders would not be paid. This would happen if there was no growth in the fund. If the fund assets lost value, capital shareholders would get nothing and the income shareholders would get back less than £1 per share.

4.5 Stepped preference shares

Stepped preference shares are an unusual type of preference shares that pays a fixed dividend. Normal preference shares pay the same dividend but stepped preference shares offer dividends that step up in value during the life of the trust. They both pay a predetermined redemption value when the trust is wound up. Commitments to pay fixed amounts would make this category of share suitable for those with a low appetite for risk.

For example, a stepped preference share might pay a dividend at 5% in year 1, 5.25% in year 2, 5.5% in year 3 etc.

4.6 Zero dividend preference shares

Zero dividend preference shares generate no dividend income but offer a fixed capital return or redemption value. The fact that they pay no income means they can be of particular interest for tax planning, especially if the annual capital gains tax allowance is used to shelter profits. For example, 'zeros' might be issued at £1, redeemable after 10 years at £2, paying no dividend in the meantime. As low-risk investments that pay a set amount at a set time, they can be appropriate for investors needing capital at certain points. Zeros rank first in the winding up of the trust together with other preference shares.

Zeros should not be considered in the same **risk category** as cash investments. This fact came very clearly to light in 2002 as fears were rising that some 'zeros' would not provide their expected return. The fact that no 'zero' had failed to pay out its predetermined return made zeros popular.

The popularity created great demand for zeros and many new ones were issued. However, the risk reduction on this type of investment is provided by the other types of split in the structure of the trust. To meet the demand, zeros were set up without the supporting structure of the other share classes, simply by cross-holdings of other zeros. This has led to problems when markets have fallen in recent years. However, zeros that are based on a 'sound' split capital structure can still be a good low risk investment.

4.7 Winding up split capital investment trusts

At the predetermined date, shareholders will be asked to agree to **wind up** the trust according to the procedure laid down in its Articles of Association. They may also be given the option of **continuing** the life of the trust or of rolling their investment over into a new trust.

If the trust is **wound up**, the different classes of share are **repaid** in order of priority, after **repayment** of any loans or debentures, out of the **assets** and according to their entitlement after expenses have been deducted.

If there are **warrants** (discussed below), these are ranked last and are paid after all other classes of share. Each share class follows in a particular order, both in respect of dividends, paid from the income earned by the trust during its life, and in respect of capital, paid from the assets of the trust at the winding-up date.

	Share class	
Highest priority	Zero Stepped preference Income	Zero Stepped preference
Lowest priority	Capital	Income and residual capital

Although split capital trusts have a limited life (which may be extended if the shareholders vote in favour), shares are tradeable and can be sold at the prevailing market rice at any time during the life of the trust. The price will reflect market conditions of demand and supply at the time.

4.8 Analysing performance

The **performance measures** used to analyse current and potential future performance on split capital investment trusts include:

- Asset cover
- Hurdle rate
- Gross redemption yield (GRY)

Which measures are most relevant will depend on which factors influence the price of the class of share.

INVESTMENT AND RISK

Class of share	Influences on price	Relevant statistics
Zero	Interest rates Proportion of underlying investment in other zeros	Asset cover Hurdle rate Gross redemption yield
Stepped preference	Interest rates	Asset cover Hurdle rate Gross yield of share Gross redemption yield
Income	Interest rates Dividend growth prospects Portfolio yield of trust	Asset cover Hurdle rate Gross redemption yield Gross yield of share
Income and residual capital	Dividend growth prospects Portfolio yield of trust Structure of trust Capital growth prospects	Hurdle rate Gross redemption yield Gross yield of share Level of gearing
Capital	Portfolio yield of trust Capital growth prospects Structure of trust	Hurdle rate Gross redemption yield Level of gearing

Source: AIC

4.9 Asset cover

Asset cover is the ratio of the value of the investment trust assets to its liability for repayment of each class of share. It is used primarily with zeros, stepped preference and income shares.

If the **asset cover** is 1 or more, it means that there are already sufficient assets to repay that class of share at the predetermined price. However, as there is a priority order for repayment this may not be the case for other classes. The higher the asset cover, the greater the chance of repaying that class of share on winding up. If a share has an asset cover of less than 1, it indicates that in the event of a wind-up at that time, the share class is not covered and the capital is therefore at risk.

4.10 Hurdle rate

The **hurdle rate** measures the level of growth on the NAV on a compound basis required to repay each individual share class at the predetermined price.

If the hurdle rate is 4%, then the trust's investment portfolio must grow in value by 4% each year in order to repay the redemption price in full.

A high hurdle rate indicates that significant growth is required between the time the statistic was calculated and the winding up date.

If the asset cover is greater than 1, the hurdle rate will be negative. A negative hurdle rate indicates that the market could fall and the shares would still be repaid in full.

4.11 Gross redemption yield

The **gross redemption yield (GRY)** is the total annual return from both income and capital, expressed as a percentage. The figure can be used to compare returns between different classes of share and different types of investment.

Certain classes of share will provide a **variable return** on winding up (eg capitals, income, income and residual capital shares, warrants) and, as such, it is not possible to calculate an exact figure for GRY. In order to provide a basis of comparison, notional rates of growth are applied and the GRY is calculated assuming the capital return based on those rates of growth.

4.12 Gearing

'Gearing' is a term generally used to refer to the extent of **borrowings** but, in a **split capital trust**, it also relates to the effect of the share structure of the company on the relative share price. Gearing exposes the investor to higher levels of risk. The higher the gearing, the greater the risk and the higher the potential reward.

With a **split capital trust**, the level of gearing depends on the entitlement to repayment of the class of share. The lower the priority for repayment, the higher the gearing.

5 Warrants and other share classes

Learning outcome

4.2.9 Warrants.

5.1 Introduction

In addition to conventional unit trusts and splits, there are a number of additional securities and classes of share available within the framework of an investment trust. These include **warrants**, **C shares** and **S shares**. We also discuss **packaged units**.

5.2 Warrants

We outlined the principle of warrants earlier. As mentioned earlier in this Chapter, warrants are often issued when there is an **issue of new shares** in **investment trusts**.

When new investment trust shares are issued, there will be no discount to NAV. This can be unattractive, as most investors anticipate that soon after starting trading the price will fall to a discount. In order to encourage investors to buy, warrants are issued as well. The warrants give the holder a right to buy shares in the investment trust at a later date, at the specified strike price. The warrants should have a value, even where the trusts are trading below the strike price. Over time, the price should be expected to rise and may be of interest to speculative investors. The sale price of the warrant helps to compensate the investor subscribing to the new issue of shares for the fact they are not getting a discount on NAV.

The exercise of warrants involves the creation of new shares with an entitlement to the NAV of the investment trust as well as any dividends. Therefore, the NAV per share for existing shares undergoes some **dilution** as a result of the exercise of the warrants.

Example: Investment trust warrants

A warrant gives the right to purchase a fixed number of shares on 30 April 2006 at £1.00. On that date, the share price was 93p. It would have been possible for the warrant holder to exercise their rights, but they would lose money as they are paying £1.00 for a share that they could buy in the market for £0.93. They should allow the warrant to expire worthless. If the price were £1.05, they could exercise the warrants, giving a profit of 5p each, less transaction costs.

INVESTMENT AND RISK

5.3 C shares

C shares (conversion shares) are shares floated after the original issue of ordinary shares, usually to **raise additional capital**.

C shares are quoted separately from the ordinary shares until the capital raised through their issue is fully or substantially invested in the investment trust. At this time, they are converted into the ordinary shares at a set ratio based on their **net asset value**. They are used to allow a trust to increase the number of shares and the funds under management without diluting the value of the existing shares.

The issue of **C shares** provides an alternative to using a **rights issue** to raise capital.

5.4 S shares

S shares are used to issue new shares on the market without incurring the expense of launching a new investment trust company. They form a separate investment to the original share issue and, unlike C shares, the price of **S shares** will always be quoted separately.

5.5 Packaged units

The managers of some split capital trusts arrange for a combination of their shares to be traded together in what is known as a **packaged unit** (not to be confused with units issued by unit trusts). Such units usually comprise shares in the ratio at which those shares were originally issued.

Packaged units have similar characteristics to an ordinary share issued by a conventional investment trust, although in some cases the component classes of share can be separated out and traded as separate securities if required. The discount to NAV may be lower than it would otherwise be due to the increased demand created by the split capital structure.

Packaged units provide a benefit for the investment trust managers, who are effectively getting the best of both worlds. The splitting of the units helps to reduce the discount on the shares and the recombination of them allows them to offer investors access to an investment with the more 'conventional' characteristics of an investment trust.

6 Investment trusts and taxation

Learning outcome

4.2.8 Taxation – dividends, capital gains of investment trusts and for the investors who own them.

6.1 Taxation of the trust

If the investment trust is **approved by HMRC** under s842 ICTA 1988, the tax regime for the trust is similar to that of **unit trusts**.

- The trust pays **no tax on gains** made from selling investments in their portfolio.
- The trust is not liable to tax on dividends from UK companies (**franked investment income**)
- The trust is liable to corporation tax at 30% on **unfranked income** (which includes foreign dividends, gilts and bank interest, and underwriting commission). Interest paid on borrowings and management fees can be set against unfranked income, with the result that a trust may not have to pay any tax at all.

To obtain approval by HMRC, the investment trust:

- Must be a UK-resident company, with its ordinary shares quoted on the London Stock Exchange
- Must not be a 'close' company (which means broadly that it cannot be controlled by five or fewer persons)
- Must get 75%+ of its income from shares and securities
- Must have no more than 15% of its assets invested in one company
- Must not distribute its capital gains (except for Venture Capital Trusts)
- Must distribute ≥ 85% of its gross income from shares and securities

Some **offshore-registered** investment companies that are managed in the UK and listed on the London Stock Exchange have s.842 ICTA 1988 approval.

6.2 Taxation of the investor

UK investors are liable for **income tax** on **dividends** in the same way as they would be with shares in any other company, and will be liable for **capital gains tax** on **disposal of shares**. There will be CGT to pay on any gain if the individual has exceeded his or her annual CGT allowance.

As already mentioned, the dividends received from shares in an investment trust are like any other dividend on shares and carry a tax credit of 10%. The investor is also subject to CGT on disposal of shares.

As with unit trusts and OEICs, CGT and additional (higher rate) income tax on dividends can be avoided where the shares are held in an **ISA**.

Stamp duty reserve tax (SDRT) of 0.5% is charged on purchases of shares in investment trusts, as for other equities.

7 Comparison of fund types

The following table summarises the differences between the various types of collective investment scheme in the UK.

	Unit Trust	Open-Ended Investment Company	Investment Trust and Venture Capital Trust
Legal Structure	Trust	Company	Company (plc)
Investors' Holdings	Units	Shares	Shares
Nature of Fund	Open-ended	Open-ended	Closed-ended
Pricing System	Dual price (bid/offer)	Single price (no bid/offer spread)	Dual price (bid/offer)
Pricing Calculation	Precise value of the underlying investments, charges calculated within spread	Precise value of the underlying investments, charges shown separately	Reflects value of underlying investments but driven by supply and demand for the shares, charges shown separately
Stock Exchange Listing	No	Listing optional	Listed
Secondary Market	None	Unlikely	As for Ordinary shares
Regulator	FSA	FSA	UKLA/LSE/HMRC

INVESTMENT AND RISK

	Unit Trust	Open-Ended Investment Company	Investment Trust and Venture Capital Trust
Investment Restrictions			
– General Rules	Clearly defined rules on what investments the manager may make	Clearly defined rules on what investments the manager may make	Almost unlimited, subject to board approval
– Maximum in Unlisted Securities	10%	10%	No limit (Minimum 70% for venture capital trusts)
– Maximum in One Investment	10%	10%	15%
– Maximum Stake in One Company	10%	10%	No limit
Maximum Borrowing	10% (Temporarily only)	10% (Temporarily only)	No limit

Key chapter points

- Investment trusts are a form of collective investment offering diversification in various sectors and in stock markets around the world. Investment trusts are set up as listed public limited companies (plcs) that invest in securities.

- Investment trusts are closed-ended (fixed number of shares in the market) and their shares are priced according to the supply and demand for them in the market. This price may be at a discount or sometimes at a premium to the net asset value (NAV) of the trust.

- Investment trusts do not have the restrictions on investments that apply to unit trusts and OEICs. They can borrow money to increase their gearing, which in turn increases their volatility and risk for the investor.

- The AITC lists the various categories within which investment trusts can be classified.

- The Board of Directors of an investment trust may delegate management to an external fund management company. Some trusts have a specified limited life, and a trust may be wound up by a vote of shareholders.

- An investment trust is bound by its Memorandum and Articles of Association and must be listed on the Stock Exchange.

- Provided that it is approved by HMRC, an investment trust is exempt from tax on capital gains from its investment portfolio. Taxation of the investor is similar to that applying for other equities.

- Investment trusts can issue different classes of share and can have a split capital structure. Zeros can provide capital growth at low risk while income shares can provide an above average yield.

- The investment trust must comply with the Companies Act and with FSA listing rules. External investment managers and firms operating savings schemes need authorisation by the FSA under FSMA 2000.

- An investor may buy shares in an investment trust through a broker or through an investment trust manager who operates a savings scheme or ISA. A financial adviser may be used.

Chapter Quiz

1. What do the initials 'AIC' stand for? .... (see para 1.5)
2. Outline the principles set down by the FSA for a company seeking a listing as an investment trust. .... (1.7)
3. What is meant by 'share exchange' in the context of an investment trust savings scheme offered to private investors? .... (2.3)
4. What is meant by an investment trust share 'trading at a premium'? .... (3.3)
5. What are the rules governing share buybacks by investment trusts? .... (3.5)
6. What is the full term for a 'zero', and what is a 'zero'? .... (4.6)
7. What is 'asset cover'? .... (4.9)
8. What does a negative hurdle rate imply for a split capital trust? .... (4.10)
9. Define a warrant. .... (5.2)
10. Distinguish between C shares and S shares. .... (5.3, 5.4)
11. What is the tax treatment of capital gains when an investment trust sells securities in its portfolio? .... (6.1)
12. What is the tax treatment when an individual disposes of investment trust shares? .... (6.2)

chapter 12

Life assurance company products

Chapter topic list

1	Life assurance products for investment	250
2	With-profits and unit-linked	251
3	Regular savings plans	258
4	Lump sum investments	261
5	Traded endowment policies	265
6	Friendly Society policies	268
7	Taxation of life assurance policies	268
8	Annuities	275
9	A comparison of unit trusts, OEICs, investment trusts and life assurance as saving schemes	278
	Key chapter points	279
	Chapter quiz	280

INVESTMENT AND RISK

Chapter Learning Outcomes

4   **Understand** the following packaged products, their main features and suitability for different consumer circumstances

    4.4   Onshore and offshore life assurance company products

        4.4.1   Structure and characteristics of life assurance funds and products.
        4.4.2   Qualifying policies – maximum investment plans and other endowments.
        4.4.3   Traded endowments.
        4.4.4   Charges – initial and annual.
        4.4.5   Taxation – onshore and offshore, within the fund and for the investor.
        4.4.6   Differences between life assurance bonds and OEICs/unit trusts.
        4.4.7   Structure and characteristics of purchased life annuities.

10.   **Understand** how other issues affect investment planning

    10.8   Implications for the consumer of closed and/or underperforming funds.

1 Life assurance products for investment

Learning outcome

4.4.1   Structure and characteristics of life assurance funds and products.

1.1 Protection and investment

The term **life assurance** implies some form of protection in the event of death. There are broadly two types of life assurance contract:

- Contracts that are only for **protection** (insurance) purposes (eg term assurance, which pays out only on death and only if death occurs within a fixed term)
- Contracts with both **protection and investment** elements

In this chapter, we will be looking primarily at **life assurance policies** as investment products.

1.2 Life assurance products v unit trusts/OEICs

We should bear in mind that, particularly as tax relief is not available on premiums on new life assurance policies, alternative investments such as **ISAs** and other **unit trust** and **OEIC** savings schemes now tend usually to be more tax efficient and/or less costly in charges than life assurance products. Ownership of unit trusts and OEICs can also be more flexible, allowing investments to be built up with variable amounts and to be sold relatively flexibly as required.

Advisers are of course expected by regulators to take these factors into account.

1.3 The protection element

With a policy that has both protection and investment elements, part of premiums paid must go towards providing for the **life insurance cover** element. The premiums required for this cover will be based on actuarial assumptions based on mortality statistics.

Some policies, such as **single premium bonds**, have a relatively low life insurance element and are primarily designed for **investment**. For example, the life insurance cover may be only slightly above the level of premiums paid and then almost all of the premiums will be attributable to the investment element of the policy.

2 With-profits and unit-linked

> **Learning outcome**
> 4.4.1 Structure and characteristics of life assurance funds and products.
> 10.8 Implications for the consumer of closed and/or underperforming funds.

2.1 With-profits policies

The investment element of life assurance products originally developed as a method of distributing underwriting profits to **with-profit** policyholders. In the 1970s, new forms of life assurance investment were developed based on **unit-linking**. Unit-linked funds are effectively **open-ended investments**, where the value of the unit is directly related to the underlying assets of the fund.

With-profits investors with policies in mutual insurers have ownership rights in the life office, and may gain from a windfall distribution from reserves if the company **demutualises**. However, demutualisation is not often more than a possibility and so should not generally influence the investor's choice of policy.

The market for with-profits policies is now mainly in **unitised with-profits** policies.

2.2 Conventional with-profits policies

The traditional non-unitised type of with-profits policy has received criticism in recent years because of the lack of transparency inherent in the **bonus** system that applies to such policies. The policy will specify a **minimum sum assured**, generally payable on death or on maturity, with bonuses payable in addition.

A **conventional with-profits policy** is set up for a **fixed term** and the return is in the form of an increase in capital value between purchase and maturity. This increase in value is based upon the sum assured of the policy and the bonuses added during the life of the policy.

Annual ('reversionary') bonuses are declared and added to the policy (for example, at a 3% compound rate). Annual bonuses broadly reflect the income yield from investments. **Terminal bonuses** are paid when a policy matures or on death. Their level is more variable because it depends more on the capital growth of the underlying investment funds.

Bonus type	When payable
Reversionary/ Normal bonuses	Paid **annually** in arrears: once added, they cannot be removed.
Special bonuses	These are declared under **extraordinary circumstances** (eg on demutualisation or takeover), or to reflect an unexpected exceptional increase in funds.
Interim bonuses	These are paid where **death** occurs between reversionary bonus payments and are proportional to the unpaid bonus.

INVESTMENT AND RISK

Bonus type	When payable
Terminal bonuses	These are paid at the **end of the term (or on death)** and reflect the growth of the underlying assets over the term of the policy, over and above those previously distributed.

An **advantage** of a conventional with-profits policy is that the investor is aware of bonuses building up towards maturity. However, the declared bonuses are not likely to be paid in full if the policy is surrendered and so the bonuses do not indicate the current value of the policy.

The size of bonuses is set to reflect the performance of the underlying investments over the long term, rather than over a single year. This system is intended to '**smooth**' the effects of fluctuations in underlying investment values and profits. For mutual insurers, the with-profits policyholders are the owners of the business and so are affected by fluctuations in the profits of the business arising from its other insurance business, including profits from its unit-linked business. For insurers that are plcs, there are shareholders to whom dividends will be paid from profits.

The smoothing effect of bonuses means that investors will not see the total of bonuses applied to the policy fall when the stock market falls, but it also means that bonuses applied will not rise greatly in periods when the stock market is booming.

The level of bonuses declared is set by the insurance company's Actuary. Because of relatively poor stock market performance in recent years, the level of bonuses has fallen. This has caused problems for many who have held endowment policies which they had expected would repay interest-only mortgages at the end of their term: many are now expected to show a shortfall below the amount required to repay the mortgage.

Investments underlying the with-profits funds of the company are likely to include a range of asset classes, including equities, fixed interest securities, property and cash. The typical asset allocation is similar to that of unit-based **managed funds**. Some companies have however made significant shifts of their allocation in or out of equities in recent volatile stock market conditions.

The performance of a **with-profit investment** will depend on:

(a) The performance of the **underlying investments**, for example equities, fixed interest securities, cash and property

(b) Whether the company is **mutual or proprietary**: proprietary companies must distribute some profits to shareholders

(c) Profits from **other areas of the business** (particularly for a mutual company)

(d) The **strength of the company** (the level of reserves, measured by the free asset ratio) affects the company's ability to continue bonus payments when investment performance is low

(e) The **reserves**, which affect the ability of the company to increase the proportion of equities in the fund as life companies are required to have certain minimum levels of liquidity

2.3 Unitised with-profits

With a **unitised with-profits** policy, the policy value is shown in units, each of which has a specified initial value. Bonuses are declared annually and are added proportionately to each unit. Normally, unlike other types of unit-linked fund, the price of units will never fall. The underlying principle of unitised with-profits investments is similar to that of conventional with-profits policies in that returns are 'smoothed': the surplus returns from good years are held in reserve to enable unit price increases to be made in bad years.

Advantages of unitised with-profits

- The investor can more easily appreciate the value of the investment, and has the reassurance that the price of units will not normally be reduced.

- Switches can be made to or from unit-linked funds of other types (although a **market value adjustment** may be charged, to reflect the fact that with-profit units do not have their value cut when investment markets fall – see below).

2.4 Market value reductions

The insurer generally reserves the right to make a **market value reduction (MVR)**, alternatively known as a **market value adjustment (MVA)**, to **with-profits** policies if they are surrendered early. This is applied if market conditions are adverse and is intended to protect those remaining with the fund. Such an adjustment may be considered necessary because bonuses declared are supposed to reflect the long-term trend of investment performance. If there has been a recent severe drop in performance, then an adjustment made to those withdrawing their policies should protect those who remain in the fund and should make surrender values more closely reflect the actual performance of policies.

An MVR will not usually apply on death or on maturity of the policy.

2.5 Free asset ratio

The **free asset ratio** of an insurance company is of interest to the with-profits investor as it is a measure of the strength of the company's reserves. Although the free asset ratio can be measured in different ways, it indicates the market value of the company's assets relative to its liabilities to policyholders. The average free asset of the major with-profits life funds was calculated as 6.6% in 2002, down from 22.5% in 1999, when the equities market reached its peak.

2.6 Unit-linked funds

A life assurance policy may have its value linked to the performance of unit-linked funds selected by the investor.

Through their unit-linked funds, **insurance companies** aim to cater for a wide range of investment objectives that an investor may have. The investment vehicle can be employed to satisfy a requirement for **income** (distribution funds) or for **capital growth**.

The insurance company may also offer unit trusts operated by other companies that investors may select for their policies.

The value of the policy is determined by the number of units allocated to it and their price. There will be a spread between the buying and selling prices of units which will typically be around 5%. This spread means that the surrender value immediately after the policy is commenced will be lower than the initial premium paid. There may also be additional surrender penalties. During the life of the policy, its value will fluctuate according to the prices of the units on which it is based.

The **Association of British Insurers Investment Classification Group** has looked at the hundreds of funds available in conjunction with Life Assurance and Pension plans and put them into groups (or categories). The aim is that all the funds in one category are broadly comparable, making it easier for investors to compare like with like when deciding which fund is most suitable for them.

The categories are set according to a variety of factors, including:

- Equity (shares) content
- Spread of assets
- Type of assets
- Geography, ie where funds are invested
- Currency

INVESTMENT AND RISK

The categories are not specifically designed to grade funds according to **risk**. The broader categorisations (equities, fixed interest, deposit) provide some indication of risk as this varies by asset type. The four categories of **Managed Funds** are differentiated mostly by their equity content, and this could be viewed as a form of risk grading.

ABI Investment Classification Group Fund Categories

MIXED ASSET SECTORS

Defensive Managed
- Maximum of 35% total equity (including convertibles)
- Minimum of 85% sterling based assets.

Cautious Managed
- Maximum of 60%, minimum 20%, total equity (including convertibles)
- Minimum of 60% sterling based assets.

Balanced Managed
- Maximum of 85%, minimum 40%, total equity (including convertibles)
- Minimum of 50% sterling based assets.

Flexible Managed
- Maximum of 100%, no minimum, total equity (including convertibles)
- Minimum of 20% sterling based assets.

DISTRIBUTION FUNDS
- Maximum 60%, minimum 20%, total equity (including convertibles)
- Minimum of 50% sterling based assets
- Yield of at least 110% of the FTSE All Share Index gross yield before deduction of management charges
- Fund must be capable of distribution.

UK EQUITY FUNDS

UK All Companies
- Funds which invest at least 80% of their assets in UK equities which have a primary objective of achieving capital growth.

UK Equity Income
- Funds which invest at least 80% of their assets in UK Equities and which aim to have a yield in excess of 110% of the yield of the FTSE All Share Index.

UK Smaller Companies
- Funds which invest at least 80% of their assets in UK Equities forming the bottom 10% by market capitalisation.

Additional Notes (UK Equity Funds)

There is currently no separate category for ethical type funds. Such funds – where they are primarily UK based – will be found in the category most suited to the nature of the underlying assets. They will however be separately "flagged".

Tracker funds will be treated in a similar way to ethical funds.

FIXED INTEREST FUNDS

UK Gilt
- At least 80% in UK Gilts.

Sterling Fixed Interest

- At least 80% in sterling denominated investment grades (BBB or above) fixed interest securities.
- Fixed Interest defined as Gilts, Bonds, Preference Shares and Permanent Interest Bearing Shares (convertibles are not treated as fixed interest investments).

Global Fixed Interest

- At least 80% of investments to be held in non-UK based assets.
- All other criteria identical to UK Fixed Interest criteria.

UK Index-linked

- At least 80% in UK Index-linked Gilts.

Sterling Long Bond

- Fund (used in conjunction with pension plans) with a specific objective of investing primarily in sterling denominated long duration bonds so that the movement in the value of units in the fund approximates to movements in annuity purchase prices.
- As least 80% held in bonds with a duration of 10 years or more.

Sterling Other Fixed Interest

- At least 80% of their assets in sterling-denominated (or hedged back to sterling) fixed interest securities.
- Funds with investment policy permitting significant changes in asset allocation between broad investment grade and sub-investment grade securities.

Sterling Corporate Bond

- Funds which invest at least 80% of their assets in sterling-denominated (or hedged back to sterling) broad investment grade corporate bond securities.
- This excludes Preference shares, Permanent Interest Bearing shares and convertible securities.

Sterling High Yield

- At least 80% in sterling-denominated Government Sovereign Bonds and Corporate Bonds.
- Funds which invest at least 50% of their assets in sub-investment grade fixed interest securities.

Global High Yield

- At least 80% in non-UK Government Sovereign Bonds and Corporate Bonds.
- At least 50% of their assets in sub-investment grade Government Sovereign Bonds and Corporate Bonds.

OVERSEAS EQUITY SECTOR FUNDS

Global Equities

- At least 80% of investments in equities and no more than 50% in any equity region.

Europe including UK Equities

- At least 80% of investments in European equities which include UK equities (but excluding those which would otherwise qualify for a UK Equity sector).

Europe excluding UK Equities

- At least 80% of investments in European equities, but which normally hold no UK Equities.

North America

- At least 80% of investments in United States or Canadian equities.

Asia Pacific including Japan

- At least 80% of investments in Far Eastern equities, but which include Japanese equities (but excluding those which would otherwise qualify for the Japan sector).

Asia Pacific excluding Japan

- At least 80% of investments in Far Eastern equities, but which normally hold no Japanese equities.

Japan

- At least 80% of investments in Japanese equities.

Global Emerging Markets

- At least 80% in equities from emerging markets (as defined by the FTSE World Index Indices) across a number of different regions
- Funds with more than 50% of assets in any one geographical region, eg China, India and Latin America will be flagged

PROPERTY

UK Direct Property

- At least 80% in UK property.

UK Property Securities

- A least 80% in property securities quoted on the UK stock market and direct property located in the UK.
- Property securities include real estate investment trusts, shares issued by companies that own, develop or manage direct property and Property Index Certificates.

Global Property

- A least 80% in direct property and property securities.
- Minimum 50% non-UK assets.

OTHER FUNDS

Sterling preference shares and convertibles

- At least 80% in sterling-denominated preference shares, PIBS and convertibles.

Protected/Guaranteed Funds

- Funds, other than money market funds, which principally aim to provide a return of a set amount of capital back to the investor (either explicitly guaranteed or via an investment strategy highly likely to achieve this objective) plus some market upside. Funds that offer a guaranteed minimum return of original capital will be flagged.

Money Market

- At least 95% of assets in Sterling money market instruments (cash and near cash, such as bank deposits, certificates of deposit, very short term fixed interest securities or floating rate notes).

Commodity/Energy

- Funds investing at least 80% in commodity and/or energy related investments

Specialist

- Funds that do not meet any other sector interest.

Unclassified

> - Any funds that do not provide sufficient data for the Investment Classification Group to monitor its classification effectively.

Many funds are similar to non-assurance based funds or are the same as unit trusts and OEIC funds run by the same financial institution. However, the following types of fund are found mainly in life assurance based investments.

- With-profits funds
- Property funds holding direct property investments (rather than property shares)
- 'Managed funds' containing a balanced mix of different asset classes such as equities, fixed interest securities, property and cash deposits.

Like unit trusts and OEICs, unit-linked prices are based on valuations (daily, in the case of equities) of the underlying assets.

2.7 Pound cost averaging in unit-linked funds

Making **regular savings** in unit-linked products gives investors the advantage of **pound cost averaging**. This can boost the return and reduce risk because more units will be purchased when the price of units is lower. More volatile funds will show this effect to a greater extent.

2.8 Switches and redirections

The **unit-linked funds** underlying the investment can be **changed** at the request of the investor. A **switch** will change the units already purchased to other available units, whereas a **redirection** changes the funds in which future contributions will be invested. To make a complete change from one fund to another, **switching and redirection** is combined. For example, with a switch from a company's European fund to the Managed fund, the switch exchanges existing European units for Managed fund units while the redirection ensures that future contributions buy Managed fund units. These switches usually involve **minimal cost**. Redirection is usually free and many companies offer unlimited free switches. In contrast, switches between investment trusts or unit trusts in non-life assurance based investment plans would incur charges and constitute a chargeable transfer for capital gains tax purposes.

2.9 Distribution bonds

Unit-linked bond funds generally do not treat income and capital separately. Returns from invested income are added to the price of units. If an 'income' is required, this can be provided by the **encashment of units** on a regular basis. However, **distribution bonds** do separate income and capital.

In order to produce **income**, a **distribution bond** will invest in a mixture of **gilts, fixed interest securities, convertibles** and **high yielding equities**. The difference between a distribution bond and an ordinary bond is that a distribution bond has a separate fund into which the income from the main fund is placed. The income in the separate fund can be distributed on a regular basis, eg quarterly or half yearly. The advantage of this is that it allows investors to encash units representing just the income rather than both income and capital.

As shown in the Box above, the ABI defines **distribution funds** as funds with a maximum 60% equity content (including convertibles), a minimum of 50% sterling based assets, and a yield of at least 110% of the FT All Share Index gross yield before deduction of management charges.

All **encashments**, whether from the **income units** or the **main fund**, are deemed by HMRC to be return of capital and are taxed in accordance with the normal rules relating to non-qualifying life insurance funds.

INVESTMENT AND RISK

2.10 Compensation

Holders of long-term with-profits and unit-linked policies will be covered by the **Financial Services Compensation Scheme** which provides that, in the event of an insurance company going into liquidation, the policyholders will be protected to the extent of up to 90% of their benefits.

2.11 Closed funds

Some providers have decide to **close with-profits funds to new business**. Research has show that some closed funds perform better than open funds, and some have worse performance.

There has been a tendency for many closed funds to have a lower exposure to equities and a higher content of fixed interest securities than open funds, particularly where the provider of the closed fund lacks financial strength. A higher fixed interest content generally reduces risk arising from shorter term volatility in equities prices, but over the long term it may result in relative underperformance.

The decision about what action a policyholder should take depends on individual circumstances and there are no easy generalisations.

A policyholder considering exiting from a fund should consider whether a penalty in the form of a **market value reduction (MVR)** is applied to the policy values of those exiting the fund. When market value reductions are low or zero, those exiting may be in a relatively advantageous position. A high MVR is designed to protect those remaining within the fund, to the relative disadvantage of those exiting.

A policyholder with an endowment policy can seek a quotation to sell their policy on the traded endowment policy market. This could, depending on the circumstances, provide proceeds up to one-third higher than the surrender value available from the life company.

3 Regular savings plans

Learning outcomes

4.4.1 Structure and characteristics of life assurance funds and products.
4.4.4 Charges – initial and annual.

3.1 Introduction

Insurance companies moved away from their traditional role of providing primarily protection policies to a position market investment products to meet various needs. In this section, we will look at products which can be used for regular savings purposes.

However, there is very little new business in the category of with-profits endowment policies. Such policies are most likely to be encountered as existing policies, which may be traded as second-hand policies.

3.2 Endowment policies

The **with-profits endowment policy** is a regular premium savings policy for a fixed term. The term may be between 10 and 25 years.

Premiums may be paid monthly, quarterly, half-yearly or annually. Only policies taken out before 14 March 1984 benefit from **life assurance premium relief (LAPR)** on the premiums paid. The premiums are paid net of life assurance tax relief at 12.5% to a limit being the greater £1,500 or one sixth of income.

The with-profits endowment policy offers the investor a guaranteed sum assured. This is normally quite low as the main aim of the policy is to provide a savings medium.

A bonus is added each year to the sum assured: this is the reversionary or annual bonus. Once added this bonus cannot be taken away. On maturity or earlier death an additional bonus, known as a vesting or terminal bonus, is added to the accrued sum assured and reversionary bonus. The terminal bonus can be a high percentage of the total return.

Before declaring the reversionary bonus, the insurance company values its life fund and declares a surplus for the year. The actuaries then recommend how much of the surplus can be allocated to the with profit policyholders with the balance going to reserves. (In the case of a proprietary office provision will need to be made for the shareholders' dividends.) Although the performance of the life fund can vary from year to year depending on investment performance, nevertheless by calling on reserves, if necessary, the insurance company should be able to declare a smooth pattern of bonus over the years. The terminal bonus reflects more directly the insurance company's returns in its life fund close to the maturity of the policy.

The Financial Services Authority (FSA) allows insurance companies to quote the returns on endowment policies assuming **growth rates** of 4%, 6% and 8% pa.

3.3 'Low cost' endowment policies

A **'low cost' endowment policy** combines two aspects of two products: a with profit endowment and a reducing term assurance. In the construction of the package, the actuary assumes that a certain level of bonus is added to the with-profits endowment element each year. The term assurance reduces annually by an equal amount. If bonus levels are greater than assumed, a profit will be achieved.

A 'low cost' endowment policy is most likely to be used in connection with a mortgage. The aim of the policy is to provide maximum cover for a given premium. As a large part of the premium is being applied to term assurance, the investment returns will be lower than with a full endowment policy.

3.4 Flexible endowment policies

Flexible endowment policies overcome the inflexibility of fixed term policies.

The policy runs to a maturity date, normally the policyholder's 65th birthday. In addition the policy is broken down into **segments**; for example if there is a monthly investment of £100, there may be ten segments of £10 each. From year ten onwards it is possible for the policyholder to encash segments of his policy without penalty. He will still be eligible for terminal or vesting bonus (which is normally not paid on early surrender).

3.5 Unit-linked endowment policies

The features of this type of policy are as follows.

(a) It is a fixed term policy into which regular premiums are made.

(b) Most contracts have minimum life cover, set at 75% of the premiums paid over the term of the policy in order to maintain the qualifying status of the policy.

(c) Some policies are designed only to accept large premium payments, say over £100 per month with the minimum amount of life cover to keep the policy qualifying. These policies are known as **maximum investment plans**.

(d) Whatever the size of the premium, the investor has a choice of funds into which his premiums can be invested, including for example UK Equity, Property, European, Pacific, America, Fixed Interest and Cash.

INVESTMENT AND RISK

(e) The premium is invested in the chosen fund or funds and units are then cancelled to pay for the life assurance and charges. The choice of fund will of course depend on the client's attitude to risk.

(f) The use of monthly premiums means that the client can make use of **pound cost averaging**, which has been mentioned earlier. The effect of pound cost averaging in the purchase of units is shown below. You will see that the unit price varies, so the number of units purchased by the same premium varies from month to month. Fewer units are purchased when the units are more expensive.

Monthly contribution of £30.00 purchasing units in a Far Eastern Fund

Month	Offer price	Units purchased
August	208.40	14.395
September	201.20	14.911
October	210.50	14.252
November	201.40	14.896
December	181.40	16.538
January	182.30	16.456

(g) Switches between funds are possible. Normally there is one free switch each policy year and subsequent switches can be made at a small cost such as £20.

3.6 Whole of life and endowment policies

Endowment policies normally have payment term of at least ten years, with an option to extend them if required. At the end of the ten-year period, or at a later date, a lump sum can be taken equal to the bid value of the units.

Although the endowment type is more common, unit-linked savings plan can be written as either an endowment policy or a **whole of life policy**. After an initial period, of perhaps ten years, premiums can continue to be paid indefinitely, or the units can be encashed at their bid value at any time.

As mentioned above, unit-linked savings plans usually have enough life cover to make sure that they are qualifying policies. Accordingly, there is typically a guaranteed sum assured of 75% of the premiums payable over the whole term, or up to age 75 in the case of a whole of life policy.

3.7 Charging structure

There is a different charging structure depending on whether the policy is with-profits or unit-linked.

The advent of commission disclosure was one of the factors leading to many insurance companies abandoning traditional **with-profits** policies. This is because of the problem of having to quantify the costs of the policy to the policyholder in the Key Features Document.

As a savings vehicle, the traditional endowment policy is relatively expensive in charges. Additionally, he policyholder is paying for life assurance which he may not need. A simpler method is to separate out an individual's protection and savings needs. Protection can then be provided by term assurance and regular investment could be by a regular contribution to an ISA or a unit trust or investment trust savings plan.

The charges on a **unit-linked** policy are more transparent. There is typically a 5% to 6% bid/offer spread on the purchase of units, a monthly policy fee, which may be indexed, and an annual management charge, of perhaps 1%. Insurance companies have used the following methods to extract setting-up charges.

(a) Low allocation of units for the first 12 to 24 months.

(b) The use of initial and accumulation units. The first 12 or 24 months premiums are used to purchase the initial units, which carry a heavier charge. Thereafter premiums are invested in the accumulation units.

3.8 Risk

A **unit-linked policy** carries the risk arising from the fact that the price of units will rise and fall with market conditions and with the performance of the individual investments making up the underlying investments.

The investment risk involved in a **with-profits** endowment policy is relatively low. The policyholder has a guaranteed sum assured to which a reversionary bonus is added and, once added, cannot be removed, however poor future performance may be. There are however the risks that future bonus rates will drop and that the terminal or vesting bonus may be low or non-existent.

There is also a risk of a poor return on early encashment. The surrender or paid-up values will include penalties which cannot easily be assessed in advance. With many with-profits policies, there will be no surrender value at all if the policy is surrendered within the first year or so. There could also be a tax implication on early encashment of such a policy.

3.9 Purchase and sale

Endowment policies are purchased from an insurance company following a recommendation from a company direct salesman, a tied agent or an independent financial adviser.

The products are designed to be held to maturity. Early encashment brings penalties which normally cannot be quantified until the time of withdrawal. The **surrender values** for traditional with profit policies are calculated by the actuary at the time of request. As an alternative to surrender, the policy may be sold on the **traded endowment policy market**. The amount obtained from selling could be around one-third more than the surrender value quoted by the insurance company.

4 Lump sum investments

> **Learning outcomes**
>
> 4.4.1 Structure and characteristics of life assurance funds and products.
> 4.4.4 Charges – initial and annual.

4.1 Investment bonds

Insurance companies offer non-qualifying single premium policies as a lump sum investment vehicle. Such non-qualifying policies are variously advertised as investment bonds, property bonds, **single premium bonds** or single premium life assurance bonds. The term **single premium bond** or **single period life assurance** bond refers to the fact that a single payment is made and units are purchased in a fund or funds of the investor's choice. A **property bond** would be one where the underlying asset generating fund income and gains is property.

The investor has the choice of a typical range of **unit-linked funds**. Bonds based on **unitised with-profits funds** are also available. The bond normally allows the investor to spread his capital between a number of funds and to switch between funds. The charges to use the switch facility are nominal. Typically the investor may be allowed one free switch per annum and subsequent switches are at a flat charge of, say, £25.

The investor can withdraw his money from the bond at the bid price at any time, normally without penalty. There may be a restriction imposed on withdrawal from a property fund, because of the relative illiquidity of the underlying assets of property funds.

The investor can simulate an income from his investment bond by making use of a **withdrawal facility**. Such a facility allows for up to 5% of the original investment to be withdrawn each policy year with no immediate tax charge. The withdrawals are taken into account when calculating the final gain when the bond is encashed (see later in this Chapter). The 'income' might be taken monthly, quarterly, half-yearly or annually.

In the event of death the units will be sold at the bid price and the funds paid to the policyholder's estate.

An investment bond is a non-qualifying whole of life policy for tax purposes. A higher rate taxpayer should ensure that the investment bond is **segmented** as this may be advantageous if he wishes to take surrenders, the taxation on total surrender being more advantageous than partial surrenders (see later in chapter).

For unit-linked policies, there is normally an **up-front charge** which is a 5% bid/offer spread. In addition there will be an **annual management charge** typically of around 0.75% to 1.0% of the value of the fund.

Bonds are purchased directly from the insurance company. The insurance company is responsible for making withdrawal and final encashment payments.

Advisers should take care when recommending a bond rather than, say, an investment or unit trust. They should be aware of the **compliance requirement** that 'you must not advise a client to buy a packaged product if you are aware of a generally available packaged product which would *better* meet his needs and circumstances'. The charges levied on an investment bond are generally higher than for unit trusts or investment trust. In addition, the insurance company pays capital gains tax within the life fund whereas unit trusts and investment trusts do not. For these reasons, the performance of an investment bond may be inferior to a similar unit trust or investment trust.

An investment bond offers certain tax advantages for a higher rate taxpayer. The insurance company fund pays tax at 20% on investment income whereas the client would have a personal tax rate of 40%. The client can take advantage of the 5% withdrawal facility (see later in this chapter) to defer taxation until, possibly, a time when he is a basic rate taxpayer. If an investment bond is held by a higher rate taxpayer and his or her spouse is a basic rate taxpayer, consideration should be given to assigning the policy to the spouse prior to encashment.

The **Trustee Act 2000** permits **trustees** to invest in investment bonds and other life assurance policies. Under the previous Trustee Investment Act 1961, these were only permitted investments for trustees if the trust deed gave appropriate powers to the trustees.

4.2 Guaranteed income bonds

A **guaranteed income bond** is a single premium investment scheme. The level of income is guaranteed and so too is the return of the original investment.

The bond can be constructed in a number of ways, as follows, although the outcome for the investor is much the same.

- A **single premium investment bond**.
- A **series of non-qualifying endowment policies**. Using this method, one bond is encashed each year to pay the income and the encashment of the final bond repays the capital.
- A **combination of a temporary annuity and a deferred annuity**. Using this method the temporary annuity pays the income and the deferred annuity repays the capital at maturity. This method may have advantages for non-taxpayers, basic rate and higher rate taxpayers.

Whichever construction method is used, a guarantee of the return of the original investment on death must be incorporated in the bond.

Some insurance companies simply offer a tranche of guaranteed income bond money and once this is exhausted the bond is withdrawn. These promotions often offer a rate in excess of the current interest rates. Other insurance companies offer guaranteed income bonds on a regular basis. However, the rate of guarantee they offer varies according to changes in interest rates. Once a client purchases the bond, the income is guaranteed for the term of the contract, whatever happens to base rates in the meantime.

The bond runs for a fixed term, say one to five years. The investor selects the term to suit his needs. The bond guarantees a fixed rate of income for the selected period. The income is normally paid annually in arrears although some bonds offer a monthly income.

The **income** from the bond is paid net of basic rate tax, so there is no further tax liability for an investor who is a basic rate taxpayer. A non-taxpayer cannot reclaim the tax. The 'gross equivalent' rate of return can be compared with current National Savings & Investments (NS&I) and building society rates in order to make a fair comparison.

The bond guarantees the return of the capital at the end of the selected period.

There is no explicit **charging** structure. The insurance company's charges are taken into account before declaring the interest rate to be offered on the income bond.

The **risk** the investor takes is that interest rates will rise, in which case he is locked into a contract which must run its full course. Surrender values are available but are usually poor.

The bond is purchased from the insurance company. The insurance company is responsible for repaying the capital at the end of the fixed term and also paying the regular income to the client.

4.3 High income bonds

High income bonds can produce guaranteed income levels, at levels depending on market conditions when the bond is purchased. The total returns will be based on the movements in one or more equity indices. Derivatives (call options) are used to enhance income. If the indices rise, the options will generate profits. If the indices fall, the premium is lost, but the capital invested is protected.

The **guaranteed** minimum return will typically be the value of the original investment less the income paid out over the term. The typical expectation for this type of investment is to get a **return** of the original investment at the end of the term (in addition to the income paid out), but again this is **not guaranteed**. Growth on top of this may be a possibility for some bonds, but it is unrealistic to expect much.

This type of investment will appeal to those needing a high guaranteed income. The additional risks taken with this type of investment can lead to a return of the original capital as well as the income, where similar income levels with other investments would almost certainly deplete the capital.

4.4 Guaranteed growth bonds

Guaranteed growth bonds have features, tax treatment, charging structure, risk and methods of purchase and sale similar to guaranteed income bonds, except that the income is allowed to roll up and is paid out with the capital at the end of the term.

The net return from a guaranteed growth bond could be compared with the tax free return from NS&I products. The bond should probably only be used if the interest rate is better or the client already has the maximum holding in the current issue of NS&I Certificates.

4.5 Guaranteed equity bonds

The **guaranteed equity bond** or **protected equity bond** is yet another type of investment bond.

There are various versions.

- The capital may be invested in an equity-linked fund with a guarantee that at the end of a specified period, usually five years, the investor will at least get the return of his capital. The insurance company arrange the guarantee usually by use of traded options.

- The capital may be invested in a scheme which offers a return linked to the growth in an index such as the FTSE 100 Index over the given period or return of the original capital, whichever is greater. The fixed term is usually five years.
- The capital may be invested in a scheme which offers the opportunity to lock into the growth in the FTSE 100 Index if the index exceeds a certain limit. These 'lock-ins' occur regularly during the term of the scheme.

The schemes detailed above are all geared to growth. Schemes can also be offered giving a guaranteed income. Such incomes are usually high when compared with current interest rates. The guaranteed return of capital at the end of the period takes into account the income already paid. For example, if such a bond offered an income of 8% net for five years, the guaranteed capital return would be 60% of the original investment.

As the schemes are based on investment bonds and are non-qualifying products, the return, if greater than the original investment, could be subject to tax for a higher rate taxpayer. A basic rate or non-taxpayer would have no tax to pay.

A guaranteed equity bond might be used by a cautious investor who is interested in stock market investments but wishes to restrict his risk.

Such a bond should only be used by an investor who intends and is likely to be able to hold the bond for the full term. If the investor encashes early, he or she will only receive the value of the units, which could be low.

A less cautious investor should receive a better return by direct investment into a FTSE 100 or equity fund. With a guaranteed equity bond, the investor is paying for the guarantee in the guaranteed equity fund, which restricts the potential performance. Another disadvantage is that many schemes do not credit the investor with the income generated by the FTSE 100 shares, which makes a significant difference in any comparison with direct equity investments.

4.6 Personal portfolio bonds

A **personal portfolio bond** allowed an investor with an amount in excess of say £50,000 to choose his own stockbroker to run his bond portfolio, rather than buying units in the insurance company's various funds. If the client already had an equity portfolio the shares would have to be sold before investment in the bond took place. This could give rise to a charge to capital gains tax.

The personal bond operated in all other respects exactly like a normal bond. For example, the investor could make use of a 5% withdrawal facility.

The points made above about personal portfolio bonds have been written in the past tense because they were effectively extinguished for UK residents by changes in the Finance Act 1988, which imposed a punitive tax on the deemed gains.

For those bonds which were 'caught' by the legislation, the tax charges are draconian. They take effect from policy years ending after 6 April 2000 and extend to impose an annual 'deemed' gain of 15% of the premiums paid plus deemed gains from previous years. There will be a further deemed gain on any chargeable event in addition to the normal chargeable event gains. When the bond is surrendered, however, the amount of the termination chargeable event gain will be reduced by the amount of previous deemed gains.

Holders of these bonds will probably have already have encashed them. Personal portfolio bonds are now only offered by offshore offices to non-UK residents.

4.7 Offshore bonds

Features of **offshore bonds** are as follows.

(a) UK life offices, such as Standard Life, Scottish Widows and Sun Life who have offshore subsidiaries, issue insurance bonds from their offices in the Channel Islands, Isle of Man, Dublin and Luxembourg.

(b) The bonds they issue are still non-qualifying life policies with the same facilities as onshore policies.

12: LIFE ASSURANCE COMPANY PRODUCTS

(c) The advantage of the offshore bond is that the underlying life funds suffer little or no tax (gross roll up) compared with UK life funds which are taxed at 20%. This tax situation may be advantageous for UK higher rate taxpayers.

(d) However, the costs of offshore products are typically higher than onshore because the insurance company is unable to offset expenditure against income for tax purposes. A typical charging structure could be 6% initial charge with 1.5% annual management charge.

(e) An offshore bond should be maintained for as long a period as possible. Because of the charges it can take five years for the value of the offshore fund to start to edge ahead of the UK fund for a basic rate taxpayer and longer for a higher rate taxpayer.

(f) Withdrawals of up to 5% of the original investment may be taken for 20 years without an immediate tax liability. If the 5% allowance is not used in one year it can be carried forward to the next.

The 1998 Finance Act made overseas insurers who write in excess of £1 million of gross premiums with UK residents appoint a UK tax representative. This representative must be approved by HMRC. The duties of the tax representative will be to provide HMRC with information in relation to chargeable events on offshore policies under Section 552 of the Income and Corporation Taxes Act 1988.

The tax treatment of offshore bonds on encashment is covered later in this chapter.

A non-taxpayer might use an offshore bond. In this case money could roll up in a virtually tax-free fund and on encashment any chargeable gain will not be subject to tax. However, this may not be a worthwhile exercise because the high charges imposed on the bond may wipe out the tax advantage.

High net worth clients previously used offshore products within a trust to mitigate income and inheritance tax. One of the best known reasons for writing an offshore bond in trust was to take advantage of the **'dead settlor provision'**.

If a policy has been **settled on trust** and the **settlor** is still alive, the gain on a chargeable event is taxable on the settlor, as above. If the settlor is non-resident or dead, the gain is assessed on the UK-resident trustees at the rate of 20% (40% less a tax credit of 20%). If the trustees are non-resident, a charge is made on the beneficiaries who receive benefits. For policies settled in trust where the settlor died before 17 March 1998, there is no tax to pay as the only charge on such policies could have been on the settlor who is, of course, not taxable if he is dead – this is the **'dead settlor provision'**.

Capital redemption bonds are the offshore equivalent of guaranteed growth bonds, guaranteeing a specified value at a set future date. **Portfolio bonds** are the offshore equivalent of personal portfolio bonds, offering the investor access to investment markets through a range of professionally managed funds.

5 Traded endowment policies

Learning outcome

4.4.3 Traded endowments.

5.1 Introduction

Because of changing financial circumstances, such as those following redundancy, divorce or early retirement, policyholders may wish to encash their endowment policies. They may need the cash or alternatively they may no longer be able to afford to pay the premiums.

- Their first course of action is to approach the insurance company for a surrender value quotation.
- A second option is to sell the endowment policy on the traded market. It may be possible to beat the quoted surrender value by up to 35%.

INVESTMENT AND RISK

The traded policy market has grown tremendously in recent years. The policies sold in this way are sometimes referred to as **Traded Endowment Policies (TEPs)** or second hand endowment policies (SHEPs).

It is possible to buy into the traded endowment market via an **investment trust** that holds a portfolio of such policies. This provides a more liquid investment than buying individual policies.

5.2 Type of policies suitable for trading

The policies bought and sold are generally with-profits endowment policies – normally those which have been in force for five years or more and have varying maturity dates. The policies may be either qualifying or non-qualifying.

5.3 Valuing a policy

A policy should only be sold in the market if a higher price can be achieved than the surrender value quoted. The market value of a traded endowment policy will depend on:

- The current surrender value quoted, maturity date of the policy and reversionary bonus paid to date
- The long-term outlook for bonus payouts and in particular terminal bonus of the company in question and the financial strength of the company

The purchaser of the endowment policy needs to calculate a possible maturity value based on current terminal and reversionary bonus rates. He or she then needs to see what effect there would be if the bonus rate changed. Most market makers will provide tables to assist the investor in this calculation.

The yields on those policies with fewer years to run until maturity will be less affected by falls in reversionary bonus. These are the policies which are most attractive to investors.

5.4 Selling and buying

After the necessary research, the policyholder would agree to sell the policy through a market maker, broker or auctioneer. Once the policy had been sold, it would be handed over to the purchaser. The sale price would be paid and a deed of assignment would be executed in favour of the purchaser.

The purchaser would then serve the notice of assignment on the insurance company (Policies of Assurance Act 1867) so that in the event of a claim the proceeds would be paid to him rather than the life assured. The purchaser would be responsible for payment of future premiums.

The purchaser will need some method of ensuring that he was informed if the life assured dies before the policy matures. Upon the death of the life assured prior to maturity, the benefits would be paid to the purchaser. If the policy ran its course, the proceeds would be paid to the purchaser on maturity.

Endowment policies can be bought and sold *via*:

    (a)   Market makers
    (b)   Brokers
    (c)   Auctioneers

We will now consider the function of each member of the market.

The **market maker** buys policies and holds them on his books until a suitable buyer can be found. Market makers are **regulated** in respect of both the **sale and purchase of policies** by the FSA under the Financial Services and Markets Act 2000 (FSMA 2000).

There will be no charges for the buyer or the seller to pay. The market maker will make his profit on the difference between the buying and selling price of a particular policy. If the client has been introduced by an independent financial adviser (IFA), commission will normally be paid to the intermediary.

The **brokers** approach a number of market makers on behalf of a client who is either buying or selling a policy. The idea is to achieve the highest price for the client who is selling or the best investment for the client who is buying. The market maker's commission is then split between the broker and the IFA.

The oldest method of buying and selling policies is through **auctioneers**, first introduced in 1843 by Foster and Cranfield. Fees of one-third of the excess over the insurance company's surrender value are typically charged to the seller. Sellers can decide to impose a reserve price below which they will not sell.

5.5 Investing in TEPs

In making recommendations for the use of these policies within a portfolio it is important to consider the following.

(a) The **investor's likely tax situation** on encashment.

(b) The **lack of liquidity** in the scheme: once the policy is purchased the investor will normally hold it for the balance of the term. This objection could be overcome by the purchase of a traded endowment investment trust. In this way the investor participates in a fund of many policies with different maturity dates. He should be able to encash all or part of his shares at any time.

The adviser is responsible for **compliance** even when the relevant information is provided by a market maker. The adviser must ensure that a second hand bond is a suitable recommendation taking into account other options. He must explain the method of assignment of the policy, the claims procedure and the tax situation.

The taxation of TEPs is covered later in this chapter.

5.6 Viatical settlements

A terminally ill person may sell a life policy to a viatical company for cash in what is called a **viatical settlement**. The viatical company will want to see medical evidence of the illness. As with other life policies that are sold, the policy will be assigned to the purchaser – the viatical company.

Viatical companies' activities are regulated by the FSA under the FSMA 2000.

A policy that is under trust or a 'life of another' policy cannot be sold in a viatical settlement because they do not belong to the person whose life is insured.

Because the person whose life is insured has only a short life expectancy, the price will probably be higher than both the secondhand market value and the surrender value of the policy. The settlement will also enable the ill person to make use of the cash generated in the last few months of their life, although receipt of the sum might affect rights to State benefits.

The viatical company will claim the sum assured from the insurance company and so the death cover is forfeited.

The tax treatment for the seller will be as for sale of other endowment policies on the open market (see Section 7 of this chapter).

The individual's circumstances should be carefully assessed before a viatical settlement is made, to evaluate whether it is the best course of action for that person.

INVESTMENT AND RISK

6 Friendly Society policies

6.1 Friendly Society tax-exempt plans

Friendly societies were established in the 18th and 19th centuries as mutual organisations and they were awarded exemption from tax. The friendly societies offer **savings plans** with investment into a **tax exempt** fund, which may be cash-based, unit-linked or with-profits.

The friendly society's total **tax exemption** on their business in such policies potentially increases the rate of return to policyholders. (Ordinary life assurance companies have to pay corporation tax.) However, the generally high **charges** on the policies may erode part of the tax advantage.

The normal maximum total premium which an individual may pay in a 12 month period on all his friendly society policies is **£270**. However, if premiums on a policy are payable more frequently than annually, only 90% of the premiums are taken into account for the purposes of this limit, so the maximum total contribution is then £300 pa. For example, £25 a month can be paid in: £25 × 12 × 90% = £300.

The friendly societies generally offer 10-year plans. The plans include life cover equal to 75% of total premiums, thus ensuring that they are qualifying policies. The life cover element may be paid for by periodic cancellation of some units.

The Financial Services Authority (FSA) allows friendly societies to provide quotations showing returns of 5% and 9% pa. This is higher than the usual 4% and 8% because of the assumed effect of the societies' tax exemption.

Friendly societies have not been able to reclaim the 10% dividend tax credit since April 2004.

Parents can take out friendly society policies for their children, and the profit will **not** be taxable income of the parent (or the child).

Baby Bond is a registered service mark of the Tunbridge Wells Equitable Friendly Society and is the name for a savings plan with that society marketed for purchase on behalf of a child.

6.2 Ordinary business

Friendly societies can also write **ordinary business** of any amount in a taxed life fund.

Some of the friendly societies also offer a wider range of savings and investment services such as unit trusts, OEICs, ISAs and mortgages through subsidiaries.

7 Taxation of life assurance policies

> **Learning outcome**
> 4.4.2 Qualifying policies – maximum investment plans and other endowments.
> 4.4.5 Taxation – onshore and offshore, within the fund and for the investor.

7.1 General points

Unlike a pension fund, a **life assurance fund** is not a tax-free vehicle: it suffers corporation tax on its income and gains at a rate of 20%.

As the fund itself suffers tax, payouts from policies are often completely free of income tax and capital gains tax. This is the case if it is a **qualifying policy**. If it is a **non-qualifying policy**, there may be an income tax charge levied on encashment, as explained below.

7.2 Definition of a qualifying policy

A policy is **qualifying** if:

(a) The policy secures a capital sum on death, earlier disability, or a date not before the tenth anniversary of taking out the policy

(b) The premiums are reasonably even and are payable annually or at shorter intervals, ie it must be a regular premium policy, and

(c) At least a certain capital sum is assured:
   (i) for endowment policies, 75% of the total premiums payable.
   (ii) for whole life policies, 75% of the premiums payable up to age 75.

7.3 Encashment of a qualifying policy

In order for the payout from a qualifying policy to be tax-free, premiums must have been paid for a minimum of one of the following:

(a) Life of the life assured
(b) 10 years
(c) Three quarters of the term

Example: Qualifying policies

A 20 year endowment policy is taken out. Decide whether the policy will qualify for a tax-free payout on encashment in each of the following circumstances.

(a) Life assured dies after seven years
(b) Policy is surrendered after seven years
(c) Policy is surrendered after 12 years

Solution

(a) Yes (premiums paid for life of life assured)
(b) No
(c) Yes (premiums paid for at least 10 years)

Any gain on the policy in (b) above would be taxed under the non-qualifying policy rules (see below).

7.4 LAPR

Qualifying policies taken out before 14 March 1984 qualify for **Life Assurance Premium Relief (LAPR).** This gives relief at source on the premium payments at a rate of 12½% to a limit being the greater of £1,500 or one sixth of income. The relief is lost if the cover or term are extended but not if they are shortened.

Policies taken out from 13 March 1984 do not generally attract tax relief on premiums paid. (The exception is term assurance linked to a pension policy, which is not part of the exam syllabus.)

7.5 Definition of non-qualifying policies

Non-qualifying policies are any policies that do not satisfy the above definition and include what are commonly called **single premium bonds**, **investment bonds** or **property bonds**. A lump sum is invested in a life fund, a small part of

INVESTMENT AND RISK

which buys cover in the event of death and the balance is invested. As this is not a 'regular premium' investment, it does not meet the definition of a qualifying policy given above.

7.6 Maturity or full surrender of policy

The encashment of such a policy, whether due to full surrender, sale (but not assignment without consideration) or death of the life assured, is classified as a **chargeable event** for **income tax** purposes. Depending on the circumstances, this event may produce an additional income tax charge in the year in which the event occurs.

When a chargeable event occurs, the life office must issue a **certificate** to the policyholder and send a copy to HMRC.

The following detailed example takes you through the principles and mechanics of these calculations.

Example: Non-qualifying policy

Joe bought a single premium bond for £15,000 on 17 May 2003. In July 2007 he withdrew £1,500 from the policy and on 18 August 2010 he encashed the policy for £26,000.

Explain the tax implications in July 2007 and August 2010, given the hypothetical 2010/11 salaries shown below.

- Case 1: Salary of £53,000
- Case 2: Salary of £33,000
- Case 3: Salary of £43,000

Solution

During the bond's life, up to 5% of the original premium for each year of the bond's life (**including the year of the chargeable event**) may be withdrawn from the bond with no **immediate** tax implications ie £750 pa.

This 5% runs cumulatively, so that in July 2007 the £1,500 withdrawn is within the allowable limit (ie limit is 17.5.03 – 16.5.07 = 4 years, × £750 = £3,000). Thus no 'chargeable event' occurs at this time. Note that this does **not** mean that the withdrawal is exempt from tax, merely that no charge is made at the time.

The encashment in August 2010 is a chargeable event. The overall profit on the bond must be calculated, as follows:

	£
Encashment	26,000
Previous withdrawals	1,500
Total withdrawn	27,500
Original cost	(15,000)
Profit on bond	12,500

The exact tax charge arising on this profit depends upon the person's tax position in 2010/11 (ie the year of encashment), as follows.

(a) *Case 1:* **Joe has a salary of £53,000.** Since Joe is (without considering the bond profit) a higher-rate income tax payer, the full bond profit is taxed at 20% ie £2,500.

(b) *Case 2:* **Joe has a salary of £33,000.** This means that his taxable income is £33,000 – £6,475 = £26,525.

As Joe is not yet a higher rate taxpayer, a 'top slicing' calculation is required, as follows.

The bond profit is divided by the number of **complete policy years** since the last chargeable event (ie since inception, since there have been no chargeable events prior to encashment in August 2010) ie 7 years from 17.5.03 to 17.5.10.

ie $\frac{£12,500}{7}$ = £1,786 pa

> This is added to the existing taxable income for the year, as an additional slice, to take it from £26,525 to £28,311. Since this figure is below £37,400 (see Tax Tables) he is still not a higher rate taxpayer, therefore he has no further tax to pay at all on the bond profit. The rationale for this is that the corporation tax suffered by the life fund is deemed to be meeting the basic rate liability of Joe.
>
> (c) *Case 3:* **Joe has a salary of £43,000.** This means that his taxable income is £43,000 – £6,475 = £36,525, so he is not yet a 40% income tax payer, and a top slicing calculation is once again necessary.
>
> 'Top slice' (as in (b)) = £1,786
>
> If added on to the taxable income of £36,525 it adds to £38,311, £911 above the higher rate threshold of £37,400. As a result, the first £875 (£37,400 – £36,525) of the 'slice' would fall in the basic rate band and the balance (£911) would be in the higher rate band.
>
> There will be no further tax due on the £875 but a further 20% will be due on the £911.
>
> ie Total tax on this slice = £911 × 20% = £182.20.
>
> However, there are seven such slices, therefore the total tax due on the bond profit is 7 × £182.20 = £1,275.40.
>
> Note that it is only the investor's tax position in the year of encashment that is relevant to these calculations. If Joe had been a non-taxpayer in previous years, he would still suffer this tax in 2010/11.

If the investor has savings or dividend income, the bond profit is still treated as the top slice of income, for the purposes of **top slicing relief**. When working out capital gains tax bands, only the 'slice' of income is included when working out the total income.

7.7 Partial encashment

Where there is a **partial encashment** that exceeds the cumulative 5% withdrawal allowance, a chargeable event occurs and a calculation similar to those above is required. In this case, the event is deemed to be made at the end of the policy year, rather than at the date of the partial encashment itself.

7.8 Segmentation of policies

In practice, whole of life or endowment policies are usually written in **segmented** form. For example, rather than pay £150 per month into an endowment policy, the contract is drawn up such that the person pays £15 per month into each of ten equivalent contracts.

When encashments are made, the choice is then between doing a partial encashment of all policies or fully encashing some of the segments.

Example: Segmented policy

Manuel is aged 62. His income is £26,000 pa. He invested £100,000 into a single premium investment bond of Easy Life plc, a UK insurance company on 12 February 2004. The bond consisted of 20 identical policies. He has made no previous withdrawals from the bond.

Owing to a family crisis, Manuel will have to take £50,000 from the bond on 3 March 2010. This can be done by encashing eight policies (£6,250 surrender value each) or simply by a withdrawal of £50,000 across all policies.

Calculate **showing all workings** the top slice of the gain arising, assuming the £50,000 is raised by:

(a) Encashing eight policies – top slice determined by complete policy years to encashment
(b) Withdrawing £50,000 across all policies equally – top slice determined by years including year of chargeable account

and state in which tax year the gain will be taxed.

INVESTMENT AND RISK

Solution

(a) **Encashing eight policies** £
Surrender value of eight policies 50,000
Less cost of eight policies (8/20 of £100,000) (40,000)
Gain 10,000

Top slice = £10,000 ÷ 6 years (12.2.04 – 11.2.10) = 1,666.67
Taxed in 2009/10

(b) **Partial withdrawal** £
Withdrawal value 50,000
Cumulative tax deferred allowance (12.2.04 – 11.2.11 = 7 years)
5% × 7 years × £100,000 = (35,000)
Gain 15,000

Top slice = £15,000 ÷ 7 years = 2,142.86
Taxed in 2010/11 (treated as made on 11 February 2011)

7.9 Topping up investment bonds

If an investor wanted to invest a further amount in an investment bond, it can be preferable to add it to an existing unit-linked bond rather than effecting a second bond if the life office concerned offers a topping up facility.

Example: Topping up investment bonds

Bill purchases one single premium bond for £20,000 in 2000 and a second bond for £20,000 in 2005. The bonds are with separate insurance companies. In 2010, Bill wishes to withdraw his money. The first bond purchased is now worth £30,000 (a gain of £10,000, which will be divided by 10 for top-slicing purposes). The second bond is worth £25,000 (a gain of £5,000, which will be divided by 5 for top-slicing purposes). Therefore the top-slice will be £1,000 + £1,000 = £2,000.

If, however, Bill had added the second £20,000 to the original bond, the situation would be different. The top-slicing relief is based on the full policy term, even if some of the profit is provided by a premium paid in the middle of the term. The gain would be £15,000 which would be divided by 10 for top-slicing purposes. Therefore the top-slice would now be £1,500. If Bill is close to the higher rate tax band and he used this second method, this may mean he has no tax to pay as he has a smaller 'slice' to add to his income.

7.10 Effect on child tax credit and age allowances

The full gain from surrender of an investment bond, without any top-slicing, is counted as income for the purposes of calculating entitlement to **child tax credit**.

People aged 65 or over are normally entitled to a **higher personal allowance** for income tax purposes. However, when working out **'statutory total income'** for age allowance restriction purposes, the full bond profit (again, without any top slicing) must be included, and so some or all of the age allowance, and married couple's allowance if applicable, may be lost.

12: LIFE ASSURANCE COMPANY PRODUCTS

Example: Age allowances

Joanne makes a profit of £5,000 on encashment of a property bond. After 'top slicing', the profit is £1,000.

Joanne is aged 67 and has the following sources of income in 2010/11:

Pensions (various)	£13,500 gross
Building society interest received	£3,000
Dividends received	£2,000

Calculate Joanne's income tax liability for 2010/11.

Solution

	Other income £	Interest £	Dividends £
Pensions	13,500		
Building society interest 3,000 × 100/80		3,750	
Dividends × 100/90			2,222
Personal age allowance (W)	(8,704)		
Taxable	4,796	3,750	2,222

Tax charge:

			£
(1)	On pensions	4,796 at 20% =	959
(2)	On building society interest	3,750 at 20%	750
(3)	On dividends	2,222 at 10%	222
Income tax charge			1,931

Note. Although the bond profit has affected the age allowance given, there is no actual income tax charge on the profit as, by adding in the 'top slice', Joanne would still only be a basic rate taxpayer.

Working

STI for age allowance purposes

	£
Pensions	13,500
Building society interest	3,750
Dividends	2,222
Bond profit	5,000
STI	24,472

	£
Basic age allowance (65–74)	9,490
Less ½ (24,472 – 22,900 income limit)	(786)
Adjusted PAA	8,704

7.11 Guaranteed income bonds and guaranteed growth bonds

These products, which take in a lump sum and pay out either a regular income or a larger lump sum at some specified time in the future, are usually made up of non-qualifying life policies. In that case, the tax treatment is simply the tax

INVESTMENT AND RISK

treatment of the underlying policies. For example, a chargeable event happens each year on a guaranteed income bond if the income paid out exceeds 5% of the premium.

7.12 Traded life policies

When whole of life or endowment policies are **traded**, there could be tax implications for the vendor and the purchaser.

(a) If the policy being sold is non-qualifying, or has been in force for less than ten years or three-quarters of the term, then a chargeable event will occur for income tax purposes. If the price raised exceeds the premiums paid then a charge to higher rate income tax could occur for income tax purposes. If a chargeable event has occurred, the vendor's disposal would be subject to an 20% income tax charge for higher rate taxpayers under the 'top slicing' rules.

(b) The purchaser acquires a chargeable asset for CGT purposes, with the gain or loss arising on eventual sales or encashment calculated under normal CGT rules.

7.13 Jointly held policies

The rules described above generally apply to **policies held jointly** by two or more people. Each person is treated as though he holds a separate policy equivalent to his proportionate interest in the jointly held policy.

An assignment of his interest by one party to the policy to the other party (unless made for no consideration) is a chargeable event. This is on the share in the rights under the policy that the person making the transfer is giving up. Any gain arising is attributed to that person.

7.14 Tax treatment of offshore bonds

The taxation of offshore policies on encashment is more stringent than for a similar onshore product. The chargeable gain on a bond is subject to **income tax** at **basic and higher rate tax**.

The gain is calculated using the formula:

Chargeable gain = [Encashment value + Previous withdrawals] *less* [Original investment + Previous chargeable excesses]

This calculation is best understood by studying an example.

Example: Tax on encashment of an offshore bond

In June 2000 Mr Stevenson purchases a bond for an amount of £100,000. He takes a withdrawal of 7% of the original investment each year for nine years (£63,000) giving rise to a chargeable excess of 2% for each of nine years (18,000). In September 2010 he encashes the bond for £140,000.

The tax calculation is:

Chargeable gain = (£140,000 + £63,000) − (£100,000 + £18,000)

£203,000 − £118,000 = £85,000

The gain of £85,000 would be top sliced by the number of complete years (10 years) and £8,500 would be added to the investor's income to see if higher rate tax applied. If it did, then the whole of the gain (£85,000) would be subject to tax at the higher rate.

There is a difference on top slicing an offshore bond. The divider used is always the years since inception, not the years since the last chargeable event, as with an onshore bond.

If the investor had been non-resident for tax purposes for part of the time that he had held the bond, then he would be given relief for the time he was non-resident. For example, if he were non-resident for five of the ten years that he held the bond, then the chargeable gain on encashment would be reduced by 50%.

If the investor is non-UK resident when the bond is encashed, there are no UK tax consequences.

8 Annuities

Learning outcome

4.4.7 Structure and characteristics of purchased life annuities.

8.1 General points

An **annuity** is a contract whereby a capital sum is paid to an insurance company, which in return pays a guaranteed income, either for a specific period or for the rest of a person's life.

The amount of income paid is based on the **investor's age**, ie the mortality factor, and interest rates on long-term gilts.

The **income payment frequency** is agreed between the insurance company and the investor at the outset. It may be annually, half yearly, quarterly or monthly. Obviously, the greater the frequency, the lower the income. Payments can be made in advance or in arrears. For example, it may be that a female client of 75, buying an annuity for a purchase price of £10,000, will receive an income of £1,366.80 per annum by monthly amounts or £1,408.20 per annum half-yearly.

Payments can be made with or without proportion. What does this mean? A client has chosen **with proportion** and has an annuity payable half yearly in arrears, with payments on 15 December and 15 June. The annuitant dies on 15 March and a payment of three months' income will be made. If the scheme is without proportion, then no such payment is made.

Annuities can be on **one life or two lives**. On two lives, the annuity will normally continue until the death of the second life. These are known as **last survivor annuities**.

8.2 Investment-linked annuities

Some offices offer annuities where the 'performance' of an annuity is to some extent **linked either to a unit linked or with-profits fund,** to give additional inflation proofing to the income.

A with profits annuity is an annuity that has many of the same options as a conventional annuity, for example, on payment frequencies, spouse's annuities and guaranteed periods. The difference is that the amount of each instalment depends on investment returns.

The funds for a with-profit annuity are generally invested in a **mixed with-profit fund**, rather than just gilts or fixed interest funds. The actuary of the fund declares a reversionary bonus (or annual bonus) and funds are set aside for years when investment performance is not so good. This smoothes out the volatility of the investment returns. In good years there may not be as much growth as with unit linked annuities but in bad years there should not be dramatic falls in income. Typically, the price of with profits units increases at the current bonus rate, and cannot fall. There may also be a built in guarantee that a market value adjustment will not be applied.

Where a **bonus rate** has been anticipated on the annuity, there is a risk that the bonus rate may be lower than predicted and in these circumstances the guaranteed income could reduce. In order to ensure that this is not the case, it is wise to use an anticipated bonus rate that is below the current rate, so that if bonuses do fall there is some in built leeway.

INVESTMENT AND RISK

8.3 Immediate and guaranteed annuities

With a **purchased life annuity** (or **immediate annuity**), the purchase price is paid to the insurance company and the income commences immediately and is paid for the lifetime of the annuitant.

An annuity may be **guaranteed**, in which case the annuitant selects a guaranteed period of say 5 or 10 years. The annuity is paid for the annuitant's life but, in the event of early death within the guaranteed period, the income is paid for the balance of the term to the beneficiaries.

8.4 Compulsory purchase and open market option annuities

Compulsory purchase or open market option annuities are purchased with the proceeds of pension funds. The client will exercise an option to move a fund to a provider offering better annuity rates. The fund arising from an occupational scheme or buy-out (s32) policy will purchase a compulsory purchase annuity. A fund arising from a retirement annuity or personal pension will purchase an open market option annuity.

8.5 Temporary annuities

With a **temporary annuity,** a lump sum payment is made to the insurance company and income commences immediately but is only paid for a limited period, say 5 years. Payments cease at the end of the fixed period or on earlier death.

8.6 Level and increasing annuities

A **level annuity**, of whatever type, provides a level income at all times. This of course does not keep pace with inflation.

With an **increasing or escalating annuity,** the annuitant selects a rate of increase and the income will rise each year by a set amount, say 5% or 10% or even the RPI.

For a given purchase cost, an increasing annuity will of course provide a lower starting income than a level annuity for the same purchase cost.

8.7 Capital protected annuities

One of the problems with annuities is that the capital is lost, even if the annuitant dies relatively early. This can be overcome, to some extent, by buying a **capital protected annuity**. The workings are best explained by use of an example.

(a) An annuity is purchased for £10,000. The annual income or annuity is £1,000.

(b) The annuitant dies after 6 years.

(c) The total payments of the annuity have been only £6,000, so £4,000 is returned to the estate (ie original investment less payments made).

If, however, the annuitant died in year 11, then no payment would be made because the whole of the original purchase price would have been used up.

The capital protection has a cost, and so a capital-protected annuity will provide a lower income than an annuity without capital protection for the same purchase cost.

8.8 Tax treatment of purchased life annuities

Purchased life annuities have a capital and interest element. The split is pre-agreed between HMRC and the insurance company.

- (a) The capital element is based on expectation of life tables and is tax-free.
- (b) The interest element is taxable (in the same manner as interest on a bank account).

This means that a non-taxpayer can obtain a gross income from an annuity.

The tax treatment of the annuity is agreed between the insurance company and HMRC by completion of the form **PLA1**, or **R87** for a non-taxpayer. The insurance company will submit the form PLA1 to HMRC. If they agree that the annuity qualifies, HMRC will send form PLA3 to the annuitant confirming the situation and a form PLA4 to the insurance company, giving them authority to deduct tax only from the interest content of the annuity.

The insurance company will then tax the interest content as follows.

- If the annuitant is a basic rate taxpayer he will be paid the capital content plus the interest content net of 20% tax.
- If the annuitant is a higher or additional rate tax payer, the insurance company will make the same level of payments and the annuitant will account to HMRC for the higher rate tax after the submission of his annual tax return.
- If the annuitant is a UK-resident non-taxpayer, the insurance company will pay out the total annuity gross. In order for this to happen, the annuitant will have completed an R87 for submission to HMRC, confirming that his income is below a certain limit.

If the annuity is held on a **joint** basis and one of the annuitants is a non-taxpayer, then the insurance company will pay 50% of the income tax-free and tax the balance on the capital and interest basis.

8.9 Risk

Risk arises from the possibility of early death, since the capital is lost; unless a capital protected policy is used.

8.10 Back-to-back arrangements

Sometimes insurance companies package annuities and other qualifying policies or investments to provide clients with an income or growth investment funded from capital. These are known as **back-to-back arrangements**.

Examples of income/growth product packages are as follows.

- (a) 5 year temporary annuity and unit trust
- (b) 5 year temporary annuity and ISA
- (c) 5 year temporary annuity and 5 year endowment

The original capital investment is split between the two investments.

- (a) If income is required, the annuity pays out the income and it is hoped that the growth on the investment will be sufficient to repay the original capital. **There is no guarantee**.
- (b) If growth is required, the income from the annuity is used to **'boost' the investment**.

Sometimes back-to-back arrangements are used for **inheritance tax planning**. In this instance, the combination of contracts is: **immediate annuity** and **whole of life policy.**

- (a) The capital sum is split to purchase the annuity and pay the first premium under the whole of life policy.

INVESTMENT AND RISK

(b) Subsequent annuity payments are used to pay the premiums under the whole of life policy. The policy is written in trust so that on the death of the policyholder, the benefits pass to the beneficiaries free of inheritance tax.

9 A Comparison of unit trusts, OEICs, investment trusts and life assurance as savings schemes

> **Learning outcome**
> 4.4.6 Differences between life assurance bonds and OEICs/unit trusts.

	Life Assurance – With Profits	Life Assurance – Unit Linked	Unit Trust and OEIC Savings Plan	Investment Trust Savings Plan
Final Proceeds	Guaranteed minimum sum on death. Value on maturity depends on bonuses declared	Guaranteed minimum sum on death. Value of units on maturity depends on fund performance	Value of units depends on fund performance up to realisation	Sum received depends on share price when shares are sold
Taxation	Proceeds are tax free for investor, but fund suffers tax	Proceeds are tax free for investor, but fund suffers tax	Tax payable on distributions received and on sales of units, unless held within a PEP/ISA	Tax payable on dividends received and on sale of shares, unless held within a PEP/ISA
Investment Policy	Fund has discretion over its investment policy	Wide range of investments possible	Restricted to authorised investments	Can only invest in shares and securities
Significance of Missed Premiums	Missing a premium means life cover is lost	Missing a premium means life cover is lost	Missing a premium only means that no units are purchased	Missing a premium only means that no shares are purchased
Significance of Early Surrender	Low surrender value, especially in earlier years	Low surrender value, especially in earlier years	Value at realisation depends on unit offer price	Value at realisation depends on share offer price
Commission Costs	Commission paid to salesman	Commission paid to salesman	Some trusts pay commission to salesman	No commission paid
Charges	Charges incurred difficult to identify	Charges incurred difficult to identify	Front end or exit charges and annual management fees suffered	Share dealing costs are suffered

Key chapter points

- Life assurance based investments may be with-profits, unitised with-profits, or unit-linked.
- With-profits funds usually reflect a mix of assets similar to that of a unit linked Managed Fund, but returns are delivered as bonuses which cannot be taken away and thus smooth the pattern of returns as reported to the investor.
- Unit-linked funds share similarities with other collective funds such as unit trusts and OEICs. The unit holder is exposed to rises and falls in market prices of the underlying investments as they change from day to day.
- Endowment policies were once a common vehicle for linking to a mortgage repayment. Although many existing policies remain in force, little new business is being written. Saving through unit trusts and OEICs, including through ISAs, will be a preferable route on grounds of flexibility, cost and tax efficiency for many people.
- The market for traded endowment policies (TEPs) often provides a means of selling an unwanted policy for more than the surrender value. The purchase and sale of policies by marketmakers is regulated under **FSMA 2000**.
- A terminally ill person may be able to unlock the value of a policy through a viatical settlement.
- The taxation of life assurance policies is subject to top slicing and special income tax rules.
- With purchased life annuities, a capital sum is used to buy an income.

Chapter Quiz

1. What different types of bonus are payable on conventional (non-unitised) with-profits policies? ...... (see para 2.2)
2. What is meant by a market value reduction (MVR)? .... (2.4)
3. What does the free asset ratio measure and what is its importance? .... (2.5)
4. Distinguish between a switch and a redirection in the context of unit-linked funds. .... (2.8)
5. How is a distribution fund defined in the ABI's Investment Classification Group categories? .... (2.9)
6. What is the typical range of terms to maturity for endowment policies? .... (3.2)
7. What is a guaranteed equity bond? .... (4.5)
8. For what type of person is a viatical settlement possible, and what does it involve? .... (5.6)
9. What are the contribution limits for Friendly Society tax-exempt plans? .... (6.1)
10. Define a 'qualifying policy'. .... (7.2)
11. Outline the tax treatment of partial encashments of non-qualifying policies. .... (7.8)

chapter 13

Tax incentives, tax wrappers and tax planning

Chapter topic list

1	Introduction	282
2	Individual Savings Accounts	283
3	Child Trust Funds (CTF)	288
4	Venture Capital Trust (VCT)	289
5	Enterprise Investment Scheme (EIS)	292
6	Pension contribution	295
7	Employee Incentive Schemes	296
8	Tax planning and advice	299
	Key chapter points	304
	Chapter quiz	305

INVESTMENT AND RISK

Chapter Learning Outcomes

3. **Understand** the following asset classes, their main features and suitability for different consumer circumstances.

    3.3 Equities.

    3.3.10 Employee share schemes and incentives.

4. **Understand** the following packaged products, their main features and suitability for different consumer circumstances.

    4.3 ISAs.

    4.3.1 Structure – components

    - Stocks and shares, cash.
    - Annual investment limits.

    4.3.2 Charging – initial and annual charges for direct investments and collectives, stakeholder standards.

    4.3.3 Tax treatment – interest dividends, mixed bond funds, capital gains.

    4.3.4 Eligibility – age, residence.

    4.3.5 Transfers – restrictions, rules.

    4.3.6 Death of the investor.

    4.6 Venture Capital Trusts (VCTs) and Enterprise Investment Schemes (EIS) – structure, tax characteristics, past performance in terms of risk and returns.

    4.8 Child Trust Funds.

9. **Understand** tax planning strategies.

    9.2 Basic investment tax planning – use of personal allowances, spouses' personal allowances, children's tax position, pension contributions, use of ISAs, use of Capital Gains Tax exemptions, tax deferral, use of life assurance bonds, entrepreneurs' relief.

    9.3 Criteria for selecting a tax planning strategy.

    9.6 Legal requirements applying to confidentiality and disclosure of personal tax information.

1 Introduction

In the previous chapters we have considered the basics of taxation, the characteristics of various asset classes and the application of the basic tax rules to the income and gains derived from those assets.

In this chapter we examine in detail the various tax incentives and wrappers that may be of relevance to an investor. The expressions tax incentives and tax wrappers are often used quite interchangably, however we make a distinction for the convenience of discussion in this chapter as follows

- **Tax wrappers** – We use this expression to refer to investor-based tax efficient vehicles, ie available to all investors in a specific product. This will include

    - Individual Savings Accounts (ISAs)
    - Child Trust Funds (CTFs)
    - Venture Capital Trusts (VCTs)

- Enterprise Investment Schemes (EIS)
- Personal pensions

- **Tax incentives** – We use this expression to refer to employee-based tax efficient share ownership plans. This will include
    - Company pension schemes
    - Employee share/share option schemes

Once we have considered these tax efficient incentives/wrappers we will ten be in a position to consider the issue of tax planning.

2 Individual Savings Accounts

Learning outcomes

4.3.1 Structure – components
- Stocks and shares, cash.
- Annual investment limits.

4.3.2 Charging – initial and annual charges for direct investments and collectives, stakeholder standards.

4.3.3 Tax treatment – interest dividends, mixed bond funds, capital gains.

4.3.4 Eligibility – age, residence.

4.3.5 Transfers – restrictions, rules.

4.3.6 Death of the investor.

2.1 Introduction

The **Individual Savings Account (ISA)** is a tax-advantaged 'wrapper' within which investments can be held. **ISAs** have been available since 6 April 1999.

From 6 April 2008, ISAs take one of two forms:
- Cash ISAs
- Stocks and shares ISAs

Both of which are defined below. Each year an investor can decide to invest in either or both types of ISAs

An **ISA manager** must have HMRC approval and securities are registered in the manager's name.

2.2 Eligible investors

An individual can invest in an ISA only if they satisfy the following criteria

- Is aged **18 or over**, or **aged 16 or over in the case of a cash ISA**, and
- Is **resident and ordinarily resident** in the UK for tax purposes, or
- Is a **Crown employee working abroad** and subject to UK tax on earnings or is the **spouse** or **civil partner** of such a person, and
- Has not already subscribed to any ISA of the same type as is to be applied for, in the same tax year

INVESTMENT AND RISK

If the ISA holder ceases to be resident and ordinarily resident in the UK, the ISA can remain open and retain the UK tax benefits, but no new contributions can be made. There may, however, be tax to pay in the foreign jurisdiction to which the investor emigrates.

It is not possible to hold an ISA jointly or as a trustee for someone else.

2.3 Tax advantages

2.3.1 Income tax

Income received from investments in an ISA is **free of income tax** (but see below regarding interest on cash). However, the 10% tax credit attached to UK dividends on shares or distributions from equity funds held within an ISA cannot be reclaimed.

There is a tax credit of 20% that is reclaimable on bond interest paid in the stocks and shares component of an ISA or an insurance ISA.

Interest in the **cash ISA** is tax-free. Interest paid on cash held temporarily in a **stocks and shares** ISA is subject to a flat rate 20% charge before being credited to the account, but higher rate taxpayers will suffer no further liability to income tax.

2.3.2 Capital gains tax

Disposal of ISA investments is **exempt from capital gains tax**. However, the other side of the coin is that there is no allowance for ISA losses to be offset against gains made elsewhere.

2.3.3 Other tax points

There is no minimum holding period to obtain the tax advantages, but this does not stop ISA providers from offering better interest rates to those willing to accept such terms.

There is no requirement to declare ISA income or capital gains on a tax return to HMRC.

The tax advantages of stocks and shares ISAs are limited given that tax credits on dividends can not be reclaimed. The main tax advantages of such ISAs are for:

- Higher rate taxpayers, who are liable to additional tax on dividends received outside the tax-advantaged ISA wrapper
- Those whose capital gains exceed, or would otherwise exceed, the annual CGT allowance. (Remember that such people will include some basic rate taxpayers, as well as some higher rate taxpayers.)

2.4 Investment limits

The ISA contribution limits (**2010/11**) are summarised in the Table below.

ISA	2010/11
Cash	£5,100
Stocks and shares	£10,200 *less* amount invested in cash ISA

Once funds are withdrawn from an ISA, they cannot be paid back in without counting as a new subscription. The ISA subscription limits apply to the total **payments in** to the account during the tax year.

Shares acquired from an approved profit-share scheme, share incentive plan or all-employee share option scheme may be **transferred directly** into the stocks and shares ISA. The value of the shares at the date of transfer will count towards the normal stocks and shares annual limit. They must be transferred within 90 days of the exercise of the option or release from the profit-sharing scheme.

Other subscriptions to ISA managers must generally be in the form of cash rather than, for instance, by means of existing shares. If an investor wants to continue to hold shares he or she currently holds, but within the ISA wrapper, it is necessary to sell the shares, and then re-purchase within the ISA. This will normally incur dealing costs, although some providers may waive some of the costs. Subscriptions can be either lump sum or via regular savings schemes.

> **Example: Cash ISA**
>
> During the tax year 2010/11, a young investor opens a cash ISA and pays in £2,000. He then withdraws £1,000. How much more can the investor pay in during 2010/11?
>
> The investor can pay in a further £3,100. (The answer would be the same if the investor had not made any withdrawal.)

2.5 Types of ISA

2.5.1 Cash ISA

The Table below shows investments a cash ISA can hold.

✓	Building society and UK or European bank deposits – such accounts will have interest credited gross
✓	ISA-eligible money market funds or qualifying funds of funds that invest solely in money market funds
✓	ISA-eligible unit trusts and OEICs meeting the 5% test – see below
✓	Stakeholder deposit products meeting the 5% test – see below
✓	Life assurance products meeting the 5% test – see below

2.5.2 Stocks and shares ISA

A stocks and shares ISA may invest in the following

(a) **Shares** issued by a company (other than an investment trust or fund - see below for rules on collective investment schemes) which are listed on a recognised stock exchange. Shares that are only on the Alternative Investment Market (**AIM**) **cannot** be held in an ISA. However, shares with a dual listing on another recognised exchange – for example, an overseas Stock Exchange – can be held in an ISA.

(b) **Corporate bonds** (secured or unsecured loan stock) issued by a company incorporated anywhere in the world, with a residual term of at least five years when first held in the ISA. Either the securities themselves must be listed or the company issuing them must be listed.

(c) **Gilts and government bonds**, including strips, from any country in the European Economic Area (EU plus Norway, Iceland and Liechtenstein) with a minimum residual term of five years when first held in the ISA.

(d) UK authorised **unit trusts and OEICs**. Money market funds, futures and options funds, geared futures and options funds, property funds and feeder funds are specifically excluded.

(e) Shares in UK-listed **investment trusts** that do not have any property income.

INVESTMENT AND RISK

- (f) Shares acquired from an **approved profit-share scheme, share incentive plan** or **all-employee share option scheme**, if transferred within 90 days of the exercise of the option or release from the profit-sharing scheme.
- (g) Since **6 April 2005**, medium-term **stakeholder products** and **life assurance products** qualifying for the stocks and shares component under the 5% test.
- (h) **Cash**, but only **for the purposes of investing** in qualifying 'stocks and shares' (interest received on cash within the 'stocks and shares' component being subject to a 20% charge).

2.6 Stakeholder products and the 5% test

From April 2005, expanded ranges of **'stakeholder' products**, which can be sold with a simplified advice regime, became available. Some of these can be held in ISAs.

To qualify for inclusion in the stocks and shares component of an ISA, medium-term stakeholder products and life assurance products must be similar to equity investments (shares) rather than cash investments.

The 5% test is applied to decide whether a **fund** or **stakeholder or life assurance product** is more like a cash investment (qualifying for the **cash component**) or like an equity investment (qualifying for the **stocks and shares component**).

- Investments guaranteeing a return of at least 95% of the original capital invested qualify for the cash component
- Others qualify for the stocks and shares component of an ISA

Collective investment schemes and **linked long-term funds** meeting stakeholder requirements must be single-priced. They must have no more than **60%** of their value in riskier assets such as equities, and must be appropriately diversified.

2.7 Transfers between ISA managers

ISA managers are required to allow transfers, although a manager is not required to accept a transfer in. The investor may transfer an ISA to a different manager in the year of subscription, but then the entire ISA subscription for that year must be transferred.

After the first year, partial (or full) transfers between ISA managers are permitted.

Securities within the ISA can be re-registered in the new manager's name. They do not have to be sold and re-purchased. If a manager returns ISA proceeds to the investor, this will be treated as a withdrawal.

Transfers between different types of ISA are allowed at any time. It is possible to transfer funds from a cash ISA to a stocks and shares ISA at any time without losing the tax relief. Transfers from a stocks and shares ISA to a cash ISA cannot be made.

2.8 Termination of an ISA

There are no tax penalties for cashing in the investment. The plan manager may however impose a closure fee. There is no set time period that the investment must be established before it may be encashed.

If an ISA holder **dies**, the tax benefits of the ISA cease and the underlying assets form part of the estate of the deceased, for inheritance tax purposes. The investor's personal representatives must account for any income and gains after death, for tax purposes.

2.9 Invalid ISAs

It may occur that someone opens a second ISA for which they are ineligible within the same tax year as the first ISA they opened. The second ISA is then **invalid**. The investor must report any gains made on an invalid ISA to their tax office.

The ISA manager must:

- Arrange with HMRC for repayment of excess tax relief given on an invalid cash ISA
- Terminate policies in an invalid insurance ISA, which could give rise to a capital gains tax charge if the proceeds exceed premiums paid

2.10 ISA types

The following are types of ISA.

- **Self-select ISAs.** The investor selects his own equity or bond investments, generally on an execution-only basis. There is likely to be a periodic charge made by the Plan Manager, but dealing costs are likely to be similar to those for trading securities outside an ISA.
- **Managed ISAs.** A stockbroker may use an ISA as the wrapper for part of a larger equity portfolio, principally to take advantage of the capital gains tax exemption.
- **Unit trust and OEIC/ICVC ISAs.** ISAs are a popular means of investing in unit trusts and Open Ended Investment Companies. High yield bond funds have proved particularly popular. There is now often a wide choice of funds available from which the investor might choose one or more for the ISA. Additionally, ISAs may be invested in any UCITS that has FSA recognition.
- **Investment trust ISAs.** There is a narrower choice of investment trusts than unit trusts / OEICs, but many groups offer investment trust ISAs. There may be management charges in addition to those levied within the trust itself, to pay for administration of the ISA wrapper. Of course, it is possible to invest in unit trusts, OEICs and investment trusts within the same ISA, if the Manager permits it.
- **Corporate ISAs.** Some listed companies offer ISAs for investment in their own shares. The ISA will normally be administered by external managers. Charges may be kept low by a subsidy from the company concerned, to reflect the costs that would otherwise be incurred on registration of individual shareholdings.
- **'Guaranteed' ISAs.** Some ISAs 'guarantee' a stockmarket index-linked return at the end of a specified period. These ISAs are generally based on funds holding derivatives and cash deposits.
- **Cash ISAs.** Various instant access and term accounts are available. Particularly in the case of TOISAs, some offer a stockmarket index-linked return instead of a return linked to interest rates.

2.11 Charges

Unit trust and OEIC/ICVC funds held in ISAs may carry initial charges of up to 5%, but commonly this charge is discounted, down to zero in some cases.

Investment trust ISAs may carry a management charge in addition to the charges internal to the trust.

Charges on **direct investments** in an ISA may be paid to the manager separately from and on top of the ISA subscription. Dealing commissions and stamp duty must come out of the invested subscriptions.

Annual charges of 0.5% to 1.5% of the fund value are typical. Some managers make a fixed charge, for example £25 plus VAT per half year, irrespective of the value of the investments.

INVESTMENT AND RISK

There may be a charge on **termination** or on **transfer** of the ISA.

Purchase and sale of shares, including shares in investment trusts, will generally incur **broker's commission**, which may be at a percentage rate, possibly with a minimum and maximum charge per deal, or it may be at a fixed rate per deal.

There are charges for **dividend collection** in some self-select ISAs.

Many managers levy a charge if holders of ISAs with direct shareholdings wish to receive copies of **annual reports** via the manager or want to vote in or attend shareholders' meetings.

3 Child Trust Funds (CTF)

> **Learning outcome**
>
> 4.8   Child Trust Funds.

The Government aims to promote positive attitudes to saving and to improve financial capability by funding a **Child Trust Fund (CTF)** account for each child born on or after 1 September 2002.

CTF accounts first became available from April 2005. The CTF is initially funded by a **Government contribution** (£250, plus an age-related enhancement for children born between 1 September 2002 and 5 April 2005, plus £250 extra for lower income families with household income within the Child Tax Credit threshold).

Every eligible child is given £250 voucher by the government that can be deposited in a CTF account. If the voucher is not invested within a year the government will invest it with a randomly chosen provider which can be changed later if wanted. There is a further Government contribution of £250 (plus £250 more for lower-income families) when the child is **seven years old**.

It will also be possible for **friends and family** (including parents) to contribute up to £1,200 a year to the account. For many, this additional contribution will be the most significant part of the CTF scheme.

Child Trust Funds may include:

- Cash accounts
- Life products
- Collective funds (unit trusts and Open Ended Investment Companies)
- Equity-based schemes, including stakeholder or non-stakeholder investments and including self-selected equities

No income tax or capital gains tax is payable on the CTF. This applies even if parental contributions have been made.

The CTF will be held for the child until he or she **reaches 18**, when the money becomes available to the child and the tax benefit ceases. There will be **no restriction** on how the accountholder uses the money in their CTF account.

The rules for CTFs involve the following provisions on **charges, access** and **terms.**

- The annual management charge is capped at 1.5% of the fund value.
- Penalty-free transfers between accounts and between CTF providers must be permitted (except for any stamp duty and dealing expenses resulting from the transfer).
- Minimum subscriptions must be set at a level of no more than £10.

All CTF providers are required to publicise their **policy about social, ethical and environmental investments**, if they have such a policy.

A range of institutions, including banks, insurance companies and Friendly Societies provide CTF accounts.

13: TAX INCENTIVES, TAX WRAPPERS AND TAX PLANNING

CTFs are required to provide **asset diversification** and **'lifestyling'** options. ('Lifestyling' means switching progressively to less risky investments, as an investment gets closer to maturity.)

There are three types of CTF account, a stakeholder account, a shares account (non-stakeholder) and a savings account (non-stakeholder).

A stakeholder account is an investment in shares or OEICs that must follow government rules with respect to diversification and asset allocation. A stakeholder fund must be spread over a range of investments to spread the investment risk and following the child's 13th birthday it must move towards safer investments. The maximum permitted charge for such a fund is 1.5% p.a. with minimum new investment level of £10.

A shares account is an investment in shares that is not constrained by government rules and may, therefore, be riskier. In addition there are no rules governing management charges and minimum new investment levels.

A savings account is a cash investment which will return the funds invested plus accumulated interest when the child is 18. As with a shares account there are no rules governing management charges and minimum new investment levels.

Once the child reaches the age of 16 they can take over the management and operation of the fund. They cannot, however, draw on the funds until they are 18 when they have complete control of the use of the fund.

In its June 2010 Budget, the new Coalition Government announced that, subject to legislation, **Government contributions to CTFs at age 7 would cease** from **August 2010**. **New CTFs would cease** from **1 January 2011**. There is no immediate effect for those with existing accounts.

4 Venture Capital Trusts

Learning outcome

4.6 Venture Capital Trusts (VCTs) and Enterprise Investment Schemes (EIS) – structure, tax characteristics, past performance in terms of risk and returns.

4.1 Introduction

Venture capital trusts (VCTs) are listed companies that invest in unquoted trading companies and meet certain conditions. The VCT scheme differs from EIS in that the individual investor may spread his risk over a number of higher-risk, unquoted companies. An individual investing in a VCT obtains the following tax benefits.

- A tax reduction of **30%** of the amount invested to the 'permitted maximum' of £200,000, in the year of making the investment (was 40% tax reduction in 2005/06 and earlier)
- Dividends received from the VCT are exempt from further taxation within the 'permitted maximum' of £200,000
- Capital gains on the sale of shares in the VCT are exempt from CGT (and losses are not allowable) within the 'permitted maximum' of £200,000

In addition, capital gains which the VCT itself makes on its investments are not chargeable gains, and so are not subject to corporation tax.

The above reliefs are not available if shares were acquired other than for bona fide commercial purposes or for the purpose of tax avoidance.

4.2 Conditions to qualify as a VCT

A VCT must be **approved by HMRC**. Approval is withdrawn if a VCT fails any of the following detailed conditions.

The VCT must not be a **close company**. A close company is, broadly, one which is under the control of its shareholder-directors or of five or fewer shareholders.

The VCT's **income** must be wholly or mainly **derived from shares or securities**.

(a) At least 70% by value of the VCT's investments (from 6 April 2007, this includes cash held) must be in shares or securities which are qualifying holdings (see below). Loans, loan stock and debentures only count as securities if no-one can require their repayment or redemption within five years of their being made or issued (except in cases of default by the borrower). Loans and securities must not be guaranteed by a third party.

(b) At least 30% by value of the VCT's qualifying holdings must be in the form of eligible shares. These are ordinary shares carrying no preferential rights in respect of dividends, assets or redemption. At least 10% of the total investment in any company must be held in ordinary, non-preferential shares.

(c) No holding in any company (other than another VCT) may exceed 15% by value of the VCT's investments.

Holdings are valued when they are acquired, or when they were last added to or further money was spent on them (for example in paying a call on shares). Thus holdings do not need to be sold merely because their market values have changed.

All of the VCT's ordinary shares must be quoted on the Stock Exchange (not the Alternative Investment Market).

The VCT **must not retain more than 15%** of the income it derives from shares and securities.

4.3 Qualifying holdings

Shares and securities are **qualifying holdings** if:

(a) They were issued to the VCT (that is, the VCT did not acquire them secondhand), and
(b) All of the conditions set out below are satisfied.

The issuing company must be unquoted. (It may be on the AIM.)

The company (or its group, which must only include 75% subsidiaries) must exist wholly to carry on qualifying trades, or research and development intended to lead to qualifying trades. Trades are qualifying if they would qualify for the purposes of the Enterprise Investment Scheme (covered below). However, the EIS exclusions of leasing and of oil extraction do not apply, so such trades are permitted.

The money raised by the issue of the shares or securities must be used at least 80% for the purposes of the qualifying trade within twelve months and the remainder within the following twelve months. If only part of the money raised is used for the trade, the issue is treated as two separate issues, a qualifying holding (corresponding to the money used for the trade) and a non-qualifying holding.

The value of the trading company's assets must not have exceeded £15m immediately before the issue of shares or securities or £16m immediately afterwards. Where there is a group of companies, the limits apply to the group's assets.

4.4 Tax reduction on investment in a VCT

An individual who is at least 18 years of age and subscribes for new VCT shares can claim **a reduction in their tax liability of up to 30% of the amount subscribed**, in the tax year of issue. This tax 'reducer' is given in priority to other tax reducers but it cannot exceed the individual's tax liability for the year.

The shares must be new ordinary shares, which for at least three years from issue carry no preferential rights to dividends, assets or redemption.

The investment which can qualify as a tax reducer is limited to **£200,000 (2010/11) per individual per tax year**. More can be invested in VCTs, but the excess will not be a tax reducer.

If a loan is made to the individual, within the period from incorporation of the VCT (or two years before the issue, if later) to five years after the issue, and the loan is linked to the investment in the VCT, the investment does not qualify as a tax reducer and any tax reduction obtained must be repaid to HMRC.

There is a **minimum qualifying holding** period in order to obtain the tax benefit: if the shares in the VCT are disposed of (except to a spouse or civil partner) within **five years** of their issue, the **tax reduction is withdrawn**. Tax is not charged when the individual to whom the shares were issued died before the event which would have led to a withdrawal.

4.5 Tax-free dividends

Dividends on ordinary shares in VCTs are **tax-free** income, and they are not included in the shareholder's personal tax computation.

The shareholder must be aged at least 18, and must have acquired the shares at a time when the company qualified as a VCT.

The profits in respect of which the dividend is paid must have arisen in an accounting period, at the end of which the company qualified as a VCT.

Dividends will only be tax-free on a limit of up to £200,000 by value of VCT shares acquired in one tax year.

4.6 CGT exemption

If an individual disposes of ordinary shares in a company that was a VCT when he acquired the shares and is still a VCT at the time of disposal, there is **no chargeable gain**, but also **no allowable loss**.

The shareholder must be aged at least 18 at the time of the disposal.

A share only qualifies for the CGT exemption if, at the time of the disposal, it would also meet the £200,000 test for tax-free dividends set out above.

4.7 Performance of VCTs

As VCTs invest in smaller unquoted companies, there is likely to be higher **risk** of poor performance and capital loss than for investments in larger listed companies.

The past performance record has **varied widely** between different VCTs, as could have been expected given the high-risk nature of the investments.

As VCT tax relief is only available on subscriptions for new shares, demand for VCT shares if the investor wishes to **exit** at the end of three years may be weak, even though the shares are listed.

INVESTMENT AND RISK

5 Enterprise Investment Schemes (EIS)

Learning outcome

4.6 Venture Capital Trusts (VCTs) and Enterprise Investment Schemes (EIS) – structure, tax characteristics, past performance in terms of risk and returns.

5.1 Introduction

The **Enterprise Investment Scheme (EIS)** is a scheme designed to promote enterprise and investment by helping unlisted trading companies raise finance by the issue of ordinary shares to individual investors who are unconnected with that company.

Potential returns may be good, but investments in smaller unquoted companies like those eligible for the EIS can be **high risk**, so losses could be suffered. Investments may be made directly in companies, or through approved or unapproved EIS funds. To spread risk, investors should consider diversifying their investments across a number of companies, or to use one or more funds which have diversified holdings.

Individuals who subscribe for EIS shares are entitled to both income tax and capital gains tax reliefs.

5.2 Income tax relief

Individuals can claim a reduction in income tax payable (a tax 'reducer') amounting to the lower of:

(a) 20% of the amount subscribed for qualifying EIS investments (maximum annual qualifying investments are £500,000, for the 2010/11 tax year)

(b) The individual's tax liability for the year after deducting any Venture Capital Trust relief (covered elsewhere in this Study Text) but before deducting any other tax 'reducers'

Example: EIS relief

Mr Matthews, a married man aged 40, has income (Statutory Total Income, for tax purposes) of £47,000 (all non-savings income) for 2010/11. He subscribes £75,000 for shares and he claims EIS relief. The shares are issued to him in December 2010. What is his 2010/11 income tax liability?

Solution

	£
Statutory Total Income	47,000
Less: Personal allowance	(6,475)
Taxable income	40,525

	£
Starting rate £2,440 × 20%	488
Basic rate £34,960 × 20%	6,992
Higher rate £3,165 × 40%	1,750
	8,730
Less: EIS relief (£75,000 × 20% = £15,000, limited to £8,730)	(8,730)
Income tax liability	Nil

To be eligible for relief, the minimum subscription of shares in any company is £500. Although the maximum EIS investments qualifying for income tax relief is £500,000, individuals can invest in excess of this amount if they wish.

If an investor subscribes for different EIS issues, or full relief is not available in a tax year because the annual limit is exceeded, the tax reducer is attributed to the various shares according to the amounts subscribed. For different issues, the relief attributed to each issue is apportioned equally between the shares in that issue and any bonus shares subsequently added to the holding. Attribution rules are needed in case the relief is subsequently withdrawn.

If shares are issued in the first six months of the tax year (ie before 6 October), the investor may claim to have up half of the shares treated as issued in the previous tax year. This is subject to a maximum carry back of £50,000 (2010/11).

When carrying back relief, relief given in the previous year must not exceed overall EIS limits for that year.

EIS relief can be claimed by an individual who subscribes wholly in cash for new ordinary shares in a qualifying company. All the shares issued must be issued to finance a qualifying business activity. The shares must be subscribed, and issued, for *bona fide* commercial purposes and not as part of a scheme to avoid tax.

For broadly three years after issue, the shares must have no right to redemption, nor preferential right to dividends or to the company's assets in a winding up.

Relief must be claimed by the 31 January which is nearly six years from the end of the tax year of investment. A certificate that the investment qualifies for relief must be issued to the taxpayer by the company before the claim can be made.

5.3 Capital gains reliefs

Where shares qualify for income tax relief under the EIS, there are also special rules that apply to those shares for capital gains purposes.

(a) Where shares are disposed of after three years any gain is exempt from CGT. If the shares are disposed of within three years any gain is computed in the normal way.

(b) If EIS shares are disposed of at a loss at any time, the loss is allowable but the acquisition cost of the shares is reduced by the amount of EIS relief attributable to the shares.

EIS reinvestment relief may be available to defer chargeable gains if an individual invests in EIS shares in the period commencing one year before and ending three years after the disposal of the asset.

INVESTMENT AND RISK

5.4 Qualifying individuals

The investor must not be 'connected with' the company during the 'designated period' starting two years prior to the share issue (or from incorporation if later) and ending three years after the share issue (or the commencement of trade, if later). This rules out employees, directors or partners of the company. The investor may subsequently become a paid director.

It is not necessary for the investor to be UK resident or ordinarily resident (although he must have income which is taxable in the UK in order to benefit from the relief).

5.5 Conditions to be satisfied by the company

In outline, a qualifying company is an unquoted trading company which exists wholly to carry on a qualifying business activity for a minimum of three years. The company must not be a subsidiary of, or be controlled by, any other company. Any subsidiary it has must be at least 90% owned and the group taken as a whole must qualify in respect of its business activities.

5.6 Qualifying business activity

The shares must be issued to finance a qualifying business activity. The following are a 'qualifying business activity'.

(a) A qualifying trade

(b) Research and development or oil exploration from which it is intended to derive a qualifying trade

(c) Activities preparatory to carrying on a qualifying trade, providing the trade commences within two years after the share issue

The company must carry on the qualifying business activity wholly or mainly (more than 50%) in the UK for a period of three years from the date of the share issue.

The company must exist wholly to carry on **qualifying trades** or to act as a holding or financing company for qualifying subsidiaries. The trade must be conducted on a commercial basis with a view to making profits. Most trades are qualifying trades. However, the following are prohibited.

(a) Dealing in commodities, shares, securities, land and futures

(b) Dealing in goods otherwise than in the course of an ordinary trade of wholesale or retail distribution

(c) Banking, insurance, money lending, debt factoring, HP financing or other financial activities

(d) Leasing (other than short-term leasing of ships), including letting assets on hire, or receiving royalties or licence fees

(e) Providing legal or accountancy services

(f) Property development

(g) Farming or market gardening

(h) Holding or managing woodlands or any other forestry activity

(i) Ship building, coal production, steel production

(j) Operating or managing hotels, nursing homes or residential care homes

The company must use at least 80% of money from the share subscription for its qualifying business activity generally within twelve months of the share issue and the remaining money within the next twelve months. Where the company intends to carry on a qualifying trade and that trade is commenced up to two years after the subscription date, the money must be used within twelve months/twenty four months from the commencement of trade.

13: TAX INCENTIVES, TAX WRAPPERS AND TAX PLANNING

The **assets of the company** (including assets of group companies) must **not exceed £7 million** immediately before the share issue and must **not exceed £8 million** immediately afterwards.

6 Pension contribution

> **Learning outcome**
>
> 3.3.10 Employee share schemes and incentives.

Tax relief is available on pension fund contributions, but the way it is received depends on whether the scheme is a company pension or a personal pension.

6.1 Company pension schemes

In a contributory company scheme the employer takes the pension contributions from your pay before deducting tax and tax is only paid on what is left. As a result a higher rate taxpayer will get the full relief immediately.

6.2 Personal Pension Plan (PPP)

With a Personal Pension Plan (PPP), the pension provider claims tax back from the government at the basic rate of 20% per cent. In practice, this means that for every £80 paid into a pension, £100 is added to the pension pot. A higher rate taxpayer can claim the difference through Self Assessment or by claiming a refund.

6.3 Small Self-Administered Schemes (SSAS)

A SSAS is a company scheme where the members are usually the company directors and/or key staff. A SSAS is set up by a trust deed and allows scheme members, greater flexibility and control over the scheme's assets than in a PPP.

Contributions paid to a SSAS are subject to the same rules as other pension schemes.

6.4 Self-Invested Personal Pension (SIPP)

A Self-Invested Personal Pension is similar in to a normal Personal Pension Plan and comes under the same basic rules as far as contributions, tax relief, eligibility etc are concerned. The difference arises out of what the investments underlying the arrangement can consist of and who manages those assets. SIPPs provide a much broader range of investments than can be held in a PPP.

In addition, in a SIPP the plan holder can choose to manage his own pension investment portfolio or he can appoint a fund manager or stockbroker to manage the investments on his behalf.

6.5 Non-tax payer

For a non-tax payer, the most you can pay in to a pension scheme with the benefit of tax relief is £2,880 net which the government will top up to £3,600.

Contributions can also be made into someone else's personal pension, such as a spouse or civil partner, a child or grandchild's. If they have no income, up to £2,880 a year (which becomes £3,600 with tax relief) can be contributed each year. In this situation they will get tax relief added to at the basic rate, but this won't the contributor's tax bill.

INVESTMENT AND RISK

6.6 Limits to tax relief

Tax relief is available on contributions of up to 100 per cent of earnings (salary and other earned income) each year, to age 75 subject an annual allowance (it is not possible to carry annual allowances forward). For the tax year 2010/11 the annual allowance is £255,000.

6.7 Other tax advantages of pension funds

Pensions fund do not pay tax on any capital gains or investment income and, as such, are highly tax efficient. In addition, on retirement up to 25% may be withdrawn as a tax-free lump sum provided the total savings fall within the lifetime allowance for the year in which you take your benefit. For the tax year 2010/11 this is £1.8 million. Lump sums or income drawn from savings above the lifetime allowance will be subject to tax.

7 Employee incentive schemes

> **Learning outcome**
>
> 3.3.10 Employee share schemes and incentives.

7.1 Introduction

Successive governments have recognised the need to encourage schemes that broaden share ownership among employees or reward personnel. A number of tax-efficient schemes exist.

7.2 Employee share ownership plans (ESOPs)

Under **ESOPs**, shares may be distributed to employees through a specially established trust. Shares must be distributed to employees within a maximum of 20 years of their acquisition by the trust. Broadly, all employees (except part-time directors, who must be excluded) must be eligible on similar terms.

The trust established by the ESOP can receive funds to buy shares from a number of sources, principally from the company establishing the ESOP (the founding company), from subsidiaries of the founding company and by borrowing.

The shares can be transferred to employees exercising options under **savings-related share option schemes** (see below). The shares can also be transferred by the trustees to a share incentive plan (see below) without a chargeable event occurring.

7.3 Savings-related schemes

An employer can set up a **savings-related share option scheme**, under which employees can choose to make regular monthly investments in special bank or building society accounts called **Sharesave** accounts.

- Employees can save a fixed **monthly** amount of between **£5** and **£250**.
- The investments are made for three or five years, and a tax-free bonus is then added to the account by way of interest.
- The employee may either withdraw the money or leave it for another two years. If he or she leaves it in the account, another tax-free bonus is added.

At the withdrawal date, the employee may take the money in cash. Alternatively, he may use it to buy ordinary shares in his employer company or its holding company. The price of these shares is fixed when the employee starts to save in the account, by granting the employee options to buy shares. The option price must be at least 80% of the market value at the date the options are granted.

The only tax charge is to capital gains tax, on the gain on the shares when they are finally sold. This gain is computed as if the employee bought the shares for the price he actually paid for them.

A scheme must be open to all employees and full-time directors, and on similar terms. Part-time directors may be included, but can be excluded. However, a minimum qualifying period of employment (of up to five years) may be imposed, and there may be differences based on remuneration or length of service.

Anyone who has within the preceding 12 months held over 25% of the shares of a close company which is the company whose shares may be acquired under the scheme, or which controls that company either alone or as part of a consortium, must be excluded from the scheme.

7.4 Company share option plans

An option is the right, but not the obligation, to buy shares at a particular price at a specified date.

An employee can be granted options on shares under a **Company Share Option Plan (CSOP)**. There is no income tax on the grant of an option, on the profit arising from the exercise of an option between three and ten years after the grant or on the disposal of the option. Capital gains tax will, however, arise on the gain made when an employee eventually sells his shares.

To obtain HMRC approval schemes must satisfy the following **conditions**.

(a) The shares must be fully paid ordinary shares.

(b) The price of the shares must not be less than their market value at the time of the grant of the option.

(c) Participation in the scheme must be limited to employees and full-time directors. Options must not be transferable. However, ex-employees and the personal representatives of deceased employees may exercise options; personal representatives must do so within one year after the death. The scheme need not be open to all employees and full-time directors.

    (d) No options may be granted which take the total market value of shares for which an employee holds options above £30,000. Shares are valued as at the times when the options on them are granted.

    (e) If the issuing company has more than one class of shares, the majority of shares in the class for which the scheme operates must be held other than by:

        (i) Persons acquiring them through their positions as directors or employees (unless the company is an employee-controlled company)

        (ii) A holding company (unless the scheme shares are quoted)

(f) Anyone who has within the preceding 12 months held over 25% of the shares of a close company which is the company whose shares may be acquired under the scheme, or which controls that company either alone or as part of a consortium, must be excluded from the scheme.

The tax exemption is lost in respect of an option if it is exercised earlier than three years or later than ten years after grant. However, this three year waiting period does not need to be observed when personal representatives exercise the options of a deceased employee (but the ten-year rule still applies). In addition, if the options are exercised before three years after the grant they will remain tax exempt if the exercise (and exit from the scheme) arises from the injury, disability, redundancy or retirement of the employee.

Schemes may be altered so that in the event of the company concerned being taken over, employees may exchange their existing options for equivalent options over shares in the acquiring company.

INVESTMENT AND RISK

The costs of setting up approved share option schemes (both savings-related and company share option plans) are deductible provided they are paid within nine months of the end of the accounting period.

7.5 Enterprise Management Incentive

The **Enterprise Management Incentive (EMI)** is intended to encourage experienced people to 'take the plunge' and leave established careers in large companies for riskier jobs in smaller, start-up or developing firms.

Under the EMI scheme, a qualifying company can grant each of its employees options over shares worth up to £120,000 at the time of grant, subject to a maximum of £3m in total.

No income tax or national insurance is chargeable on either the grant or exercise of the options provided the exercise takes place within 10 years of the grant and the exercise price is the market value of the shares at the date of the grant. If options are granted at a discount, the discount is taxed at the date of exercise as normal.

An employing company may set a target to be achieved before an option can be exercised. The target must clearly be defined at the time the option is granted.

When the shares are sold, the gain is subject to CGT.

To be a **qualifying company**, the company (which may be quoted or unquoted) must have:

- 250 or fewer employees.
- Have gross assets not exceeding £30m.
- Not be under the control of any other company.
- Carry out one of a number of qualifying trades.
- Not be involved in shipbuilding, coal production, or steel production.

For **employees** to be **eligible**:

- Employees must be employed by the company or group for at least 25 hours a week, or, if less, for at least 75% of their working time (including self-employment).
- Employees who own 30% or more of the ordinary shares in the company (disregarding unexercised options shares) are excluded.
- Employees who participate in EMI cannot hold options under a CSOP although they can participate in savings related schemes.

The shares must be **fully paid up irredeemable ordinary shares.** The rules permit restrictions on sale, forfeiture conditions and performance conditions.

At any one time, an employee may hold EMI options over shares with a value of **up to £100,000** at the date of grant. Restrictions and conditions attaching to the shares may not be taken into account when valuing shares. Where options are granted above the £100,000 limit, relief is given on options up to the limit. Once the employee has reached the limit, no more EMI options may be granted for 3 years ie the employee may not immediately top up with new options following the exercise of old options.

There are a number of **disqualifying events** including an employee ceasing to spend at least 75% of his working time with the company. EMI relief is available up to the date of the event.

It is not necessary to submit schemes to HMRC for **approval**. Instead, HMRC must be notified of the grant of options within 92 days. HMRC then has 12 months to check whether the grants satisfy the EMI rules.

7.6 Share Incentive Plans

Under a **Share Incentive Plan (SIP)**, which must be operated through a UK-resident trust, employers can give **up to £3,000 of 'free shares'** a year to employees with no tax or NICs.

Employees can purchase **'partnership shares'** at any time in the year. These shares are funded through deductions of **up to £125 or 10% (whichever is lower)** from monthly salary. There is an overall **maximum** therefore of **£1,500**.

Employers offering free shares must offer a minimum amount to each employee on 'similar terms'. Between the minimum and the maximum of £3,000, the employer can offer shares in different amounts and on different bases to different employees. Employers can set performance targets as long as rewards are not concentrated on directors and more highly paid employees.

Free and matching shares must normally be held in a plan for **at least three years.** If shares are withdrawn within three years (because the employee leaves) there is a charge to income tax (as specific employment income) and NIC on the market value of the shares at the time of withdrawal. If shares are taken out of the plan after three years but before five years, there is a charge to income tax and NIC based on the lower of the initial value of the shares – and their value at the date of withdrawal so any increase in value is free of income tax and NIC. If one of the specified reasons applies, eg redundancy or retirement, there is no tax or NIC charge. Once the shares have been held for five years there is no income tax or NIC.

Partnership shares can be taken out at any time. If the shares are held for less than three years, there is a charge to income tax and NIC on the market value at the time the shares are removed. If the share are removed after three years but before five years, the charge to income tax and NIC is based on the lesser of salary used to buy the shares and the market value at the date of removal. Once the shares have been held for five years there is no income tax or NICs.

Provided they were held in the plan for at least three years, there is no charge to CGT on shares taken out of a plan and sold immediately. A charge to CGT will arise on sale to the extent that the shares increase in value after they are withdrawn from the plan.

Stamp duty is not payable when an employee purchases shares from a SIP trust. The trust must pay stamp duty when it acquires the shares. No taxable benefit arises on an employee as a result of a SIP trust or an employer paying either stamp duty or the incidental costs of operating the plan.

Shares used in the plan must be fully paid up irredeemable ordinary shares in a company either:

(a) Listed on a recognised stock exchange (or in its subsidiary), or
(b) Not controlled by another company

A plan established by a company that controls other companies, may be extended to any or all of these other companies. Such a plan is called a group plan.

A plan need not include all the components – it is possible to have a plan with only free shares.

Companies must offer **all full and part-time employees** the opportunity to participate in the plan. A minimum qualifying period of employment may be specified, but not more than 18 months. If a minimum period is specified it, can be satisfied by working for any company within a group.

8 Tax planning and advice

Learning outcomes

9.2 Basic investment tax planning – use of personal allowances, spouses' personal allowances, children's tax position, pension contributions, use of ISAs, use of Capital Gains Tax exemptions, tax deferral, use of life assurance bonds, entrepreneurs' relief.

9.3 Criteria for selecting a tax planning strategy.

9.6 Legal requirements applying to confidentiality and disclosure of personal tax information.

INVESTMENT AND RISK

8.1 Tax planning

Tax planning refers to the process of organising one's affairs so as to take best advantage of tax rules.

The practice of organising one's affairs so as to minimise tax liabilities, within the constraints of the law, is sometimes called **tax avoidance**. To make changes to one's affairs in order to avoid tax that one might otherwise have to pay is a legal activity, provided that no tax rule is being breached. However, caution is necessary with some of the more complex ways of taking advantage of tax rules: the **HMRC** may raise objections to schemes whose main objective is tax avoidance.

Tax evasion, on the other hand, is illegal. Tax evasion means failing to disclose one's affairs fully to the tax authorities, or breaching tax rules in other ways so as to evade the payment of tax. Penalties can be severe, and conviction for tax crimes could carry a prison sentence.

8.2 Confidentiality and disclosure

As a financial adviser, you have a general professional duty to maintain the **confidentiality** of your clients' affairs, including clients' tax affairs. You will often be in a position in which you have a great amount of detailed information relating to clients' finances.

In spite of the professional reasons for maintaining confidentiality, there are circumstances in which **disclosure** of information of clients' affairs is required. The requirement concerns situations in which a financial adviser becomes aware that information held on a client indicates possible breaches of the law. The legal provisions on this are included in the Proceeds of Crime Act 2002.

It is a criminal offence under the Proceeds of Crime Act 2002 for anyone working in a regulated financial firm not to report any dealing that they suspect, or ought to suspect, involves the proceeds of crime. This would include an act of tax evasion by an individual. Under the Money Laundering Regulations 2007, the report should be made to the firm's **Money Laundering Reporting Officer (MLRO)**. The MLRO must report appropriate cases to the **Serious Organised Crime Agency (SOCA)**.

8.3 Selecting a tax planning strategy

A **tax planning strategy** should recognise that:

- The after-tax returns from different investments can be affected by tax rules
- Taxation should therefore be considered when choosing investments and how they are held

Favourable tax status should not however be treated as the first priority, over and above the choice of investments appropriate to the individual's risk profile and objectives. Possible tax savings should not generally be used a reason to choose bad investments.

8.4 Investment tax planning

Giving **tax advice** can be a specialist matter and may require the involvement of a qualified tax adviser. It is additionally important for the financial adviser to be familiar with the tax rules concerning the adviser's field of work. There is hardly an area of investment where tax considerations do not play a part.

Some particular **investment tax planning** points are set out in the following paragraphs.

13: TAX INCENTIVES, TAX WRAPPERS AND TAX PLANNING

Personal allowances and spouses / civil partners

The general position on allowances has been set out earlier in this Chapter. **Husband and wife**, and those in same-sex **civil partnerships** are taxed as separate people. If one spouse's or civil partner's **marginal rate of tax** (the rate on the highest part of his or her income) is higher than the other's marginal rate, it could be chosen to transfer income-yielding assets to the individual with the lower rate.

The year of marriage

In the year of marriage or the year of establishing a civil partnership, the married couple's / civil partners' age allowance for those eligible will be the full amount less 1/12 for each complete tax month during which the couple were unmarried. A tax month runs from the 6th of one month to the 5th of the next month.

The year of death

The deceased person will get their full tax-free personal allowance for the year of their death. They will also get a full year's entitlement to any blind person's or married couple's allowance for the full year.

Jointly owned property

Where spouses or civil partners jointly own income-generating property, it is assumed that they are entitled to equal shares of the income.

If, in fact, the couple are not entitled to equal shares in the income-generating property (other than shares in close companies), they may make a joint declaration to HMRC, specifying the proportion to which each is entitled. These proportions are used to tax each of them separately, in respect of income arising on or after the date of the declaration.

Capital gains tax exemption

As we have seen, each individual has an **annual CGT exemption**. An investor with significant investments (outside the tax-free wrapper of ISAs) may choose to plan disposals of investments that are subject to CGT so as to make use of the annual exemption, using the rules set out earlier in this Chapter.

Use of ISAs

The use of **Individual Savings Accounts (ISAs)** as an investment wrapper is particularly important for individuals who could have a capital gains tax liability either now or in the future. ISAs are covered in detail earlier in this Chapter.

Higher rate taxpayers also benefit from the fact that they have no further tax to pay on dividends in a stocks and shares ISA.

Venture capital trusts (VCTs) and Enterprise Investment Schemes (EISs)

The characteristics of VCTs and EISs are covered earlier in this Chapter.

With respect to tax, however, VCTs offer the following tax reliefs

- Income tax
    - No income tax on dividends paid by the VCT.
    - Tax relief at 30% on the cost of any new subscriptions to a limit of £200,000 provided the shares are held for 5 years.
- CGT relief
    - No CGT on gains on disposal of VCT shares.

- CGT deferral
  - CGT deferral on gains from other asset disposals was available in 2003/04 and earlier.

EISs offer the following tax reliefs

- Income tax
  - Tax relief at 20% on the cost of any new subscriptions to a maximum of £500,000, offering a potential £100,000 relief.
- CGT relief
  - No CGT on gains on disposal of EIS shares provided the purchase attracted income tax relief and the shares were held for at least three years.
- CGT deferral
  - CGT deferral on gains from other asset disposals is available so long as the EIS investment is made between one year before and three years after the gain is made. This gain becomes taxable on the disposal of the EIS shares.

Pension contributions

Tax relief is available on pension fund contributions but the way it is received depends on whether the scheme is a company pension scheme or a personal one. Consideration should be given to maximizing the use of any available allowances.

Annuities

An **annuity** is a contract whereby a capital sum is paid to an insurance company, which in return pays a guaranteed income, either for a specific period or for the rest of a person's life.

The amount of income paid is based on the **investor's age**, ie the mortality factor, and interest rates on long-term gilts.

Purchased life annuities have a **capital element** and an **interest element**, with the split being pre-agreed between the HMRC and the insurance company.

(a) The capital element is based on expectation of life tables and is **tax-free**.
(b) The interest element is **taxable** (in the same way as interest on a bank account).

This means that a non-taxpayer can obtain a gross income from an annuity.

Pre-owned assets

If the gift with reservation rules do not apply, an **income tax** charge under **'pre-owned assets' rules** may apply (from **6 April 2005**) where individuals have entered into tax planning to reduce their inheritance tax liability without completely divesting themselves of the asset.

These could affect certain tax planning schemes involving the family home.

Children's tax position

There is legislation to prevent the parent of a minor child transferring income to the child in order to use the child's personal allowance and starting and basic rate tax bands. Income which is directly transferred by the parent, or is derived from capital so transferred, remains income of the parent for tax purposes.

This applies only to parents, however, and tax saving is therefore possible through gifts from other relatives.

Even where a parent is involved, the child's income is not treated as the parent's if it does not exceed £100 a year.

This legislation is concerned with **gifts from a parent to a child.** It could be possible to use the child's personal allowance and starting and basic rate bands if the child is employed in the parent's trade.

A parent can however make contributions to a child's **Child Trust Fund** account and the income will not be subject to tax. We discuss CTFs in the next section below.

Child Trust Fund (CTF)

Child Trust Funds (CTFs) were established by the Government in 2005 to promote long-term saving, CTFs are covered in detail earlier in this Chapter.

For children born on or after 1 September 2002, the Government contributes £250 at birth to be deposited in a CTF and a further £250 on the child's seventh birthday. In addition to the Government contribution, family and friends may contribute up to £1,200 p.a. to the account.

In its June 2010 Budget, the new Coalition Government announced that, subject to legislation, **Government contributions to CTFs at age 7 would cease** from **August 2010. New CTFs would cease** from **1 January 2011**. There is no immediate effect for those with existing accounts.

No income tax or capital gains tax is payable on CTF income or gains.

Key chapter points

- The Individual Savings Account is a tax-efficient investment vehicle for limited amounts of cash, and stocks and shares.

- Particularly as the tax credit on dividends can not be reclaimed, the advantages of a stocks and shares ISA are mainly for two types of investor. Firstly, there are taxpayers who pay or would otherwise pay capital gains tax. Secondly, higher rate taxpayers avoid additional tax on dividends.

- ISAs can hold unit trusts or OEICs, as well as listed shares and some corporate bonds and gilts. AIM shares cannot be held in an ISA unless they have a dual listing on a recognised exchange.

- 'Stakeholder' products can be held in an ISA. Products are subject to a '5% test' to establish whether they are eligible for the cash component or the stocks and shares component of an ISA.

- Venture Capital Trusts comprise a scheme that is designed to encourage investment in small unquoted companies. Tax reliefs are available, but investment in such companies can be risky.

- There are various approved tax-efficient employee share schemes which can make rewarding staff and helping them to acquire a stake in the business.

- The EIS and VCTs are schemes designed to encourage investment in small unquoted companies. Various tax reliefs are available, but investment in such companies can be risky.

- There are various tax planning opportunities when an individual's investment strategy is being planned.

Chapter Quiz

1. Outline the investments eligible for the stocks and shares component of an ISA. ....(See para 2.5.2)
2. What is the '5% test'? .... (2.6)
3. Outline the rules applying to transfers of ISAs. .... (2.7)
4. What is the tax position regarding dividends on ordinary shares in a Venture Capital Trust? .... (4.5)
5. What is the capital gains tax position regarding holdings in Venture Capital Trusts? .... (4.6)
6. What is the maximum monthly payment an individual may pay into an employee Sharesave share option scheme? .... (7.3)
7. What are the tax advantages of the Enterprise Management Incentive scheme? .... (7.5)
8. What are the maxima per employee for 'free shares' and 'partnership shares' in Share Incentive Plans? .... (7.6)
9. How would you characterise the expected performance of Enterprise Investment Scheme investments? ...... (5.1)
10. What is the rate of tax relief obtainable on an investment in an Enterprise Investment Scheme? .... (5.2)

chapter 14

Socially responsible and ethical investment

Chapter topic list

1	Ethical investment and its origins	308
2	Ethical/socially responsible strategies	310
3	Evaluating ethical investments	314
	Key chapter points	316
	Chapter quiz	317

Chapter Learning Outcomes

5 **Understand** the role of ethical investment and socially responsible investment in financial advice.

    5.1 Socially responsible investment – definition of socially responsible investment.

    5.2 Ethical investment – definition of ethical investment and the criteria used for including or excluding companies in ethical funds.

    5.3 Implications for investment performance.

1 Ethical investment and its origins

Learning outcomes

5.1 Socially responsible investment – definition of socially responsible investment.

5.2 Ethical investment – definition of ethical investment and the criteria used for including or excluding companies in ethical funds.

1.1 The basis of ethical investment

An investor, whether an individual or an organisation, may wish to make investment decisions in the light of the investor's **ethical beliefs** or **social values**. Churches and charities that have wished to invest on stock markets have often sought to avoid companies involved in activities such as alcohol and gambling and have run into controversy when companies in which they have invested have been found wanting by ethical standards.

The individual or corporate investor may want to avoid having investments in their portfolios that place funds in the hands of businesses of which the investor does not approve. Some investors may wish to ensure that their investments are made in areas of which they positively approve: for example, enterprises that exhibit a degree of social responsibility or are pro-active in certain desirable activities. It is possible for the adviser to take account of such motives, whether investments are within a **portfolio** of **individual stocks** or **collective funds**.

When did modern ethical investing get started?

- The first ethically screened mutual fund in the USA was set up in 1971 in response to a demand for investments that did not benefit from the Vietnam War.
- The oldest ethical fund in the UK is the Friends Provident Stewardship Fund, which was launched in 1984.
- The first 'green' UK unit trust was established in 1988 with the launch of the Merlin Ecology Fund (now the Jupiter Ecology Fund).

1.2 Ethical investing versus Socially Responsible Investment

Definition of Ethical Investment

Ethical investment is commonly used to describe the purchase of shares in companies that have been selected by combining ethical screening with conventional financial criteria.

How extensive is ethical investing now?

- The **Ethical Investment Research Service (EIRIS)** is an independent UK charity set up in 1983 that researches companies on behalf of other charities and fund managers. The EIRIS guide for financial advisers covers listed companies satisfying certain criteria (see below) and their Ethical IFA Directory lists IFAs with ethical experience.
- The Social Investment Forum in the USA has stated that the amount of assets under management invested according to social responsibility principles has passed the level of US$2 trillion.

EIRIS figures released in June 2010 showed the amount of money in the UK ethical investment sector was at an all time high of £9.5billion.

The idea of **socially responsible investment (SRI)** broadens the idea of ethical aspects of investment decisions by promoting a pro-active view of how social and environmental aspects can be brought into the investment decision, beyond the traditional approach of avoiding unethical investments.

Definition of Socially Responsible Investment SRI focuses on investments in companies that are making a positive contribution to the world, together with the active engagement with a company's management to promote best practice on social or environmental issues.

For investors, SRI allows them to combine their personal values and social concerns with investment decisions.

1.3 Engagement

As SRI has developed, new approaches have been adopted.

The traditional approach involved excluding companies engaged in undesirable activities. Many ethical investors now seek to adopt a more **'pro-active'** stance. Such a stance may involve not just selecting companies whose activities could improve the world, but also becoming involved by exercising shareholder rights and occasionally applying the pressure of publicity to encourage companies to develop more socially responsible policies and practices. Such involvement is often called **'engagement'**.

The movement in favour of investments that promote social responsibility in a pro-active way is in line with the 2001 **Myners Review of Institutional Investment**, which advocated a greater degree of shareholder activism.

The idea of **engagement** goes beyond mere selection criteria and involves an active process of shareholder activism and lobbying, by investors or institutional fund managers. A fund manager with a substantial stake in a company may be in a position to enter into dialogue with the company in an attempt to encourage the company to pay attention to ethical and SRI objectives where there is a good business case for them, and improved corporate reporting.

Those who favour an engagement-based approach argue that high standards in **corporate governance** and **corporate reporting** are vital to the financial success of companies and to the long-term sustainability of the economic system.

1.4 Issues for financial advisers

Advisers need to be aware of a number of issues if they are discussing and considering screened ethical investments with clients.

(a) The investor needs to be made aware of the other **various criteria for evaluating investments** – such as the financial criteria by which direct equity investments are judged, and the track record of funds. Some investors see any under-performance relative to the market as an acceptable price to pay for having made an ethical investment. However, many ethical funds do have a relatively good **investment performance** record, and it should not be assumed that there must be a sacrifice of performance in return for a fund meeting ethical criteria.

(b) **Every ethical fund is different** and an investor who has developed firm opinions on the criteria they wish to adopt in selecting investments will need to find a fund or other investment that meets these criteria closely.

INVESTMENT AND RISK

(c) As with other types of fund investment, consideration should be given to the **financial strength of the provider**. The amount of resources that a fund management group is able to devote to ethical research will also be relevant.

(d) The companies that pass the ethical screening of fund managers may well be smaller than an average stock market listed company. Shares in larger companies have, in the past, tended to be under-represented in ethically selected funds compared with many mainstream funds. This may mean that the share price of ethically selected investments could be relatively volatile because of their relatively high weighting of smaller company stocks, resulting in the possibility of increased **risk**.

(e) Restricting choices by applying ethical criteria means a **narrowing of the field of companies** in which a fund or an individual can invest.

Although the choice of ethical investments used to be relatively limited, there is now a much **wider choice**, if a client is able to consider various providers. Ethical or SRI funds exist which invest in **corporate bonds** and **property** as well as **equities**, and funds with various risk profiles are available. Clients can also choose to keep their **cash deposits** in interest-bearing accounts with financial institutions that pay attention to ethical issues.

1.5 Is there a typical 'ethical investor'?

The UK Social Investment Forum suggests that, compared with the bulk of investors, ethical investors are more likely to be female and younger, to work in a caring profession and to belong to at least one major organisation promoting conservation, environmental protection or social change. Beyond this stereotype, a financial adviser should be alert to any ethical concerns that clients might wish to take account of in their investment choices.

2 Ethical/socially responsible strategies

Learning outcomes

5.2 Ethical investment – definition of ethical investment and the criteria used for including or excluding companies in ethical funds.

5.3 Implications for investment performance.

2.1 Introduction

2.1.1 Ethical investment strategies

There are four basic strategies that can be applied by ethical or socially responsible funds when selecting investments for their portfolios

- **Screening** – The inclusion (positive screening) or exclusion (negative screening) of investments based on ethical or social reasons. Negative screening looks to filter out investments with an unacceptable ethical or social performance, positive screening aims to identify investments with a superior ethical/social stance.

- **Positive engagement** – Identifying investments that could improve their ethical, social or environmental behaviour and encouraging them to do so through exercising their shareholder power.

- **Best of class** – Rating investments in the same sector based on ethical, social or environmental issues with the fund manager biasing his selection based on this '**best in class**'.

- **Thematic investment** – Where key themes (eg pollution, education) are used to identify investment opportunities that are seeking to improve the ethical and social wellbeing of the world.

An ethical or SRI-oriented fund must state clearly the criteria it uses in selecting investments, so that investors can decide if that particular fund meets their needs.

A fund may use either **negative criteria** or **positive criteria** in the process of **screening** the companies it is considering investing in. Once it has been established whether a company meets the criteria of the fund, investment managers can decide whether the company is worth investing in at the current price based on other financially-based criteria.

Each ethical/SRI fund has its own set of criteria. Some funds may predominantly use a more 'traditional' approach of excluding companies because of their negative aspects. Other funds balance an application of such negative criteria with a set of positive criteria.

2.2 Screening

2.2.1 Negative screening

The oldest forms of ethical investment involved negative screening, avoiding investment in business/sectors with a poor ethical value. A fund may decide to **avoid** investments that are involved in or have a poor record in some or all of the following areas.

- Alcohol production or sale
- Animal exploitation
- Animal testing in cosmetics
- Animal testing for pharmaceutical products
- Environmental degradation and damage
- Gambling
- Genetic engineering and modern biotechnology
- Genetically modified organisms (GMO)
- Health and safety breaches
- Human rights breaches
- Intensive farming
- Military-related enterprises
- Nuclear power
- Offensive or misleading advertising
- Oppressive regimes
- Pesticides
- Pollution breaches
- Pornography
- Third World exploitation
- Tobacco production or sale
- Tropical hardwoods
- Water pollution

2.2.2 Positive screening

As an alternative to negative screening, a fund may choose to monitor how enterprises comply with certain positive ethical and social governance criteria and may decide to choose some or all of its investments from companies that serve positive ethical and social responsibility concerns, such as the following.

- Community involvement
- Training and education policies

INVESTMENT AND RISK

- Full disclosure and openness about activities
- Good relations with customers and suppliers
- Equal opportunities
- Good employment practices
- Environmental improvement
- Environmental management: energy and resource conservation
- Positive goods and services produced

Example: Ethical criteria of a fund

The ethical criteria adopted by the Friends Provident Stewardship Fund are summarised below.

Positive criteria. The Stewardship Fund actively looks to support companies involved in the following:

Supplying the basic necessities of life
Providing high quality products and services which are of long term benefit to the community
Conservation of energy or natural resources
Environmental improvements and pollution control
Good relations with customers and suppliers
Good employment practices
Training and education
Strong community involvement
A good equal opportunities record
Openness about company activities

Negative criteria. The Stewardship Fund aims to avoid companies involved in the following:

Environmental damage and pollution
Manufacture and sale of weapons
Trade with or operations in oppressive regimes
Exploitation of developing countries
Unnecessary exploitation of animals
Nuclear power
Tobacco or alcohol production
Gambling
Pornography
Offensive or misleading advertising

2.2.3 Applying and interpreting criteria

Clearly the application of negative and positive criteria such as those listed above requires fairly detailed policies to be followed if the ethical principles guiding a fund's strategy are to be followed consistently.

Investors should read the stated ethical policies of funds carefully in order to ensure that a given fund meets their requirements.

- Some investors may be quite specific in their requirements, if they have specific opinions on the relevant issues.
- Other investors may be content to choose funds that have a broadly 'positive' ethical policy, as an acceptable alternative to a fund that has no specific ethical policy.

> ### Example: 'Community involvement'
>
> When considering a criterion such as '**community involvement**', clearly investors will differ widely in their views on what kind of activities comprise the kind of community involvement they favour.
>
> Many funds mention the following organisations that seek to promote community involvement in different ways in their statements on ethical criteria:
>
> (a) **Business in the Community (BiC):** 'an association of major UK businesses which are committed to working in partnership with each other, with central and local Government, voluntary organisations and trade unions to promote corporate social responsibility and revitalise economic life in local communities'.
>
> (b) **Per Cent Club:** 'a group of some 300 leading companies which are committed to making a significant contribution to the communities in which they operate. The Per Cent Club has no written constitution, nor does it attempt to influence its members' contributions. The qualification for membership is the contribution of no less than half a per cent of pre-tax (UK) profits or one percent of dividends to the community.'

2.3 Positive engagement

A fund may also adopt an approach of positive engagement, whereby it uses its stake in the company to enter into dialogue with management and, thereby, influence their attitude to SRI.

2.4 'Best of class' approach

Using a best in class approach rates all investments in the same sector by ethical, social and environmental factors and factors this rating into the stock selection decision.

Considering pollution, for example, there must be only a very few companies which have a totally 'clean' record, since virtually all economic activity pollutes the environment to some extent. The **best of class** approach identifies those companies that have the best record, which may mean that they produce a low level of pollution compared with other companies and that they take the most positive steps on improvements related to pollution.

The 'best of class' approach is sometimes called a **preference** approach.

2.5 Thematic approach

The **thematic investment** approach concentrates on companies that are thought to be bringing about improvements in particular areas. 'Themes' that might appeal to different investors include education, health care, renewable energy or public transport. In many cases, the companies involved may be companies seen to have a potential for future growth: as such, there may be a relatively high risk of failure.

The thematic investment approach is often regarded as an alternative to using traditional positive screening criteria.

2.6 Implications for investment performance

The big question about ethical investments is whether you have to suffer for your principles in terms of lower returns and higher levels of risk.

Such investments tend to be in smaller companies, particularly those with stricter criteria, since large firms are more likely to break the negative screening tests due to the diversity of their operations. These small company shares can be more volatile, though the effects of this volatility may be mitigated through broad diversification.

INVESTMENT AND RISK

Diversification, however, is often restricted by the fact that many industry sectors will be discounted by strict ethical funds due to the very nature of the business. Examples here include tobacco, mining and livestock. Funds leaving out key industry sectors can bear more risk than others – losing out, say, when those sectors boom. But on the other side of the argument they will not lose out when these sectors slump.

2.7 Regulation

Evidence suggests that ethical funds have performed much in line with their non-ethical equivalents over the last 15 years, albeit slightly less well.

There is no specific regulation of ethical funds as such, but issues to consider would include

- Compliance with the trust deed (or similar).
- Providing adequate (and not misleading) information in the scheme particulars for the customer to make a balanced and informed decision.
- Advertisements are fair and not misleading.

3 Evaluating ethical investments

Learning outcome

5.3 Implications for investment performance.

3.1 How green is an ethical investment fund?

As SRI has developed over time to suit investors' demands, funds have expanded the range of SRI criteria that they use to include or exclude companies from their investment portfolio. Depending on how strict are the fund's investment criteria, funds can be seen as falling into one of three **shades of 'greenness'**:

- **Dark green:** using predominantly negative screening methods and applying them strictly
- **Medium green:** adopting a moderate approach between 'dark green' and 'light green'
- **Light green:** less restrictive in its policies, possibly only using positive criteria or a policy of positive shareholder engagement

3.2 FTSE4Good Indices

The share indices organisation FTSE produces a range of ethical or SRI share indices called **FTSE4Good** that are designed to identify and measure the performance of companies working towards:

- Environmental sustainability
- Positive relationships with stakeholders, and
- Upholding and supporting universal human rights

The establishment of the FTSE4Good indices follows earlier development in the USA of the Dow Jones Sustainability Group Indices.

FTSE4Good selects its constituents in the following way.

- The **starting universe** comprises companies in the FTSE All-Share Index, the FTSE Developed Europe Index, the FTSE US Index and the FTSE Developed Index.

- **Exclusions** are made for: tobacco producers, nuclear weapon manufacturers, nuclear power stations, uranium mining companies.
- **Selection criteria** then applied are: working towards environmental sustainability, upholding and supporting universal human rights and positive relations with stakeholders.
- The performance of manufacturers marketing breast milk substitutes in developing countries is evaluated to decide if they are eligible for inclusion.

A company is included in the index if it meets FTSE4Good standards, and excluded if it does not. This process gives rise to a series of FTSE4Good indices for the UK, for Europe, for the USA, and for global investing.

3.3 Uses of SRI indices

From the investor's point of view, **SRI indices** such as FTSE4Good might be a useful research tool. The investor may find that they produce ideas of companies to consider further for direct equity investment in building a portfolio along SRI lines. However, most investors would wish to look at many more criteria than purely SRI considerations, such as those we looked at earlier in this Study Text. Indeed, an adviser should ensure that clients are aware of the possible risks of investing purely on SRI criteria without considering other aspects of proposed investments.

FTSE also aims that such indices will be used by asset managers as a basis for developing index-linked products such as **tracker funds** or derivative products. An example is the CIS UK FTSE4Good Tracker.

Key chapter points

- Ethical investment involves a process of applying negative and positive criteria in selecting candidate companies for investment.
- Just as there are diverse ethical concerns of investors, so there are many different ways that funds can apply ethical criteria.
- In the past, ethical funds have tended to have a relatively low weighting in larger capitalisation stocks.
- 'Best of class' and 'thematic' describe different approaches to applying ethical criteria.
- Socially responsible investing (SRI) encompasses various aspects of ethical, social and environmental concern and may involve pro-active shareholder involvement as a form of engagement in the companies in which investments are made.
- EIRIS provides research services for many fund managers and publishes a guide to choosing ethical funds for financial advisers.
- SRI indices identify baskets of shares that have passed particular ethical criteria.

14: SOCIALLY RESPONSIBLE AND ETHICAL INVESTMENT

Chapter Quiz

1. What is the full name of EIRIS? .... (see para 1.2)
2. What is meant by 'engagement' in the context of ethical investment? .... (1.3)
3. Give five examples of negative criteria that an ethical fund might apply. .... (2.2.1)
4. Give five examples of positive criteria that an ethical fund might apply. .... (2.2.2)
5. Distinguish 'best of class' and 'thematic' ethical investment approaches. .... (2.4, 2.5)
6. What are the FTSE4Good indices? .... (3.2)

chapter 15

Risks and return

Chapter topic list

1	Introduction	320
2	Measuring returns	321
3	Types of risk	325
4	Measuring risk	329
5	Diversification	330
6	Relating risk and return	334
	Key chapter points	338
	Chapter quiz	339

INVESTMENT AND RISK

CHAPTER LEARNING OUTCOMES

6 **Understand** how investment returns are related to investment risk and how that risk is measured

    6.1   Principles of investment risk.

    6.2   Inflation and investment returns – the difference between nominal and real returns.

    6.3   The effects of compound and simple interest.

    6.4   The time value of money.

    6.5   Varying investment returns from the main different asset classes – risk-free rates of return and the risk premium.

    6.6   Measuring risk – volatility, the significance of standard deviation as a measure of volatility, the importance and limitations of performance data.

    6.7   Sharpe ratio.

    6.8   Measuring total return and the significance of beta and alpha.

    6.9   Investment portfolio planning and reducing risk through diversification – systemic and unsystematic risk, diversification across shares, sectors, markets and asset classes.

7.   **Understand** the risks faced by investors and how an investor's risk profile is determined

    7.2   Main types of risk for investors – equity capital risk, currency risk, interest rate risk, institutional risk, regulatory risk, income risk, inflation risk, shortfall risk, legislative risk, counterparty risk;

1 Introduction

Learning outcome

6.1   Principles of investment risk.

In a certain world, the return from an investment would always be exactly as expected and there would be no risk. The investor would merely have to compare the returns available on different investments and choose those which offered the highest returns.

Unfortunately, the existence of uncertainty means that the returns from investments are not always as expected – there is some risk involved.

Almost all investment opportunities involve a risk. All securities quoted on the Stock Exchange are subject to risk. Different types of security will have different kinds of risk associated with them, for example, UK government securities do not suffer the risk of default, but are vulnerable to changes in interest rates. However, the effect of all these different kinds of risk is the same, that is, the actual returns achieved may differ from those expected by the investor. The riskier the investment, the more likely it is that the hoped-for return will not be reached or the greater the shortfall from the expected return.

One of the fundamental assumptions of investment appraisal is that investors are rational and risk averse, ie they will demand a higher return if they are to face a higher risk, or the return that investors demand will be commensurate with the risk that they face.

But how can we use this idea to rationally appraise any investment alternatives?

15: RISKS AND RETURN

If we are to undertake a systematic appraisal of an investment opportunity, we must be able to incorporate all relevant factors. In order to incorporate these factors into our analysis, we must be able to answer the following questions.

- How can we measure/quantity returns
- What causes risk?
- How can we measure/quantify risk?
- Can risk be avoided?
- How can we relate risk and return?

2 Measuring returns

2.1 Calculating total return

Learning outcomes

6.2 Inflation and investment returns – the difference between nominal and real returns.
6.3 The effects of compound and simple interest.
6.4 The time value of money.
6.8 Measuring total return and the significance of beta and alpha.

The **total return** or **holding period return** on an investment is a measure of the percentage **gain** or **loss** on the investment relative to the purchase price. The gain or loss will be the difference between the total cash return (sale price + dividends) and the original cost giving

$$\text{Total return} = \frac{(\text{Sale value of the investment} + \text{dividends received}) - \text{cost of the investment}}{\text{Cost of the investment}}$$

Example: Total return

An investor purchased £15,000 in value of Bondweed plc shares, and incurred £250 in additional costs (Stamp Duty Reserve Tax plus broker's commission)

She received £800 cash dividends during the period for which she held the shares.

The investor sold the shares for £24,000, net of broker's commission. What was her total return?

Solution

$$\text{Total return} = \frac{(£24,000 + £800) - £15,250}{£15,250} = \frac{£9,530}{£15,250} = 0.6262 \text{ or } 62.62\%$$

What factors might affect whether we view the total return in the Example above as a good investment return?

Two such factors are the **time period** of the investment and the **relative performance of other investments** over the period.

- If the return of 62% were achieved over one or two years, this would generally be seen as a very good investment. If such a 62% return were earned over 20 years, it would represent a poor investment, since it probably would not even have kept pace with inflation.
- If a return of 62% is achieved over a period over which the FTSE 100 Index fell by 25%, then this investment has performed extremely well: it has outperformed the wider market spectacularly. If the

INVESTMENT AND RISK

return of 62% was over a period of, say, six years in which the FTSE 100 Index rose by 90%, then the investment has been unimpressive, since it has underperformed the wider market.

Note that, in our assessment of the investment in the Example, we have been considering only **past performance**. Nothing has been said about whether the investment might perform well in the future. Past share price performance cannot be taken as an indication simply that a similar performance can be expected in the future. Some companies, with good management and the right market conditions, manage to grow their share price over a long sustained period but, equally, many do not.

2.2 The time value of money

The time value of money is a way of appraising the value of investment based on their expected future returns.

If a person has a choice between (A) £1,000 now, and (B) £1,000 in one year's time then he or she will have a preference for (A). If you have £1,000 now, then you could invest it and earn interest, so that you would have a greater sum in one year's time. You might alternatively have other uses for the money.

This example shows that money has a '**time value**'. The option of having money now is of more value than the option of having money at a date in the future. **Interest** can be seen partly as the return required by the lender to compensate for the time value of money that the lender is supplying to the borrower.

2.3 Nominal and real rates of return

Nominal rates of interest or **return** are rates expressed in money terms. The nominal rate of interest might also be referred to as the **money rate of interest**, or the **actual money yield** on an investment.

Real rates of return are the returns that investors get from their investment, adjusted for the rate of inflation.

The relationship between the **rate of inflation**, the **real rate of return** and the **nominal (money) rate of return** is as follows, with rates expressed as a fraction (eg 5% would be expressed as 0.05).

(1+ real rate of return) × (1+ inflation rate) = 1+ money rate of return

If the nominal rate of return is 12% per annum and the annual rate of inflation is 8% per annum, the real rate of return is the return earned after allowing for the return needed just to keep pace with inflation.

We may rearrange the equation above to find the real rate of return.

$$\frac{1+ \text{money rate}}{1+ \text{inflation rate}} = 1 + \text{real rate}$$

$$\frac{1.12}{1.08} = 1.037$$

The real rate of return is thus 3.7%.

The real rate of return is commonly measured **approximately**, however, as the difference between the nominal rate of return and the rate of inflation. In our example, this would be 12% − 8% = 4%.

2.4 Simple interest

Simple interest is interest (or return) which is earned in equal amounts every year (or month) and which is a given proportion of the original investment (the principal).

If a sum of money is invested for a period of time, then the amount of simple interest which accrues is equal to the number of periods × the interest rate × the amount invested. We can write this as a formula.

The formula for **simple interest** is as follows.

S = X + nrX

where X = the original sum invested
       r = the interest rate (expressed as a proportion, so 10% = 0.1)
       n = the number of periods (normally years)
       S = the sum invested after n periods, consisting of the original capital (X) plus interest earned.

Example: Simple interest

How much will an investor have after five years if he invests £1,000 at 10% simple interest per annum?

Solution

Using the formula S = X + nrX

where X = £1,000
       r = 10%
       n = 5

∴ S = £1,000 + (5 × 0.1 × £1,000) = £1,500

2.5 Compound interest

2.5.1 Annual compounding

Interest is normally calculated using the method of **compounding**.

If a sum of money (the **principal**) is invested at a fixed rate of interest such that the interest is added to the principal and no withdrawals are made, then the amount invested will grow by an increasing number of pounds in each successive time period, because **interest earned in earlier periods** will itself earn interest **in later periods**.

Example: Compound interest (1)

Suppose that £2,000 is invested at 10% interest. What will be the value of the investment at the end of each of the next three years.

One year

After one year, the original principal plus interest will amount to £2,200.

	£
Original investment	2,000
Interest in the first year (10%)	200
Total investment at the end of one year	2,200

Two Years

After two years the total investment will be £2,420.

	£
Investment at end of one year	2,200
Interest in the second year (10%)	220
Total investment at the end of two years	2,420

INVESTMENT AND RISK

> The second year interest of £220 represents 10% of the original investment, and 10% of the interest earned in the first year.
>
> **Three years**
>
> Similarly, after three years, the total investment will be £2,662.
>
> | | £ |
> |---|---|
> | Investment at the end of two years | 2,420 |
> | Interest in the third year (10%) | 242 |
> | Total investment at the end of three years | 2,662 |

Instead of performing the calculations in the box above, we could have used the following **formula**.

The basic formula for **compound interest** (or compound return) is $S = X(1 + r)^n$

where X = the original sum invested
       r = the interest/return rate, expressed as a proportion (so 5% = 0.05)
       n = the number of periods
       S = the sum invested after n periods

Using the formula for compound interest, $S = X(1 + r)^n$

where X = £2,000
       r = 10% = 0.1
       n = 3
       S = £2,000 × 1.10^3
         = £2,000 × 1.331
         = £2,662.

2.5.2 Compounding over non-annual periods

In the previous examples, interest has been calculated **annually**, but this isn't always the case. Interest may be compounded **daily**, **weekly**, **monthly** or **quarterly**.

Interest rates are expressed as per annum figures even when the interest is compounded over periods of less than one year. In such cases, the given interest rate is called a **nominal rate**. The **effective annual rate of interest** or **return**, when the interest or return is compounded at shorter intervals, is given the official names of **Annual Equivalent Rate (AER)** for savings or **Annual Percentage Rate (APR)** for mortgages, credit cards and personal loans.

Information on the AER / APR of financial products helps consumers to make comparisons between products.

The AER/APR is sometimes called the **compound annual rate (CAR)**.

> ### Example: Nominal and effective rates of interest (1)
>
> A building society offers investors 10% per annum interest payable half-yearly. If the 10% is a nominal rate of interest, the building society would in fact pay 5% every six months, compounded so that the effective annual rate of interest would be:
>
> $[(1.05)^2 - 1] = 0.1025 = 10.25\%$ per annum.
>
> Similarly, if a bank offers depositors a nominal 12% per annum, with interest payable quarterly, the effective rate of interest would be 3% compound every three months, which is
>
> $[(1.03)^4 - 1] = 0.1255 = 12.55\%$ per annum.

Now work out the answer for yourself to the following example.

> ### Example: Nominal and effective rates of interest (2)
>
> A bank adds interest monthly to investors' accounts even though interest rates are expressed in annual terms. The current rate of interest is 12%. Fred deposits £2,000 on 1 July. How much interest will have been earned by 31 December (to the nearest £)?
>
> A £123.00 B £60.00 C £240.00 D £120.00
>
> ### Solution
>
> The nominal rate is 12% pa payable monthly.
>
> ∴ The effective rate = $\dfrac{12\%}{12 \text{ months}}$ = 1% compound monthly.
>
> ∴ In the six months from July to December, the interest earned = (£2,000 × $(1.01)^6$) – £2,000 = £123.04.
>
> The correct answer is A.

This can be expressed mathematically as

Annual Equivalent Rate (AER) = $[(1+r)^{\frac{12}{n}} - 1]$ or $[(1+r)^{\frac{365}{y}} - 1]$

where r is the rate of interest for each time period
       n is the number of months in the time period
       y is the number of days in the time period

> ### Example: Annual equivalent rate of interest
>
> Calculate the annual equivalent rate of interest for:
>
> (a) 1.5% per month, compound
> (b) 4.5% per quarter, compound
> (c) 9% per half year, compound
>
> ### Solution
>
> (a) $(1.015)^{12} - 1$ = 0.1956 = 19.56%
> (b) $(1.045)^4 - 1$ = 0.1925 = 19.25%
> (c) $(1.09)^2 - 1$ = 0.1881 = 18.81%

3 Types of risk

> ### Learning outcomes
>
> 6.1 Principles of investment risk.
>
> 7.2 Main types of risk for investors – equity capital risk, currency risk, interest rate risk, institutional risk, regulatory risk, income risk, inflation risk, shortfall risk, legislative risk, counterparty risk.

INVESTMENT AND RISK

3.1 Distinguishing types of risk

There are several different factors that give rise to risk, ie lead to variability in the return on an investment. Some investments, such as gilts, will have few risks associated with them, whereas company shares will be subject to many possible reasons for fluctuations in return. Factors contributing to risk in investment returns include

- Interest rate risk
- Income risk
- Inflation risk
- Shortfall risk
- Capital risk
- Currency risk
- Liquidity risk
- Institutional risk
- Political risk
- Regulatory risk

3.2 Interest rate risk and income risk

The possible future movement of interest rates affects borrowers and savers in conversely different ways.

The following cases are examples of **interest rate risk** (which you may find called **interest risk** in an exam question).

(a) A rise in interest rates is a risk for a **borrower** who is borrowing at a **variable** rate.
(b) A **saver** with a **variable** rate account faces the risk that interest rates will fall in the future.

A borrower who locks into a fixed rate mortgage rate is protected against a rise in rates of interest for the fixed period. However, the possibility that the fixed rate he locks into could be higher than prevailing variable rates, if rates fall in the future, could be seen as a 'risk' he takes on if he locks into the fixed rate deal.

Conversely, a saver who locks into a fixed rate account without instant access, or carrying penalties for withdrawals, may be worse off than he might have been with a variable rate account, if interest rates rise during the period of the investment.

The term 'income risk' can be used to refer to the possibility that the **income from a fund** will fluctuate due to **changes in interest rates**. Another use of the term 'income risk' concerns the risk carried by individuals that their salary or wages will fall (see the next paragraph).

3.3 Income risk

It has been estimated that for someone in the UK with a gross household income of £400 per week, their income is likely to be above £620 or below £260 per week for approximately ten per cent of the time. This illustrates the **income risk** that an average household carries. An example of the types of circumstance causing this is that the individual may have a period with no wages, when between jobs. Most self-employed people will experience fluctuating incomes throughout their self-employed career. Although some protection products can reduce the adverse effects of redundancy or having to stop work due to ill-health or disability, to some extent labour income risk will be an uninsurable risk.

Total **income risk** is found be lower for older individuals and is slightly less for women than men. Better-off individuals are likely to have lower **income risk** than those at the lower part of the income distribution.

3.4 Inflation risk

Rising prices can reduce the purchasing power of an amount of capital, or income. By investing money, the investor may be risking loss in purchasing power during the period of the investment.

We discussed in Chapter 3 of this Study Text how **inflation in prices** erodes the purchasing power of money.

Imagine also the situation of an economy with **deflation in prices**, as has affected Japan in recent years. If prices are deflating, one could say that buying goods now bears the 'risk' that the same goods could have been bought for less later. There is then a strong incentive for people to save, since the purchasing power of cash, even if no interest were being earned, would increase through time. This is one reason why deflation can be an economic problem: if people have a strong incentive to save, demand for goods and services may be weak.

3.5 Shortfall risk

Shortfall risk is the risk that an amount invested will not reach a target financial goal at some time in the future. For example, a couple might start a savings plan to support the future education expenses of a child. There could be a risk that the plan does not grow enough to pay these expenses. Another example is that of a holder of an interest-only mortgage who has an investment that is intended to pay off the full amount of the mortgage at the end of its term. There is a shortfall risk that the investment will have generated insufficient returns to pay off the full target amount at the intended date.

Choosing riskier investments is likely to increase the shortfall risk. If reaching a particular target level is important to the investor, then the shortfall risk can be reduced by choosing lower risk investments. However, choosing lower risk investments is likely to mean a higher probability that returns will be relatively low, and so more may need to be invested than might have been required with more risky investments, assuming that such investments had produced higher returns.

3.6 Capital risk

Capital risk is the possibility of loss of some or all of the original capital invested. This can be a very significant form of risk, with potentially devastating results to the unwary investor.

Holding **equities** presents a **capital risk**. With purchases of individual shares, there is the risk that the value of the investment will fall, and it could be totally wiped out. This can be particularly so for shares in newer smaller companies without a track record and without a full Stock Exchange listing. A company might be set up to develop a new product, such as a new type of hydraulic pump, with no revenues expected for four to five years after the company is set up. If revenues fail to materialise and the company is liquidated, all of investors' capital could be lost. If an investor had invested half of his savings in the company, the personal effect on that investor would be great.

Especially for **derivative** investments, such as futures contracts, options or contracts for differences (CFDs), it is possible to lose **more** than the original capital invested. Such investments can be **geared** so that they offer the prospect of magnified gains, but also the risk of magnified losses.

3.7 Currency risk

Currency risk is the risk arising from fluctuations in the value of currencies against each other. A UK resident (that is, someone whose home currency is sterling) who buys stocks or bonds in other currencies, for example the euro or the US dollar, faces currency risk.

Suppose that a UK investor buys shares in a US company which does most of its trading in the US. The share price in US dollars fluctuates on the US stock market. Additionally, the value of sterling fluctuates against the US dollar. Therefore, the sterling value of the investment will fluctuate in time as a result of two effects: the changing dollar share price, and the changing US dollar / sterling exchange rate.

Exposure to currency risk is not totally avoided by investing within the UK. Many UK companies do much of their business abroad. This means that their earnings will be affected by exchange rate fluctuations. If a UK company manufactures goods in the UK using domestically sourced raw materials, and exports much of its products to the European 'Eurozone' countries, then it is exposed to a rise in the value of sterling against the euro. If sterling rises in value, the euro-priced receipts from the company's Eurozone sales will buy fewer pounds sterling than before.

Some companies **hedge** their foreign exchange earnings or their foreign raw materials costs, to give them greater certainty about future earnings and to reduce currency risks. This may be done, for example, by entering forward currency contracts, fixing the value of future transactions of the company in advance.

Some larger **multinational** companies have costs and revenues in many different countries, and they may also have shareholders in many different countries. Since shareholders will be based in various currency areas, there may be no currency hedging strategy that serves all shareholders equally. In general, a company may seek to hedge currency exposures in such a way that currency risks between input (raw materials) costs and the income from that production are hedged. Then, each production unit should have a chance of meeting its profit targets without being affected too much by exchange rate fluctuations.

3.8 Liquidity risk

An investor in **property** suffers from the risk associated with **illiquidity**. A sale can only be made if a buyer can be found and this can prove a great problem. During the early 1990s, with a stagnant housing and property market few buyers of residential property could be found and prices fell. Many homeowners had negative equity: the value of their house fell to below the value of their debt (mortgage). If a client invests in property via the medium of a property unit trust or investment bond he may suffer similar, although not such acute, illiquidity. Under the terms of these investments the proceeds of a sale may be delayed for up to six months to allow the managers to realise assets to pay the investor.

3.9 Institutional risk

In a financial market, there are different types of investor and participant, often including both individuals and financial institutions. There are regulations and laws that aim to make information freely available to all potential participants, in many markets. In practice, and particularly in overseas markets for example, it may be difficult for 'outsiders' to become fully aware of the institutional structure.

There may be '**institutional risks**' arising from the fact that a market is relatively immature (as with so-called **emerging markets**) or with other institutional factors such as market liquidity (How easy is it to buy and sell the investment?), regulation and the availability of information.

3.10 Political risk

Political risk describes the risk that unexpected action by the government in the country where the investment is located may devalue an investment. This might occur, for example, if the government introduces new currency controls or new taxes, or if it nationalises assets.

3.11 Regulatory risk

The term **regulatory risk** can be defined as the risk associated with the potential for laws related to a given industry, country, or type of security to change and impact relevant investments. There is clearly a degree of overlap among regulatory risk and institutional and political risk. However, regulatory risk is present within any economy, affecting all domestic investments: regulations may change, affecting how an investment performs. Taxation and other laws may change, possibly to close a 'loophole' that some investments have set out to exploit.

Clearly, some degree of regulation is a positive thing for the investor. However, a government that minimises the amount of unexpected change to regulation may be able to create a more attractive environment for investors.

4 Measuring risk

> **Learning outcome**
>
> 6.6 Measuring risk – volatility, the significance of standard deviation as a measure of volatility, the importance and limitations of performance data.

4.1 Standard deviation

The variability or **volatility** of investment values can be seen by looking at almost any graph of a daily share price or share index over a period of time in a copy of a newspaper such as the *Financial Times*. A smooth line is unusual to find.

The volatility in value of an investment can be quantified mathematically by calculating the **standard deviation** of the values.

The standard deviation measures how widely the value of an investment fluctuates around the **mean** or **average.** The more volatile the variations in the value of an investment are, the greater is the standard deviation.

- An investment with returns that do not vary much from its average return has a low standard deviation. **Low standard deviation** implies **low risk.**
- An investment with returns that do vary greatly from its average return has a high standard deviation. **High standard deviation** implies **high risk.**

The standard deviation can be calculated on the basis of past data, on the assumption that a similar level of volatility will be found in the future too, for that investment.

Knowing the standard deviation can help us to know the range of different values of return we might expect from an investment. For about **two-thirds** of the time, we can expect the return to be within one standard deviation above or below the average return.

For example, suppose that an investment has an average annual return of 9% and a standard deviation of returns of 4%. Then we can expect that, if we make the investment:

- There is a chance of 2/3 that the annual return will be between 5% and 13%
- There is a chance of 1/3 that the annual return will be below 5% and above 13%

4.2 Volatility of collective funds

Although holding **collective funds** such as unit trusts, open ended investment companies (OEICs) and investment trusts, is a means of diversifying a portfolio (see later), the volatility of different funds varies.

Figures are published for the standard deviations of the performance of collective funds. In the case of funds whose performance has a relatively high standard deviation, the fund manager would appear to be taking greater risks than fund managers with a lower standard deviation.

Standard deviation data provides additional insight into how volatile a fund's performance might be in future.

The volatility of a fund can be compared with:

- The volatility of other funds in the sector
- The volatility of the benchmark for the fund

Funds with high volatility involve higher risk: there will be a greater variation in returns than for a lower-volatility fund.

An investor will be particularly interested to invest in funds that produce **higher than average returns** but with **low volatility.**

INVESTMENT AND RISK

4.3 Using past performance data

Measuring volatility in order to appreciate the risk of an investment is possible when we have **data on past performance**. For a fund, positive past performance data may be an indicator of good management of the fund.

If a fund has turned in 4th quartile performances (ie, in the bottom 25% of funds, in its sector) for the last ten years, it is unlikely to be recommended. On the other hand, a fund that is in 1st quartile performance for the last year should not generally be recommended solely on that basis, without looking at the consistency of the performance. To be sure of the track record of a fund, an investor will want to look back over several periods.

The following are **limitations** of past performance data.

- Even a well managed fund may underperform in some periods
- Changes in fund management personnel could have a significant effect on performance
- Fund strategy may change in the future
- Performance of markets, and of funds, varies through time

5 Diversification

Learning outcome

6.9 Investment portfolio planning and reducing risk through diversification – systematic and unsystematic risk, diversification across shares, sectors, markets and asset classes.

5.1 What is diversification?

Diversification in investments means including a spread of investments in a portfolio.

Diversification can reduce **risk** because a portfolio that includes only one investment is of greater risk of loss than if the portfolio includes a number of investments having different characteristics. If an investor puts all of his money in shares in X plc, then he stands to lose substantially if that investment fails. If he spreads his investment between X plc, Y plc and Z plc, then the chances of all three companies failing to the same extent is smaller.

5.2 Types of diversification

Two types of diversification can be distinguished:

- **Diversification by asset class.** This is achieved by holding a combination of different kinds of asset within a portfolio, possibly spread across: cash, fixed interest securities, equity investments, property-based investments, and other assets.
- **Diversification within asset classes.** An investor can diversify a portfolio by holding a variety of investments within the particular asset types that he holds. This may be achieved by holding various fixed interest securities, by holding equities in a number of different companies, by spreading investments across different industry sectors and geographical markets, and by holding a number of different properties or property-based investments.

5.3 Diversification by asset class

Cash can be useful as an emergency fund or for instantly accessible money. At times when the future for interest rates is uncertain, it may be wise to hold some cash in variable rate deposits, in the hope of a rate rise and some in fixed rate deposits as a hedge against a possible fall in the rate.

Fixed interest securities, such as government bonds, National Savings & Investment certificates or guaranteed income bonds give a secure income and known redemption value at a fixed future date.

Equities can be used to produce a potentially increasing dividend income and capital growth. For example, a share yielding 3% income plus capital growth of 6% gives an overall return of 9% compared with a building society deposit account yielding, say, 4%.

Collective investments such as unit trusts, investment trusts or unit linked insurance products spread the risk still further. In this case the client is participating in a pool of shares. He may chose a fund investing in a number of different economies, thereby reducing risk still further. Pooled investments may be a sensible method of obtaining exposure to some of the less sophisticated world markets where there is a high risk in holding one company's shares.

The use of **property**, whether residential or commercial and **other types of assets** such as antiques, coins or stamps might help to spread risk further.

5.4 Diversification within asset classes

A portfolio that includes a collection of securities will be less exposed to any loss arising from one of the securities.

Using a **spread of shares** across different **sectors** of the market can also reduce risk. In this way there is a reduced concentration of capital in any one sector.

Diversification across different **markets** can also be achieved within an asset class. For example, a portfolio of shares or equity-based collective investments may be spread across different national markets and regions, perhaps with holdings in Asia as well as North America, Europe and the UK. Gaining exposure to particular markets can be relatively difficult – for example, there are currently relatively few investment vehicles providing exposure to China, although new collective investments (such as **exchange-traded funds** or **ETFs**, based on the shares in an index) covering China are now becoming available.

Sometimes a client will have a large holding in one share, perhaps because of an inheritance or as the result of a share option scheme. Such a client should be made aware of the potential risk of such a large holding.

Although different economies and stock markets influence each other, there are differences in how well different regions and national markets perform. Different economies will be at different stages of the **business cycle** than others at any particular time. On the same principle as that of different companies' shares, a **portfolio spread across different markets or regions of the world** will be less exposed to poor performance of a particular economy such as the UK.

5.5 Balance in a portfolio

A portfolio can be designed reflect a **balance** between types of investment with different levels of **risk** – cash deposits, fixed interest and equities. The percentage in each sector would depend upon the client's need and attitude to risk.

A very cautious investor may wish to be 100% invested in cash. An **investor's experiences** may have made them particularly cautious. At the other end of the spectrum, an investor may wish to take great risks with his or her money, which some might consider to be reckless.

As well as past experiences, investors' **personality traits** can be significant in their attitude to risk-taking.

It may be argued that no investor should be totally invested in equities so that he has no other liquid funds: he will need some accessible funds and should probably also have an exposure to fixed interest securities. Ultimately, what investments are held should accord with the **investment objectives and attitudes** of the investor, but the more the investor can be informed and educated about the possible consequences of the courses of action they are considering, the better.

The use of **cash** in a portfolio is obviously to give easy access to funds. There are also reasons for fixed interest securities as well as equities. Although equities should give a real rate of return over inflation over long periods, there are times in the economic cycle when a client would obtain a better short-term return from a fixed interest security. The relative proportion of equities and fixed interest securities held may vary depending on the investor's or adviser's view of what may happen in the market. If the view is that interest rates may fall, it may be time to hold a higher percentage of gilts to take advantage of a capital gain in the holding when the rates reduce.

If a portfolio has been constructed to produce **income**, there is again an argument for having the portfolio balanced between fixed interest and equity investments. The equities may have a lower yield at the outset but over a period the income should increase. The income may, however, be more volatile. The income from fixed interest securities may be higher, but it is fixed. This income may from time to time look less attractive if interest rates rise. If the client holds a balanced portfolio, he should be able to maintain a smoother income pattern than could be produced from a 100% fixed interest or a 100% equity portfolio. Companies may pay low dividends but make use of share buy-backs or special dividends. This could result in a need for a change in the balance of equities and fixed interest in a portfolio.

5.6 Diversifiable and non-diversifiable risk

As we have seen, diversification can reduce the risk of uncertain returns from a portfolio of investments. However, not all risk can be 'diversified away'.

- **Diversifiable risk: non-systematic or specific risk.** The risk that can be diversified away is that relating to or **specific** the particular investment. As we saw earlier in this Chapter, this kind of risk is called **non-systematic** or **unsystematic risk** as well as **specific risk**. In the case of an equity investment, the company concerned might, for example, lose a major customer, or it might suffer a loss in its share of sales in its particular market. Such events can adversely affect the share price of that particular company.

- **Non-diversifiable risk: systematic or market risk.** Suppose that the economy generally is performing poorly. Consumer demand may be weak, affecting companies generally. The international political situation may be seen as fragile. Such factors can affect market confidence and investment values generally. If share prices generally are falling and returns are declining, then a wide and diversified portfolio of shares is very likely to fall in line with the wider market. The risk of this happening affects the whole 'system' – the market. **Systematic** or **market risk** cannot be diversified away by holding a range of investments in that particular market.

An investor with limited funds to invest can achieve a high degree of diversification by investing in collective funds such as unit trusts and investment trusts. This can reduce non-systematic, specific risk to very low levels. However, systematic risk cannot be eliminated.

5.7 Diversification and correlation

How much will diversification reduce risk in a portfolio? This depends on the degree to which the prices of the different investments chosen move in line with each other – that is, the degree of **correlation** between their prices. If two companies are in the same sector and are relatively similar, then their share prices may move closely in line with each other. If two companies have activities that are complementary in some way, there may be a high degree of correlation resulting from that. For example, personal computer (PC) manufacturers and retailers, as well as micro-chip manufacturing companies, should stand to gain from a surge in demand for PCs.

There is **positive correlation** between investments, such as the share prices of two companies, if their prices move up and down together. There is **negative correlation** if the prices tend to move in opposite directions to each other. If prices bear no relationship to each other, then there is **no correlation** between them.

Diversification is most effective when the investments combined are negatively correlated. The fluctuations or volatility in the price of each investment will then tend to cancel each other out.

5.8 How much diversification?

Research has shown that almost all the investment-specific risk is eliminated in a portfolio of as few as **15 to 20 securities**. What remains in such a portfolio is market risk. The diagram below illustrates the components of risk and the decline of risk as the number of investments increases.

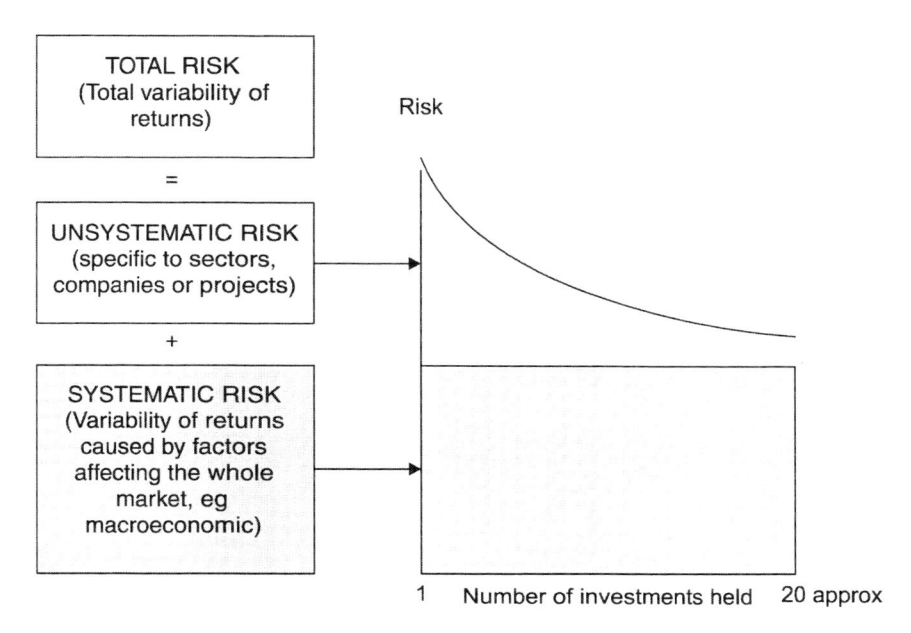

Once a portfolio contains about 20 shares in different companies in different sectors, most (but not all) of the unsystematic risk is diversified away. However, systematic risk is not affected by diversification.

5.9 Beta factors

The **beta factor** measures the **volatility of a security or fund relative to the market** as a whole or more specifically it measure the systematic risk at an investment against that of the market. The higher the value of beta for a security, the greater the movement in its return relative to the market. Where the standard deviation is an absolute measure of risk, the beta is relative measure.

(a) A security with a **beta factor of 1** moves in line with the market. If the market (for example, as indicated by a share price index such as the FTSE-100) moves up 5%, the price of this security is likely to move up 5%.

(b) A security with a **beta factor greater than 1** varies more widely than the market. If the market moves up 5%, the price of a security with a beta of 2 is likely to move up 10%.

(c) A security with a **beta factor of less than 1** fluctuates less than the wider market. If the market moves up or down 10%, the price of a security with a beta of 0.5 is likely to move up or down respectively by 5%.

5.10 Beta factors for collective funds

Beta factors are calculated for collective funds as well as for individual securities. The beta factors for funds measure the fund's volatility against a benchmark such as the FT-SE All-Share Index, or some other benchmark appropriate to the fund.

INVESTMENT AND RISK

Betas for fund are generally calculated over a 36-month period, from monthly data.

- A fund with a beta factor of 1 moves in line with its benchmark.
- A fund with a beta factor greater than 1 is more volatile than its benchmark.
- A fund with a beta factor of less than 1 is less volatile than its benchmark.

As with standard deviations, the beta factors are calculated from historical data. Changes in the strategy of a fund, or changes resulting from a change in manager, may mean that future performance and volatility differ from the past.

5.11 Alpha

Alpha is a measure of the risk-adjusted return of a security or of a fund.

Alpha measures the difference between the actual return and its expected performance, given its level of risk as measured by beta.

A positive alpha indicates the investment has performed better than expected, given its level of risk (beta). A negative alpha indicates the investment has underperformed for a security or fund with its level of risk.

In practice, for funds, a negative alpha is more likely because of the effect of fund management charges in reducing the overall return.

5.12 Conclusion

We can summarise at this point by observing that the overall risk of a portfolio depends upon:

- The risk of each individual investment
- The diversification of the portfolio across different investments, and
- The correlation of returns between the investments which is lower when a portfolio invests in a greater spread of asset classes, markets and sectors.

6 Relating risk and return

Learning outcomes

6.5 Varying investment returns from the main different asset classes – risk-free rates of return and the risk premium.
6.7 Sharpe Ratio.

6.1 Risks and reward

Risks and **reward** are important aspects of investment decisions. It is true that low-risk investments generally carry a low return. To believe, however, that taking on a high level of risk is a sure way to produce higher returns is to misunderstand the meaning of 'risk'. Risk is present when there is a possibility of poor performance. A risky investment can offer the possibility of relatively high rates of return, but the other side of the coin, from which the 'riskiness' arises, is that the return might instead be low or negative.

We can say that **risk** and **potential reward** are generally positively correlated: investments with a higher **potential** return generally carry a higher risk.

Both financial advisers and their clients need to understand clearly the connection between risk and return.

(a) High risk investments generally have the potential for a higher reward, plus a greater possibility of loss.
(b) Low risk investments generally have a lower reward, with a lower possibility of loss.

6.2 Higher returns with low risk?

An investment strategy that provides a way to invest money to produce a high return while bearing a low risk would clearly be valuable.

The skill of a fund manager or an individual investor can be viewed in terms of how they manage to achieve higher returns than others, without incurring greater risks. We would all like to know of high-return low-risk investments. Some equity investors try to seek out companies whose shares are neglected and undervalued by the market, anticipating that eventually the value of the shares will be noticed more widely by the market and will therefore rise in price. Such a strategy, if it involves a portfolio of a number of such shares, seeks to produce good returns with relatively low risk.

In broad terms however, seeking higher returns generally involves taking on a higher level of risk. For the private investor, we might think of the best interest rate on an instant access account from a large retail domestic bank or major building society as a baseline. This is an investment with virtually no risk of loss of capital. From this baseline, the investor is likely to need to take on some risk, if he or she is to have the possibility of improving on the return from the deposit account.

6.3 The risk-free rate of return

How much can investor earn by taking no risk? While a complete absence of risk may be only a theoretical concept, an investment in a UK government security (a gilt) can be treated as virtually free from risk of default by the government, and therefore provides a benchmark for what is a **risk-free rate of return**. If we hold a gilt from now up to its redemption, or if it is an undated gilt which will never be redeemed, then we know exactly what return we will get if we continue to hold it.

The risk-free rate of return will vary through time, just as interest rates generally vary.

The **Government Consol** is a term for the government's 4% Consolidated Stock, which is an undated or 'perpetual' stock. There is no redemption at par, and the instrument is effectively a government promise to pay the owner £4.00 for each £100 of the stock each year, indefinitely. For example, when 4% Consols are priced at around £80, they give a yield of 5% indefinitely – a virtually risk-free rate of return if we simply hold on to the stock. The yield on this undated stock indicates the market's view of the **long-term interest rate**.

Required rates of return on other investments will vary from the risk-free rate, reflecting the additional return or 'risk premium' that is required by investors who are taking a risk on the outcome of the investment.

6.4 Risk premium

The additional return that investors expect from a risky investment, as compared with an investment carrying virtually no risk, is the **risk premium**.

An **individual** may find that such a 'premium' is required from him or her when taking out a mortgage, for example. The housebuyer seeks an 'investor' (lender) from whom to borrow money. If the individual's mortgage proposal carries higher than average risk, then they may find that they have to pay a higher rate of interest than if the risk were lower. If the individual's credit rating is below average, or if the amount to be borrowed is a relatively high percentage of the value of the property, then the individual may find that some lenders will not offer their most favourable terms. The borrower is effectively having to pay a risk premium in order to borrow the money.

For **companies** seeking finance, the principle is similar. For example, lending to companies with relatively low credit ratings will generally be available at higher rates of interest (carrying a risk premium relative to the interest rates that would be available to companies with higher creditworthiness ratings.

For the UK during the twentieth century, it has been calculated that equities have produced a return 5.6% per annum higher than the return from gilts, on average. This can therefore be treated as the **risk premium** from investing in

INVESTMENT AND RISK

equities. Equity holders bears the risk that, over the period of their shareholding, the return will be much lower than average, and below the rate on risk-free assets such as gilts held to redemption. The risk premium from investing in shares can be seen as compensating them for taking that risk.

6.5 The spectrum of risk

The table below gives a broad indication of where various investments can be placed in a 'spectrum' of overall investment risk.

NEGLIGIBLE RISK	NS&I deposit products Gilts (income) Gilts (redemption)
LOW RISK	Bank deposits Building society deposits Cash ISAs Annuities
LOW / MEDIUM RISK	Gilts (pre-redemption capital) With-profits funds
MEDIUM RISK	Unit-linked managed funds Unit trusts and OEICs/ICVCs (UK funds) Investment trusts (UK) Residential and commercial property
MEDIUM / HIGH RISK	Unit-linked overseas funds Unit trusts and OEICs/ICVCs (overseas funds) UK single equities Commodities
HIGH RISK	Venture Capital Trusts Unlisted shares Warrants Futures and Options when used to speculate Enterprise Investment Scheme Enterprise Zone Property

6.6 Sharpe measure

We are aware that risk and return go hand in hand. The risk-free rate of return may be achieved at zero risk (by definition), to achieve a higher return, however, will require the acceptance of risk. We may, therefore, ask how much extra return we are getting for each unit of risk taken on, the higher the better.

The Sharpe measure answers this question. The Sharpe measure compares the excess return (over and above the risk-free rate) to the investment/portfolio total risk or standard deviation.

The Sharpe measure is calculated as

$$\text{Sharpe measure} = \frac{r_p - r_f}{\sigma_p}$$

where

r_p = portfolio return

r_f = risk-free return over the same interval

σ_p = portfolio risk (standard deviation of the portfolio returns)

This measure is appropriate where this portfolio represents the full set of investments of the client. In isolation, the measure is of little value however the higher the measure, the better the performance of the fund when we take account of risk.

Example

Two fund managers are employed to manage portions of a large pension fund. They both have the same objectives etc. Details about their portfolios are given below.

Fund	Return %	Total Risk σ_p %
A	19.5	20
B	22	30

Over the same period the risk-free rate was 8% and the stock market generated a return of 18% at a risk of 19%.

Solution

Sharpe measure = $\dfrac{r_p - r_f}{\sigma_p}$

Gives

Fund A = $\dfrac{19.5 - 8}{20} = 0.575$

Fund B = $\dfrac{22 - 8}{30} = 0.467$

Index = $\dfrac{18 - 8}{19} = 0.526$

Hence, we can say that on a risk-adjusted basis (total risk) fund manager A has outperformed fund manager B and the index. Manager B underperformed the index.

Key chapter points

- Money has a 'time value': having money now is of more value than a promise of money at a date in the future.
- Inflation erodes the value of money and savings. The real rate of return measures how much is being earned, over and above the rate of inflation.
- Compounding and discounting are key concepts in calculating returns through time.
- Compounding means that, as income is earned, it is added to the original investment and starts to earn interest itself. The basic formula for compounding is $S = X(1 + r)^n$.
- There are various different types of risk that investors may face.
- In general, having the chance of a higher return involves taking higher risks. This means that, instead of the higher return hoped for, losses could be incurred instead. Investors in risky investments, such as equities, require a 'risk premium'. The risk premium is reflected in the amount by which the long-term higher average rate of return exceeds the risk-free rate of return on a very safe investment.
- Diversification involves choosing investments in different asset classes, and choosing different investments within a particular asset class.
- Overall risk can be measured from the variability or volatility of investment returns.
- Volatility arises from:
  - The 'systematic' fluctuations in the wider market, which cannot be diversified away, and
  - The 'non-systematic' investment-specific risks of the particular investment.
- Standard deviations of returns from an investment measure their variability.
- Beta factors measure how much returns from an investment vary relative to the market or a sector benchmark.
- Alpha measures the difference between the actual return of a fund and its expected performance, given its level of risk as measured by beta.
- Data on past performance has its uses in checking the track record of certain types of investment, but the future performance of risky investments may differ significantly from the past.
- Standard deviations of returns from an investment measure their variability. Beta factors go further and measure how much returns from an investment vary relative to the market or a sector benchmark.

Chapter Quiz

1. What is the approximate relationship among the nominal rate of return, the rate of inflation and the real rate of return on an investment?.. (see para 2.3)
2. Give a formula for calculating compound interest. .... (2.5.1)
3. Give two alternative terms that are used to measure the effective annual rate of interest. .... (2.5.2)
4. Distinguish between interest rate risk and inflation risk .... (3.2, 3.4)
5. Distinguish between two types of diversification .... (5.2)
6. 'Diversification reduces systematic risk.' True or False? .... (5.6)
7. What does it mean if two investments are negatively correlated? .... (5.7)
8. What does a beta factor measure? .... (5.9)
9. What is meant by the 'risk-free rate of return'? .... (6.3)
10. What is the 'risk premium'? .... (6.4)

chapter 16

Investment planning and management

Chapter topic list

1	Investment management – an overview	344
2	Asset allocation	347
3	Client circumstances and objectives	349
4	Attitude to risk	354
5	Meeting client needs	355
6	Reporting to clients	358
	Key chapter points	359
	Chapter quiz	360

INVESTMENT AND RISK

Chapter Learning Outcomes

7. **Understand** the risks faced by investors and how an investor's risk profile is determined.

    7.1 The importance of affordability and suitability in making financial planning decisions.

    7.3 Objective factors to determine an investor's risk tolerance – timescale of investment, age, commitments, wealth, life cycle.

    7.4 Subjective factors to determine an investor's risk tolerance – attitudes and experiences.

    7.5 Methods of assessing an investor's risk tolerance.

8. **Understand** the importance of asset allocation in the investment process

    8.1 The definition and importance of asset allocation – achieving objectives, reducing risk, need for review.
    8.2 The underlying composition of funds – managed funds, with-profits funds, and other funds.
    8.3 Sample asset allocations for different types of investors.
    8.4 Different approaches to asset allocation.
    8.5 Quantitative and qualitative statistical data.

10. **Understand** how other issues affect investment planning.

    10.2 Active investment management.
    10.3 Passive investment managements.
    10.4 The relationship between investing and borrowing.
    10.7 Advantages and disadvantages of using aggregation and consolidation services.

12. **Analyse** consumers' circumstances and suitable investment products, taking account of any existing arrangements.

    12.1 Factors shaping consumers' circumstances.
    12.2 Affordability and suitability.
    12.3 Methods of identifying and reviewing suitable product solutions.
    12.4 The impact of new solutions on existing arrangements.

13. **Apply** suitable investment product solutions to specific consumers' circumstances.

    13.1 The range of solutions available to suit different types of circumstance.
    13.2 The criteria for matching solutions to consumer needs and demands.
    13.3 Factors influencing the way in which recommendations are presented.

1 Investment management – an overview

Learning outcomes

8.4 Different approaches to asset allocation.
8.5 Quantitative and qualitative statistical data.
10.2 Active investment management.
10.3 Passive investment management.
12.1 Factors shaping consumers' circumstances.

1.1 Investment management: Definition

Investment management is the management of an investment portfolio on behalf of a private client or an institution, the receipt and distribution of dividends, and all other administrative work in connection with the portfolio.

This management may be conducted on either

- A discretionary basis, in which case the investment manager acts at his own discretion in the management of the portfolio, without referring to the client; or
- A non-discretionary basis, in which case the manager recommends investment sales and purchases to the client and awaits the latter's approval.

1.2 Purpose and considerations of investment management

Investment management involves the investment of a client's assets in order to meet a number of key objectives. The objectives will vary from investor to investor and consequently the process of investment management must start with a detailed consideration of the fund's objectives in order to determine the appropriate investment policies.

Broadly speaking, the fund **objectives** fall into one of two categories.

- To maximise their returns, ie positive net worth individuals looking for a portfolio to match their risk/return preferences.
- To match liabilities, eg pension funds where the aim is to match asset and liabilities or minimise any mismatch.

To satisfy these funds' objectives, the investment manager needs to know the fund **constraints** he must operate within based on the requirements of the client, ie

- Time horizons.
- Liabilities to be met.
- Liquidity needs.
- Risk aversion/risk tolerances.
- Tax status.
- Other preferences and legal constraints, eg ethical considerations.

This is needed for at least three reasons.

- It is a prerequisite to the initial portfolio structure.
- It influences the kinds of portfolio adjustment that can be made.
- It consequently influences portfolio performance.

1.3 Overview of the fund management process

The objectives and constraints of the fund lead the fund manager to consider a variety of strategies or possible asset allocations, and within these to select specific stocks that meet the fund objectives. The fund manager will be judged by his performance with regard to the objectives of the fund and, in the highly competitive world of fund management, an under-performing manager will not be given many second chances.

The Approach to Fund Management

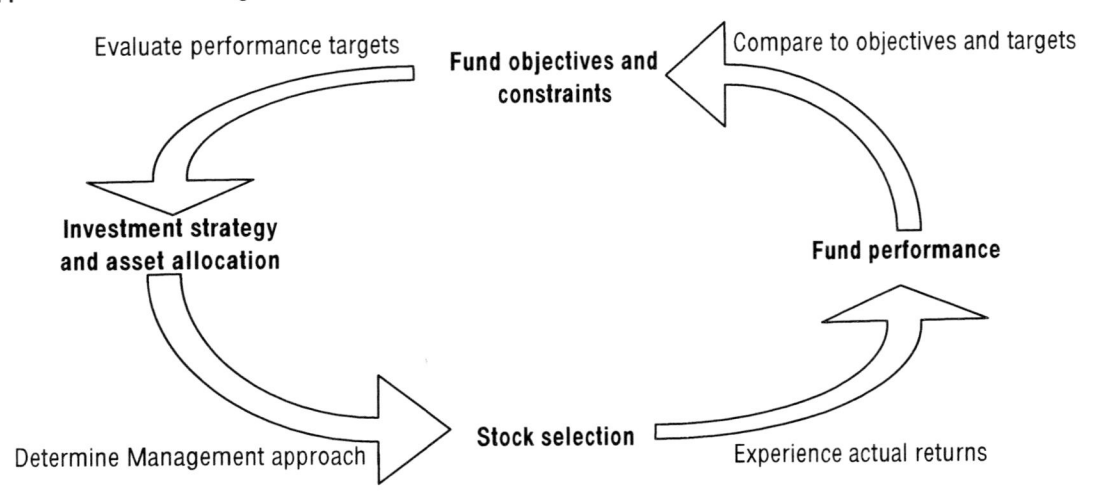

```
Evaluate performance targets          Fund objectives and          Compare to objectives and targets
                                         constraints

   Investment strategy                                              Fund performance
   and asset allocation

   Determine Management approach    Stock selection    Experience actual returns
```

Once the objectives and constraints of the particular fund have been established, the next stage is to develop the investment policy/strategies that will be used in order to achieve these objectives. All these considerations will be detailed as recommended investment policy/strategy options.

These recommendations must then be submitted to the client for approval. In simple situations there may be one obvious approach for the manager to adopt, in more complex situations, several alternatives may be presented to the client forming the basis of a discussion leading to the finally agreed investment policy/strategy statement.

The resultant investment policy/strategy statement forms the basis of the management approach. This strategy will determine the long term strategic asset allocation options selected to achieve the client's objectives. Asset allocations should not, however, be set in stone. Different asset categories perform better in different economic situations and the fund manager must be ready to respond to such circumstances.

Along with the long term strategic asset allocation, the strategy may also detail market timing/tactical asset allocation options that may be adopted by the fund in those differing circumstances. The strategy details asset allocations and limits but will not detail stock or product recommendations.

Finally, the investment strategy will probably detail any performance benchmarks against which the fund performance is to be assessed.

When the overall strategy and policy of the fund have been determined, the final stage is to select the stock that will make up the portfolio and approaches to this are discussed later.

The final stage of the investment process is to evaluate whether the fund is achieving its objectives through a consideration of its performance. Fund performance should be reviewed no less than once a year, certainly more regularly for short term funds, and will look to achieve a number of objectives.

- **Client circumstances** – we should firstly look to determine whether any client circumstances have altered as this may result in an alteration of the client's objectives. Any significant changes may require a modification to the investment strategy.

- **Performance review** – we need to monitor the performance of the fund against the selected benchmark to ensure that it is achieving its objectives.

- **Portfolio rebalancing** – following on from the performance review we should consider whether there is any need to update the agreed asset allocations. Care needs to be taken here in respect of the tax liabilities that may arise from the effects of any rebalancing.

The fund management process cannot, however, be thought of as a step by step process that finishes at this stage, rather it is an ongoing process. This review will establish the strategy for the next period and the process will continue.

Throughout this process there are, however, a number of considerations that must be kept in mind in carrying out this fund management process. These include

- Should the fund management be conducted on an active or a passive basis?
- Should fund management be conducted top-down or bottom-up?
- Should the fund manager be conducting a value or growth style of management?

1.4 Active versus passive

There are two overall styles that the investment manager can adopt. On the one hand, an active investment manager is one who intervenes with the portfolio on a regular basis, attempting to use individual expertise in order to enhance the overall return of the fund. Passive investment management, on the other hand, establishes a strategy which, once established, should guarantee the appropriate level of return for the fund. These are, perhaps, two extreme versions of investment management. There are alternatives that represent hybrids between the two extremes.

1.4.1 Active

As mentioned above, active investment management means the fund manager constantly takes decisions and appraises the value of investments within the portfolio. While, to many, this may seem the only thing a fund manager could do, it has to be appreciated that in practice, there are costs involved with all transactions, and hence limits on the number of active interventions taking place are likely to be to the advantage of the fund holder.

Moreover, from a more theoretical point of view, there are a number of theories (such as efficient market hypothesis) that indicate that the market itself is efficient and therefore the prices currently quoted in the market contain within them all available information. If this is so, then the only reason that a price will move is because of information which is not already known to the market and, as such, fund managers buying and selling (switching between stocks) will only make money if they are 'lucky' and switch to the right stock at the right time.

Active fund managers do not believe that the securities markets are continuously efficient. Instead, they believe that securities can be misvalued and that at times **winners** can be found. They also attempt to correctly **time** their purchase or sale on the basis of specific stock information, market information, economic factors, etc.

Active fund managers may obtain research from external sources such as investment banks. In this instance analysts are referred to as 'sell-side' analysts. Alternatively they may establish an in-house research department, made up of 'buy-side' analysts. The benefit of generating unbiased internal research needs to be weighed against the costs of setting up the department.

1.4.2 Passive

Introduction

Passive management involves the establishing of a strategy with the intention of achieving the overall objectives of the fund. Once established, this strategy should not require active intervention, but should be self-maintaining. The simplest strategy is to 'buy and hold'. However, perhaps the most common form of passive management is indexation.

Indexation

With indexation, the fund manager selects an appropriate index quoted in the market place. Having established the index, the fund manager builds a portfolio which mimics the index, the belief being that this portfolio will then perform in line with the index numbers. Such funds are known as **index** or **tracker** funds.

Overall, the likelihood is that the fund will underperform the index for a number of reasons. First, there is the initial cost of creating the portfolio. Second, and perhaps more importantly, all index funds tend to be based on a sampling approach and consequently exhibit a degree of **tracking error**.

It should be noted that indexation itself is not a totally passive form of investment management since the constitution of each index will, over time, change and the portfolio will also be required to change. Tracker funds will, however, incur lower transaction costs as a result of the lower levels of turnover, an advantage over actively managed funds.

1.4.3 Hybrids

Increasingly, fund managers are being requested to outperform indexes, rather than merely track them, and this inevitably requires a less passive, more interventionist approach, potentially with an **indexed core fund** and a **peripheral** or **satellite fund** (which is more actively managed and potentially involves the use of derivatives in order to establish larger trading positions than the fund itself can obtain). The regulator of collective investment schemes such as unit trusts, the FSA, has established a number of important rules limiting the extent to which a fund can invest in futures and options.

Alternatively, the fund manager may combine both active and passive fund management methods by **tilting** the fund. Tilting involves holding all (or a representative sample) of the constituents of an index (like a passive tracker fund), but with larger proportions in areas that the manager favours. This asset allocation decision constitutes the active management component.

1.5 Analysing assets

1.5.1 Introduction

In theory, all investment managers should have undertaken a complete analysis of all available investment assets to be in a position to assess them in relation to a client's portfolio.

There are, broadly, four approaches that are adopted.

- Fundamental analysis.
- Technical analysis.
- Quantitative analysis.
- A combination.

1.5.2 Fundamental analysis

Fundamental analysis concentrates on the economic strengths or weaknesses of the market in question and the individual features of the stock within that market. The basic idea behind this approach is that every security has an **intrinsic value** that can be determined from a consideration of these factors.

With government bonds, this form of analysis entails reviewing the economic outlook for the economy and the funding requirement.

With corporate securities, in addition to assessing the economic environment and interest rate profile, it involves assessing the individual credit and operational risk, along with details of its dividend yield and P/E ratio.

1.5.3 Technical analysis

Technical analysts, rather than looking at the fundamentals of the economy, look to the pattern and trading history to determine the appropriate strategy to adopt.

Frequently, through the use of charts, technical analysts develop patterns of market behaviour that they expect to be repeated time and time again. By charting the daily price movement in a stock, they believe they can predict the eventual out-turn of the market. To an extent these predictions will be self-fulfilling because, for example, if the charts predict the price will fall and investment managers react to this sell signal, then undoubtedly the supply and demand factors will force the price down.

The intellectual justification for the use of technical analysis is based on the behaviour of crowds. Basically, the same group of people exposed to the same circumstances will react in the same way: 'history repeats itself.'

1.5.4 Quantitative analysis

Quantitative analysis involves analysing portfolio/investment instruments according to expected levels of return and risk. It is generally accepted that higher returns can only be obtained at the expense of higher risk, however, investment managers can use computers to generate strategies which allow them to invest at the most cost-effective and efficient trade-off between risk and return.

1.5.5 The combination approach

Many houses tend to use a combination of all three approaches, with fundamental and quantitative analysis dictating the markets and stocks which they need to buy and technical analysis being used to determine the timing of entry into the market place.

Regardless of whether the investment manager believes in technical analysis or not, he will have to keep an eye on the charts, since if sufficient numbers do believe the technical analysts, the market will move in line with their predictions.

2 Asset allocation

Learning outcomes

8.1   The definition and importance of asset allocation – achieving objectives, reducing risk, need for review.
8.2   The underlying composition of funds – managed funds, with-profits funds and other funds.

2.1 Objectives of asset allocation

Asset allocation is a term used to describe the choices made about the proportions of different types of asset included in a portfolio. The fundamental role of asset allocation when constructing a managed portfolio is to balance inherent risks and potential returns.

The asset allocation of a portfolio can be designed to fit with the investor's **personal circumstances**, **investment objectives** and **attitude to risk**. Whether the investor has a need for **income** of a particular level can influence the asset allocation decision. However, an investor who seeks a regular income from a portfolio could achieve this from assets that do not produce an income, by incrementally selling assets to create an income flow.

By striking a **balance** between different types of assets, the investor has some protection against the possibility of cyclical under-performance. Such under-performance is likely to be confined to particular asset classes, and some investments may be counter-cyclical.

We looked in the previous Chapter at the purpose of **diversification**, both across asset classes and within asset classes. The desired balance needs to be achieved within asset classes as well as between asset classes. For example, within the equities section of a portfolio, there is much to be said for diversifying across different sectors. Concentration of

INVESTMENT AND RISK

investment within a particular sector, such as retailing, or technology stocks, makes the portfolio vulnerable to a downturn within those particular sectors.

Asset allocation is also influenced by the need for **liquidity** and **accessibility** of investments. A portfolio containing equities that is being actively managed is likely to need a cash component in order to provide liquidity in making equity purchases when opportunities arise. An investor or portfolio manager who takes a view on the general immediate future direction of equities prices might wish to vary the proportion of cash held through time, so that cash holdings are low when it is believed that the prices of equities will rise but high when general share price falls are expected.

2.2 Asset classes

Investments in the following **asset classes** have typically produced **long-term historical returns** in approximately the following ranges.

- Cash deposits – 2% to 4% (low risk)
- Fixed interest – 5% to 7% (low/medium risk)
- Equities/property – 6% to 9% (medium/high risk)

These ranges indicate that, if a return of 8% or 9% is required, then only equities are likely to be able to produce that level of return. Why not recommend an all-equity portfolio in all cases? Because equities carry risk, and therefore are more likely to produce actual returns beyond the range of 6% to 9% return than are the lower-risk asset classes of cash deposits or fixed interest. Although equities therefore stand a chance of outperforming a 9% rate of return, they also stand a chance of underperforming, and returns could be negative.

Whether an investor is willing to carry the risk of a negative return – loss of capital – depends on various factors, including the investor's attitude to risk, the timescale of the investment, and the extent to which their personal circumstances will suffer from a loss.

2.3 Fund composition

The **composition of a fund** is a breakdown of the fund by asset class or investment type, and this information is generally summarised in factsheets provided by fund managers.

Here is an example of the allocation of assets in a particular **with profits fund**, at a particular date.

Asset type	Percentage
UK equities	41.4
International (non-UK) equities	9.3
Fixed interest	26.1
Overseas bonds	4.4
Property	14.5
Cash	4.3
Total	100.0

A **managed fund** is likely to have a spread of investments across the main asset classes, as does the with profits fund above. The proportions of the different asset classes will vary between funds and at different times, according to the investment strategy of the fund.

One of the purposes behind a managed fund or a with profits fund is to provide a spread of assets within a single product. Such a product may suit the risk profile of an investor, so that the investor may not need to construct a tailor-made portfolio from different elements.

Many other **collective funds**, such as many unit trusts and OEICs, are more specialised in their composition. Some funds may be almost entirely invested in equities, except for cash held for liquidity purposes. Fund factsheets may show a fund's top ten individual holdings at a particular date, although the information may already be out-of-date because of purchases and sales of investments by the fund in the meantime.

Funds of funds are available that package together a number of funds – for example, a fund of funds might include an income fund, a growth fund and a global growth fund. There may be a fund of funds that covers closely enough the particular investment needs of a particular fund investor, avoiding the need for a number of fund holdings. The investor should check whether there are two layers of charges being imposed by a fund of fund arrangement.

As already mentioned, a unit trust or OEIC/ICVC may hold **cash** only to provide liquidity and cash flow. Therefore, cash holdings must of necessity be low. Investment trusts have greater investment freedom, and may be **geared** – so there may be **borrowings** in their capital structure.

Index-tracking funds, you will recall, aim to reproduce the composition of an index, such as a share price index. They will therefore carry weightings of index constituents according to their weightings in the index that is being tracked.

2.4 Effect on risk

Mixing different asset classes in a portfolio can have the effect of **reducing risk**.

- If a proportion of lower-risk classes of asset are chosen (such as deposits or fixed interest), this will reduce the overall risk weighting of a portfolio, compared with an all-equity portfolio.
- If the performances of asset classes chosen tend to move against each other, the asset classes are said to be non-correlated, and this non-correlation reduces risk still further.

3 Client circumstances and objectives

Learning outcomes

7.1	The importance of affordability and suitability in making financial planning decisions.
7.3	Objective factors to determine an investor's risk tolerance – timescale of investment, age, commitments, wealth, life cycle.
7.4	Subjective factors to determine an investor's risk tolerance – attitudes and experiences.
8.1	The definition and importance of asset allocation – achieving objectives, reducing risk, need for review.
8.3	Sample asset allocations for different types of investors.
10.4	The relationship between investing and borrowing.
12.1	Factors shaping consumers' circumstances.
12.2	Affordability and suitability.

3.1 Client objectives

Any individual is likely to have a number of **objectives**, for which some financial provision may be required. Having a particular view of risk does not imply that the same attitude to risk should be applied to all of the individual's objectives.

An individual might have investments that they wish to use for specific purposes or objectives and which they cannot easily afford to bear a great degree of **shortfall risk**. In such cases, the individual may wish to choose low risk investments, so that they can be reasonably certain that their objective will be achievable by the desired date.

Examples of such purposes or objectives could include:

- Saving for a deposit on a house
- Payment of a child's school fees
- Payment of university costs
- Provision to cover care of a baby
- Replacement of a car

The same individual who has investment objectives such as those above might have other possibilities in mind for which the person would be prepared to tolerate a higher level of risk. The objective may be seen as less essential to the individual, and may be something that the person accepts that they will have to do without if investment returns are not sufficient.

Examples of purposes or objectives for which an individual might typically be prepared to take on higher risk could include:

- Purchase of a vintage car
- A second home
- The possibility of an early retirement
- A 'dream' holiday

Of course, every individual is different, and the ways in which people rank their objectives and their risk tolerance in relation to different objectives vary. For one person, having enough money to spend on a comfortable home may take a higher priority than having the funds to travel widely. Another person may treat travelling as a higher priority than spending on a home. In general, the objectives that an individual sees as having the highest priority are those for which they will want to take the lowest risk if they are investing to achieve those objectives. Lower priority objectives can generally be more easily foregone if investments suffer losses.

3.2 Factors shaping individual circumstances

We can identify various life stages, with differing financial needs, but bear in mind that every case is different, and there may be many variations in individual circumstances that cannot easily be fitted into easily formulated categories.

Wealth and investment exposure

When considering investment, the **wealth** of the investor is clearly an important consideration. If there is free capital to invest, then clearly it is sensible for the individual to take steps to make the best use of that capital.

It is possible, although not generally advisable, for someone with little wealth to gain exposure to investment markets, for example by **borrowing money to invest**, or by using investments such as derivatives or spread betting to gain a greater exposure than the individual's free resources. When investing in **risky assets** such as **equities**, a good principle is the often-stated one that **someone should only invest what they can afford to lose**. Someone who borrows to invest without having other capital to back it up if things go wrong, has the problem that they may end up with liabilities in excess of their assets.

An investor who uses instruments such as derivatives to increase their exposure should maintain other accessible resources (for example, cash on deposit) that can be used to meet losses that may arise. Clearly, it is also important that they understand the risks they are undertaking.

Life cycle, age and commitments

The **age** of an investor, the stage of **life cycle** that he is at, and his **commitments**, all affect the investor's risk profile.

Adventurous risk-taking may be unwise for someone with heavy financial **commitments**, for example to children and other dependants. Another aspect of an investor's commitments is that of how much time he has available: if he works full-time and has a family, there may be little time left for him to manage his own investments even if he has an interest and knowledge to do so, and his commitments may mean that he is more likely to wish to seek professional financial advice.

Individual circumstances may differ widely, but some aspects of common **life stages** encountered in different typical **age groups** are described below.

- **Minors (under 18).** Someone who is under 18 may have very little in the way of direct investment needs as an individual. He is likely to be dependent on one or two parents and nobody is going to suffer financially if his bank balance runs out.

- **Single and still young (18 to 30).** If your client is in his early or mid twenties, he may not yet have any dependants. He may now be financially independent of his parents even if he is still living at home. Alternatively, your client may be renting a flat or possibly even buying a house. Such a client will probably not have accumulated much capital as he could be spending everything that he earns. He is also more likely to be an employee than to be self employed.

- **Married or cohabiting (20 to 30)** The client will have ceased to be dependent on parents at this stage and will be earning and either renting or buying a house.

- **Couple working but no dependants (20 to 30).** This is the time when a couple will be building up their income at the fastest possible rate before the expenses of looking after children begin.

- **One of a couple working, with no dependants (20 to 30).** The client's financial life could be a little bit more fragile. Dependence upon the earnings of one of the couple increases the possibility of difficulties if there is a fall in the earnings of the one person working.

- **One of a couple working, with dependants (25 to 40).** With all the earnings concentrated in the hands of one of the couple and with there being both a partner and at least one dependant to look after, the burden of dependency has now begun to reach its maximum with the welfare of an entire family.

- **Married or cohabiting, with older children (35 to 50).** This is the point when the expenses are probably at their highest, even without school fees. Higher education costs can increase the burden especially if it takes the form of university. The couple may again have two incomes and possibly even have a higher net income despite the higher level of expenses.

- **After children: 'empty nesters' (45 to 60).** When children have left home, their parents have a higher net income as a result of lower expenses relating to children.

- **Retired (60 or 65 plus).** Retirement income may be significantly lower than when working, but there may be savings that have been built up. Investors may now have more free time, which they may or may not wish to devote to managing their own investments.

Timescale and risk

An investor's **investment timescale** can, and arguably should, affect the investor's attitude to risk. The timing of buying and selling investments can have a significant effect on the outcome and any gain or loss incurred.

The effect of the investment timescale is particularly important for equity or equity-backed investments. Over the very long term, equities have shown a high appreciation in value. Over short time periods, price levels in equities markets tend to fluctuate markedly, and the effects of this can be most significant over shorter periods.

The **time period** over which someone is considering investing affects the level of risk that it is prudent to take on.

If an individual has a sum of money they are seeking to invest over a period of a few months, at the end of which they need to use it, for example as a deposit for a house purchase, then it would generally be inadvisable to invest the money in higher-risk investments such as equities. Given the **volatility of equity markets**, the investments might have to be sold at a loss.

Over a longer time period, an investment in equities is more likely to achieve strong positive real growth, though a lower but more secure real return can be generated by index linked bonds.

INVESTMENT AND RISK

The timescale for the **accessibility** of investments should also be considered. For example, notice or term bank deposit accounts may be an inferior choice to an easy access account if the money might be needed in a hurry. Notice accounts typically carry penalties if the notice period cannot be honoured, and the penalty may be greater than the interest advantage that was obtained by choosing a notice account in the first place.

The effect of the risk of buying or selling an investment at a disfavourable time can be reduced by using the method of **pound cost averaging**, which involves staging the investment, or its encashment, over a period of time, rather than buying or selling the investment as a single lump sum.

Pound cost averaging

A regular or periodically staged investment can take advantage of the fact that fewer units will be purchased when the price is relatively high. This is **pound cost averaging**, which we have mentioned earlier in this Study Text.

The need for liquidity

The **liquidity** of an investment is the ease with which the investment is readily convertible into cash.

An asset that can be traded in substantial quantity without the transaction moving the price up or down is a **liquid asset**.

A '**portfolio**' of investments can be defined as a collection of investments held by an investor, investment company, or financial institution. For our purposes here, we are considering the portfolio of an investor. Within such a portfolio, there should be an appropriate level of liquidity so that anticipated and unanticipated needs can be met by maturing investments or by encashing investments when necessary.

With the need for **liquidity** in mind, it is wise for an investor to have sufficient **funds held on deposit** at any time to meet likely cash needs. Keeping funds liquid brings the benefit of accessibility, for which there is usually a cost: the most liquid investments, such as cash or instant access accounts, may have lower returns.

Some investments face a degree of **liquidity risk** whose impact can be difficult to predict. For example, investors in **unquoted shares** may find it difficult to find a buyer for their shares when the time comes when they wish to sell, particularly if this is a time at which the stock is less favoured or if there is a general market downturn. Only one or two market makers may be in the market for a share, and spreads between buying and selling prices can widen unpredictably for less liquid shares.

Affordability and accessibility

The **affordability** of any investments for the client must be considered. Existing assets and policies, such as life assurance contracts and other savings need to be taken into account in quantifying the sizes of investments needed to meet client needs.

Some investments are constrained in their **liquidity** and **accessibility** in that they tie the investor in for a specified period. In some cases, the investment cannot be realised early even if the investor wishes it. In many other cases, early redemption may be possible, but at the expense of a penalty or a significant reduction in returns. It is sometimes possible to sell an investment before maturity on the open market, as for example with **traded endowment policies**. Although this should achieve a higher price than surrendering the policy to the insurance company, there is still likely to be a loss in the rate of return compared with retaining the investment until maturity. It is generally prudent to plan so as to avoid such '**forced selling**' of investments, so that the losses and costs incurred on such selling can be avoided or minimised.

- Possible changes in a client's circumstances may change his or her investment needs.
- Is any course of action being considered adaptable enough to change to fit new changed circumstances?
- How easy is it for any investment contract or arrangement being considered to be cancelled?

16: INVESTMENT PLANNING AND MANAGEMENT

- To the extent that most individuals must risk changes in their income (**income risk**), can the investment strategy accommodate salary changes easily?

The adviser and client should consider such affordability questions, in the light of information about any investments being considered.

Paying off a mortgage

Many people with capital available to invest will also be **owner-occupiers** (home owners) with a **mortgage**.

Should such a person use free capital to pay off all or part of their mortgage rather than invest the money?

The cost of maintaining the mortgage can be quantified in terms of the interest cost.

Suppose that an individual has a repayment mortgage for £50,000 and also has £50,000 in cash. If the interest rate on the mortgage is 5% and the after-tax rate of interest paid on deposits is 3%, then the net cost of keeping the mortgage rather than using the money to pay it off is 2%. (£50,000 × 2% = £1,000 per annum.)

What if the individual is considering investing the available sum of £50,000 in equities? This obviously involves taking a risk with the money, and the sum could either grow or get smaller.

Generally, it is well worth someone considering paying off part of their mortgage if they can. This will reduce their interest repayments in the future, and may bring forward the day when they are free of mortgage debt. The alternative of investing the money will also be considered by some, and is a valid strategy for someone who is not risk-averse.

It is worth bearing in mind that a home buyer who has an **interest-only mortgage** backed by a **repayment vehicle** such as an **equity ISA** is effectively choosing to take the risk of investing in equities (through the ISA) rather than withdrawing and using those funds to partially repay the mortgage.

In conclusion, there are different ways that an individual can consider balancing the relationship between **borrowings** and **capital** for investing. The availability of **offset mortgages** which allow the net outstanding borrowing to be set against cash balances has increased the flexibility that can be employed in reaching a balance that suits the individual.

4 Attitude to risk

Learning outcomes

7.1 The importance of affordability and suitability in making financial planning decisions.
7.5 Methods of assessing an investor's risk tolerance.
8.1 The definition and importance of asset allocation – achieving objectives, reducing risk, need for review.

4.1 An investor's risk profile

The financial adviser must recognise that each client has their own views, aspirations and attitudes. **Attitudes to risk** vary widely, and accordingly investment choices vary widely too. Some individuals will be reluctant to take on any significant risk of loss of their capital while others are prepared to 'gamble' with their savings.

People are likely to take notice of the growth potential of an investment while some could be less willing to appreciate the risk involved. The adviser needs to take especial care to make such a client aware of risks.

Attitudes to risk vary according to the different objectives of the investor. An investor may have a core holding of deposits that he wishes to keep as an emergency fund, while he may be prepared to take greater risks with other funds he holds.

INVESTMENT AND RISK

If a client has a specific target for a particular investment – for example, to pay for children's education, or to pay for a vacation – then he may choose lower risk investments for the funds intended to reach that target than for his other investments. A frequently quoted saying about exposure to the equities market is that someone should not invest in equities what they cannot afford to lose. If an individual is prepared to take on risks for a proportion of his savings and does not require those funds for a specific purpose, then equities may be an appropriate choice for that individual.

4.2 Risk levels

Different firms have different descriptions for the risk levels that are appropriate for different investors.

The scale of risk as appropriate to different investors could be divided up as follows.

- **Cautious** – The most appropriate investments are deposit based investments where capital is secure even if it means giving up potential growth.
- **Cautious/Medium** – A balance of investments is appropriate, offering some security with potential for long term growth/ income. The capital value can go up and down.
- **Medium** – A balance of investments is appropriate, offering a wide spread of investment with potential for long-term growth/income. The capital value can go up and down.
- **Medium/Adventurous** – At this risk level, there is a narrower spread of investment in such areas as UK shares and international shares. The value of the funds can go up and down.
- **Adventurous** – This category of risk level involves investing in areas considered to be specialised, with a correspondingly high degree of volatility.

An adviser will assess the appropriate level of risk in discussion with the client, having ascertained by interview the client's various circumstances, level of experience as an investor, and attitudes.

4.3 Assessment of risk profile

In order to produce consistent results, standard **methods of assessment** can be developed by firms in order to evaluate an individual's risk profile.

One approach is to have a **written questionnaire** which the individual is then asked to complete. Alternatively, a set of questions could be asked in an interview with the client. The different possible answers to questions can be **scored**, so that someone who has a more conservative or cautious attitude to risk has a low score, while an adventurous or aggressive risk-taker would show a high score.

The questions asked to assess an individual's risk profile could include the following examples.

- How long do you expect to leave your investment in place until you sell it?
- Which outcome is most important to you from an investment portfolio: Preserving asset value/Generating income/Long-term growth ?
- Which of the following investments have you owned before or do you now own: Bank or building society deposit account/Government stocks ('gilts')/Unit trusts or OEICs/Investment trusts/Individual company shares?
- Which of the following best describes your experience of investment: 'I have little investment experience beyond bank or building society savings accounts'/'I have had some experience of investment (such as unit trusts or individual shares)'/'I am an experienced investor with a portfolio managed by a financial adviser'/'I am an experienced investor and I prefer to manage my own portfolio'.
- Which of the following best describes your main objective in investing: The education of my children/Savings/Capital growth and returns/My retirement/To leave money in my will?

- How large is your investment plan in proportion to your total savings? (Less than 10%/Between 10% and 20%/Between 20% and 30%/Between 30% and 40%/40% or more)

If the **client declines to complete an assessment** of their risk profile, then they should be asked to sign a **statement** indicating that they have been given the opportunity to complete the assessment but have declined to do so.

5 Meeting client needs

Learning outcomes

8.4 Different approaches to asset allocation.
10.1 Charges, their impact on returns, reduction in yields.
10.7 Advantages and disadvantages of using aggregation and consolidation services.
12.2 Affordability and suitability.
12.3 Methods of identifying and reviewing suitable product solutions.
12.4 The impact of new solutions on existing arrangements.
13.1 The range of solutions available to suit different types of circumstance.
13.2 The criteria for matching solutions to consumer needs and demands.

For your examination, you need to be able to analyse suitable investment products, taking account of existing arrangements.

In analysing the overall circumstances of an individual client, you will be taking a **holistic approach** in reaching solutions which take into account the client's needs for:

- Investment products
- Retirement planning products
- Protection products

Each of these product types is covered in separate Appropriate Examination papers, but they are brought together in the final 'holistic' case-study based module.

For the purposes of the *Investment and Risk* exam, you should ensure that you are aware of the features, advantages and disadvantages of the various investment alternatives that we have analysed in the previous individual Chapters of this Study Text:

- Cash deposits
- Government securities and corporate bonds
- Equities
- Property – residential and commercial
- OEICs/ICVCs and unit trusts
- Investment trusts
- Individual Savings Accounts (ISAs)
- Life assurance products (UK and offshore)

The **client's needs and demands** should be considered in order to **match possible appropriate solutions** to these needs and demands, in the light of the features of the various investment alternatives. It is not necessarily the case that only one possible solution should be recommended: there may be a number of feasible solutions that can be discussed with the client.

INVESTMENT AND RISK

5.1 Sample asset allocations

The percentage of a portfolio invested in different asset classes can be varied to fit with the level of risk an investor chooses.

The asset allocations below are typical examples, but these are only 'rules of thumb', and slightly different proportions might be seen recommended as **sample asset allocations**.

- **Very low risk**: 100% cash deposits and fixed interest
- **Low risk**: 40% equities; 60% cash deposits and fixed interest
- **Medium risk**: 60% equities; 40% cash deposits and fixed interest
- **Medium to higher risk**: 80% equities; 20% cash deposits and fixed interest
- **High risk**: 100% equities (apart from some cash for short-term liquidity)

5.2 Existing portfolios

The considerations involved when taking over an existing portfolio and reconstructing it are similar to those involved when constructing an entirely new portfolio. There will be the same need to consider the individual's need for accessibility and liquidity, income needs, attitude to risk, timescale, tax position and so on.

Where clients have investments that no longer meet current requirements and circumstances, they should be changed.

An adviser may face a dilemma if there are existing life assurance policies, over the issue of whether to advise that the policies be retained or surrendered. Ethical considerations require that the advice accords with the client's best interests and is not swayed by any commission that the adviser may earn. Law and regulation require that advisers do not 'churn' a client's investments: **churning** means trading or switching investments on behalf of clients too frequently in the circumstances.

There may be **tax penalties** if investments are disposed of. For property, shares and collective investments not sheltered within an ISA, there may be a capital gains tax charge. Encashment of a life assurance investment bond may create a chargeable event, resulting in a possible higher rate tax liability.

5.3 Suitability

Whether an investor is making his or her own **financial planning decisions**, or is being advised by a financial adviser, it may seem obvious to state that investments chosen should meet a test of **suitability**. An adviser clearly needs to follow the regulatory principle of 'Know your client' in order to be able to assess the suitability requirements of a client.

In more detail, the following guidelines should be followed by an adviser in making recommendations of **suitable** investments.

The aim should be to give conscientiously thought-out, considered advice, only in the best interests of the client.

Client needs should be quantified and the shortfall (if any) between needs and the client's existing arrangements should be assessed.

For each quantified need, the adviser should draw up a list of suitable products from those available.

From the list of suitable products, the most suitable should be identified: this can generally be achieved by a process of elimination.

The adviser must ensure that the client understands the disadvantages as well as the advantages of recommended products or courses of action, and the **risks** involved.

Where **past performance figures** are used to illustrate investment projections, it should be stated that past performance is no guarantee of future performance.

5.4 Customer understanding

It is a basic regulatory requirement that a firm should not recommend a transaction or act as an investment manager for a customer unless it has taken reasonable steps to help the customer **understand the nature of the risks** involved.

In the case of **warrants** and **derivatives**, the firm must obtain from the customer the appropriate **warrants and derivatives risk warning**.

If recommending to a private customer transactions in investments that are not readily realisable, the adviser should explain the difficulties in establishing a market price.

Following the recording of recommendations in a **report**, the adviser can check whether the client has read and understood the contents of the report, and can be asked whether he has any **questions** to ask about it.

5.5 Charges and adviser remuneration

The **charges** attached to an investment should be considered. An investor may be willing to pay above average charges for a superior level of investment management. However, relatively high charges that are not matched by a benefit to the investor are obviously less attractive.

The declared **reduction in yield** indicates the amount by which the investment yield is reduced, in percentage terms, by charges.

The relative levels of charges are one basis on which different investment **products** from different **providers** can be compared.

As well as (or instead of) **product-related commission**, financial advisers may charge **fees**.

A financial adviser's remuneration may take the following forms:

- Product-related commission, including regular '**trail commission**'
- Fees, charged by the hour
- Fees, dependent on the value of investments
- Regular retainers paid by the client

HMRC has indicated (in SP4/97) that **rebated commissions** are generally **not taxable**.

5.6 The need for review and consideration of new solutions

Regular review of a portfolio, on at least an annual basis, can take account of various changes:

- Changes to investor circumstances
- Changes in investor's attitudes and objectives
- The record of investment performance to date
- Changes in the availability investments

Although **annual review** might be appropriate for an investor who invests in funds (such as unit trusts and OEICs) and has therefore delegated fund management to professional fund managers, **more frequent review** may be more appropriate for an investor who as made direct investments and is managing them himself or herself. The review of a directly invested portfolio should look at the changing circumstances of the various investments, to check what sales or purchases should be made in line with the investment objectives. An investor making direct investments has to do the job of the fund manager himself.

More frequent review may also be prompted by an unexpected change in circumstances.

Where new investment products have been developed it will be necessary to determine whether these represent a more suitable investment than the currently held products.

5.7 Aggregation services

An online **aggregation service** is a service designed to allow users to organise and track the value of all their financial accounts and assets, with virtually all financial institutions, through a single secure online site using a single password.

The user chooses a single username and password, and can then choose the service to collect information from the online services of the institutions where the user's accounts are held. Where the accounts are held at institutions other than the company providing the aggregation service, this requires the user to supply their login information to the aggregation service. An aggregation service potentially offers time savings for investors who are accustomed to using online services and who want to review their overall financial position and check account balances and investment performance.

6 Reporting to clients

> **Learning outcome**
>
> 13.3 Factors influencing the way in which recommendations are presented.

6.1 The importance of written reports

Providing a **written report** to clients is an important part of the process of giving financial advice.

A written report provides a way of putting across **recommendations** that have already been made **orally** in meetings with clients. The written format makes some aspects of observations and recommendations easier for the client to understand.

Furthermore, providing a written report is clearly an important way of providing a **record** of what is being recommended, and on what key information it is based. A report in writing should avoid the potential for misunderstandings about the advice that has been given, thus acting as a safeguard for the adviser in justifying his work, as well as a document of record for the client.

6.2 Presenting a report

The **parts of a financial planning report** to a client are normally as follows.

- A statement of the client's objectives
- A summary of the client's income and assets and other relevant circumstances or problems
- Recommendations, including any proposals for immediate action as well as longer-term suggestions for the client to consider in the future
- Appendices, including any data that is best presented separately, if appropriate

Product quotations, illustrations and brochures should be presented in an orderly way, possibly with an index listing the various items being sent to the client.

The **language** in the report should be written as concisely as possible. The language used should not include jargon except where necessary to explain points being made.

When a client has agreed a set of recommendations, there will be a considerable amount of work involved in arranging investments, along with any pension arrangements and protection policies also being taken out.

Key chapter points

- A diversified portfolio can be based on a range of investments giving balanced exposure to different asset classes.

- It is important to understand the fund composition of collective investments. A single packaged product may span different asset classes.

- Clients may have existing portfolios. Which existing investments should be retained or surrendered? The adviser must take care to avoid recommendations that amount to 'churning' of a client's investments.

- An individual's risk profile may be established through asking questions covering investment timescale, attitudes to risk, client circumstances and objectives and the client's investment experience.

- Individual circumstances including commitments, experience, life cycle stage, age and wealth are factors to consider in designing a portfolio.

- Investment portfolios need to be affordable, taking into account changes in circumstances as far as possible, and they need to be suitable for the client. The level of accessibility must be assessed, to allow liquidity when it is needed.

- Risk tolerance and risk attitude may be graded, for example using the terms 'cautious', 'medium' and 'adventurous'. The proportion of risky asset types in a portfolio may be varied according to the desired overall level of risk.

- Risky investments should not generally be undertaken if the investment timescale is short, as short-term fluctuations could lead to losses. Pound cost averaging is an advantage when regular amounts are invested.

- Recommendations to a client on investments or portfolios should generally be recorded in written correspondence or a report sent to the client.

INVESTMENT AND RISK

Chapter Quiz

1. What are typical long-term historical rates of return for major asset classes? .... (see para 2.2)
2. List five typical 'life stages'. ....(3.2)
3. What is meant by 'pound cost averaging'? ....(3.2)
4. Outline five categories into which an individual's risk profile might fall. ....(4.2)
5. State three questions that might be used to assess an individual's risk profile. ....(4.3)
6. What approximate asset allocation between equities and cash deposits / fixed interest might be appropriate for a client with a low risk profile?..(5.1)
7. What is meant by 'reduction in yield'? ....(5.5)
8. Outline the scope of aggregation services...(5.7)
9. Outline suitable sections of a financial planning report for sending to a client..................................(6.2)

chapter 17

Regulation

Chapter topic list

1	The FSA regulatory regime	362
2	FSA rules	367
3	COBS: Application and general provisions	368
4	Client categorisation	370
5	Client agreement and information provision	374
6	Communicating with clients	380
7	Advising and selling	385
8	Dealing and managing	388
9	Product disclosure and cancellation rights	391
10	Regime for basic advice on stakeholder products	394
11	Reporting to clients	396
12	Customer complaints procedures	398
13	The Financial Ombudsman Service	402
14	Compensation	403
	Key chapter points	405
	Chapter quiz	407

Chapter Learning Outcomes

10. **Understand** how other issues affect investment planning.

    10.6 Advantages and disadvantages of using past performance.

11. **Understand** the importance of keeping up to date with trends and changes in the legal framework for providing advice.

    11.1 Existing regulations and forthcoming changes in regulation and legislation affecting investment advice and the investment market.

    11.2 Trends in case law affecting investment advice.

12. **Analyse** consumers' circumstances and suitable investment products, taking account of any existing arrangements.

    12.2 Affordability and suitability.

13. **Apply** suitable investment product solutions to specific consumers' circumstances

    13.4 Confirm consumers' understanding of recommendations.
    13.5 Consumer rights and the regulatory requirements that apply to the provision of investment advice.

1 The FSA Regulatory Regime

Learning outcomes

11.1 Existing regulations and forthcoming changes in regulation and legislation affecting investment advice and the investment market.

11.2 Trends in case law affecting investment advice.

13.5 Consumer rights and the regulatory requirements that apply to the provision of investment advice.

1.1 Development of the UK regulatory system

1.1.1 Creation of a single regulator

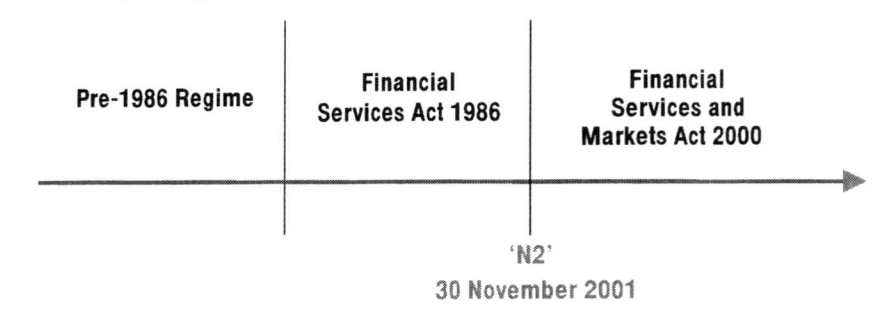

Pre-1986 Regime | Financial Services Act 1986 | Financial Services and Markets Act 2000

'N2'
30 November 2001

Before the advent of the **Financial Services Act 1986**, the UK financial services industry was entirely self-regulating. Standards were maintained by an assurance that those in the financial services industry had a common set of values and were able, and willing, to ostracise those who violated them.

The 1986 Act moved the UK to a system which became known as **'self-regulation within a statutory framework'**. Once **authorised**, firms and individuals would be regulated by self-regulating organisations (SROs), such as IMRO, SFA or PIA. The Financial Services Act 1986 only covered investment activities. Retail banking, general insurance, Lloyd's of London and mortgages were all covered by separate Acts and Codes.

When the Labour Party gained power in 1997, it wanted to make change to the regulation of financial services. The late 1990s saw a more radical reform of the financial services system with the unification of most aspects of financial services regulation under a **single statutory regulator**, the **Financial Services Authority (FSA)**. The process took place in two phases.

1.1.2 Phases of the reforms

First, the Bank of England's responsibility for banking supervision was transferred to the **Financial Services Authority (FSA)** as part of the **Bank of England Act 1998**. Despite losing responsibility for banking supervision, the **Bank of England** ('the Bank') gained the role in 1998 of **setting official UK interest rates**.

The Bank is also responsible for maintaining stability in the financial system by analysing and promoting initiatives to strengthen the financial system. It is also the financial system's **'lender of last resort'**, being ready to provide funds in exceptional circumstances.

The **second phase** of reforms consisted of a new Act covering financial services which would repeal the main provisions of the Financial Services Act 1986 and some other legislation. The earlier 'patchwork quilt' of regulation would be swept away and the FSA would regulate investment business, insurance business, banking, building societies, Friendly Societies, mortgages and Lloyd's.

On 30 November 2001, the new Act – the **Financial Services and Markets Act 2000 (FSMA 2000)** – came into force, to create a system of **statutory regulation**. While practitioners and consumers are actively consulted, it is the FSA that co-ordinates the regulation of the industry.

1.2 FSA as the UK statutory regulator

The creation of the FSA as the UK's **single statutory regulator** for the industry brought together regulation of investment, insurance and banking.

With the implementation of FSMA 2000 at date 'N2' in 2001, the FSA took over responsibility for:

- Prudential supervision of all firms, which involves monitoring the adequacy of their management, financial resources and internal systems and controls, and
- Conduct of business regulations of those firms doing investment business. This involves overseeing firms' dealings with investors to ensure, for example, that information provided is clear and not misleading

Arguably, the FSA's role as **legislator** has been diminished by the requirements of EU Single Market Directives – in particular, the far-reaching **Markets in Financial Instruments Directive (MiFID)**, implemented on 1 November 2007 – as the FSA has increasingly needed to apply rules which have been formulated at the **European level**.

1.3 The FSA's statutory objectives

Section 2 of the Financial Services and Markets Act (FSMA 2000) spells out the purpose of regulation by specifying the FSA's four **statutory objectives**.

INVESTMENT AND RISK

The FSA's original statutory objectives per FSMA 2000

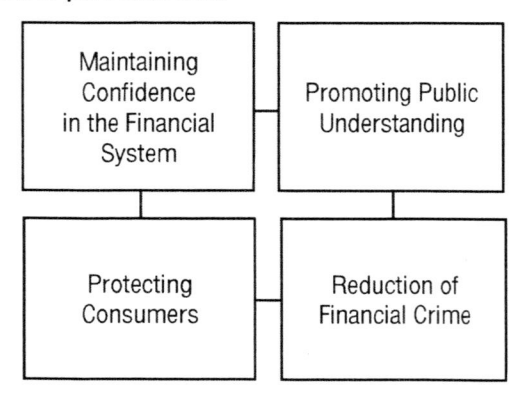

```
┌─────────────────┐   ┌─────────────────┐
│   Maintaining   │   │                 │
│   Confidence    │───│ Promoting Public│
│ in the Financial│   │  Understanding  │
│     System      │   │                 │
└─────────────────┘   └─────────────────┘
         │                     │
┌─────────────────┐   ┌─────────────────┐
│                 │   │                 │
│    Protecting   │   │   Reduction of  │
│    Consumers    │   │  Financial Crime│
│                 │   │                 │
└─────────────────┘   └─────────────────┘
```

The emphasis placed on these objectives makes FSMA 2000 unusual compared to the Acts that it supersedes – none of which clearly articulated their objectives. FSMA 2000 is seeking to inject much needed clarity into what the regulatory regime is trying to achieve and, perhaps more importantly, seeking to manage expectations regarding what it cannot achieve.

1.3.1 Financial Services Act 2010

The Financial Services Act 2010 gave the FSA a fifth statutory objective of financial stability. The Act also requires to FSA to create an independent consumer financial education body (CFEB) with a mandate from Parliament to improve consumer financial education in the UK. As a result, promoting public understanding will be removed as an objective of the FSA in due course.

1.4 Status of the FSA

The FSA is not a government agency. Its members, officers and staff are not Crown servants nor civil servants. It is a private company limited by guarantee, with HM Treasury as the guarantor. The FSA is financed by the financial services industry.

The Board of the FSA is appointed by the Treasury and the Chancellor of the Exchequer is ultimately responsible for the regulatory system for financial services under FSMA 2000.

1.5 Functions of the FSA

The FSA's **principal powers** include the following.

- Granting **authorisation** and permission to firms to undertake regulated activities
- **Approving** individuals to perform controlled functions
- The right to issue under **S138 FSMA 2000:**
  - General rules (such as the *Conduct of Business* rules) for authorised firms which appear to be necessary or expedient to protect the interests of consumers
  - Principles (such as the *Principles for Businesses*)
  - Codes of conduct (such as the *Code of Practice for Approved Persons*)
  - Evidential provisions and guidance
- The right to **investigate** authorised firms or approved persons

17: REGULATION

- The right to take **enforcement** action against authorised firms and approved persons
- The right to **discipline** authorised firms and approved persons
- The power to take action against any person for **market abuse**
- The power to **recognise** investment exchanges and clearing houses
- As the **UK Listing Authority**, approval of companies for stock exchange listings in the UK

Note that the term 'firm' is used generally in the FSA regulations to apply to an authorised person, whether the person is an individual, a partnership or a corporate body.

1.6 Risks for consumers

The FSA has identified the following **consumer risks** in the financial services industry.

(a) **Prudential risk** – for example the risk of a company collapsing through poor management

(b) **Bad faith risk** – the risk of loss due to mis-selling, non-disclosure, fraud and misrepresentation

(c) **Complexity/unsuitability risk** – the risk that a customer chooses unsuitable products through lack of understanding

(d) **Performance risk** – the risk that investment do not provide the returns that had been hoped for

The FSA has a **Consumer Panel** to monitor how the FSA fulfils its objectives in relation to consumers.

1.7 Market abuse

The new regime brought with it the new offence of **market abuse**, complementing legislation covering insider dealing and market manipulation.

Market abuse could consist of, for example:

(a) Knowingly buying shares in a takeover target before a general disclosure of the proposed takeover

(b) Market distortion: dealing on an exchange just prior to the exchange closing with the purpose of positioning the share price at a distorted level in order to avoid having to pay out on a derivatives transaction

(c) Posting an inaccurate story on an internet bulletin board in order to give a false or misleading impression

These provisions relate particularly to participation in equity markets.

1.8 FSA Principles for Business

The FSA's eleven **Principles for Businesses** (PRIN) of the FSA are a general statement of authorised firms' obligations. Although they may be invoked when the FSA disciplines firms, they cannot themselves give rise to actions for damages. The Principles are important to the FSA's more detailed rules, and we shall be referring back to some of the Principles later in this chapter.

FSA Principles for Businesses		
1:	Integrity	A firm must conduct its business with integrity.
2:	Skill, care and diligence	A firm must conduct its business with due skill, care and diligence.

INVESTMENT AND RISK

FSA Principles for Businesses

3:	**Management and control**	A firm must take reasonable care to organise and control its affairs responsibly and effectively, with adequate risk management systems.
4:	**Financial prudence**	A firm must maintain adequate financial resources.
5:	**Market conduct**	A firm must observe proper standards of market conduct.
6:	**Customers' interests**	A firm must pay due regard to the interests of its customers and treat them fairly.
7:	**Communications with clients**	A firm must pay due regard to the information needs of its clients, and communicate information to them in a way which is clear, fair and not misleading.
8:	**Conflicts of interest**	A firm must manage conflict of interest fairly, both between itself and its customers and between a customer and another client.
9:	**Customers: relationships of trust**	A firm must take reasonable care to ensure the suitability of its advice and discretionary decisions for any customer who is entitled to rely upon its judgment.
10:	**Clients' assets**	A firm must arrange adequate protection for clients' assets when it is responsible for them.
11:	**Relations with regulators**	A firm must deal with its regulators in an open and co-operative way, and must disclose to the FSA appropriately anything relating to the firm of which the FSA would reasonably expect notice.

1.9 Breaches of the Principles

The consequence of breaching a Principle makes the firm liable to **enforcement or disciplinary sanctions**. The FSA may bring these sanctions where it can show that the firm has been at fault in some way. The definition of 'fault' will depend upon when Principle has been breached.

S150 FSMA 2000 creates a right of action in damages for a '**private person**' who suffers loss as a result of a contravention of certain **rules** by an authorised firm. However, a 'private person' may not sue a firm under S150 FSMA 2000 for the breach of a **Principle**.

1.10 Treating customers fairly (TCF)

In addition to meeting the regulatory objectives, the FSA aims to maintain efficient, orderly and clean markets and help retail customers achieve a fair deal. Since 2000, the FSA has been examining what a fair deal for retail customers actually means. This has led to much discussion of the concept of **TCF** – 'treating customers fairly'.

The FSA does not define **treating customers fairly (TCF)** in a way that applies in all circumstances. By adopting a '**Principles-based approach**' to TCF through Principle 6, the FSA puts the onus on firms to determine what is fair in each particular set of circumstances. Firms therefore need to make their own assessment of what TCF means for them, taking into account the nature of their business.

The FSA wants firms to focus on delivering the following six TCF consumer outcomes.

- Consumers can be confident that they are dealing with firms where the fair treatment of customers is central to the corporate culture.

- Products and services marketed and sold in the retail market are designed to meet the needs of identified consumer groups and are targeted accordingly.

- Consumers are provided with clear information and are kept appropriately informed before, during and after the point of sale.
- Where consumers receive advice, the advice is suitable and takes account of their circumstances.
- Consumers are provided with products that perform as firms have led them to expect, and the associated service is both of an acceptable standard and also as they have been led to expect.
- Consumers do not face unreasonable post-sale barriers imposed by firms to change product, switch provider, submit a claim or make a complaint.

2 FSA Rules

> **Learning outcomes**
>
> 11.1 Existing regulations and forthcoming changes in regulation and legislation affecting investment advice and the investment market.
>
> 11.2 Trends in case law affecting investment advice.
>
> 13.5 Consumer rights and the regulatory requirements that apply to the provision of investment advice.

2.1 Primary and secondary legislation

FSMA 2000 – the **primary legislation** – only provides the skeleton of the regulatory system, with much of the detail being provided by **secondary legislation**. Both FSMA 2000 and the secondary legislation are drafted by **HM Treasury**.

Secondary legislation links into various sections of FSMA 2000, fleshing out the requirements and, thus, requiring the two to be read in conjunction. An example of this concerns the authorisation requirement. FSMA 2000 requires that any firm undertaking a **regulated activity** must be authorised or exempt from authorisation. While the routes that a firm may follow to obtain authorisation are contained in FSMA 2000, the meaning of the term 'regulated activity' and the exemptions are found in secondary legislation – namely the Regulated Activities Order.

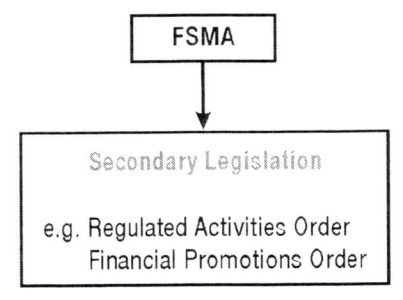

```
         FSMA
           |
           v
   Secondary Legislation

 e.g. Regulated Activities Order
      Financial Promotions Order
```

2.2 The role of the FSA Handbook

Earlier we highlighted the link between FSMA 2000 and the secondary legislation. In the day-to-day running of a firm, it will not generally be necessary to pay attention to the legislation and secondary legislation directly. The principles, rules and regulations to which a firm must adhere when running the business are generally found in the **FSA Handbook**. Indeed, even where standards are imposed by FSMA 2000 itself, such as in the case of market abuse and financial promotion, the *FSA Handbook* is used to provide additional requirements.

INVESTMENT AND RISK

```
      ┌──────────┐
      │   FSMA   │
      └────┬─────┘
           ▼
  ┌──────────────────────────────┐
  │    Secondary Legislation     │
  │ e.g. Regulated Activities Order │
  │    Financial Promotions Order │
  └──────────────┬───────────────┘
                 ▼
         ┌───────────────┐
         │  FSA Handbook │
         └───────────────┘
```

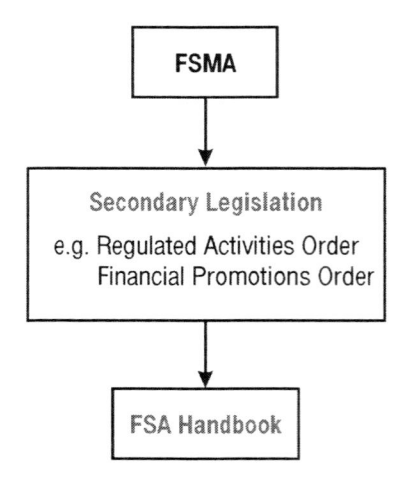

Since 1997, when the move to the new regime was first announced, FSA has undergone a massive consultation exercise. Indeed, hundreds of consultation papers have been released dealing with all aspects of the new regulatory regime. One of the main functions of the consultation process was to alleviate concerns regarding accountability of the FSA and practitioner involvement under FSMA 2000.

The consultation papers resulted in the *FSA Handbook* – a final set of rules, principles and guidance that a firm must adhere to. The FSA derives its power to make rules in the FSA Handbook from FSMA 2000. Therefore, it includes *Principles for Businesses* and various rules contained in the *Conduct of Business Sourcebook*.

Given the range of financial services activities covered, it is hardly surprising that the *FSA Handbook* is a lengthy document. However, as already mentioned, the Handbook is undergoing a process of simplification, in line with the move towards principles-based regulation. This process is partly being carried out in conjunction with the implementation of the Markets in Financial Instruments Directive (MiFID), which has resulted in major changes to the content of the Handbook with effect from 1 November 2007.

3 COBS: Application and general provisions

Learning outcomes

11.1 Existing regulations and forthcoming changes in regulation and legislation affecting investment advice and the investment market.

11.2 Trends in case law affecting investment advice.

13.5 Consumer rights and the regulatory requirements that apply to the provision of investment advice.

3.1 COBS

The FSA includes various rules in a large section of its Handbook called the **Conduct of Business Sourcebook**. The Conduct of Business Rules have been revised extensively, and shortened, with the implementation of the Markets in Financial Instruments Directive (MiFID), with effect from November 2007. The new Sourcebook has sometimes been referred to as 'NEWCOB', but is now referred to by the abbreviation '**COBS**'.

3.2 General application rule

The **general application rule** is that COBS applies to an authorised **firm** in respect of the following activities when carried out from one of its (or its **appointed representative's**) **UK** establishments.

- Accepting deposits

- Designated investment business
- Long-term life insurance business

Many rules (except the financial promotion rules) only apply when the firm is doing **designated investment business** with customers.

The term **'designated investment business'** has a narrower meaning than the concept of **'regulated activities'** by excluding activities relating to Lloyd's business, deposits, funeral plans, mortgages, pure protection policies and general insurance contracts. Following the implementation of MiFID, operating a **multilateral trading facility (MTF)** is designated investment business.

In the context of FSA regulation, the official FSA definition of an investment manager is a person who, acting only on behalf of a client:

- Manages **designated investments** in an account or portfolio on a discretionary basis under the terms of a **discretionary management agreement**, or
- Manages **designated investments** in an account or portfolio on a non-discretionary basis under the terms of a **non-discretionary management agreement**.

The term 'discretionary' does not have an official FSA definition. With **discretionary portfolio management**, the investment manager makes and implements decisions to buy and sell investments in the portfolio without referring to the client each time. In contrast, the **non-discretionary portfolio manager** provided advice to the client to assist the client in making their own investment decisions.

3.3 The investment manager

In the context of FSA regulation, the official FSA definition of an **investment manager** is a person who, acting **only on behalf of a client**:

- Manages **designated investments** in an account or portfolio on a discretionary basis under the terms of a **discretionary management agreement**, or
- Manages **designated investments** in an account or portfolio on a non-discretionary basis under the terms of a **non-discretionary management agreement**.

The term 'discretionary' does not have an official FSA definition. With **discretionary portfolio management**, the investment manager makes the implements decisions to buy and sell investments in the portfolio without referring to the client each time. In contrast, the **non-discretionary portfolio manager** provides advice to the client to assist the client in making their own investment decisions.

3.4 Further general provisions

The **territorial scope** of COBS is modified to ensure compatibility with European law: this is called the '**EEA territorial scope rule**'. One of the effects of the EEA territorial scope rule is to override the application of COBS to the overseas establishments of EEA firms in a number of cases, including circumstances covered by MiFID, the Distance Marketing Directive or the Electronic Commerce Directive. In some circumstances, the rules on financial promotions and other communications will apply to communications made by UK firms to persons located outside the United Kingdom and will not apply to communications made to persons inside the United Kingdom by EEA firms.

3.5 Communications by electronic media

Where a rule requires a notice to be delivered in writing, a firm may comply using **electronic media**. The COBS rules often specify that communication must be in a **durable medium**.

Durable medium means:

- Paper, or
- Any instrument (eg an email message) which enables the recipient to store information addressed personally to him in a way accessible for future reference for a period of time adequate for the purposes of the information and which allows the unchanged reproduction of the information stored. This will include the recipient's computer hard drive or other storage devices on which the electronic mail is stored, but not internet websites unless they fulfil the criteria in this definition.

Some communications are allowed to be delivered either in a durable medium or via a website, where the **website conditions** are satisfied.

The **website conditions** are specified as follows:

- The provision of the information in that medium must be appropriate to the context in which the business between the firm and the client is, or is to be, carried on (ie there is evidence that the client has regular access to the internet, such as the provision by the client of an e-mail address).
- The client must specifically consent to the provision of that information in that form.
- The client must be notified electronically of the address of the website, and the place on the website where the information may be accessed.
- The information must be up-to-date.
- The information must be accessible continuously by means of that website for such period of time as the client may reasonably need to inspect it.

4 Client categorisation

Learning outcomes

11.1 Existing regulations and forthcoming changes in regulation and legislation affecting investment advice and the investment market.

11.2 Trends in case law affecting investment advice.

13.5 Consumer rights and the regulatory requirements that apply to the provision of investment advice.

4.1 Levels of protection

Within any cost-effective regulatory system, protection provided ought to be **proportionate** to the need for protection. This is because there is not only a cost element to protection but also an inverse relationship with freedom. It is desirable that those who do not require high protection are given more freedom to trade without the restrictions that the rules inevitably bring.

The **size** and **financial awareness** of **clients** will determine the level of protection. As the size/knowledge increases, protection will decrease. A system of categorising clients can help determine that the level of protection is appropriate to the client.

```
            Low                              High
            ────────── Protection ──────────▶

            ◀────────── Size/Knowledge ──────────
            High                             Low
```

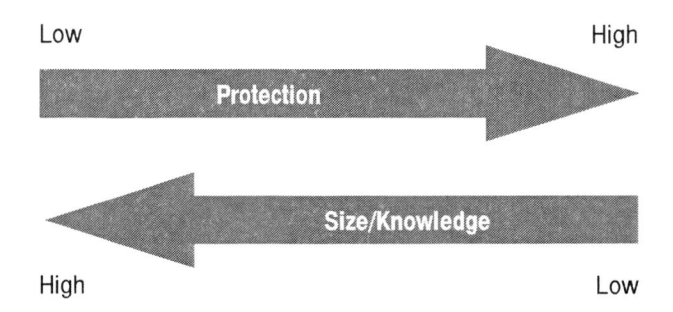

While this would ideally be a continuous process, gradually moving from full protection to no protection, in practical terms this is an impossibility.

4.2 Client categories

The terms used to classify clients has changed following the implementation of **MiFID** and the introduction of the new COBS.

Firms (unless they are providing only the special level of **basic advice** on a **stakeholder product**) are obliged to classify all clients who are undertaking **designated investment business,** before doing such business.

MiFID creates three client categories:

- **Eligible counterparties** – who are either *per se* or **elective** eligible counterparties
- **Professional clients** – who are either *per se* or **elective** professional clients
- **Retail clients**

As well as setting up criteria to classify clients into these categories, MiFID provides for clients to **change** their initial classification, on request.

4.2.1 Clients

A **client** is a person to whom an authorised **firm** provides a service in the course of carrying on a **regulated activity** or, in the case of MiFID or equivalent third country business, a person to whom a firm provides an **ancillary service**.

4.2.2 Retail clients

Retail clients are defined as those clients who are not professional clients or eligible counterparties.

4.2.3 Professional clients

Some undertakings are automatically recognised as **professional clients**. Accordingly, these entities may be referred to as *per se* professional clients. (An **undertaking** is a company, partnership or unincorporated association.)

Clients who are *per se* **professional clients** are as follows.

- Entities that **require authorisation or regulation** to operate in the financial markets, including: credit institutions, investment firms, other financial institutions, insurance companies, collective investment schemes and pension funds and their management companies, commodity and commodity derivatives dealers, 'local' derivatives dealing firms, and other institutional investors
- In relation to **MiFID** or equivalent third country business, a **large undertaking** – meaning one that meets two of the following size requirements:

INVESTMENT AND RISK

- €20,000,000 Balance sheet total
- €40,000,000 Net turnover
- €2,000,000 Own funds

- In relation to business that is not **MiFID** or equivalent third country business, a **large undertaking** meeting **either** of the following requirements:

    - Called up share capital of at least £5,000,000 or equivalent, or

    Two of the three following size tests:

    - €12,500,000 Balance sheet total
    - €25,000,000 Net turnover
    - 250 average Number of employees in the year

- Central banks, international institutions, and national and regional government bodies
- Institutional investors whose main activity is to invest in financial instruments

A firm may treat a retail client as an **elective professional client** if the following tests are met.

- **Qualitative test.** The firm assesses adequately the client's **expertise**, **experience** and **knowledge** and thereby gains reasonable assurance that, for the transactions or services envisaged, the client is capable of making his own investment decisions and understanding the risks involved.

- **Quantitative test.** In the case of **MiFID** or equivalent third country business, at least **two** of the following three criteria must apply:

    - The client has carried out at least ten 'significant' transactions per quarter on the relevant market, over the last four quarters
    - The client's portfolio, including cash deposits, exceeds €500,000
    - The client has knowledge of the transactions envisaged from at least one year's professional work in the financial sector

Additionally, for professional client status to apply:

- The client must agree in writing to be treated as a professional client
- The firm must give written warning of the protections and compensation rights which may be lost
- The client must state in writing, separately from the contract, that it is aware of the consequences of losing protections

It is the responsibility of the professional client to keep the firm informed about changes (eg in portfolio size or company size) which could affect their categorisation.

COBS states that an elective professional client should not be presumed to have market knowledge and experience comparable to a *per se* professional client.

4.2.4 Eligible counterparties

In relation to MiFID or equivalent third country business, a client can only be an eligible counterparty in relation to eligible counterparty business.

The following, and their non-EEA equivalents, are *per se* **eligible counterparties** (ie they are automatically recognised as eligible counterparties).

- Investment firms
- Credit institutions
- Insurance companies

- UCITS collective investment schemes, and their management companies
- Pension funds, and their management companies
- Other financial institutions authorised or regulated under the law of the EU or an EEA state
- Certain own-account commodity derivatives dealers and 'local' derivatives firms
- National governments
- Central banks
- Supranational organisations

A firm may treat an undertaking as an **elective eligible counterparty** if the client:

- Is a *per se* professional client (unless it is such by virtue of being an institutional investor), or
- Is an elective professional client and requests the categorisation, but only in respect of the transactions and services for which it counts as a professional client, and
- In the case of MiFID or equivalent third country business, provides 'express confirmation' of their agreement (which may be for a specific transaction or may be general) to be treated as an eligible counterparty

If the prospective counterparty is established in another EEA state, for MiFID business the firm should defer to the status determined by the law of that other state.

4.3 Agent as client

One area that has proved complicated in the past is where a firm is dealing with an **agent**. For example, suppose that a solicitor is acting for his client and approaches a firm to sell bonds on his client's behalf. Clearly, it is important that the firm establish whether it owes duties to the solicitor or to the solicitor's client.

The agent is the client of the firm, unless an agreement in writing treats the other person as the client.

The relevant COBS rule applies to designated investment business and ancillary services. The rule states that the firm may treat the agent as its client if the agent is another authorised firm or an overseas financial services institution **or** if the agent is another person, provided that the arrangement is not to avoid duties which the firm would otherwise owe to the agent's clients.

An agreement may however be made, in writing, to treat the other person (in the above example, the solicitor's client) as the firm's client.

4.4 Providing a higher level of protection to clients

Firms must allow **professional clients** and **eligible counterparties** to re-categorise in order to get more protection. Such clients are themselves responsible for asking for higher protection if they deem themselves to be **unable** to assess properly or manage the risks involved.

Either on its own initiative or following a client request or written agreement:

- A *per se* **eligible counterparty** may be re-categorised as a **professional client** or **retail client**
- A *per se* **professional client** may be re-categorised as a **retail client**

The **higher level of protection** may be provided through re-categorisation:

- On a general basis
- Trade by trade
- In respect of specified rules
- In respect of particular services, transactions, transaction types or product types

The client should (of course) be notified of a re-categorisation. Firms must have written internal policies and procedures to categorise clients.

INVESTMENT AND RISK

4.5 Policies, procedure and records

Firms must have written internal **policies and procedures** to categorise clients.

The firm must keep records of client categorisations, with supporting information. It must also keep records of all notices and agreements related to categorisation, with evidence of despatch to clients.

The records must be **kept** for **five years** in the case of MiFID or equivalent third country business, and for life policies or pension contracts, **indefinitely** for pension transfers, pension opt-outs and free-standing additional voluntary contributions (FSAVC), and for **three years** in any other case.

5 Client Agreements and Information Provision

> **Learning outcomes**
>
> 11.1 Existing regulations and forthcoming changes in regulation and legislation affecting investment advice and the investment market.
>
> 11.2 Trends in case law affecting investment advice.
>
> 13.5 Consumer rights and the regulatory requirements that apply to the provision of investment advice.

5.1 Client agreements: designated investment business

If a firm carries on **designated investment business**, other than advising on investments, for a **new retail client,** the firm must enter into a **basic agreement** with the client. Although little guidance is given in the rules as to the contents, the agreement will set out the essential rights and obligations of the firm, and must be in writing – on paper or other durable medium. For a **professional client**, there is no requirement for an agreement, although most firms will wish there to be one.

In good time, normally **before** the client is bound by any agreement relating to designated investment business or ancillary services, the firm must provide to the retail client – either in a durable medium or on a website, if the website conditions are satisfied:

- The terms of the agreement
- Information about **the firm and its services** (see below), including information on communications, conflicts of interest and authorised status

The agreement and information may be provided **immediately after** the client is bound by the agreement if the agreement was concluded using a means of distance communication (eg telephone).

Relevant material changes to the information provided must be notified to the client in **good time**.

5.2 Information disclosure before providing services

A firm must provide to clients appropriate information in a comprehensible form about:

- The **firm and its services**
- Designated investments and proposed investment strategies, including guidance and warnings on risks associated with designated investments and investment strategies
- Execution venues
- Costs and associated charges

The information on designated investments and proposed investment strategies must be provided for MiFID business, and also for non-MiFID designated investment business in relation to **derivatives, warrants** and **stock lending activity**.

5.3 Information about a firm and its services

Information about a firm and its services which must be provided to a **retail client** comprises the following general information:

- The firm's **name and address**, and **contact details** which allow effective communication
- For MiFID and equivalent third country business, the **languages** the firm uses for documents and other communication
- **Methods of communication with clients** which are used by the firm, including those for sending and receiving orders where relevant
- Statement that the firm is **authorised**, and the name of the authorising **competent authority** (e.g. the Financial Services Authority) – with the authority's contact address, in the case of MiFID business
- If the firm is acting through an **appointed representative or tied agent**, a statement of this fact specifying the EEA state in which the representative/agent is registered
- The nature, frequency and timing of **performance reports** provided by the firm (in accordance with rules on reporting to clients)
- For a common platform firm or a third country (non-EEA) investment firm, the firm's **conflicts of interest policy** (or a summary of it)
- For non-common platform firms, details of **how the firm will ensure fair treatment** of clients when material interests or conflicts of interest arise

5.4 Information about designated investments

The provisions in this section apply to **MiFID** and equivalent third country business, and also to the **following regulated activities** when they involve a **retail client**.

- Making a personal recommendation about a designated investment
- Managing designated investments
- Arranging or executing a deal in warrants or derivatives
- Stock lending activity

Firms must provide to clients a **general description of the nature and risks** of the type of designated investments involved, taking into account the client's categorisation as a **retail** or **professional** client.

Each of a series of transactions involving the same type of investment does not need to be treated as a new or different service. However, if product charges differ from those already disclosed, the new details must be given. A **key features document** or **simplified prospectus** may meet the requirements of this section. Information must be provided in a durable medium, or via a website meeting the website conditions.

The description must be in enough detail to enable the client to make investment decisions on an informed basis, including where relevant for the investment type and status and knowledge of the client:

- **Risks** associated with that type of designated investment, explaining **leverage** and its effects, and the risk of losing the entire investment
- **Price volatility** of designated investments and any **limitations on the available market**
- Financial commitments such as **contingent liabilities** which may be assumed as a result of transactions

- Any applicable **margin requirements** (e. g. money which must be deposited to cover potential losses as the price of derivatives changes)

For a designated investment subject to a current offer to the public, where a **prospectus** has been published, the firm must inform the client that the prospectus has been published.

Where a designated investment is **composed of two or more designated investments** and is likely to carry greater **risks** than the components, the firm must describe how the **interaction** of the components increases risk.

For a designated investment incorporating a **guarantee by a third party**, sufficient information must be given about the guarantor and the guarantee to enable the retail client to assess it.

5.5 Provision of information: managing investments

A firm **managing investments** must establish a **benchmark** or other appropriate method of evaluation and comparison, based on the client's investment objectives and the designated investments in their portfolio, to enable the client to assess the firm's performance.

Firms proposing to **manage investments** for a **retail client** must provide the following information to the client:

- Method and frequency of valuation of designated investments in the client's portfolio
- Details of any delegation of the discretionary management of the investments
- Specification of any benchmark used to compare performance
- Types of designated investments and transactions that may be included in the portfolio
- Management objectives, the level of risk reflected, and any constraints in the manager's discretion

5.6 Information on safeguards and client money

A firm holding **designated investments** or **client money** for a **retail client** subject to MiFID custody and client money rules must provide the following information to clients where applicable:

- That the investments/money may be held by a third party on behalf of the firm
- The responsibility of the firm for acts or omissions of the third party, under national laws
- Consequences for the client of the insolvency of the third party
- If the designated investments belonging to the retail client are held in an omnibus account by a third party (in which case, there should be a prominent warning of the resulting risks)
- If the designated investments cannot, under national law, be separately identified from the firm or the third party, a prominent warning of the resulting risks
- Client rights relating to accounts subject to jurisdiction outside the EEA
- Summary of steps taken to protect the client's investments/money, including summary details of any investor compensation scheme which applies (professional clients must also be given this information)
- Any security interest, lien or right of set-off held by a depositary (again, for professional clients as well as retail, in this case)

Before **using clients' designated investments for its own account**, a firm must provide in good time and in a durable medium clear full and accurate information on the firm's obligations and responsibilities with respect to that use, including terms for restitution and risks involved.

5.7 Information about costs, charges and compensation

5.7.1 Information about costs and charges

Firms must provide information on **costs and associated charges** to retail clients, including:

- The total price to be paid by the client (or the basis for calculation, if an exact price cannot be indicated) for the designated investments or ancillary services including all related fees, commissions (separately itemised), charges, expenses and taxes payable via the firm (with currency exchange rates where relevant)
- Notice of the possibility that other costs not paid via the firm, including taxes, may arise
- Payment arrangements

5.7.2 Compensation information

For MiFID business, the firm must tell the client about the applicable **investor compensation scheme**, giving information in a durable medium or via a website meeting the website conditions and in the language of the EEA state:

- On the amount and scope of cover offered
- At the client's request, on conditions and formalities involved in claiming compensation

5.8 Medium of disclosure and changes to information

Information we have described so far in this chapter is to be provided **in good time before providing** designated investment business or ancillary services, or **immediately after starting** to provide the **services** if the agreement was concluded using a means of distance communication.

The information should be provided in a **durable medium**, or via a **website** where the website conditions are satisfied.

The firm must keep the client **notified** in good time of material relevant changes, using a durable medium if that was used initially.

5.9 Information disclosure for packaged products

5.9.1 Packaged products

'**Packaged products**' relates to products that can be bought 'off-the-shelf', with the terms and conditions and price identical for all potential investors. These are typically products sold through an intermediary, for example an Independent Financial Adviser (IFA).

A **packaged product** is defined as one of the following:

- A life policy
- A unit in a regulated collective investment scheme
- An interest in an investment trust savings scheme
- A stakeholder pension scheme
- A personal pension scheme

Whether or not (in the case of the first three types listed above) it is held within a PEP, an ISA or a Child Trust Fund (CTF) and whether or not the packaged product is also a stakeholder product.

INVESTMENT AND RISK

> **Exam tip**
>
> Use the word **CLIPS** to remember the types of packaged product.
>
> **C**ollective Investment Schemes (regulated)
> **L**ife policies
> **I**nvestment trust savings schemes
> **P**ersonal pensions
> **S**takeholder pensions

There are disclosure rules, described below, which apply when a firm makes a **personal recommendation** to a **retail client** to buy a **packaged product**. These rules do not apply when special rules on (scripted) **basic advice** for stakeholder products are being followed.

These rules apply to a UK firm's business carried out in another EEA state for a retail client in the UK, subject to certain exclusions. They also apply to business carried out in the UK for a client in another EEA state.

5.9.2 Selling products from the scope

The firm's disclosures should indicate whether it expects its **scope** to be:

- The whole of the market or market sector
- Limited to several product providers
- Limited to a single product provider

What is meant by the **scope** and **range** of a firm's advice?

- The **scope** relates to the **product providers** whose products it sells
- The **range** relates to which **products** from those providers it sells

A firm must maintain an up-to-date **record** of the **scopes and ranges** it uses, and must keep the records for at least **five years**.

If a firm holds itself out as independent or with a scope across the whole market or a whole market sector, the firm's selection will need to be '**sufficiently large**' to satisfy the client's best interests rule and the fair, clear and not misleading rule. (Note how, similarly to many other cases, the rules do not specify the meaning of 'sufficiently large'. In line with principles-based regulation, it is up to the firm to come to a judgement on how it can comply.)

In accordance with the **client's best interests rule** and the **fair, clear and not misleading rule**, a firm must ensure that:

- Its representatives consider, based on adequate knowledge, products across its scope
- Products outside the scope are not recommended
- All representatives advising on packaged products and making recommendations can recommend and sell each product in the relevant range. (If a representative is not competent to advise on a product or category, a client to whom a recommendation ought to be made should be referred to a representative who is competent.)
- The scope disclosed to the client is not narrowed without appropriate new disclosure to the client
- The scope is not extended in a way that alters remuneration arrangements unless it provides new disclosures on inducements, charges and costs (e. g. by providing a further '**menu**')

5.9.3 Disclosure documents for retail clients

For packaged products business, the FSA gives guidance on the format of appropriate disclosures. Clients have generally been provided with an **initial disclosure document (IDD)** and a **fees and commissions statement** (alternatively called the **menu**). Standard wordings are provided by the FSA for those drafting IDDs and menus. However, these documents are (since November 2007) no longer mandatory: the required information could be provided in another way.

The firm should consider whether an IDD or menu needs to be provided if they were provided previously and still apply.

The IDD for investments and the proposed new services and costs disclosure document both contain the following sections.

- **Financial Services Authority**. This section explains the purpose of the document to consumers.
- **Whose products do we offer?** This section explains the scope of the services that a firm is offering on packaged products to a particular client.
- **Which service will we provide you with?** This section tells consumers whether they are receiving advice and recommendations from the adviser; have to make a choice for themselves; or are receiving basic advice on a limited range of stakeholder products.
- **Who regulates us?**
- **Loans and ownership**. This section tells consumers of interest held in (share capital, voting rights or both) and/or loans provided to firms by product providers and *vice versa*.
- **What to do if you have a complaint**
- **Are we covered by the Financial Services Compensation Scheme?**

The FSA considers that the disclosure requirements are met if the firm's representatives provide these documents '**in good time**' before the client is bound by an agreement to provide a personal recommendation, or the firm performs an act preparatory to providing a recommendation.

The standard **menu** is entitled '**Key Facts: A guide to the Cost of our Services' and includes:**

- A section on the FSA, and the purpose of the required menu
- A section in which the firm gives details of 'Our services'
- The payment options offered (whether paying by fee or by commission/product charges)
- The typical fees or maximum commission the firm is likely to receive for a transaction
- An indication of the market average commission (for commission-based work)

The **market average (MA)** is designed to give consumers a benchmark for what might be a competitive level of commission.

An advisor should not start charging until after the consumer has been given a menu and has agreed the **payment option** for the client.

A firm may have different 'menus', and firms are free to offer different charging structures to different groups of clients.

If a firm did not provide information on expected commission arrangements in the menu, it would be unlikely to be in compliance with the **clients' best interest rule**.

The menu was highly prescriptive, requiring the inclusion of many figures (eg market averages and maximum commission shown in a precise way). The new **services and costs disclosure document** does not mandate this type of information. Instead, firms will have much greater flexibility about how they explain the cost of their services and without using the 'tick box' approach.

Accordingly, the new document includes a section on 'costs', removing the need for a separate 'menu'.

INVESTMENT AND RISK

5.9.4 Providing requested information

A firm's representative should provide a **copy** of the appropriate range of packaged products to the client, on the client's **request**.

5.9.5 Ongoing disclosure

Firms should not arrange to retain commission in excess of the maximum rate previously disclosed without providing **further inducements information** to the client, and obtaining the client's informed consent to the alteration, in a durable medium.

6 Communicating with clients

> **Learning outcomes**
>
> 10.6 Advantages and disadvantages of using past performance.
>
> 11.1 Existing regulations and forthcoming changes in regulation and legislation affecting investment advice and the investment market.
>
> 11.2 Trends in case law affecting investment advice.
>
> 13.5 Consumer rights and the regulatory requirements that apply to the provision of investment advice.

6.1 Introduction

A **financial promotion** is an **invitation** or **inducement** to engage in investment activity. The term therefore describes most forms and methods of marketing financial services. It covers traditional advertising, most website content, telephone sales campaigns and face-to-face meetings. The term is extended to cover **marketing communications** by MiFID.

The purpose of regulation in this area is to create a regime where the quality of financial promotions is scrutinised by an authorised firm who must then comply with lengthy rules to ensure that their promotions are **clear**, **fair and not misleading** and that customers are treated **fairly**.

6.2 Application of the financial promotions rules

The **financial promotions rules** within COBS apply to a firm:

- Communicating with a **client** in relation to **designated investment business**
- **Communicating** or **approving** a **financial promotion** (with some exceptions in respect of: credit promotions, home purchase plans, home reversion schemes, non-investment insurance contracts and unregulated collective investment schemes)

Firms must also apply the rules to promotions issued by their **appointed representatives**.

6.3 Territorial scope

For financial promotions, the **general application rule** applies. This indicates that the rules apply to a firm in respect of designated investment business carried out from an establishment maintained by the firm or its appointed representative in the UK. Additionally, in general the rules apply to firms carrying on business with a client in the UK from an establishment overseas.

The financial promotions rules also apply to:

- Promotions communicated to a person in the UK
- Cold (unsolicited) calling to someone outside the UK, if the call is from within the UK or is in respect of UK business

6.4 Fair, clear and not misleading

A firm must ensure that a communication or financial promotion is **fair, clear and not misleading**, as is **appropriate** and **proportionate** considering the means of communication and the information to be conveyed.

6.5 Financial Promotions Order

Section 21 FSMA 2000 makes it criminal for someone to undertake a financial promotion, ie invite or induce another to engage in investment activity, unless they are either:

- An **authorised firm** (ie **issuing the financial promotion**), or
- The content of the communication is **approved** by an authorised firm

There are a number of exemptions from s21 set out in the **Financial Promotions Order**. The effect of being an **exemption** is that the promotion would **not** need to be issued or approved by an authorised firm. It would therefore not have to comply with the detailed financial promotion rules.

The main examples are as follows. (Other exemptions cover certain one-off and purely factual promotions.)

Exemption	Comments
Investment professional	A communication to an authorised or exempt person.
Certified high net worth individuals	Anyone may promote **unlisted securities** to persons who hold certificates of high net worth (normally signed by their accountant or employer, however, these can now be self-certified by an individual) and who have agreed to be classified as such. Requirements for a certificate are that a person must have a net income of £100,000 or more, or net assets (excluding principal property) of £250,000 or more. Note that, if applicable, the financial promotion should not invite or induce the recipient to engage in business with the firm that signed the certificate of high net worth.
Associations of high net worth individuals	Anyone can promote non-derivative products to associations of high net worth investors.
Sophisticated investors	Anyone can promote products to a person who holds a certificate indicating that they are knowledgeable in a particular stock (normally signed by an authorised firm, however, individuals can now self-certify themselves as sophisticated in relation to unlisted securities) and who have signed a statement agreeing to be such. Note that the financial promotion should not invite or induce the recipient to engage in business with the authorised firm that signed the certificate.

6.6 Communicating with retail clients

6.6.1 General rule

The general rule on **communicating with retail clients** in relation to **designated investment business** states that firms must ensure that the information:

- Includes the **name of the firm** (which may be the **trading name** or **shortened name**, provided the firm is identifiable)

INVESTMENT AND RISK

- Is accurate and does not emphasise potential benefits of investment without also giving a **fair and prominent indication of relevant risks**
- Is **sufficient** for and presented so as to be **likely to be understood** by the **average member** of the group to whom it is directed or by whom it is likely to be received
- Does **not disguise, diminish** or **obscure** important **items, statements** or **warnings**

In deciding whether and how to communicate to a target audience, the firm should **consider**: the nature of the product/business, risks, the client's commitment, the average recipient's information needs and the role of the information in the sales process.

The firm should consider whether omission of a relevant fact will result in information being **insufficient, unclear, unfair** or **misleading**.

6.6.2 Comparative information

Information comparing business / investments / persons must:

- Present **comparisons** in a meaningful, fair and balanced way
- In relation to MiFID or equivalent third country business, specify **information sources**, key facts and assumptions

6.6.3 Tax treatment

If **tax treatment** is referred to, it should be stated prominently that the tax treatment depends on the individual circumstances of the client and may be subject to change in future. (One of a couple of exceptions to this rule is that it does not apply to deposits other than cash ISAs or CTFs.)

6.6.4 Consistency

The firm should ensure that information in a financial promotion is **consistent** with other information provided to the retail client. (**Deposits** are an exception to this rule.)

6.7 Past, simulated past and future information

6.7.1 Introduction

Rules on **performance information** apply to information disseminated to retail clients, and to financial promotions. In the case of non-MiFID business, the rules do not apply to deposits generally nor to pure protection long-term care insurance (LTCI) contracts.

6.7.2 Past performance information

Past performance information must:

- **Not** be the most prominent feature of the communication
- Include appropriate information covering at least the **five preceding years**, or the whole period the investment/service has been offered/provided or the whole period the financial index has been established, if less than five years
- Be based on and must show complete **12-month periods**

- State the **reference period** and **source of the information**
- Contain a **prominent warning** that the figures refer to the past and that past performance is not a reliable indicator of future results
- If denominated in a foreign **currency**, state the currency clearly, with a warning that the return may increase or decrease as a result of currency fluctuations
- If based on gross performance, disclose the effect of **commissions**, fees or other charges

The above provisions are to be interpreted in a way that is '**appropriate and proportionate**' to the communication. For example, in a periodic statement issued for investments managed, past performance may be the most prominent feature, in spite of the first bullet point immediately above.

For a **packaged product** (except a unitised with-profits life policy or a stakeholder pension scheme), information should be given on:

- An **offer to bid** basis (which should be stated) for an actual return or comparison with other investments, or
- An **offer to offer**, **bid to bid** or **offer to bid** basis (which should be stated) if there is a comparison with an index or with movements in the price of units, or
- A **single pricing** basis with allowance for charges

6.7.3 Simulated past performance information

Simulated past performance information must:

- Relate to an investment or a financial index
- Be based on actual past performance of investments/indices which are the same as, or underlie, the investment concerned
- Contain a **prominent warning** that figures refer to simulated past performance and that past performance is not a reliable indicator of future performance

6.7.4 Future performance information

Future performance information must:

- **Not** be based on nor refer to simulated past performance
- Be based on **reasonable assumptions** supported by **objective data**
- If based on gross performance, disclose the effect of **commissions**, fees or other charges
- Contain a **prominent warning** that such forecasts are not a reliable indicator of future performance
- Only be provided if **objective data** can be obtained

6.8 Financial promotions containing offers or invitations

A **direct offer financial promotion** is a form of financial promotion which enables investors to purchase investments directly 'off the page' without receiving further information.

A direct offer financial promotion to retail clients must contain whatever **disclosures** are relevant to that offer or invitation (as outlined earlier, such as information about the firm and its services, and costs and charges) and, for non-MiFID business, additional appropriate information about the relevant business and investments so that the client is reasonably able to understand their nature and risks, and consequently to take investment decisions on an informed basis. This information may be contained in a separate document to which the client must refer in responding to the

INVESTMENT AND RISK

offer or invitation. Alternatively, information disclosures may be omitted if the firm can demonstrate that the client referred to the required information before making or accepting the offer.

A firm may wish to include in a direct offer financial promotion a summary of **tax** consequences, and a statement that the recipient should seek a **personal recommendation** if he has any doubt about the suitability of the investments or services.

6.9 Unwritten promotions and cold calling

An **unwritten financial promotion** outside the firm's premises may only be initiated if the person communicating it:

- Does so at an appropriate time of day
- Identifies himself and his firm, and makes his purpose clear
- Clarifies if the client wants to continue or terminate the communication, and terminates it on request at any time
- If an appointment is arranged, gives a contact point to a client

Firms may only make **cold (unsolicited) calls** if:

- The recipient has an established client relationship with the firm, such that the recipient envisages receiving them, or
- The call is about a generally marketed packaged product (not based on a high volatility fund), or
- The call relates to controlled activities by an authorised person or exempt person, involving only readily realisable securities (not warrants)

6.10 Promotion of collective investment schemes

Section 238 FSMA 2000 permits promotion of authorised unit trust schemes and open ended investment companies (OEICs) and other recognised schemes. **Section 241** provides that to promote, or approve promotions of, an unauthorised scheme could give rise to an action for damages under section 150 FSMA 2000.

Section 38 FSMA 2000 states that an authorised firm must not communicate a financial promotion regarding an unregulated collective investment scheme unless permitted by the FSA's rules.

The **Promotion Collective Investment Schemes (Exemptions) Order 2001** (as amended) then sets out persons to whom a firm may communicate such promotions. These include:

- Persons who **participants** (or have been participants in the last 30 months) in a substantially similar scheme
- Established or newly accepted customers of the firm for whom the firm has taken reasonable steps to ensure the investment is **suitable**
- **Eligible counterparties** and **professional clients**
- Certain person covered by **FPO** exemptions, eg certified sophisticated investors

What is the difference between a **regulated** and **unregulated** collective investment scheme? A regulated collective investment scheme would include an authorised unit trust, an authorised OEIC or other scheme recognised and granted authorisation. To gain authorisation, the manager and trustee of the scheme must apply to the FSA and show they have complied with requirements such as those set out in the **New Collective Investment Schemes (COLL)** Sourcebook found in the Specialist Sourcebook block of the FSA handbook. All other schemes are generally considered 'unregulated' and as such have restricted marketing.

COLL created a definition of a '**qualified investor scheme**' (aimed at sophisticated investors) which would be subject to the same promotional restrictions as unregulated collective investment scheme described above.

Note that an investment trust is a listed company and thus is covered by the rules of UKLA.

6.11 Financial promotions for the business of overseas persons

An 'overseas person' here means a firm carrying on regulated activities who does not do so within the UK.

Any financial promotion for the business of such an **overseas person** must:

- Make clear which firm has approved or communicated it
- Explain that rules for protection of retail clients do not apply
- Explain the extent and level of any available compensation scheme (or state that no scheme applies)
- Not be issued if the firm has any reason to doubt that the overseas person will deal with UK retail clients in an honest and reliable way

An example would be an offshore or overseas investment fund that is being marketed by a UK firm to all UK clients.

6.12 Record keeping: financial promotions

Adequate records must be kept of all financial promotions, except those made during personal visits, telephone conversations or other interactive dialogue. If continuously updated market information is included, that information does not need to be recorded. For a **telemarketing** campaign, copies of **scripts** used must be kept.

Subject to certain exclusions, the **five-year** record keeping rule applies for MiFID and equivalent third country business.

In other cases, **three years** is the normal rule, with some exceptions relating to life policies and pensions requiring longer periods.

7 Advising and Selling

Learning outcomes

11.1 Existing regulations and forthcoming changes in regulation and legislation affecting investment advice and the investment market.

11.2 Trends in case law affecting investment advice.

12.2 Affordability and suitability.

13.4 Confirm consumers' understanding of recommendations.

13.5 Consumer rights and the regulatory requirements that apply to the provision of investment advice.

7.1 Assessing suitability

Suitability rules apply when a firm makes a **personal recommendation** in relation to a **designated investment** (but not if the firm makes use of the rules on basic scripted advice for stakeholder products).

The firm has obligations regarding the assessment of **suitability**: the firm must take reasonable steps to ensure that, in respect of designated investments, a personal recommendation or a decision to trade is **suitable for its client**.

To meet this obligation, the firm must **obtain necessary information** regarding the client's:

- **Knowledge and experience** in the relevant investment field (including: types of investment or service with which the client is familiar; transactions experience; level of education and profession or former profession; understanding of risks)
- **Investment objectives** (including: length of time he wishes to hold the investment; risk preferences; risk profile; purposes of the investment)
- **Financial situation** (including: extent and source of regular income; assets including liquid assets; investments and real property; regular financial commitments) (Is he able to bear any investment risks, consistent with his investment objectives?)

The firm is entitled to **rely** on **information provided by the client**, unless it is aware that the information is out of date, inaccurate or incomplete.

A **transaction** may be **unsuitable** for a client because of:

- The risks of the designated investments involved
- The type of transaction
- The characteristics of the order
- The frequency of trading
- It resulting in an unsuitable portfolio (in the case of **managing investments**)

For non-MiFID business, these rules apply to business with **retail clients**. When making personal recommendations or managing investments for **professional clients**, in the course of MiFID or equivalent third country business, a firm is entitled to assume that the client has the necessary experience and knowledge, in relation to products and services for which the professional client is so classified.

7.2 Suitability report

7.2.1 Requirement

A firm must provide a **suitability report** to a retail client if the firm makes a personal recommendation and the client:

- Buys or sells shares/units in a regulated collective investment scheme
- Buys or sells shares through an investment trust savings scheme or investment trust ISA or PEP
- Buys, sells, surrenders, cancels rights in or suspends contributions to a personal or stakeholder pension scheme
- Elects to make income withdrawals from a short-term annuity
- Enters into a pension transfer or pension opt-out

A suitability report is required for all personal recommendations in relation to **life policies**.

A suitability report is **not** required:

- If the firm acts as investment manager and recommends a regulated collective investment scheme
- If the client is habitually resident outside the EEA and is not in the UK when acknowledging consent to the proposal form
- For small life policies (not >£50 p.a.) recommended by friendly societies
- For recommendations to increase regular premiums on an existing contract
- For recommendations to invest further single contributions to an existing packaged product

7.2.2 Timing

The suitability report must generally be provided to the client **as soon as possible after the transaction is effected**. For personal or stakeholder pension schemes requiring notification of cancellation rights, the report must be provided no later than 14 days after the contract is concluded.

7.2.3 Contents

The suitability report must, at least:

- Specify the client's **demands and needs**
- Explain the firm's **recommendation** that the transaction is suitable, having regard to information provided by the client
- Explain any possible **disadvantages** of the transaction to the client

The firm should give details appropriate to the **complexity** of the transaction.

For **income withdrawals** from a **short-term annuity**, the explanation of possible disadvantages should include **risk factors** involved in income withdrawals or purchase of a short-term annuity.

7.3 Appropriateness

The **appropriateness** rules we outline here apply to a firm providing **investment services** in the course of **MiFID** or equivalent third country business, **other than** making a personal recommendation and managing investments. The rules thus apply to 'execution only' services which are available in the UK, where transactions are undertaken at the initiative of the customer without advice having been given. (Note that, as we have seen, the **suitability** rules apply where there is a personal recommendation.) One firm may rely on another MiFID firm's assessment of appropriateness, in line with the general rule on reliance on other investment firms.

The rules apply to arranging or dealing in **derivatives** or **warrants** for a **retail client**, when in response to a **direct offer financial promotion**.

To **assess appropriateness**, the firm must ask the client to provide information on his knowledge and experience in the relevant investment field, to enable the assessment to be made.

The firm will then:

- Determine whether the client has the necessary **experience and knowledge** to understand the **risks** involved in the product/service (including the following aspects: nature and extent of service with which client is familiar; complexity; risks involved; extent of client's transactions in designated investments; level of client's education and profession or former profession)
- Be entitled to assume that a **professional client** has such experience and knowledge, for products/services for which it is classified as 'professional'

Unless it knows the information from the client to be out-of-date, inaccurate or incomplete, the firm may rely on it. Where reasonable, a firm may infer knowledge from experience.

The firm may seek to increase the client's level of understanding by providing appropriate information to the client.

If the firm is satisfied about the client's experience and knowledge, there is **no duty to communicate** this to the client. If, in doing so, it is making a personal recommendation, it must comply with the **suitability** rules. But if the firm concludes that the product or service is **not appropriate** to the client, it must **warn** the client. The warning may be in a standardised format.

INVESTMENT AND RISK

If the client provides insufficient information, the firm must **warn** the client that such a decision will not allow the firm to determine whether the service or product is appropriate for him. Again, the warning may be in a standardised format.

If a client who has received a warning asks the firm to go ahead with the transaction, it is for the firm to consider whether to do so 'having regard to the circumstances'.

7.4 When is an assessment of appropriateness not needed?

A firm does **not** need to seek information from the client or assess appropriateness if:

- The service consists only of execution and receiving / transmitting client orders for particular **financial instruments** (see below), provided at the initiative of the client
- The client has been informed clearly that in providing this service the firm is not required to assess suitability and that therefore he does not receive protection from the suitability rules, and
- The firm complies with obligations regarding conflicts of interest

The particular **financial instruments** are:

- Shares on a regulated or equivalent third country market
- Money market instruments, bonds and other forms of securitised debt (excluding bonds and securitised debt which embed a derivative)
- Units in a UCITS scheme
- Other non-complex financial instruments (among the requirements to qualify as 'non-complex' are that they cannot lead the investor to lose more than they invested, adequate information is freely available, there is a market for them with prices made available independently of the issuer, and they do not give rise to cash settlement in the way that many derivatives do)

For a **course of dealings** in a specific type of product or service, the firm does not have to make a new assessment for each transaction.

If a client has engaged in a **course of dealings before 1 November 2007**, he is presumed to have the necessary experience and knowledge to understand the risks involved.

A firm need not assess appropriateness if it is receiving or transmitting and order for which it has assessed **suitability** under the COBS suitability rules (covered above). Also, a firm may not need to assess appropriateness if it is able to rely on a recommendation made by a **different investment firm**.

8 Dealing and Managing

Learning outcomes

11.1 Existing regulations and forthcoming changes in regulation and legislation affecting investment advice and the investment market.

11.2 Trends in case law affecting investment advice.

13.5 Consumer rights and the regulatory requirements that apply to the provision of investment advice.

8.1 Application of rules

COBS rules on **dealing and managing** apply to **MiFID business** carried out by a **MiFID investment firm**, and to equivalent third country business.

17: REGULATION

The provisions on **personal account dealing** apply to designated investment business carried on from a UK establishment. They also apply to passported activities carried on by a UK MiFID investment firm from a branch in another EEA state, but not to the UK branch of an EEA MiFID investment firm in relation to its MiFID business.

8.2 Conflicts of interest

Inevitably, authorised firms, particularly where they act in dual capacity (both broker and dealing for the firm itself), are faced with **conflicts** between the firm and customers or between one customer and another.

Principle 8 of the *Principles for Businesses* states: 'A firm must manage conflicts of interest fairly, both between itself and its customers and between a customer and another client'.

Principle 8 thus requires that authorised firms should seek to ensure that when **conflicts of interest** do arise, the firm **manages** the conflicts to ensure that customers are treated **fairly**.

8.3 Inducements

A firm must **not** pay or accept any fee or commission, or provide or receive any non-monetary benefit, in relation to designated investment business, or an ancillary service in the case of MiFID or equivalent third country business, other than:

- Fees, commissions and non-monetary benefits paid or provided to or by the client or a person on their behalf
- Fees, commissions and non-monetary benefits paid or provided to or by a third party or a person acting on their behalf, if the firm's duty to act in the best interests of the client is not impaired, and (for MiFID and equivalent business, and where there is a personal recommendation of a packaged product, but not for 'basic advice') clear, comprehensive, accurate, understandable disclosure (except of 'reasonable non-monetary benefits', listed later) is made to the client before the service is provided (Thus, the rule on inducements does not apply to disclosable commissions.)

This rule supplements Principles 1 and 6 of the *Principles for Businesses*. It deals with the delicate area of inducements and seeks to ensure that firms do not conduct business under arrangements that may give rise to conflicts of interest.

Inducements could mean anything from gifts to entertainment to bribery. The rules provide a test to help judge whether or not something is acceptable.

In the case of packaged products business with retail clients, there are rules to prevent a product provider from taking a **holding of capital** in the firm or providing **credit** to a firm unless stringent terms are met, including a condition requiring the holding or credit to be on commercial terms.

In relation to the sale of **packaged products**, the following are broadly deemed to be **reasonable non-monetary benefits**.

- Gifts, hospitality and promotional competition prizes of reasonable value, given by product provider to the firm
- Assistance in promotion of a firm's packaged products
- Generic product literature which enhances service to the client, with costs borne by the recipient firm
- 'Freepost' envelopes supplied by a product provider
- Product specific literature
- Content for publication in another firm's magazine, if costs are paid at market rate
- Seminar / conference attendance by a product provider, if for a genuine business purpose, with costs paid being reasonable

INVESTMENT AND RISK

- 'Freephone' links
- Quotations and projections, and advice on completion of forms
- Access to data and data processing, related to the product provider's business
- Access to third party dealing and quotation systems, related to the product provider's business
- Appropriate informational software
- Cash or other assistance to develop computer facilities and software, if cost savings are generated
- Information about sources of mortgage finance
- Generic technical information
- Training facilities
- Reasonable travel and accommodation expenses, eg to meetings, training and market research participation

If a product provider makes benefits available to one firm but not another, this is more likely to impair compliance with the **clients' best interests rule**.

Most firms deliver against the inducements requirements by drafting detailed '**gifts policies**' (although the rule does **not** explicitly require firms to have a gifts policy). These contain internal rules regarding disclosure, limits and clearance procedures for gifts.

8.4 Best execution

The basic COBS rule of **best execution** is as follows.

A firm must take all reasonable steps to obtain, when executing orders, the best possible result for its clients taking into account the execution factors.

When a firm is **dealing on own account with clients**, this is considered to be execution of client orders, and is therefore subject to the best execution rule.

If a firm provides a best quote to a client, it is acceptable for the quote to be executed after the client accepts it, provided the quote is not manifestly out of date.

The obligation to obtain best execution needs to be interpreted according to the particular type of financial instrument involved, but the rule applies to **all types of financial instrument**.

The **best execution criteria** are that the firm must take into account **characteristics of**:

- The client, including categorisation as retail or professional
- The client order
- The financial instruments
- The execution venues

The '**best possible result**' must be determined in terms of **total consideration** – taking into account any costs, including the firm's own commissions in the case of competing execution venues, and not just quoted prices. (However, the firm is not expected to compare the result with that of clients of other firms.) Commissions structure must not discriminate between execution venues.

8.5 Churning and switching

Churning and switching are similar wrongs. They involve the cynical **overtrading** of customer accounts for the purpose of generating commission. This would clearly contravene the **client's best interests rule**.

The difference between the two lies in the **different products** in which the transactions are undertaken.

- **Churning** relates to investments generally
- **Switching** describes overtrading within and between packaged products

Churning or switching will often be difficult to isolate, unless blatant. Much would depend upon the market conditions prevailing at the time of dealing.

The **COBS rules** on churning and switching state that:

- A series of transactions that are each suitable when viewed in isolation may be unsuitable if the recommendations or the decisions to trade are made with a frequency that is not in the best interests of the client
- A firm should have regard to the client's agreed investment strategy in determining the frequency of transactions. This would include, for example, the need to switch within or between packaged products

9 Product Disclosure and Cancellation Rights

Learning outcomes

11.1 Existing regulations and forthcoming changes in regulation and legislation affecting investment advice and the investment market.

11.2 Trends in case law affecting investment advice.

13.5 Consumer rights and the regulatory requirements that apply to the provision of investment advice.

9.1 Key features documents

9.1.1 Requirement

A firm must prepare a **key features document** for each packaged product, cash deposit ISA and cash deposit CTF it produces, in good time before that document has to be provided.

The firm does **not** have to prepare the document if **another firm** has agreed to prepare it. There are some further **exceptions**, including certain collective investment schemes for which a simplified prospectus is produced instead of a key features document, and stakeholder and personal pension schemes if the information appears prominently in another document.

A **single document** may be used as the key features document for **different schemes**, if the schemes are offered through a '**funds supermarket**' and the document clearly describes the difference between the schemes.

9.1.2 Product information standards

A **key features document** must:

- Be produced / presented to **at least** the quality / standard of **sales and marketing material** used to promote the product
- Display the **firm's brand** as prominently as any other
- Include the **keyfacts logo** prominently at the top
- Include the following **statement**, in a prominent position:

INVESTMENT AND RISK

> 'The Financial Services Authority is the independent financial services regulator. It requires us, [provider name], to give you this important information to help you to decide whether our [product name] is right for you. You should read this document carefully so that you understand what you are buying, and then keep it safe for future reference.'

- Not include anything that might reasonably cause a retail client to be **mistaken** about the **identity** of the firm that produced, or will produce, the product

9.1.3 Contents of key features document

Required headings in a **key features document** are as follows. (The **order** shown below must be followed.)

- *Title:* '**key features of the [name of product]**'
- *Heading:* '**Its aims**' – followed by a brief description of the product's aims
- *Heading:* '**Your commitment**' or '**Your investment**' – followed by information on what a retail client is committing to or investing in and any consequences of failing to maintain the commitment or investment
- *Heading:* '**Risks**' – followed by information on the material risks associated with the product, including a description of the factors that may have an adverse effect on performance or are material to the decision to invest
- *Heading:* '**Questions and answers**' – (in the form of questions and answers) about the principal terms of the product, what it will do for a retail client and any other information necessary to enable a retail client to make an informed decision

The **key features document** must:

- Include **enough information** about the nature and complexity of the product, any minimum standards / limitations, material benefits / risks of buying or investing for a retail client to be able to make an **informed decision** about whether to proceed
- Explain arrangements for handling **complaints**
- Explain the **compensation** available from the FSCS if the firm cannot meet its liabilities
- Explain whether there are **cancellation / withdrawal rights**, their duration and conditions, including amounts payable if the right is exercised, consequences of not exercising, and practical instructions for exercising the right, including the address to which any notice must be sent
- For **child trust funds (CTFs)**, explain that stakeholder, cash deposit and share CTFs are available, and which type the firm is offering
- For personal pension schemes, explain clearly and prominently that **stakeholder pension schemes** are available and might meet the client's needs as well as the scheme on offer

9.2 Additional information requirements

Note the requirements to provide **general information** to clients about **designated investments**, which were explained earlier in this chapter. As we noted there, a **key features document** may meet those requirements.

9.3 Cancellation and withdrawal rights

9.3.1 Introduction

Cancellation and withdrawal rights are of relevance to firms that enter into a cancellable contract, which means most providers of retail financial products, including distance contracts, based on deposits or designated investments.

9.3.2 Cancellation periods

Minimum **cancellation periods** where a consumer has a right to cancel are summarised below (and are subject to certain exemptions in special situations which are beyond the syllabus). (Note that a **wrapper** means an ISA or CTF. Personal pension contracts, including SIPPs, and pension contracts based on regulated collective investment schemes, fall within the definition of a **pension wrapper**.)

Life and pensions contracts: 30 calendar days

- Life policies, including pension annuities, pension policies or within a wrapper (For a life policy effected when opening or transferring a wrapper, the 30-day right applies to the entire arrangement.)
- Contracts to join a personal or stakeholder pension scheme
- Pension contracts
- Pension transfers
- Initial income withdrawals from an existing personal or stakeholder pension scheme

Cash deposit ISAs: 14 calendar days

Non-life/pensions contracts (advised but not at a distance): 14 calendar days – these rights arise only following a personal recommendation

- Non-distance contracts to buy units in a regulated collective investment scheme (including within a wrapper or pension wrapper) (For units bought when opening or transferring a wrapper or pension wrapper, the 14-day right applies to the entire arrangement.)
- Opening or transferring an ISA or CTF
- Enterprise Investment Schemes

Non-life/pensions contracts (at a distance): 14 calendar days

- Accepting deposits
- Designated investment business

If one transaction attracts more than one right to cancel, the longest period applies.

The **cancellation period begins**:

- **Either:** From the day the contract is concluded (but, for life policies, when the consumer is informed that the contract has been concluded),
- **Or:** From the day when the consumer receives the contract terms and conditions, if later

9.3.3 Disclosure of rights to cancel or withdraw

Where the consumer would not already have received similar information under another rule, the firm must **disclose** – in a durable medium and in good time or, if that is not possible, immediately after the consumer is bound – the right to cancel or withdraw, its duration and conditions, information on any further amount payable, consequences of not

INVESTMENT AND RISK

exercising the right, practical instructions for exercising it, and the address to which notification of cancellation or withdrawal should be sent.

9.3.4 Exercising a right to cancel

A consumer's notification of exercise of a right to cancel is deemed to have observed the deadline if it is **dispatched**, in a durable medium, before the deadline expires.

The consumer need **not** give any **reason** for exercising the right to cancel.

10 Regime for basic advice on stakeholder products

> **Learning outcomes**
>
> 11.1 Existing regulations and forthcoming changes in regulation and legislation affecting investment advice and the investment market.
>
> 11.2 Trends in case law affecting investment advice.
>
> 13.5 Consumer rights and the regulatory requirements that apply to the provision of investment advice.

10.1 Introduction

The **Sandler Review** proposals have been put into effect in legislation and in changes to the FSA Handbook which came into force on 6 April 2005. These rules allow for firms to provide a **basic level of advice** on a range of stakeholder products. **Stakeholder products** are intended to provide a relatively simple **risk-controlled** low-cost way of investing and saving.

10.2 Stakeholder products

The range of stakeholder products includes:

(a) Stakeholder pension schemes
(b) Stakeholder Child Trust Funds (CTFs)
(c) Stakeholder-compliant deposit accounts
(d) Stakeholder-compliant collective investment schemes (CISs)
(e) Stakeholder-compliant linked long-term contracts

To be a stakeholder product, a **deposit account** must have a minimum deposit amount set no higher than £10 per occasion. Interest must accrue at a rate not less than the Bank of England base rate minus 1% per annum. The interest rate must be increased within one month of a change in the base rate. Withdrawals must be paid within 7 days, with no limit on frequency of withdrawals.

To meet stakeholder requirements, **collective investment schemes** and **linked long-term funds** must have no more than 60% of their value in listed equities, and must be appropriately diversified. The minimum contribution must be set no higher than £20. The scheme must be **single-priced** – with no spread between the buying and selling price of units.

Linked long-term contracts are assurance-based contracts. Where such contracts have **smoothed investment returns**, additional requirements apply. The fund must seek to meet a target range of investment return, which must be notified to the investor at the outset. However, no guarantee will be given. Full information must be made available about the policy and charges. The **basic level of advice cannot be provided** on smoothed linked long term products.

Medium term and pension stakeholder products have a **cap on charges** at 1.5% per year for the first ten years that the investor holds the product. After that, a cap of 1% applies.

10.3 Simplified advice

The new requirements on **basic advice on stakeholder products** are designed to enable firms to provide **simple, quick and limited** advice to people interested in buying stakeholder products.

The requirements include the following.

(a) An **Initial Disclosure Document (IDD)** is to be provided, and explained to the customer.

(b) The advice should be based on either a limited number of stakeholder product providers, or a single provider.

(c) The range of products should not include more than one of each of:

 (i) A collective investment product or linked life products
 (ii) A stakeholder pension
 (iii) A stakeholder Child Trust Fund

 (There can be more than one deposit-based product in the range. Also, a firm may operate with more than one range of stakeholder products. Proper records of the ranges must be kept, for six years.)

(d) Representatives are not to recommend one particular fund, and they are not to give advice on products outside the range while advising on stakeholder products. The firm must not hold itself out as giving **independent advice** when it is giving only basic advice on stakeholder products.

(e) Remuneration of representatives must not be likely to influence them to give unsuitable advice or induce them to refer customers to another firm.

(f) The sales process for basic stakeholder advice must use **scripted questions** put to the customer. Unless excluded at the preliminary stage, the customer must be sent a copy of the completed scripted questions and answers.

10.4 Carrying out the simplified advice regime

A firm's scripted questions should be **short, simple and in plain language** that customers will understand. The customer should be able to **exit freely and without pressure** at any stage. There should be provision for the representative to **terminate** the sale process if no products are likely to be suitable or affordable for the customer.

If appropriate, the customer should be given a warning about the desirability of meeting the following **other priorities** before making payments to a stakeholder product:

- Insurance protection for self or dependents
- Access to liquid cash in emergencies
- Reduction of the level of existing debt

Affordability may be assessed in a firm's scripted sales process by means of a threshold or indicator, for example where a customer:

(a) Has annual unsecured debt repayments of more than 20% of gross annual income
(b) Has four or more active forms of unsecured credit, or
(c) Has consistently reached his or her overdraft limit

Except in the case of stakeholder CTFs, the customer's **savings and investment objectives** should be ascertained, including:

INVESTMENT AND RISK

- The importance of early access to amounts saved or invested
- Whether the customer wishes to save or invest for retirement
- Whether the customer wants to accumulate a specific sum by a specific date

The customer's **objectives** and **risk tolerance** will influence what may be recommended. For example:

(a) If the customer wishes to save for the short term only, then a CIS, a linked life stakeholder product or a stakeholder pension would all be unsuitable and should not be recommended.

(b) If a customer is not prepared to accept any risk of reduction of capital value, then a CIS or linked life stakeholder product should not be recommended. (However, in this case, a firm may invite the customer to consider his or her attitude to risk in the light of the effect of inflation on long-term savings.)

A stakeholder pension should not be recommended under the basic advice rules if the customer:

- Already has an occupational pension scheme
- Already has a pension to which he or she can contribute further
- Wishes to retire within five years

A **software based system** may be most appropriate to provide prompts and support for representatives. It is permissible to **depart from the scripted questions** if it helps customers' understanding, if this is compatible with the representative's level of competence.

The customer is only to be **recommended** to acquire a stakeholder product if the customer's answers and circumstances have been assessed, and (except for deposit-based products) the product is believed to be **suitable**. The adviser must reasonably believe that the customer **understands** the advice given.

When providing basic advice, the customer must not be advised on the contribution levels to a stakeholder pension needed to achieve a specific income in retirement.

Before concluding the contract, the representative is to:

- Explain the **aims, risks and commitments** sections of the **key features**, together with any other explanation of the product that will help the customer make an informed decision (except for a deposit-based product).
- Provide a **summary sheet** setting out amounts the customer wishes to pay in to the product, reasons for the recommendation and other relevant information including the customer's attitude to risk. (The summary sheet may be read through by telephone if the customer requests it, with the sheet being sent to the customer after the contract is concluded.)
- Explain that the recommendation is based on limited information and that the Financial Ombudsman may take this into account in determining any subsequent complaint.

11 Reporting to Clients

Learning outcomes

11.1 Existing regulations and forthcoming changes in regulation and legislation affecting investment advice and the investment market.

11.2 Trends in case law affecting investment advice.

13.5 Consumer rights and the regulatory requirements that apply to the provision of investment advice.

11.1 Reporting executions

In respect of **MiFID** and equivalent third country business, a firm must ensure that clients receive **adequate reports** on the services provided to it by the firm and their costs.

A firm must provide promptly in a durable medium the **essential information** on **execution of orders** to clients in the course of **designated investment business**, when it is not managing the investments. The information may be sent to an agent of the client, nominated by the client in writing.

For retail clients, a notice confirming execution must be sent as soon as possible and no later than the first business day following receipt of confirmation from the third party.

Firms must supply information about the **status of a client's order** on request.

For **series of orders** to buy units or shares in a collective undertaking (such as a **regular savings plan**), after the initial report, further reports must be provided at least at six-monthly intervals.

Where an order is executed in tranches, the firm may supply the price for each tranche or an average price. The price for each tranche must be made available on the request of a retail client.

For business that is not MiFID or equivalent third country business, confirmations need **not** be supplied if:

- The client has agreed not to receive them (with informed written consent, in the case of retail clients), or
- The designated investment is a life policy or a personal pension scheme (other than a SIPP), or
- The designated investment is held in a CTF and the information is contained in the annual statement

Copies of confirmations dispatched must be **kept** for at least **five years**, for MiFID and equivalent third country business, and for at least **three years** in other cases.

Information to be included in trade confirmations to a retail client

- Reporting firm identification
- Name / designation of client
- Trading day and time
- Order type (eg limit order / market order)
- Venue identification
- Instrument identification
- Buy / sell indicator (or nature of order, if not buy/sell)
- Quantity
- Unit price
- Total consideration
- Total commissions and expenses charged with, if requested, itemised breakdown
- Currency exchange rate, where relevant
- Client's responsibilities regarding settlement, including time limit for payment or delivery, and appropriate account details where not previously notified
- Details if the client's counterparty was in the firm's group or was another client, unless trading was anonymous

INVESTMENT AND RISK

11.2 Periodic reporting

A firm **managing investments** on behalf of a client must provide a periodic statement to the client in a durable medium, unless such a statement is provided by another person. The statement may be sent to an agent nominated by the client in writing.

Information to be included in a periodic report

- Name of the firm
- Name / designation of retail client's account
- Statement of contents and valuation of portfolio, including details of:
    - Each designated investment held, its market value or, if unavailable, its fair value
    - Cash balance at beginning and end of reporting period
    - Performance of portfolio during reporting period
- Total fees and charges, itemising total management fees and total execution costs
- Comparison of period performance with any agreed investment performance benchmark
- Total dividends, interest and other payments received in the period
- Information about other corporate actions giving rights to designated investments held

For a **retail client**, the **periodic statement** should be provided once every **six months**, except that:

- In the case of a leveraged portfolio, it should be provided at least **once a month**
- It should be provided every **three months** if the client requests it (The firm must inform clients of this right.)
- If the retail client elects to receive information on a transaction-by-transaction basis and there are no transactions in derivatives or similar instruments giving rise to a cash settlement, the periodic statement must be supplied at least once every **twelve months**

A firm managing investments (or operating a retail client account that includes an uncovered open position in a contingent liability transaction – involving a potential liability in excess of the cost) must report to the client any **losses** exceeding any **predetermined threshold** agreed with the client.

Periodic statements for **contingent liability transactions** may include information on the **collateral value** and **option account valuations** in respect of each option written by the client in the portfolio at the end of the relevant period.

For **non-MiFID business**, a firm need not provide a periodic statement to a client habitually resident outside the UK if the client does not wish to receive it, nor in respect of a **CTF** if the annual statement contains the periodic information.

12 Customer Complaints Procedures

Learning outcomes

11.1 Existing regulations and forthcoming changes in regulation and legislation affecting investment advice and the investment market.

11.2 Trends in case law affecting investment advice.

13.5 Consumer rights and the regulatory requirements that apply to the provision of investment advice.

12.1 General points

Firms carrying on regulated activities may receive **complaints** from their clients about the way the firm has provided financial services or in respect of failure to provide a financial service. This could include allegations of financial loss whether or not such losses have actually yet occurred: for example, in the case of a mis-sold pension contract, future losses may be involved. Under the FSA's rules, a firm must have **procedures** to ensure complaints from eligible complainants are properly handled.

A **complaint** is defined as 'any **oral or written** expression of dissatisfaction, whether justified or not, from, or on behalf of, a person about the provision of, or failure to provide, a financial service, which alleges that the complainant has suffered (or may suffer) financial loss, material distress or material inconvenience'.

Firms are permitted to **outsource complaints handling**, or to arrange a 'one-stop shop' for handling complaints with other firms.

12.2 Eligible complainants

The rules on how firms must handle complaints apply to **eligible complainants**. An eligible complainant is a person eligible to have a complaint considered under the Financial Ombudsman Service.

Eligible complainants comprise: private **individuals**, **businesses** with a group annual turnover of less than £1m, **charities** with an annual income of less than £1m or trusts with net asset value of less than £1m (other than those who are properly classified as **professional clients or eligible counterparties**) who are customers or potential customers of the firm.

The rules do not apply to **authorised professional firms** (such as firms of accountants or solicitors) in respect of their **non-mainstream regulated activities**.

For **MiFID business**, the **complaints handling and record rules** apply to:

- Complaints from **retail clients**, but not those who are not retail clients.
- Activities carried on from a **branch** of a UK firm in another EEA state, but not to activities carried on from a branch of an EEA firm in the UK.
- If a firm takes responsibility for activities **outsourced** to a third party processor, the firm is responsible for dealing with complaints about those activities.

12.3 Consumer awareness rule

To aid **consumer awareness** of the complaints protection offered, firms must:

- Publish a **summary** of their internal processes for dealing with complaints promptly and fairly.
- Refer eligible customers in writing to this summary at, or immediately after, the point of sale.
- Provide the summary on request, or when acknowledging a complaint.

12.4 Complaints handling

Firms, and UK firms' branches in the EEA, must establish procedures for the reasonable handling of complaints which:

- Are effective and transparent.
- Allow complaints to be made by any reasonable means (which might include email messages, or telephone calls, for example).
- Recognise complaints as requiring resolution.

INVESTMENT AND RISK

In respect of non-MiFID business, firms must ensure that they identify any **recurring or systemic problems** revealed by complaints. For MiFID business, the requirement is that firms must use complaints information to detect and minimise risk of '**compliance failures**'.

Having regard to FSA **Principle 6** (*Customers' interests*), firms should consider acting on its own initiative in respect of customers who may have been disadvantaged but have not complained. (This is a good example of how, in line with its move towards 'principles-based regulation, the FSA expects firms to consider themselves how to apply the Principles for Businesses.)

12.5 Complaints resolution

For all complaints received, the firm must:

- Investigate the complaint competently, diligently and impartially
- Assess fairly, consistently and promptly:
    - whether the complaint should be upheld
    - what remedial action and/or redress may be appropriate
    - whether another respondent may be responsible for the matter (in which case, by the **complaints forwarding rule**, the complaint may be **forwarded** to that other firm, promptly and with notification of the reasons to the client)
- Offer any redress or remedial action
- Explain the firm's assessment of the complaint to the client, its decision, including any offer of redress or remedial action made – in a fair, clear and not misleading way

Factors relevant to assessing a complaint

- All the available evidence and circumstances
- Similarities with other complaints
- Guidance from the FSA, FOS or other regulators

The firm should aim to resolve complaints as early as possible, minimising the number of unresolved complaints referred to the FOS – with whom the firm must cooperate fully, complying promptly with any settlements or awards.

12.6 Complaints resolved the next day

Complaints **time limit, forwarding and reporting rules** do not apply to complaints which are **resolved by the next business day** after the complaint is made.

12.7 Time limit rules

On receiving a complaint, the firm must:

- Send to the complainant a prompt written acknowledgement providing 'early reassurance' that it has received the complaint and is dealing with it, and
- Ensure the complainant in kept informed of progress on the complaint's resolution thereafter.

By the end of **eight weeks** after receiving a complaint which remains unresolved, the firm must send:

- A final response, or

17: REGULATION

- A holding response, which explains why a final response cannot be made and gives the expected time it will be provided, informs the complainant of his right to complain directly to the FOS if he is not satisfied with the delay, and encloses a copy of the FOS explanatory leaflet

The FSA expects that, within eight weeks of their receipt, almost all complaints will have been substantively addressed.

12.8 Firms with a two-stage complaints procedure

Some firms operate a **two-stage complaints procedure** that provides for a complainant who is not satisfied with the firm's initial response to refer the matter back to the firm or to its head office.

These firms are subject to the time limits set out above, but the rules recognise that some complainants may never respond to the initial reply or may take a long time to do so. Therefore, where the firm sends a response to the complainant offering redress or explaining why they do not propose to give redress and setting out how the complainant can pursue the claim further within the firm or apply to the FOS, it is permissible for the firm to regard the matter as closed if the firm does not get a reply within eight weeks.

If the complainant does reply indicating that they remain dissatisfied, then the general time limits will resume. However, the firm can discount any time in excess of a week taken by the complainant to reply.

12.9 Time barring

Complaints received outside the FOS **time limits** (see below) may be rejected without considering their merits in a final response, but this response should state that the FOS may waive this requirement in exceptional circumstances.

12.10 Complaints record rule

Records of complaints and of the measures taken for their resolution must be retained for:

- **Five years**, for MiFID business
- **Three years**, for other complaints

after the date the complaint was received.

12.11 Complaints reporting

Firms must provide a complete **report to the FSA** on complaints received **twice a year**. There is a standard format for the report, which must show, for the reporting period:

- Complaints broken down into categories and generic product types
- Numbers of complaints closed by the firm: within four weeks of receipt; within four to eight weeks; and more than eight weeks from receipt
- Numbers of complaints: upheld; known to have been referred to and accepted by the FOS; outstanding at the beginning of reporting period; outstanding at the end of the reporting period
- Total amount of redress paid in respect of complaints

INVESTMENT AND RISK

13 The Financial Ombudsman Service

> **Learning outcomes**
>
> 11.1 Existing regulations and forthcoming changes in regulation and legislation affecting investment advice and the investment market.
>
> 11.2 Trends in case law affecting investment advice.
>
> 13.5 Consumer rights and the regulatory requirements that apply to the provision of investment advice.

13.1 Function of the Ombudsman

A **complainant** must first go to the authorised firm against which the complaint is being made. If the authorised firm does not resolve the complaint to his satisfaction, the complainant may refer it to the **Financial Ombudsman Service (FOS)**.

The FOS offers an informal method of independent adjudication of disputes between a firm and its customer, which is relatively cheap compared with the alternative of taking action through the Courts.

13.2 Powers of the FOS

The FOS is a body set up by statute and, while its Board is appointed by the FSA, it is **independent** from the FSA and authorised firms. The FOS is, however, accountable to the FSA and is required to make an annual report to the FSA on its activities.

The FOS can consider a complaint against an authorised firm for an act or omission in carrying out any of the firm's regulated activities together with any ancillary activities that firm does. This is known as the **Compulsory Jurisdiction** of the FOS.

In addition to the Compulsory Jurisdiction, the FOS can consider a complaint under its **'Voluntary Jurisdiction'**. Firms or businesses can choose to submit to the voluntary jurisdiction of the FOS by entering into a contract with the FOS. This is available, for example, to unauthorised firms, and can cover activities such as credit and debit card transactions and ancillary activities carried on by that voluntary participant where they are not regulated activities.

A further **Consumer Credit Jurisdiction** applies under the Consumer Credit Act 2006, which gives to the FOS powers to resolve certain disputes regarding loans against holders of licences issued by the Office of Fair Trading under the Consumer Credit Act 1974.

13.3 Eligible complainants

Only **eligible complainants** who have been customers of authorised firms or of firms which have voluntarily agreed to abide by the FOS rules may use the FOS.

Where an eligible complainant refers a matter to the Ombudsman, a firm has no definitive right to block the matter being referred, but may dispute the eligibility of the complaint or the complainant. In such circumstances, the Ombudsman will seek representations from the parties. The Ombudsman may investigate the merits of the case and may also convene a hearing if necessary.

13.4 Outcome of FOS findings

Where the Ombudsman finds in favour of the complainant, it can force the firm to take appropriate steps to remedy the position including to pay up to **£100,000** plus reasonable costs (although awards of costs are not common). This figure will normally represent the financial loss the eligible complainant has suffered but can also cover any pain and suffering, damage to their reputation and any distress or inconvenience caused. If the Ombudsman considers that a sum greater than £100,000 would be fair, he can recommend that the firm pays the balance, although he cannot force the firm to pay this excess.

Once the Ombudsman has given a decision, the complainant may decide whether to accept or reject that decision.

- If the complainant **accepts** the Ombudsman's decision, **the authorised firm is bound** by it
- If the complainant **rejects** the decision, they can pursue the matter further through the **Courts**

14 Compensation

> **Learning outcomes**
>
> 11.1 Existing regulations and forthcoming changes in regulation and legislation affecting investment advice and the investment market.
>
> 11.2 Trends in case law affecting investment advice.
>
> 13.5 Consumer rights and the regulatory requirements that apply to the provision of investment advice.

14.1 Purpose of FSCS

The **Financial Services Compensation Scheme (FSCS)** is set up under FSMA 2000. The FSCS is designed to compensate **eligible claimants** where a relevant firm is unable or likely to be unable to meet claims against it. Generally speaking, therefore, the scheme will only apply where the firm is declared **insolvent or bankrupt**. The FSCS is seen as part of the 'toolkit' the FSA will use to meet its statutory objectives.

The compensation scheme is independent, but accountable, to the FSA and HM Treasury for its operations and works in partnership with the FSA in delivering the FSA's objectives, particularly that of consumer protection. The FSCS is funded by **levies on authorised firms**.

14.2 Entitlement to compensation

To be entitled to compensation from the scheme, a person must:

1. Be an **eligible claimant**. This would generally cover most individuals and small businesses. Specifically, an eligible claimant is defined as a claimant who is **not**:
    - An individual with a connection to the insolvent firm, eg directors
    - A large company or large partnership/mutual association. What is meant by a large company and partnership will depend on rules established under the UK Companies Acts, which are amended from time to time
    - An authorised firm, unless they are a sole trader/small business and the claim arises out of a regulated activity of which they have no experience, ie do not have permission to carry out
    - An overseas financial services institution, supranational body, government and local authority

INVESTMENT AND RISK

2 Have a '**protected claim**'. This means certain types of claims in respect of deposits and investment business. Protected investment business means **designated investment business**, the activities of the manager/trustee of an authorised unit trust and the activities of the authorised corporate director/depository of an ICVC. These activities must be carried on either from an establishment in the UK or in an EEA state by a UK firm who is passporting their services there.

3 Be claiming against a '**relevant person**' who is **in default**. A relevant person means:
   – An authorised firm, except an EEA firm passporting into the UK (customers who lose money as a result of default by an EEA firm must normally seek compensation from the firm's home state system, unless the firm has **top-up cover** provided by the FSCS in addition to, or in the absence of, compensation provided by the home state).
   – An appointed representative of the above

4 Make the claim within the relevant **time limits** (normally six years from when the claim arose)

The scheme will normally award financial compensation in cash. The FSCS may require the eligible claimant to assign any legal rights to them in order to receive compensation as they see fit.

14.3 Compensation limits

The maximum compensation levels per claim, are summarised in the Table below.

	Limit
Protected investments	£50,000 (100% of the first £50,000)
Protected deposits	£50,000 (100% of the first £50,000)
Insurance	90% of claim with no upper limit. Compulsory insurance is protected in full.

Note that the limits are per person per claim, and not per account or contract held.

Key chapter points

- The Conduct of Business Sourcebook (COBS) generally applies to authorised firms engaged in designated investment business carried out from their (or their appointed representatives') UK establishments. Some COBS rules do not apply to eligible counterparty business.

- The level of protection given to clients by the regulatory system depends on their classification, with retail clients being protected the most. Professional clients and eligible counterparties may both be either *per se* or elective. Both professional clients and eligible counterparties can re-categorise to get more protection.

- Firms doing designated investment business, except advising, must set out a basic client agreement. Firms must provide to clients appropriate information about the firm and its services, designated investments and their risks, execution venues and costs. Firms managing investments must establish a performance benchmark and must provide information about valuations and management objectives.

- There are special disclosure rules where a personal recommendation to buy a packaged product is given to a retail client: the IDD and 'menu' will be provided to the client.

- It is generally acceptable for a firm to rely on information provided by others if the other firm is competent and not connected with the firm placing the reliance.

- A financial promotion inviting someone to engage in investment activity must be issued by or approved by an authorised firm. Communications must be fair, clear and not misleading. Prospectus advertisements must clearly indicate that they are not a prospectus. Communications with retail clients must balance information about benefits of investments with information about risks.

- Unwritten financial promotions rules cover cold calling, which must be limited to an 'appropriate time of day'.

- Rules on assessing suitability of the recommendation apply when a firm makes a personal recommendation in relation to a designated investment.

- For certain packaged products, a suitability report is required, specifying the client's demands and needs and explaining the firm's recommendation.

- There are obligations to assess 'appropriateness' – based on information about the client's experience and knowledge – for MiFID business other than making a personal recommendation and managing investments.

- Key Features Documents, which must be produced to at least the same quality as marketing material, disclose product information for packaged products.

- Retail clients must be given the opportunity to change their mind (cancel) after agreeing to the purchase of a packaged product.

- Firms must seek to ensure fair treatment if there could be a conflict of interest. Common platform firms must maintain an effective conflicts of interest policy. Conflicts of interest policies must cover financial analysts producing investment research.

- Inducements must not be given if they conflict with acting in the best interests of clients, and there are controls on the use of dealing commission.

- Firms must establish arrangements designed to prevent employees entering into personal transactions which are prohibited forms of market abuse. Staff must be made aware of the personal dealing restrictions.

- Churning (investments generally) and switching (packaged products) forms of unsuitable overtrading of customer accounts in order to generate commission.

Key chapter points (cont'd)

- There are requirements to send out confirmation notes promptly, and periodic statements (valuations) regularly.
- Firms must have transparent and effective complaints procedures, and must make customers aware of them.
- Firms must investigate complaints competently, diligently and impartially.
- Time limits apply to complaints processing, and the firm must report data on complaints to the FSA twice-yearly.
- If the firm does not resolve a customer's complaint to the customer's satisfaction, the Financial Ombudsman Service is available to adjudicate the dispute.
- The FOS has a Compulsory Jurisdiction (covering authorised firms' regulated activities) and a Voluntary Jurisdiction (for unregulated activities where a firm opts for it).
- The FOS can order a firm to pay up to £100,000, plus costs, in respect of a complaint.
- The Financial Services Compensation Scheme – set up under FSMA 2000 to help meet the FSA's statutory objectives – will pay out within the claim limits to eligible depositors and investors if a firm becomes insolvent.

Chapter Quiz

1. What are the five statutory objectives of the Financial Services Authority? .... (see para 1.3)
2. Identify six of the FSA's eleven Principles for Businesses. .... (1.8)
3. What is a 'packaged product'? .... (5.9)
4. What is the difference between churning and switching? .... (8.5)
5. Outline the requirements on scripted questions in the advice regime for stakeholder products. ..... (10.4)
6. What is the maximum award that can be made by the Financial Ombudsman Service? .... (13.4)
7. What is the maximum compensation payable by the Financial Services Compensation Scheme in respect of bank and building society deposits? .... (14.3)

Tax Tables

Income tax rates

Rate Band	2010/11 Band limits	Non-savings income	Savings income (excl div)	Dividend income	2009/10 Band limits	Non-savings income	Savings income (excl div)	Dividend income
Starting	1 – 2,440	20%	10%	10%	1 – 2,440	20%	10%	10%
Basic	2,441 – 37,400	20%	20%	10%	2,441 – 37,400	20%	20%	10%
Higher	37,400 – 150,000	40%	40%	32.5%	Over 37,400	40%	40%	32.5%
Additional	Over 150,000	50%	50%	42.5%	N/A	N/A	N/A	N/A

Income tax reliefs

		2010/11 £	2009/10 £
Personal allowance	– under 65 (see note 4)	6,475	6,475
	– 65 – 74	9,490	9,490
	– 75 and over	9,640	9,640
Married couple's allowance	– 65 – 74 (see note 1)	N/A	6,965
	– 75 and over (see note 1)	6,965	6,965
	minimum for 65+	2,670	2,670
Age allowance income limit		22,900	22,900
Blind person's allowance		1,890	1,890
Enterprise investment scheme relief limit (see note 2)		500,000	500,000
Venture capital trust relief limit (see note 3)		200,000	200,000

Notes

1. Ages relate to the elder spouse or civil partner. MCA is available to only those couples where at least one spouse or civil partner was born before 6 April 1935. Relief is restricted to 10%.

2. EIS qualifies for 20% relief.

3. Tax relief is at 30% for VCT shares issued on or after 5 April 2006.

4. Personal allowances are reduced where income is greater than £100,000. The personal allowance reduces by £1 for every £2 above £100,000.

Pensions

	Annual Allowance £	Lifetime Allowance £
2009/10	245,000	1,750,000
2010/11	255,000	1,800,000

INVESTMENT AND RISK

Working and child tax credits

Working tax credit	2010/11 £	2009/10 £
Basic element	1,920	1,890
Couple and lone parent element	1,890	1,860
30 hour element	790	775
Childcare element of WTC		
Maximum eligible cost for 1 child	175 per week	175 per week
Maximum eligible cost for 2 children	300 per week	300 per week
Percent of eligible child costs covered	80%	80%
Child tax credit		
Family element	545	545
Baby addition	545	545
Child element	2,300	2,235
Tax credits income thresholds and withdrawal rates		
First income threshold	6,420	6,420
First withdrawal rate	39%	39%
Second income threshold	50,000	50,000
Second withdrawal rate	6.67%	6.67%
First threshold for those entitled to CTC	16,190	16,040
Income disregard	25,000	25,000

Capital gains tax

	2010/11	2009/10
Rate	18% / 28% (See note 1)	Gains taxed at 18% separately from income
Individuals - exemption	£10,100	£10,100
Trusts - exemption	£5,050	£5,050

Note 1

From 6 April 2010 until 22 June 2010

Gains taxed at 18% separately from income

From 23 June 2010

Gains taxed at 18% if the individual is a basic rate income tax payer.

Gains taxed at 28% if the individual pays income tax at a higher rate.

Entrepreneur's relief for gains on or after 6 April 2009 until 5 April 2010

- First £1m of qualifying gains – 10%
- Gains in excess of £1m – 18%

Entrepreneur's relief for gains on or after 6 April 2010 until 22 June 2010

- First £2m of qualifying gains – 10%
- Gains in excess of £2m – 18%

Entrepreneur's relief for gains on or after 23 June 2010
- First £5m of qualifying gains – 10%
- Gains in excess of £5m – Taxed at applicable gains rate of 18% or 28%

Inheritance tax

Death rate	Lifetime rate	Chargeable 2010/11	Chargeable 2009/10
%	%	£'000	£'000
Nil	Nil	0 – 325	0 – 325
40	20	Over 325	Over 325

Where a spouse or civil partner dies on or after 9 October 2007, the unused portion of their nil rate bond is transferred to the surviving spouse. The nil rate band on the second death will be the full second person's nil rate bond plus the unused portion of the first persons, based on the rate applicable on the second death.

Reliefs

Annual exemption	£3,000	Marriage	– parent	£5,000
Small gifts	£250		– grandparent	£2,500
			– bride/groom	£2,500
			– other	£1,000

Reduced charge on gifts within 7 years of death

Years before death	0 – 3	3 – 4	4 – 5	5 – 6	6 – 7
% of death charge	100%	80%	60%	40%	20%

Stamp taxes

Stamp Duty Land Tax

Transfers of property (consideration paid)

Rate (%)	All land in the UK		Land in disadvantaged areas	
	Residential	Non-residential	Residential	Non-residential
Zero	£0 – £125,000	£0 – £150,000	£0 – £150,000	
1	£125,001 – £250,000	£150,001 – £250,000	£150,001 – £250,000	
3	£250,001 – £500,000	£250,001 – £500,000	£250,001 – £500,000	
4	Over £500,000	Over £500,000	Over £500,000	

A first time buyer's threshold of £250,000 applies from March 2010 until 24 March 2012 for residential property. For purchases above this value normal rates apply.

INVESTMENT AND RISK

New leases - Duty on rent

Rate (%)	Net present value (NPV) of rent	
	Residential	Non-residential
Zero	£0 – £125,000	£0 – £150,000
1% of value exceeding £125,000	Over £125,000	
1% of value exceeding £150,000		Over £150,000

Duty on lease premium is the same as for transfer of land (except special rules apply for premium where rent exceeds £1,000 annually).

Shares and securities

The rate of stamp duty / stamp duty reserve tax on the transfer of shares and securities is unchanged at 0.5% for 2010/11.

Main Social Security benefits

		2010/11 £	2009/10 £
Child benefit	– first child	20.30	20.00
	– subsequent child	13.40	13.20
Incapacity benefit	– short term lower rate	68.95	67.75
	– short term higher rate	81.60	80.15
	– long term rate	91.40	89.80
Attendance allowance	– lower rate	47.80	47.10
	– higher rate	71.40	70.35
Retirement pension	– single	97.65	95.25
	– married	156.15	152.30
Widowed parent's allowance		97.65	95.25
Bereavement payment (lump sum)		2,000.00	2,000.00
Jobseekers allowance (25 or over)		65.45	64.30

2010/11 TAX TABLES

National Insurance contributions
2010/11 rates

	Weekly	Monthly	Yearly
Class 1 (employee)			
Lower Earnings Limit (LEL)	£97.00	£420.00	£5,044.00
Upper Earnings Limit (UEL)	£844.00	£3,656.00	£43,875.00
Earnings Threshold (ET)*	£110.00	£476.00	£5,715.00
Upper Accruals Point (UAP)	£770.00	£3,337.00	£40,040.00

Employees' contributions – Class 1

Total earnings £ per week	Contracted-in rate	Contracted-out rate
Below £110.00*	Nil	Nil
£110.01 – £844.00	11%	9.4%
Excess over £844.00	1%	1%
		1.6% rebate on earnings between LEL and UAP

Employers' contributions – Class 1

Total earnings £ per week	Contracted-in rate	Contracted-out rate Final salary	Contracted-out rate Money purchase
Below £110.00*	Nil	Nil	Nil
£110.01 – £844.00	12.8%	9.1%	11.4%
Excess over £844.00	12.8%	12.8%	12.8%
		3.7% rebate on earnings between LEL and UAP	1.4% rebate on earnings between LEL and UAP

* Earnings threshold below which no NICs payable. There is a zero band between the lower earnings limit (£97 pw) and the earnings threshold (£110 pw) to protect lower earners' rights to contributory state benefits such as basic state pension.

Class 1A
(employers' contributions on most benefits) 12.8% on all relevant benefits

Class 2 (self-employed)
Flat rate per week £2.40
where earnings are over £5,075 pa

Class 3 (voluntary)
Flat rate per week £12.05

Class 4 (self-employed)
8% on profits £5,715 – £43,875;
1% on profits above £43,875

Index

INDEX

A shares, 139
ABI Investment Classification Group, 253
Accessibility, 352
Accounting Standards Board, 150
Accrued income scheme, 126
Accumulation units, 260
Acquisitions, 148
Active fund management, 213, 345
Active investment management style, 345
Affordability, 352
Age (of an investor), 350
Age allowance, 71, 272
Age structure (of the population), 3
Aggregate spread limits, 218
Aggregation services, 358
AIM share price indices, 160
AIM Shares, 145
Allowable deductions, 70
Alpha, 334
Alternative Investment Market (AIM), 24, 140
Analysts, 151
Annual bonuses, 251
Annual charges, 204
Annual equivalent rate (AER), 324
Annual exemption (CGT), 82
Annual management charge, 204, 260, 262
Annual percentage rate (APR), 324
Annuities, 275, 302
Appropriateness rules, 387
Approved money market instruments, 217
Asset allocation, 347
Asset classes, 348
Asset cover, 242
Asset strippers, 232
Association of Investment Companies (AIC), 230
Assured shorthold tenancy, 177
Attitudes (of the investor), 332, 353
Authorised Corporate Director, 207
Authorised investment funds (AIFs), 207
Authorised unit trusts, 205
Average earnings index, 10

B shares, 139
Baby Bond, 268
Baby boomers, 4
Back to back arrangements, 277
Balance of payments, 46, 57
Balance of trade, 58
Balance sheet, 150
Balanced budget multiplier, 20
Bank and building society accounts, 98
Bank deposit rates, 50
Bank of England, 22, 23, 363
Bank of England Act 1998, 363

Bank of England Brokerage Service, 118
Barriers to trade, 31
Base rate, 23, 48
Basis points, 122
Bear market, 44, 147
Bed and breakfasting (shares), 86
Benchmarks, 376
Benefits in kind, 68
Best execution, 142
Best of class, 310
Best of class approach, 313
Beta factors, 333
Bid pricing, 202, 203
Bid/offer spread, 260, 262
Blind person's allowance, 72
Bonds, 112
Bonus issues (scrip issues), 86
Borrowings, 353
Broad money, 51
Broker commission, 142
Brokers, 142
Budget, 21
Bull market, 44, 147
Bulldog bonds, 121
Business confidence, 53
Business cycle, 42, 147
Buy to let, 175
Buyback (of own shares), 139
Buyback of shares (investment trusts), 238
Buying and selling shares, 142

C shares, 244
CAC 40 index, 161
Call warrants, 165
Cancellation / withdrawal rights, 393
Cancellation rights, 391
Cancellation rules, 220
Capital account (balance of payments), 57
Capital employed, 156
Capital gains tax (CGT), 80
Capital markets, 23
Capital protected annuity, 276
Capital redemption bonds, 265
Capital risk, 327
Capital shares, 240
Carpetbaggers, 123
Cash, 331
Cash deposits, 94
Cash flow statement, 150
Cash ISAs, 102, 285
Census, 2
Central bank, 22
Certificates of Deposit, 27
Chargeable disposals, 81

419

Chargeable event, 270
Chargeable person, 80
Charges, 204, 357
Chartism, 148
Chattels, 80
Child tax credit, 272
Child Trust Funds (CTFs), 80, 303, 392, 394
Churning, 356, 390
Circular flow of income, 39
CIS Sourcebook, 217
City Code on Takeovers and Mergers, 149
Civil Partnership Act 2004, 66
Civil partnerships, 66, 83
Clean price, 125
Client agreements, 374
Client categorisation, 370
Client money (information provision), 376
Closed with-profits funds, 258
Closed-ended funds, 198, 229
Cohabiting, 351
Cold calling, 384
COLL Sourcebook, 217
Collectibles, 190
Collective investments, 196, 217, 331
Commercial property, 178
Commitments (of an investor), 350
Commodities, 188;
    Energy commodities, 188; Hard commodities, 188;
    Soft commodities, 188
Common market, 29
Communications with retail clients, 381
Companies Act, 149
Company Share Option Plans (CSOP), 297
Comparative advantage, 28
Compensation, 403
Complaints (against firms), 399
Compound annual rate (CAR), 324
Compound interest, 324
Compulsory Jurisdiction (FOS), 402
Concentration limits, 218
Conduct of Business Sourcebook (COBS), 368
Confidentiality, 300
Confirmations, 397
Conflicts of interest, 389
Consolidation services, 216
Consumer Credit Act 1974, 402
Consumer Credit Act 2006, 402
Consumer expenditure, 40
Consumer panel, 365
Consumer Prices Index (CPI), 23, 45
Contracts for Difference (CFDs), 165
Conventional with-profits policies, 251
Conversion premium, 120
Convertible loan stock, 120
Convertible preference shares, 140

Corporate bonds, 118
Correlation, 332
Costs of investing in shares, 142
Counter-cyclical share, 147
Coupon, 113
Covered warrants, 165
Creation price, 202
Creations, 201
Credit and default risk, 133
Credit ratings, 134
Creditworthiness rating, 134
CREST, 142
Cum dividend, 125
Cum interest, 125
Cumulative preference shares, 140
Currencies, 222
Currency risk, 327
Currency trading, 55
Current account (balance of payments), 57, 58
Current and savings account, 98
Current year basis, 69
Customer complaints procedures, 398
Customer understanding, 357
Customs union, 29
Cyclical shares, 147

Dark green funds, 314
DAX, 161
Dead settlor provision, 265
Debentures, 119
Debt Management Office (DMO), 115
Deep discounted security, 120
Defensive shares, 147
Deferral of tax, 221
Deferred annuity, 262
Deferred ordinary shares, 139
Deficit (on current account), 58
Deflation, 46, 59
Demography, 2
Demutualisation, 98
Deposits, 217
Derivatives, 26, 162, 217, 327
Designated investment business, 369, 371
Designated territories, 221
Dilution levy, 208
Direct offer financial promotion, 383
Dirty price, 125
Disadvantaged area, 179
Disclosure (of tax information), 300
Discount (to NAV), 236
Discretionary service, 142
Disinflation, 46
Disintermediation, 26
Distribution bonds, 257

Distribution funds, 257
Distributor status, 223
Diversifiable risk, 332
Diversification, 330
Dividend cover, 155
Dividend reinvestment, 234
Dividend yield, 155
Dividends, 143, 146
Domicile', 65
Dot com boom, 216
Double tax relief, 73
Dow-Jones Industrial Average, 160
Dual capacity, 142
Dual listing, 285
Durable medium (COBS), 369

Earnings and living standards, 10
Earnings growth, 10
Earnings per share, 153
Easy Access Savings Account (NS&I), 104
Economic growth, 18, 41
Economic policy, 18
EEA territorial scope rule, 369
Effective annual rate of interest, 324
Efficient markets hypothesis, 148
Elective eligible counterparties, 373
Elective professional clients, 372
Electronic media (COBS), 369
Eligible complainants, 399, 402
Eligible counterparties, 372
Eligible shares, 290
Emergency fund, 97
Emerging markets, 328
Employee incentive schemes, 296
Employee Share Ownership Trusts (ESOTs), 296
Employees (taxation), 68
Empty nesters, 7, 351
Endowment policies, 258
Energy commodities, 188
Engagement, 309
Enterprise Investment Scheme, 292
Enterprise Management Incentive (EMI), 298
Enterprise zone property, 181, 206
Entrepreneurs' relief, 84
Equalisation payments, 205
Equities, 47, 138, 331
Equity capital risk, 327
Ethical investment, 308
Ethical investment policy (CTFs), 288
Ethical Investment Research Service (EIRIS), 309
Ethnic minorities, 6
Eurobonds, 121
European Central Bank, 22, 32
European Economic and Monetary Union (EMU), 31

European Exchange Rate Mechanism (ERM), 56
European Union, 28, 29
Eurosterling, 121
Eurozone, 32, 327
Ex dividend, 125
Ex interest, 125
Exchange listings, 140
Exchange rate mechanism (ERM), 21
Exchange rates, 54, 327
Exchange traded funds (ETFs), 213, 331
Execution only, 142
Exempt unit trusts, 206
Existing arrangements (of the investor), 356
Exit charges, 204
Expatriates, 221
Expectational inflation, 46
Expenditure reducing policies, 59
Expenditure switching policies, 59
Experiences (of the investor), 331
Extractive industries, 11

Factor incomes, 39
Factors of production, 11
False market, 149
Family life cycle, 6
Federal Reserve Bank, 22
Financial intermediaries, 25
Financial Ombudsman Service, 402
Financial planning report, 358
Financial promotion, 380
Financial Promotions Order, 381
Financial Services Act 1986, 362
Financial Services and Markets Act 2000 (FSMA 200), 221, 226, 363
Financial Services Authority (FSA), 5, 259, 363
Financial Services Compensation Scheme (FSCS), 96, 124, 258, 403
Financial statements, 150
Firms, 365
Fiscal easing, 20
Fiscal policy, 19
Fiscal year, 65
Fisher equation, 52
Fixed charge, 119
Fixed exchange rate, 55
Fixed interest securities, 47, 113, 331
Fixed rate savings bonds, 104
Flat yield, 128
Flat yield curve, 131
Flexible endowment policies, 259
Floating charge, 119
Floating exchange rate, 55
Floating rate notes (FRNs), 122
Fonds Commun de Placement, 221

INDEX

Foreign direct investment, 31
Foreign exchange markets, 55
Form R105, 102
Form R85, 101
Forward pricing, 203
Franked investment income, 244
Free asset ratio, 253
Free shares (in SIPs), 298
Free trade area, 29
Friendly Society tax-exempt plans, 268
FSA cancellation rules, 220
FSA Handbook, 367
FSA Principles for Business, 365
FT Ordinary Share Index, 160
FTSE 100 Index, 154, 158, 264
FTSE 250 Index, 159
FTSE 350 Index, 159
FTSE AIM Index Series, 160
FTSE All-Share Index, 159
FTSE All-Small Index, 160
FTSE All-World Index, 161
FTSE Eurobloc 100, 161
FTSE Eurotop 300, 161
FTSE Fledgling Index, 159
FTSE sector indices, 154
FTSE Small Cap Index, 159
FTSE techMARK indices, 160
FTSE TMT Index, 160
FTSE4Good indices, 160, 314
Full employment, 18
Fund management process, 343
Fund supermarkets, 204, 215
Fundamental analysis, 148, 346
Funds of funds, 215, 349
Furnished holiday accommodation, 174
Futures contract, 162

Gearing, 156, 237, 243
General application rule (COBS), 368
Gift Aid, 72
Gifts policy, 390
Gilt: Bearer stock, 115;
    Coupon, 114; Maturity, 114; Name, 114; Price, 114;
    Registered securities, 115; Yield, 115
Gilt edged market makers (GEMMs), 118
Gilt repo, 116
Gilt strips, 116
Gilt yields, 25
Gilt-edged market, 25
Globalisation, 30, 147
Golden rule (fiscal policy), 19
Government economic policy, 18
Gross Domestic Product (GDP), 40
Gross interest yield, 128

Gross National Product, 40
Gross redemption yield, 129, 242
Growth, 146
Growth shares, 154
Guaranteed annuity, 276
Guaranteed Equity Bonds (NS&I), 103, 106
Guaranteed equity investment bonds, 263
Guaranteed funds, 214
Guaranteed growth bonds, 263, 273
Guaranteed income bonds, 262, 273

Hang Seng Index, 161
Hard commodities, 188
Harmonised Index of Consumer Prices (HICP), 45
Herd mentality, 147
High income bonds, 263
Historic pricing, 203
Holding period return, 321
Household expenditure, 9
Hurdle rate, 242

Immediate annuity, 276
Import quotas, 59
Income and residual capital shares, 240
Income bonds, 104
Income distribution, 8
Income equalisation, 205
Income risk, 326, 353
Income shares, 239
Income tax, 64
Income yield, 128
Incomes policy, 53
Increasing (or escalating) annuity, 276
Independent Financial Adviser (IFA), 266
Index tracker funds, 213
Indexation allowance, 81
Index-linked gilts, 116
Index-Linked Savings Certificates, 47
Index-tracking funds, 349
Indices, 157
Individual Savings Account (ISA), 283
Individual spread limits, 218
Inflation, 18, 45, 52
Inflation risk, 326
Initial charges, 204
Initial Disclosure Document, 395
Insider information, 147
Institutional, 25
Institutional risk, 328
Insurance company property funds, 181
Interbank market, 27
Interest rate risk, 326
Interest rates, 48, 147
Interest yield, 128

Interim bonuses, 251
Interim dividend, 139
International bonds, 121
International business cycle, 44
International monetary fund, 45
International trade, 27
Internet, 11
Internet stocks, 216
Inverted yield curve, 132
Investment Account (NS&I), 104
Investment bonds, 261
Investment Companies with Variable Capital (ICVCs), 197, 207
Investment expenditure, 40
Investment management, 343;
  Fund constraints, 343;
  Fund objectives, 343
Investment Management Association (IMA), 209
Investment ratios, 151
Investment trust ISAs, 287
Investment trusts, 25, 228, 331
Investor sentiment, 147
Invisibles, 57
Isle of Man, 101

Japan, 59

Key features, 396
Key Features Document (KFD), 235, 391
Keyfacts logo, 391
Keynesians, 53

Labour income risk, 326
Landlords energy saving allowance, 174
Large undertaking (MiFID), 371
Last survivor annuities, 275
Lender of last resort., 22
LIBOR (London Inter-Bank Offered Rate), 22, 27, 48
Life Assurance Premium Relief (LAPR), 258, 269
Life assurance products, 250
Life cycle, 6, 350
Lifestyling, 289
LIFFE, 162, 163
Light green funds, 314
Limited companies, 140
Limited issue funds, 220
Limited liability partnerships, 181
Linked long-term funds, 286, 394
Liquidation, 145, 201
Liquidation price, 202
Liquidity, 94, 348, 352
Liquidity preference, 49
Liquidity risk, 352

Living standards, 8, 10
London Stock Exchange, 24
Long dated gilts, 117
Losses, 82
Low cost endowment policies, 259

Managed fund, 254, 348
Management buy-outs, 25
Manager of manager schemes, 215
Manager's box, 201
Manager's role (unit trusts), 200
Mandatory cash offer, 149
Manufacturing industry, 12
Marginal propensity to consume (MPC), 41
Marginal propensity to save (MPS), 41
Marginal rate of tax, 301
Market abuse, 365
Market value reduction (MVR), 253, 258
Marketing communications, 380
Marketmakers, 142
Markets in Financial Instruments Directive (MiFID), 363
Married couple's allowance, 72
Matching rules (CGT), 85
Matching shares (in SIPs), 299
Matching solutions (to client needs), 355
Matilda bonds, 121
Maximum investment plans, 259
Mean, 329
Measuring returns, 321
Medium green funds, 314
Meeting client needs, 355
Mergers, 148
Minority, 351
Monetarists, 52
Monetary policy, 21
Monetary Policy Committee (MPC), 23
Money Laundering Reporting Officer, 300
Money market deposits, 100
Money markets, 23, 27
Money stock, 50
Money supply, 50, 52
Monthly interest account, 99
Mortgage (paying off), 353
Multilateral Trading Facilities (MTFs), 369
Multi-manager schemes, 214
Multinational enterprises, 31
Multiple, 171, 178
Myners Review, 309

Narrow money, 51
NASDAQ 100 Index, 161
NASDAQ Composite Index, 161
National income, 39, 41
National Savings & Investments (NS&I), 25, 103

INDEX

Negative correlation, 332
Negative equity, 171, 176
Negative screening, 311
Negotiated option, 164
Net asset value (NAV), 229, 236
Net asset value per share, 156
Net interest yield, 128
Net national product, 39
Net redemption yield, 130
Nikkei 225 Index, 161
Nikkei 350 index, 161
Nikkei-Dow index, 161
Nominal rate of interest, 47, 50, 324
Nominal rate of return, 322
Nominal value, 139
Non-distributor status, 223
Non-qualifying policies, 269
Non-savings income, 73
Non-systematic risk, 332
Non-UCITS retail schemes, 217
Non-voting shares, 139
Normal yield curve, 131
Notice account, 99
Notice of assignment, 266
Notifiable interest, 149

Offer and bid basis pricing, 203
Offer price, 202
Offshore bonds, 264, 274
Offshore deposit accounts, 101
Offshore funds, 221
Offshore pooled investments, 222
Offshore property funds, 181
Offshoring, 31
Open Ended Investment Companies (OEICs), 197, 206
Open market option annuities, 276
Open-ended funds, 198, 229
Opportunity costs, 28
Optimisation, 214
Options, 163
Ordinary income shares, 240
Ordinary shares, 138, 139
Organic growth, 148
Outsourcing, 11
Over the counter (OTC) markets, 24
Over-the-counter option, 164
Owner-occupation, 172, 353

P11D, 68
Pacific Basin, 31
Packaged products, 377
Packaged units (investment trusts), 244
Panel of Takeovers and Mergers Levy, 142
Parallel markets, 27

Partial encashment, 271
Participating preference shares, 140
Partly paid shares, 139
Partnership shares (in SIPs), 299
Passive fund management, 213, 345
passive management style, 345
Past performance data, 330
Past performance figures, 356
Pay As You Earn (PAYE), 68
Pension, 295
Pension contributions (taxation), 72
Pension funds, 25
Pension wrapper, 393
Pensioners Guaranteed Income Bonds, 104
Per se eligible counterparties, 372
Per se professional clients, 371
Performance-based fees, 205
Periodic statements, 398
Permanent interest bearing shares, 81
Permanent interest bearing shares (PIBS), 123
Perpetual subordinated bonds (PSBs), 123
Personal allowance, 71
Personal portfolio bonds, 264
Personal tax computation, 73
Personality traits, 331
Political risk, 328
Population, 2
Portable bonds, 265
Portfolio, 352
Positive correlation, 332
Positive engagement, 310
Positive screening, 311
Pound cost averaging, 234, 257, 260, 352
Pre-Budget Report, 21
Preference shares, 140
Premium (to NAV), 236
Premium bonds, 106
Pre-owned assets, 302
Price indices, 213
Price/earnings (P/E) ratio, 153
Primary legislation, 367
Primary market, 24
Primary sector (of the economy), 11
Principal private residence, 174
Proceeds of Crime Act 2002, 300
Product disclosure, 391
Productivity, 11
Professional clients, 371
Profitability, 12
Property, 170, 328, 331
Property bond, 182
Property investment trusts, 180
Property OEICs/unit trusts, 179
Property shares, 179
Protected claim (FSCS), 404

Protected equity bond, 263
Protection, 250
Protection (levels), 370
Protectionism, 28
Public limited company, 140
Public Sector Net Cash Requirement (PSNCR), 19
Purchased life annuities, 277, 302
Purchasing power of money, 45
Purchasing power parity, 55
Put warrants, 165

Qualified Investor Scheme (QIS), 205, 217
Qualifying corporate bonds, 80, 127
Qualifying holdings, 290
Qualifying policy, 269
Quantitative theory of money, 52
Quoted shares, 140

Range (of products advised on), 378
Ratio analysis, 150
Real Estate Investment Trusts (REITs), 180
Real rate of return, 47, 95, 322
Real rates of interest, 50
Rebated commissions, 357
Recession, 42
Record keeping, 385
Redeemable preference shares, 140
Redemption yield, 129
Redemptions, 220
Redirections, 257
Redistribution of wealth, 46
Reduction in yield, 357
Regular savings plans, 258
Regulatory News Service (RNS), 146, 149
Regulatory risk, 328
Reinvestment (of company earnings), 146
Relevant person (FSCS), 404
Remuneration (of the adviser), 357
Rent a room scheme, 174
Reports (to the client), 357, 358
Residence, 65
Residential property, 172, 175
Retail clients, 371
Retail Prices Index (RPI), 45
Reverse auction, 118
Reversionary bonus, 251, 259
Review (of a portfolio), 357
Rights issues, 87
Risk management, 26
Risk premium, 335
Risk profile, 353
Risk tolerance, 396
Risk-free rate of return, 335
Rollover relief (CGT), 84

Running yield, 128

S shares, 244
S&P 500 index, 161
Sample asset allocations, 356
Samurai bonds, 121
Savings Certificates (NS&I), 105
Savings income, 73
Savings rate, 101
Savings-related share option schemes, 296
Scope (of firm's advice), 378
Screening, 310
Scripted questions, 395
Second hand endowment policies (SHEPs), 266
Secondary legislation, 367
Secondary market, 24
Secondary sector (of the economy), 12
Securitisation, 26
Segmentation, 271
Self-assessment, 65
Self-Invested Personal Pension Plans, 171
Self-regulating organisations, 363
Self-regulation, 363
Self-select ISAs, 287
Service sector (of the economy), 12
SETS, 142
Settlements, 87
Share buybacks (investment trusts), 238
Share exchange, 200, 234
Share Incentive Plan (SIP), 298
Shareholders, 138
Shares, 85
Sharesave accounts, 296
Sharpe measure, 336
Short dated gilts, 117
Shortfall risk, 327
SICAV, 221
Simple interest, 322, 323
Single period life assurance, 261
Single premium bond, 261
Single pricing, 204
Socially responsible investment, 308
Soft commodities, 188
Sole traders, 68
Special bonuses, 251
Specific risk, 332
Speculation, 56
Speculative motives, 147
Split capital investment trusts, 239
Stakeholder products, 286
Stakeholder products (basic advice), 394
Stamp duty, 88, 142
Stamp Duty Land Tax (SDLT), 89, 142, 174, 178
Standard and Poor's, 161

Standard deviation, 329
Statutory objectives, 363
Statutory regulation, 363
Statutory total income, 74, 272
Stepped preference shares, 240
Stock Exchange, 24
Stock index futures, 162
Stock market indices, 24, 157
Stock markets, 24
Stocks and shares ISA, 285
Stratified sampling, 214
Strike price, 165
Structured products, 224
Suitability, 356, 385
Suitability report, 386
Surplus, 259
Sustainable investment rule (fiscal policy), 20
Switch facility, 261
Switches, 257
Switching, 390
Synergies, 149
Systematic risk, 332

Takeovers, 148
Taper relief, 81
Tariffs, 59
Tax advice, 300
Tax credit, 143
Tax incentives, 144, 283
Tax planning, 300
Tax return, 65
Tax wrappers, 144, 282
Taxable income, 70
Tax-free income, 67
TechMARK indices, 160
Technical analysis, 148, 346
Technological changes, 53
Technology, 11
Technology stocks, 216
Temporary annuity, 262, 276
Term accounts, 100
Term structure of interest rates, 49
Terminal bonuses, 251
Tertiary sector (of the economy), 12
The FSA Regulatory Regime, 362
Thematic investment, 311, 313
Time value of money, 322
Timescale, 351
Top slicing calculation, 270
TOPIX, 161
Total expense ratio (TER), 209, 234
Total return indices, 213
Tracker funds, 213
Tracking error, 214

Trade cycle, 42
Traded endowment policies (TEPs), 266
Traded life policies, 274
Traded options, 164
Trail commission, 357
Transferable securities, 217
Treasury shares, 139
Treating customers fairly (TCF), 366
Trust, 87
Trust deed, 119
Trustee Act 2000, 262
Trustee Investment Act 1961, 262
Trustees, 199

UCITS, 221, 222
UCITS schemes, 217
Unauthorised unit trusts, 206
Unit trusts, 25, 197, 199, 229, 331;
    Certificates, 201; Creation price, 202; Creations and liquidations, 201; Liquidation price, 202; Offer price, 202; Open-ended, 200
Unitised with-profits, 252
Unit-linking, 251
Unquoted shares, 141, 145
Unsecured loan stock, 119, 120
Unsystematic risk, 332
Unwritten financial promotions, 384

Valuation point, 203
Value investors, 154
Venture capital, 25
Venture capital trusts (VCTs), 289
Viatical settlements, 267
Visibles, 57
Void periods, 175
Volatility, 329
Volume of consumer spending, 41
Volume of fiscal investment, 41
Voluntary Jurisdiction (FOS), 402
Voting rights, 149

Wage-price spiral, 47
War Loan 3.5%, 115
Warrants, 165, 237
Warrants (investment trusts), 237, 243
Warrants and derivatives risk warning, 357
Wealth (of the investor), 350
Wealth distribution, 8
Website conditions (COBS), 370
Whole of life policy, 260
With profits fund, 348, 251
With proportion, 275
Withdrawal facility (investment bonds), 261

World economic outlook, 45
World Trade Organisation, 28
Wrap accounts, 216
Wrapper, 393

Yankee bonds, 121
Year of death, 301
Year of marriage, 301
Yield curve, 131

Zero coupon bonds, 120, 121
Zero dividend preference shares, 240

INDEX